The
Clamorgans

The Clamorgans

ONE

FAMILY'S HISTORY

OF

RACE IN AMERICA

Julie Winch

A division of Farrar, Straus and Giroux   New York

HILL AND WANG
A division of Farrar, Straus and Giroux
18 West 18th Street, New York 10011

Library of Congress Cataloging-in-Publication Data
Winch, Julie, 1953–
    The Clamorgans : one family's history of race in America / Julie Winch. — 1st ed.
      p.   cm.
    Includes bibliographical references and index.
    ISBN 978-0-8090-9517-9 (alk. paper)
    1. Clamorgan family.   2. African American families—Missouri—Saint Louis—
Biography.   3. African Americans—Missouri—Saint Louis—Biography.   4. Upper
class families—Missouri—Saint Louis—Biography.   5. Saint Louis (Mo.)—Race
relations—History.   6. Saint Louis (Mo.)—Biography.   I. Title.

F474.S29N4835 2011
305.896'073077865—dc22

                                                            2010043635

Designed by Abby Kagan

www.fsgbooks.com

1   3   5   7   9   10   8   6   4   2

For Lou

Contents

The
Clamorgans

Introduction: "The Clamorgans Are Fighters"

THERE IS, alas, no evidence that during his 1842 visit to St. Louis the famed novelist Charles Dickens ever ventured out of the Planters' House Hotel to call at an equally well-appointed establishment in the neighborhood. Another exalted English tourist would do so, some years later, in order to enjoy the amenities offered at what was acknowledged to be the finest "bathing saloon" west of the Mississippi. Edward, Prince of Wales, the heir to the British throne, just wanted a decent bath—and the Planters' House came up short in that department, at least in his estimation. He no doubt glanced at the proprietor of Clamorgans and then got on with the business at hand—wallowing in warm, scented water in a fine marble tub, attended to by Mr. Clamorgan himself. An unimaginative young man, His Royal Highness missed the opportunity to uncover a remarkable story.

Charles Dickens would have relished the Clamorgan saga had *he* patronized Clamorgans and struck up a conversation with the owner. The history of the family was replete with the kinds of characters Dickens loved to weave into his novels—hapless orphans, wily villains, women seduced and betrayed by the men they trusted, imposters of one kind or another, with an unscrupulous lawyer or two thrown into the mix.

Tying them all together was an epic court battle that has its fictional counterpart in *Bleak House*'s *Jarndyce v. Jarndyce*. At the same time, though, Dickens might have been at a loss to appreciate the nuances of the Clamorgans' story, for it is a peculiarly American one. The Clamorgans were fighting for possession of land on a scale Dickens could not have imagined—enough to make each and every member of the family a millionaire—and they were fighting against a system infinitely more rigid and oppressive than the hierarchy of class that was the hallmark of the England Charles Dickens was familiar with. All the same, the drama that surrounded the Clamorgans from the moment the family's founder first set foot on America's shores to Dickens's own era and beyond was and remains a gift to any writer.

"The Clamorgans are fighters," the editor of the *St. Louis Globe-Democrat* informed his readers in the summer of 1911, as the family embarked on yet another round of litigation. He was right . . . and he was wrong. He reported that the Clamorgans had been fighting in the courts for five decades. In fact, they had been taking on all comers for more than a century. Hardly a year went by when the Clamorgan name did not grace a court docket in some jurisdiction or another. The courtroom was the family's natural arena, although from time to time they pressed their luck on Capitol Hill as well.

The Clamorgan clan was litigious to a fault, and anyone who seeks to understand their story has to follow them through the thickets of the law as, for generation after generation, they sought justice and vindication. They fought with dogged determination. They fought their neighbors, they fought their rivals, and they fought the government. They fought any person and any entity they believed had done them wrong. Only one member of the family actually claimed to be a lawyer—and he was lying!—but every Clamorgan from youth to old age was remarkably well versed in the law, and adept at using it to his or her advantage. The practice and interpretation of the law was almost second nature to them. The complex language of common law and civil law was a language every Clamorgan spoke with remarkable fluency. They could and did play with the law, as the law so often played with them, because of who and what they were.

In recent years the study of the "borderlands" has gained in popularity among historians and scholars in related fields. It is a somewhat loosely defined term, but one that applies to so many parts of the Clamorgans' story, for they were quintessential "borderlands" people. In the most literal sense, that of geography, the family obsessed over titles to vast expanses of territory on the ever-moving American frontier. They lived on the borderlands in other senses as well. They defied many of the social conventions, and broke a good many laws along the way. The boundary between what they were *supposed* to do and what they *wanted* to do was one they often chose to disregard. Above all, they grappled with the reality that they dwelled in the racial borderlands. Their history was shaped by their status as people "in between," for the Clamorgans straddled the shifting racial fault line that, at least in theory, separated "black" from "white." They were constantly redefining themselves, or being redefined, as race became the measure of virtually every aspect of people's lives. They made and remade their identities, determined not merely to survive but to grow rich in an America where law and custom sought to thrust them to the social and economic margins.

The story of the Clamorgans is a story about inheritance. Through the generations the family pursued a vast and elusive fortune that came with strings attached. Their legacy from their white forefather could be quantified in dollars and cents, in acres and arpents. Their legacy from their black foremother had to be measured very differently. They continually had to decide for themselves which mattered more, and how much they were willing to divulge about one legacy in order to claim the other.

This is a tale about money, land, power, and the nation's obsession with race. It is also a story about personalities. Some of the Clamorgans were capable of intense loyalty and acts of selfless generosity. Others betrayed friends and family without a moment's hesitation. They were all adventurers and risk takers, but in some respects that was a characteristic forced upon them by their circumstances. They were a resilient bunch, able to bounce back from defeat and fix their eyes unwaveringly on the next battle. If they were in most instances duplicitous and double-dealing, it was because they had to be. And they proved that they could keep secrets remarkably well.

Tracking the Clamorgans has been challenging, to say the least.

They changed names and abodes, races and religions, occupations, political loyalties, and just about every other facet of their lives with abandon. While in pursuit of them, I learned more about sleuthing—online and in archives—than in any other project I have ever undertaken. The Clamorgans have at times frustrated me. Always, it seemed, when I had penetrated to the heart of one mystery, they presented me with another. Through it all, though, I have considered it a privilege to spend time in their company.

And now, with a few words of caution—for nothing in the Clamorgans' story is ever quite what it seems, and subterfuge was second nature to them—it is time for the author to step back and let the reader make the acquaintance of the founder of the family. The year is 1781 and the place is a remote spot a mile or two upriver from New Orleans. A dreamer of dreams, a man of limitless ambition, and someone most definitely not to be trusted with anyone else's money, Don Santiago Clamorgan, alias Sieur Jacques Clamorgan, is about to set off to make his fortune.

1

Sieur Jacques

I T WAS THE SUMMER OF 1781. Jacques Clamorgan was not supposed
to be in St. Louis and he knew it. He had tried to get the necessary
licenses from the Spanish authorities in New Orleans to travel upriver, but the alcalde, the city's chief administrative and judicial officer,
had forbidden him to leave until he had paid off a substantial debt he
owed. Clamorgan rarely accepted being told he could not do what he
wanted. He had his trade goods surreptitiously loaded onto a flatboat
and then sneaked out of the city to board the bateau at a remote spot,
away from the eyes of officialdom.[1]

For many weeks he followed the Mississippi north, the boatmen
straining against the current, poling the bateau and occasionally dragging it along the riverbank. Finally the vessel reached its destination, a
settlement of about a thousand people set high on a limestone bluff
overlooking the great river. Back in New Orleans, Clamorgan's friend
François Marmillon had assured him he could make his fortune in
St. Louis, but Jacques Clamorgan was beginning to have his doubts. His
first sight of St. Louis did not inspire confidence. This brash new community, with its cluster of homes and warehouses, a church, and a few

taverns, had an unfinished look, and its inhabitants, even the wealthiest of them, a decidedly backwoods appearance.[2]

A longer look and a moment's reflection restored his faith. The town was strategically located at the confluence of the Mississippi, Missouri, and Illinois rivers. The homes might be rough-hewn, but they were neat. Some families had an entire block to themselves, and others at least a quarter or a half block. Most had gardens, where the women raised vegetables and herbs, and a few had their own orchards. The site had been well chosen. When the rivers flooded, as they were bound to from time to time, the town's elevation would spare it. The street plan was coherent enough. Three largish unpaved streets, Rue Royale, Rue de l'Eglise, and Rue des Granges, ran parallel to the Mississippi and were intersected by a series of small cross streets. Beyond the town were the Great and Little Prairies, where the town's inhabitants planted crops and pastured livestock.[3] And everywhere were the very visible signs of the wealth on which the community had been built. Outside almost every home were drying racks festooned with furs of every kind—beaver, bear, wolf, and others that Clamorgan could not immediately identify. As a rule, not many native people turned up in St. Louis to exchange their furs. White voyageurs went out to their villages with a selection of trade goods and did the bargaining. Once the furs had been obtained, they were carefully dried, packed, and taken down to New Orleans to be shipped to Europe. There was also an illegal trade—illegal as far as the Spanish authorities were concerned—with British-held Montreal.[4]

Jacques Clamorgan assessed the potential of this new community. It might be possible to push farther into the interior, establish ties with more distant peoples, and even challenge the monopoly of the all-powerful Hudson's Bay and North West companies trading out of Canada. There might be other commodities worth dealing in besides furs. It was all a matter of opportunity, of talking to the right people, and of greasing a few palms. A man with vision and a modest amount of capital could indeed make his fortune here. Clamorgan's friend Marmillon had not steered him wrong.

Well traveled and well informed, Jacques Clamorgan understood that this was contested terrain. For eight decades France had laid claim to a swath of real estate that stretched from the present-day border between the United States and Canada down to the Gulf of Mexico. To the east French land extended to the "Ohio Country," the region of western Pennsylvania and Ohio so hotly disputed with the British. To the west . . . well, no one was quite sure. French authority had come to an end as a consequence of the French and Indian War. When Louis XV saw defeat staring him in the face, he secretly offered his ally Carlos III of Spain the whole of Louisiana, including the "Illinois Country," the land on the eastern side of the Mississippi. Carlos knew France was offloading an unprofitable colony. However, Spain wanted to expand its hold over Texas, and that could be jeopardized if France was forced to surrender Louisiana to the British. On the advice of his ministers, Carlos agreed in 1762 to the Treaty of Fontainebleau.[5]

Peace negotiations with Britain the following year resulted in a modification of that treaty. The British got the Illinois Country, but Spain was confirmed in its ownership of the Louisiana Territory. The news of the land swap caught many people off guard, among them Pierre Liguest Laclède. When he left New Orleans in 1763 to stake a claim to the lucrative fur trade in Upper Louisiana, Laclède carried with him a license from the French authorities. On reaching his destination he discovered two things: first, none of the existing French settlements suited his needs, and second, he was now in Spanish territory. Undeterred by the regime change or the lack of trading facilities, Laclède established his own base of operations. He marked out the site of what would become St. Louis and set his teenage stepson, Auguste Chouteau, to work to build him a store and a house. He also began attracting settlers. Many of the French in the Illinois Country were appalled at the thought of being under the dominion of Britain. If they had to swear allegiance to Carlos III in order to join Laclède in St. Louis, that was vastly preferable to becoming subjects of George III.

When Jacques Clamorgan arrived in St. Louis in 1781 he was, to all intents and purposes, in a French town, even though it was under Spanish rule. The mix of French from the Illinois Country, French from British-controlled Canada, and French from the mother country ensured that French would remain the dominant language for decades, especially since the Spanish Crown saw the wisdom of appointing officials who were themselves of French extraction. The French-speaking inhabitants did not seem resentful of Spanish authority. The most serious threat to Spanish power came from the British. Spain had backed Britain's thirteen rebellious American colonies in the War for Independence, and in the spring of 1780 the British and their Indian allies had launched an assault on St. Louis. But the attack failed, and by the time Jacques Clamorgan stepped ashore and began unloading his merchandise, things seemed to be quiet enough.

He quickly assessed where the real power lay. He was already familiar with the Spanish governmental structure. Presiding over the whole of the Louisiana Territory was a governor, a royal appointee headquartered in New Orleans. Taking into account the factor of distance and the difficulties of communication, the king of Spain and his ministers had seen the sense of splitting the Louisiana Territory in two. The northern part became Upper Louisiana. St. Louis emerged as its administrative center, and it was from St. Louis that the lieutenant governor operated. He had charge of all sorts of matters that related to the security and good order of his region, although he was ultimately answerable to the governor and was expected to send reports to him on a regular basis and to defer to him on all major issues.

Jacques Clamorgan understood that if he hoped to make his fortune in St. Louis he would need to be on good terms with the lieutenant governor, but there were other individuals besides the lieutenant governor whom Jacques quickly realized he had to cultivate. The half-brothers Auguste and Pierre Chouteau were two of the richest and most influential men in Upper Louisiana, and arguably in the whole of the Louisiana Territory. Pierre was the unacknowledged son of Pierre Laclède and his *chère amie*, Marie-Thérèse Bourgeois Chouteau. Married as a teenager to the New Orleans tradesman René Chouteau, Marie-Thérèse had found herself abandoned with a small child, Auguste, when René took off for France. Before long she had moved in with Laclède, but since she was still tied to the absent René, each of the children she bore received the last name Chouteau, although no one was in any doubt as to their true paternity.[6]

Clamorgan never met Pierre Laclède, who died in 1778, but he may have been introduced to Madame Chouteau, and he certainly made the acquaintance of her sons. Auguste and Pierre were men to be reckoned with. From their youth they had lived for months at a time with the Osage, the most powerful native people of the region. They spoke their language and knew their ways. And although both would eventually marry white women, they had Osage wives and children, too, which made them real as well as fictive kin of many of the Osage hunters they traded with. Spanish officials recognized the influence the brothers wielded, and the two men got all manner of trading licenses to work with the Osage. The Chouteau brothers could prove useful allies or dangerous adversaries if Clamorgan followed through on his plan to settle in St. Louis. First, though, he had other matters to attend to.

Once he had sold his merchandise, Clamorgan asked the lieutenant-governor, Francisco Cruzat, for permission to return to New Orleans. Cruzat refused at first, but eventually relented. Clamorgan got a passport for part of his journey, and Cruzat put into his hands some documents to be delivered to his superior in New Orleans. Clamorgan was instructed to go only as far as Arkansas Post, a fort located at the point where the Arkansas flowed into the Mississippi, and wait there while officials assessed the danger posed downriver by British Loyalists operating out of Natchez. Cruzat was not especially worried about Clamorgan's safety, but he could not allow the dispatches he'd given him to fall into enemy hands. He soon learned what kind of man he was dealing with. It did not suit Clamorgan to break his journey. Once at Arkansas Post, he pushed on to New Orleans, and Cruzat was thrown into a panic about the documents he had somewhat rashly entrusted to Clamorgan. When Cruzat learned they had been delivered safely, he was both relieved and angry. He urged the governor of the Louisiana Territory to punish such flagrant disobedience, but Clamorgan emerged from the episode unscathed, unrepentant, and determined to return to St. Louis to make his fortune.[7]

In the literature on the early days of St. Louis, Jacques Clamorgan has achieved near-legendary status, and like so many heroes and villains, his origins have been obscured by the passage of time. In Clamorgan's case even his name is a matter of contention. He was a Spaniard, declare some commentators, and in one sense he *was* a Spaniard. As a resident of the Spanish province of Upper Louisiana, he was technically a subject of the king of Spain, but that did not mean he had been born in Spain. He was not Spanish but Portuguese, insist other sources, one of which bestows on him the very un-Portuguese name of Clem Morgan. No, say others, he was not from Iberia but from Britain: he was a Welshman, and his name a corruption of the Welsh shire of Glamorgan. He was no Welshman, insist others: he was a proud Scot. He was neither, others maintain: he was an Irishman, and his name was not Clamorgan or Glamorgan but James Morgan.[8]

Then there are the reports that he was a man of color and a friend of Jean-Baptiste Point du Sable, the legendary black founder of Chicago, though there is no evidence that the two ever met.[9] No matter the origin prescribed him, Jacques Clamorgan evoked strong emotions: if some of his contemporaries praised him to the skies, others vilified him as an unmitigated scoundrel. Had he been known to be of even partial African descent, surely one of his enemies would have played the race card . . . And yet no one ever did.

Those who actually met Jacques Clamorgan identified him fairly readily as a Frenchman, and with good reason.[10] The Clamorgans were French nobility (although admittedly fairly minor nobility), and their roots were dug deep into the soil of Normandy. As one early twentieth-century chronicler observed, the family was "more distinguished for its antiquity than for its achievements."[11] The most prominent Clamorgan up to the time of Jacques's birth was Jean de Clamorgan, an officer in the embryonic French navy who in 1566 authored a treatise on wolf hunting. Curiously, Jean had more than a passing interest in the exploration of the Americas.[12] Maybe Jacques was a descendant of his and inherited his fascination with America and its peoples, although Jacques's personal papers reveal nothing whatsoever about his parentage. Just how he fitted into the family is anyone's guess, but the Clamorgans were prolific and there were plenty of branches from which he could have sprung.[13] He might have been born in France or he might have been the child of French parents born in one or another of France's overseas colonies.[14]

Jacques's date of birth is uncertain, although by his own account he was born in 1744 or 1745.[15] His education was superior to that of many of his contemporaries: the contents of his library reveal a man who was well read and had more than a passing acquaintance with the classics.[16] Beyond that, determining what his background was, where he was, and what he was doing at any one time is a challenge. This much one can say: by the 1770s, when he was in his early thirties, he was in the West Indies and dealing in any commodity likely to earn him a profit. In December 1777 he was in St. Pierre, on the island of Martinique, and while there, he contracted a substantial debt to Bernard and Jacques Texier, merchants headquartered in the Dutch Antilles. Jacques being Jacques, the debt went unpaid. The Texiers won a judgment against him in Martinique, only to spend years tracking him down. Finally, in 1781, they got word that he was in New Orleans and they applied to the alcalde for justice. That was the reason the authorities had tried (in vain, as it turned out) to keep him from making his first departure for St. Louis.[17]

Although Jacques was a frequent visitor to New Orleans, he had not been in town very long when the Texiers caught up with him. He had just returned after a failed venture as a blockade runner, trying to outwit the British Royal Navy and get cargoes of West Indian rum, sugar, molasses, and coffee to rebel-held ports along the Atlantic seaboard. His base of operations was Saint Domingue (modern-day Haiti), and his vessel was a small sloop, the appropriately named *Hazard*. Things went fairly well for Captain Clamorgan until the spring of 1780, when the *Hazard* was captured on her way to Philadelphia by a British warship and he lost both his vessel and her cargo.[18]

Both before and after his unfortunate experience at sea, Jacques Clamorgan made New Orleans a regular port of call. He was trading slaves in the city at least as early as 1778. After his first visit to St. Louis he returned to New Orleans, where he was joined by François Marmillon. Jacques did not stay put for long. Marmillon handled their slave-trading operation in New Orleans while Jacques headed off to the Caribbean again. In the spring of 1783 he was in Jamaica, arranging with the British firm of Thompson and Campbell for a shipment of slaves. Soon after Jacques's return from the Caribbean, he and Marmillon had a falling-out over the deal with Thompson and Campbell, but they patched things up, and before long they were on their way back to St. Louis.[19] They arrived toward the end of 1783. Within a year Marmillon died. He had no immediate family. He named as his principal heir the surgeon Claude Mercier, but he did remember Jacques. In token of their friendship he forgave the younger man a four-hundred-dollar debt.[20]

Even before Marmillon's death, Jacques Clamorgan was searching out other partners. In the autumn of 1784, he and Pierre Lacoste purchased a piece of land and a smallish house in St. Louis to serve as both their home and a place of business. Over the next couple of years Jacques bought other properties—a piece of land and a more substantial stone house, two adjoining lots with an even larger house and outbuildings, and yet another lot with a simple wooden structure on it.[21] It was in one of these homes, probably the largest of them, that a census taker found Jacques living in 1787, at which point his household comprised nine persons: Jacques himself, two enslaved women, a free black man, four white day laborers, and a carpenter. A year or two later Jacques took in an elderly Frenchman, Jean-Baptiste Tardif. Tardif was a childless widower with whom Jacques did business on occasion, and in gratitude for Jacques's care, Tardif left him his entire estate. With land, money, credit, and contacts, in a few short years Jacques Clamorgan had become a fixture in St. Louis.[22]

In navigating his way through the complex world of commerce in Upper Louisiana and across the river in the Illinois Country, Jacques Clamorgan had a distinct advantage over many of his rivals. French was his mother tongue, but he also had an impressive command of English, since the breadth of his business contacts in the Caribbean had demanded it. On the "American" side of the Mississippi—with Britain's defeat in the War for Independence, the Illinois Country was now U.S. territory—English was rapidly gaining ground. Not to be able to converse with buyers and sellers, or scrutinize a written agreement for loopholes and disclaimers, was to expose oneself to all manner of financial embarrassment. Jacques sometimes went over to Cahokia to do business in the court there, and the people he crossed paths with were a mixed bunch—French men and women and French-speaking Canadians, but also plenty of folks with decidedly "Anglo" names. Occasionally he wrapped up legal matters for friends back in St. Louis. Mostly, though, he was in pursuit of money he was owed, for his credit network had begun to expand in all directions.[23] Usually payment was to be made in Cahokia or St. Louis, but not always. In 1787, Pierre Lacoste entered into an agreement to pay Clamorgan almost sixteen thousand livres, and that agreement stipulated that part of the debt was to be liquidated at Michilimackinac, the old French trading post on the straits of Mackinac between Lake Michigan and Lake Huron that had been under British control since the end of the French and Indian War.[24] Promissory notes changed hands, traded like currency in a specie-poor region. Jacques assigned notes to other people and received notes from them, putting him at one remove, sometimes more, from the original debtor, and he collected his debts in many forms: a house, a shipment of furs, a quantity of flour or tobacco, even crops still in the ground.[25]

What kind of a businessman was Jacques Clamorgan? People in the Illinois Country soon discovered what others in the West Indies had already learned. He needed watching. In 1788, for instance, several American traders made a concerted effort to bring him to book. He had racked up a debt he could not pay, but as long as he stayed in Spanish territory and kept his trips to Cahokia brief, he was essentially immune from prosecution. However, his creditors got a tip that he was heading to Louisville on an extended "Speculating journey," and the chase was on. Clamorgan had no intention of being hauled into court, especially by Americans, whom he had somewhat rashly described as "nothing less than a Set of Cattle." By the time the necessary paperwork for his apprehension and prosecution reached the right people in Louisville, he had left for Nashville. From Nashville he took to the Cumberland River and traveled back to St. Louis by canoe.[26] To get Clamorgan when he was in U.S. territory and answerable to American justice, one had to move swiftly; and always, it seemed, he moved more swiftly.

During this period, chattel slavery was woven into the social and economic fabric of St. Louis, as it was into that of the other French communities of the region. Slaves were much in demand in the town: by 1787 almost a quarter of the population was classed as black or of mixed African and European descent, and the majority of those so classified were unfree.[27] Enslaved men raised crops and tended to livestock. They served as boatmen on the river and mastered all manner of skilled trades. Women did domestic work as well as field labor, and in a frontier setting where white men outnumbered white women, inevitably some became the concubines of their owners. The existence of a ready market for slaves suited Jacques Clamorgan very well. Long before he ever set foot in St. Louis, slaves had constituted a large part of his stock in trade. The Spanish, eager for good relations with native peoples, had outlawed Indian enslavement in 1769, eliciting howls of protest from Upper Louisiana's French settlers, since French law had sanctioned the practice.[28] The ban on Indian slaves did not bother Clamorgan. He had his sources for supplies of black people and had no need to deal in Indian captives. Perennial lawbreaker that he was, though, he would undoubtedly have violated that prohibition had it been in his interest to do so.

The roster of the enslaved who passed through Jacques's hands is a lengthy one. In most cases a first name and an approximate age were all that were recorded. Slaves' names were not of their own choosing, and tracking them is a lesson in the mutability of language. Françoise was "Francisca" to the Spanish clerk and "Fanny" to his English-speaking counterpart. Juan Bautista was "Jean-Baptiste" in the French records and "John" or "Jack" in an English bill of sale—assuming a new owner did not completely rename the woman or man he had purchased. [29]

Trips downriver to New Orleans to see the governor or take care of some other piece of business gave Jacques Clamorgan ample opportunity to pick up a "likely" slave or dispose of one. Closer to home, he was often in the old French settlement of Ste. Geneviève, where the inhabitants were just as eager as the residents of St. Louis to buy and sell slaves. Occasionally he ventured across the river into American territory to trade a slave or two.[30] There were many more sales in and around St. Louis, though, the earliest in 1785. Jacques purchased slaves from and sold them to his neighbors.[31] He also hired slaves. In 1787 one such arrangement led to a lawsuit when Charles Sanguinet's man Cezar drowned while in Jacques Clamorgan's employ. Sanguinet alleged negligence. Jacques responded that Sanguinet had known the risks of renting out a slave. This was purely a property dispute. Neither party cared about the loss of a human life beyond its cash value.[32]

One transaction almost landed Jacques Clamorgan in jail, however. In 1789, Daniel McElduff complained to the court in Cahokia that Jacques had broken into his home in Ste. Geneviève and made off with two slaves, a woman and her newborn baby. McElduff had agreed to sell a parcel of slaves to Clamorgan, but they had had a falling-out over payment and over when exactly the mother and child would be fit enough to travel to St. Louis. Clamorgan concluded that McElduff was trying to cheat him, and he and two of his male slaves set off to take his property by force. Housebreaking was a felony, and the court ordered Clamorgan's arrest, but matters were soon resolved.[33] As for the unfortunate woman dragged off in the middle of the night by total strangers, she became yet another of Jacques's items for sale, as did her infant.

Now and again some of Clamorgan's slaves got the better of him. In 1790 he purchased two men and a woman in Nashville for delivery to him in St. Louis, but the trio fled en route, obliging him to sue their seller. He was luckier in another matter, that of the slaves Will and Phebe: they had the decency not to abscond with their children until after Jacques had sold them to one of his neighbors. Because they waited until they had been handed over before making their escape, the loss was the purchaser's and not the seller's.[34]

Jacques Clamorgan obeyed some of the provisions of the Spanish slave code when it suited him. Although he was not noted for his piety, until he had a falling-out with the parish priest Father Didier toward the end of 1793, he was reasonably zealous about seeing that his slaves received the sacraments. Not until Didier died and another man was appointed in his stead did Jacques again start having his slaves baptized.[35] Not that his attention to his slaves' spiritual lives indicated any real solicitude for their well-being. The brief history of one family makes this abundantly clear. Charles and Catherine, an American-born couple he owned, were fairly prolific, and he arranged for the baptism of each of their children. Even so, he had no compunction about splitting up the family in 1793 when he needed cash. Charles went to one buyer and Catherine to another, while Jacques kept their children.[36]

Besides trading in slaves, Jacques saw tremendous potential in real estate. He picked up parcels of land in St. Louis, confident they would increase in value as the community grew. He was also keen to acquire property on the Meramec River, which flowed through a good part of what is present-day southern Missouri before emptying into the Mississippi twenty miles below St. Louis. Farming land along its banks was good, and those same banks were dotted with salines, or salt deposits. In an era before refrigeration, a reliable supply of salt was vital for preserving meat. Jacques was eager to monopolize the salines, and he came close to doing so, acquiring in 1791 almost 13,500 acres on the Meramec at a place called the Tête de Boeuf.[37]

Indian raids were a fact of life in these outlying areas, however, as Jacques had reason to know. In the summer of 1788 a roving band of Osage descended on one of his farms, killing one of his tenants, an Englishman by the name of Keer; Keer's wife; and three of their five children. This did not deter Jacques from buying more land in areas subject to attack.[38] The Meramec holdings were ones he was especially eager to develop. Writing to the lieutenant-governor of the territory in the spring of 1793, he detailed all that he had done to increase the prosperity of the area. He had kept local farmers supplied with essentials and paid to set up a saltworks. Then he cut to the chase. He had debts to pay off, but he did not want to lean too heavily on the farmers who owed him money. Why didn't the government establish a settlement on the Meramec? It would do much to curb the aggression of the Osage and give a real boost to the area's white inhabitants. Naturally, he did not mention that the settlement he proposed would drive up land values and benefit him personally. The answer he received was that although a settlement would do much good in the region, international tensions would have to ease before the government could bring in farming families from Europe, as Clamorgan had suggested.[39]

Despite his disappointment, Jacques continued acquiring land along the Meramec. In June 1793 he talked the lieutenant-governor into giving him 800 arpents (equivalent to 670 acres). Over the course of the next few months he got two more concessions totaling 4,800 arpents. Some of it he leased out, and another of his tenants suffered the same fate as the Keer family. Whenever Jacques Clamorgan could get a grant along the Meramec he was happy to take it, and the authorities obliged him again and again, in one instance with no less than eight thousand arpents "for the purpose of procuring wood for [his] salt-works." He also got a sizable grant on Gingras Creek, another rather exposed area to the north of St. Louis. His tenants would have to farm with one eye open for roving Osage, but that was no concern of Jacques's, as long as the rent came in. By the mid-1790s Jacques Clamorgan was one of the largest private landholders in the region, and certainly one of the most aggressive.[40]

Among Jacques Clamorgan's many talents was the talent to flatter, and he wasted no time in exercising it in 1792, when a new governor was appointed to oversee the whole of the Louisiana Territory. Jacques and other prominent citizens of St. Louis greeted the Baron de Carondelet with a flowery congratulatory address. The following year, Zenon Trudeau arrived in St. Louis to take charge of Upper Louisiana, and Clamorgan helped craft a memorial to the king of Spain in which he praised Trudeau to the skies.[41] Jacques Clamorgan meant to work himself into the good graces of Governor Carondelet and Lieutenant-Governor Trudeau, find out what policies they intended to pursue, and use that knowledge to his advantage.

From the start, the most pressing concern of the two new officers of the Spanish Crown was that of territorial integrity. The British might have suffered a humiliating defeat in the War for Independence, but they were hardly a spent force on the North American continent. They had a firm hold on Canada and every intention of exploiting it. The Spanish authorities had good reason to feel uneasy. Pushing down from Canada, by the early 1790s the British were gaining the upper hand in the fur trade, strengthening their influence among the Indian peoples who lived along the upper Mississippi and Missouri rivers, and generally reorienting business, diverting more of it up to Montreal via the straits of Mackinac.[42] Losing out in the fur trade was serious enough for the Spanish, but there was a growing fear that the British were intent on pushing farther south, working their way down the Missouri and its tributaries to New Mexico. The fears of Carondelet and Trudeau were reinforced by reports they were receiving. In the autumn of 1792 the independent trader Jacques D'Eglise recounted his venture up the Missouri. He bore the disquieting news that the British were only two weeks' travel from the Mandan villages, in the southwestern part of what is today North Dakota.[43]

Jacques Clamorgan played with consummate skill on the panic induced by news of the encroaching British. "Our New Mexico . . . continually arouses their desires, especially since they have found out that they can get there by land in fifteen or twenty days," he wrote Carondelet in 1793. Almost as ominous as the British were the Americans, who might abandon their neutral stance at any moment and decide on an incursion into Spanish territory. The solution Jacques offered for the whole of Upper Louisiana was the same one he had put forward a few months earlier on a smaller scale for the Meramec region: managed immigration. The Spanish government should recruit immigrants in Europe, ship them across the ocean in neutral vessels, land them in Philadelphia, bring them overland to Illinois, and settle them on small farms in Spanish territory, to constitute a "human rampart." Jacques even had cost estimates to show that the initial outlay could be recouped in three or four years. He capped off his proposal by making the point that he was a man of erudition, throwing in a couple of classical allusions and mangling a quote from Horace's *Epistles* to the effect that a job begun was a job already half completed. Clearly, if the governor wanted someone with the wisdom and experience to handle this resettlement program, he need look no further than Jacques Clamorgan.[44]

Carondelet did not follow up on Jacques's suggestion. He had already devised his own plan for thwarting the British. Jacques was only briefly disappointed. When he found out what the governor had in mind, Jacques Clamorgan saw a way to make his fortune and serve the interests of the Spanish Crown at the same time.

Carondelet was convinced of the necessity of encouraging Spanish commercial endeavors on the upper Missouri. His predecessors had not been sufficiently energetic or farsighted in that regard: the "old ways" had been the only ways they knew. It was time to abandon the restrictive practices that had limited the initiative of many an ambitious merchant. In 1792, Carondelet opened the Missouri trade to any Spanish subjects who wanted to engage in it, provided they got the appropriate licenses. Taking things one step further, the following summer he sent Zenon Trudeau his outline for a thoroughgoing reorganization of commerce. It was his belief that distributing the trade on the Missouri by lot each year, under the direction of a syndic (a principal agent and administrator), would be both fair and effective.[45]

Trudeau assembled the merchants in St. Louis on October 15, 1793, to share with them Carondelet's proposals. Although they reacted positively, they had a few modifications to make. They wanted the governor to give them exclusive trading rights with all the peoples north of the Ponca (who lived in what is today South Dakota) for ten years. They also insisted on permission to buy trade goods from the British and the Americans, given the difficulty they often encountered getting merchandise through officially sanctioned Spanish channels. And they wanted to set up a company to squeeze out the British and sponsor expeditions to the West. They were convinced, as were many of their contemporaries, that one could reach the Pacific Ocean by following the Missouri River. Before disbanding, they elected as their syndic Jacques Clamorgan.[46]

Through the winter months, when many of the traders were out among the various Native American peoples buying furs, Clamorgan gave a great deal of thought to Carondelet's proposal and his brother merchants' response. How should he proceed as syndic, and of course how could he make money for himself? As a first move, he sought and got Trudeau's permission to hold a meeting to distribute shares of the trade. That meeting went ahead on May 3, 1794, when the traders were back in town. There were nine trading posts already established on the Missouri, and Clamorgan oversaw their division among twenty-five merchants from St. Louis and three from Ste. Geneviève, with an additional share set aside for Trudeau.[47]

That was not the end of Clamorgan's planning, however. Again with Trudeau's consent (and very active encouragement), he held another meeting two days later at which he presented his ideas for the trading company they had talked about the previous autumn. The plan was straightforward. The company would receive from the authorities a ten-year monopoly on trade with the northern tribes. Everyone who bought in would make an initial pledge of one thousand pesos (well over twenty thousand dollars by today's reckoning) to fund expeditions. When ship-ments of furs arrived in St. Louis, there would be a general sharing out of the profits. The meeting adjourned and the assembled merchants were given a week to mull over Clamorgan's proposal. On May 12 they reconvened, and at that point nine men signed on to what became known as the Commercial Company for the Discovery of the Nations of the Upper Missouri. For his help in moving things along, Trudeau was given a share.[48] In his report to the governor, Jacques Clamorgan had harsh words for those who did not join the new endeavor. While some were reluctant to take risks, others had remained aloof, "with the intention of harming . . . the enterprise." This was no doubt a swipe at Auguste and Pierre Chouteau, who already had the Osage trade sewn up. Some men, of course, were disinclined to gamble on what seemed like a speculative venture.[49]

Zenon Trudeau earned his stake in the company. As he explained to Carondelet within a couple of weeks of that May 12 meeting, he had already pushed the partners to send out one expedition to the Man-dan. Another would be sent the following year.[50] Carondelet heartily approved, and wasted no time granting the company the asked-for ten-year monopoly. So delighted was he, in fact, that in the king's name he offered a prize of two thousand Spanish silver dollars (later raised to three thousand, equivalent to fifty thousand dollars today) to the first Spanish subject to reach the Pacific via the Missouri.[51]

Jacques Clamorgan had had some experience fitting out trading expeditions in the past, but this would be a far more ambitious under-taking than anything he had engaged in before.[52] The Missouri Compa-ny's first expedition set out in June 1794 under the command of the local schoolmaster Jean-Baptiste Truteau, who was, despite the slightly dif-ferent spelling of their last names, a relative of the lieutenant-governor's. Clamorgan and fellow company director Antoine Reihle gave Truteau specific instructions. He was to establish good relations with the Man-dan and get as much information as he could from them about more distant peoples, especially those "on the other side of the Rocky chain." Along the way he was to make notes about distances and water courses, and pick up any furs he came across. He was also to find out what trade items appealed to what peoples.[53]

Truteau's party got as far as South Dakota before disaster struck: the Teton Sioux pillaged their supplies of trade goods. The traders took refuge among the neighboring Arikara, only to find that *they* had already disposed of their furs to free-lancer Jacques D'Eglise. Truteau moved south and spent time with the Pawnee, gaining much knowledge but precious little else. He warned, though, of the energy the British were displaying. Let them once get hold of the trade on the Missouri and there would be no stopping them.[54]

Although the company had gotten off to a less than profitable start, its members remained confident through the first year or so. On July 8, 1795, Clamorgan and Reihle responded to a request from Zenon Trudeau for a progress report. They confessed to the lieutenant-governor that they were a little disappointed. Building and maintaining forts and buying the favor of the various tribes cost money, and the British and their Indian allies were proving very aggressive. However, the Missouri Company was dispatching well-organized expeditions under capable leaders, and in the next few months one of them would surely cross the Rockies and reach that elusive goal, "the Sea of the West." Before long there would be a chain of forts all the way from St. Louis to the Pacific.[55]

The company's second expedition was a failure, but planning soon started on a third. Although Jacques Clamorgan exuded confidence, Zenon Trudeau was beginning to have his doubts, telling Governor Carondelet the expense of yet another expedition had frightened off several members of the company, himself included. Trudeau was rapidly coming to the conclusion that Clamorgan "has at heart his own interests."[56]

The third expedition was the best organized. Its leader was James Mackay, a Scotsman who had worked for some years for the British trading companies before switching his allegiance and becoming a Spanish subject. Mackay reported back to Clamorgan, describing the problems he had confronted and offering suggestions about how to avoid future depredations. It was vital to win over the Oto, who lived along the Missouri in what is today southeastern Nebraska. Mackay had promised them that the company would build a fort to protect them against their enemies and supply them with guns. The company had to make good on that pledge, and of course that meant coming up with money.[57]

Jacques Clamorgan promptly embarked on an aggressive letter-writing campaign, always promising Governor Carondelet what he could achieve if he got more trading licenses and funds from the Spanish treasury. On December 15, 1795, for instance, he proposed building a fort near the mouth of the Des Moines River to beat back the British and keep the way open on the Missouri for the company's boats. Recompense would be in the form of exclusive rights for six years to trade with the peoples of the Des Moines, Skunk, and Iowa rivers. Trudeau, however, cautioned Carondelet that Clamorgan's "ambition makes him promise more than he will be able to execute."[58]

What Trudeau did not know was just how subtle a game Jacques Clamorgan was playing. He was busy cultivating an influential young Irish merchant to serve the interests of the company and, more important, the interests of the company Clamorgan himself was hoping to build. Andrew Todd was a junior partner in the Canadian firm of Todd, McGill and Co. His uncle, Isaac Todd, and his uncle's partner, James McGill, held shares in the North West Company and also ran their own fur trading concern. The younger Todd was industriously pursuing the trade in furs, partly on behalf of his uncle's firm and partly on his own account. Hitherto he had operated out of Canada through the straits of Mackinac, shipping furs to Europe via Montreal. Such dealings as he had had in the Mississippi and Missouri trade had not been very fortunate, and more than once he had fallen afoul of the Spanish authorities. Why, then, was he amenable to Clamorgan's suggestion that he reroute his trade via St. Louis and New Orleans? Because in June 1796, under the terms of Jay's Treaty, the British were obligated to hand over Fort Mackinac (the trading post that had replaced Michilimackinac) to the United States, and Todd anticipated a considerable financial loss as a result. When the young merchant visited St. Louis in the autumn of 1795, Jacques Clamorgan went to work on him. The plan they came up with was that Todd would have trade goods shipped from London to New Orleans and brought upriver to St. Louis, instead of downriver from Montreal via Mackinac.[59] Clamorgan would get commissions from the company and from Todd on all the merchandise he arranged for the company to purchase. In every way Clamorgan stood to gain.[60]

Clamorgan wasted no time letting Governor Carondelet know of the new arrangement and stressing the need to do everything possible to bind Todd to the Missouri Company. More forts were needed, and more men capable of garrisoning them. Todd had promised to recruit those men in Canada. With Todd's backing, the Missouri Company could send out more expeditions, and Clamorgan confidently predicted that a year hence he would be able to send Carondelet "the exact map of the Missouri as far as its sources and the exact voyage [to] the western sea." They must spare no effort. James Mackay had reported that the British were building forts and encroaching where they had no business to be. "It is time to close the doors to this nation if we do not wish them to kick us out."[61] And the Spanish could do just that with Andrew Todd's help.

In letter after letter, Clamorgan harped on his ties with Todd, boasting that he had single-handedly brought him on board to become the Missouri Company's "supply-house." He conceded that Todd had lavished certain favors on him, but that was only fair since, in promoting the company, "I have exposed my reputation, my credit, and my fortune." He also announced that as of May 1, 1796, there would be a new business concern, Clamorgan and Loisel. He was joining forces with Regis Loisel, a young French Canadian who had been the Chouteaus' clerk in Mackinac. Just what the relationship of this new entity would be to the Missouri Company he did not bother to explain. He was also endeavoring to persuade the other members of the Missouri Company to deal exclusively with Todd for their trade goods. Some were opposed to this, and he begged Carondelet to authorize him as director to require them to patronize Todd. No, Todd was not yet a Spanish subject, Jacques conceded, but he was willing to demonstrate his loyalty to Spain.[62] That was good enough for Carondelet. He gave Todd the exclusive right for ten years to trade with the Sac and the Fox, two peoples of the upper Midwest, and sanctioned his admittance to the Missouri Company, even though, as a foreigner, he was technically ineligible for membership.[63] Carondelet also agreed to require Missouri Company members to buy their merchandize from Todd, a move that delighted Clamorgan because it would silence the discontent and "malicious envy" of certain individuals.[64]

Jacques Clamorgan made use of his ties with Todd to gain real estate as well as money and influence. In the summer of 1796 he traveled to New Madrid, another Spanish outpost downriver from St. Louis, and petitioned Charles Dehault Delassus, the commandant of the region, for a grant of 536,904 arpents (over 450,000 acres) some 30 miles below the village of New Madrid. He explained that he had been encouraged by Carondelet to establish a rope manufactory to supply cordage to the Spanish navy. Since he was "connected . . . with a powerful house in Canada," he was in an ideal position to recruit farmers to grow and process hemp once tensions between Spain and Britain eased. (The two nations were on the brink of war, so recruiting settlers in Canada was likely to prove difficult.) Delassus reviewed the request and recommended to Carondelet that it be approved, given that "this remote country [was] so miserable on account of the . . . want of population." Jacques Clamorgan got his land. He never did get his settlers, but the grant was his, and that was all that mattered.[65]

From New Madrid, Clamorgan continued on to New Orleans. Upon his arrival he contacted Carondelet to thank him for his past favors and inform him of certain revisions he had made to the articles governing the Missouri Company, most of which, it went without saying, gave him as director far greater authority.[66] Trudeau had warned Carondelet to expect just such a move. "[D]riven by his ambition," Clamorgan "wanted to usurp everything." Trouble was already brewing over the order that the company buy exclusively from Todd. Clamorgan had contracted with him without consulting the other members, because it suited his own interests: "[H]e seeks to force his associates . . . to resign . . . in order alone to profit from the privileges . . . Your Excellency has solicited in favor of the . . . Company."[67] Still, the arrangement with Todd was Clamorgan's trump card, and he played it for all it was worth.

Especially heartening to Clamorgan was the news Carondelet had received from Spain. The Missouri Company had finally received royal approval, along with authorization to raise one hundred militiamen at a cost of ten thousand pesos a year. Jacques Clamorgan assumed, as did Carondelet at first, that the king would pay. However, Intendant Morales, who would have to sign off on the appropriation, insisted this was not what the king had in mind. The Missouri Company would be responsible for paying the men it recruited and for maintaining the forts it built.[68]

In late October 1796, Andrew Todd arrived in New Orleans to finalize arrangements with Clamorgan. He undertook to use his own contacts in Canada to get the firm of Clamorgan, Loisel and Co. all the men it needed for its expeditions. He also promised to ship in trade goods from Britain via New Orleans for the partners.[69] Just as Zenon Trudeau had warned, somewhere along the line the Missouri Company had faded out of the picture and been replaced by Clamorgan's personal company.

Todd planned on stopping in New Orleans just a week or two before heading back up north. It was not wise for those unused to the climate to expose themselves to the heat and humidity that beset New Orleans even in the fall. That particular year the summer heat lingered longer than usual, and soon the first cases of yellow fever were reported. And while Jacques Clamorgan had become inured to the deadly malady during his various sojourns in the West Indies, Todd had not. He fell ill, and by the end of November he was dead. It was a financial and personal blow for Clamorgan. Todd had advanced the now hopelessly intertwined Missouri Company and Clamorgan, Loisel and Co. over eighty thousand dollars in trade goods. Everything hinged on how Todd's heirs and creditors decided to proceed. Would they keep his business arrangements going, or would they demand their money?[70]

Jacques Clamorgan soon got his answer. He and the two companies were caught in the middle of a fight between a couple of hardheaded men of business. Daniel Clark, Jr., had been Todd's representative in New Orleans, and he wanted to maintain ties to Clamorgan, Loisel and Co. and the Missouri Company. He had advanced money and merchandise to both enterprises and faced a hefty loss if either or both failed. He asked the authorities to continue the concessions granted to Todd. Governor Carondelet was sympathetic. Clark was a longtime resident of New Orleans: he was also wealthy and well connected, and Carondelet thought it in everyone's best interests to accommodate him.[71] Clark was not, however, Todd's heir. Isaac Todd was, and he had no wish to take over his nephew's trading venture. What Todd Sr. wanted was payment in full for the trade goods.[72]

Even with disaster looming, Jacques Clamorgan pushed ahead with building up his real estate empire. On March 1, 1797, he approached Trudeau. The lieutenant-governor had been kind enough to encourage his "industrious exertions," and His Majesty, in gracious acknowledgment of Jacques's "excessive expenses," had allowed Jacques ten thousand pesos a year. (Clamorgan glossed over two crucial facts: the money was supposed to go not to him personally but to the Missouri Company, and Intendant Morales had vetoed payment anyway.) The subsidy had not been paid, and Clamorgan hoped Trudeau would recompense him with a modest land concession—not much over a half million arpents—on the Missouri, to erect sawmills and gristmills and maintain a herd of cattle so he could supply New Orleans with salt provisions. Trudeau complied, and Carondelet signed off on the grant. It seemed a simple enough way of saving a business enterprise neither of them wanted to see fail.[73]

Buoyed up by his success, Clamorgan kept asking. Could he have a few thousand arpents here? What about a concession there? He pledged to put the land to good use. And always there was the promise that, with enough land, he would have the means to launch another expedition up the Missouri, to the greater glory of Spain and the undoing of the British. By the autumn of 1798, Trudeau had received nine separate requests from Clamorgan, and he was getting a little irritated. Clamorgan also had to reckon with a change in personnel in New Orleans. Carondelet had been replaced, and the new governor, Manuel Gayoso de Lemos, was less generous.[74]

At this point, the one remaining independent shareholder in the Missouri Company, Joseph Robidoux, launched an attack on Clamorgan. The petition Robidoux submitted to Gayoso de Lemos put a very negative spin on the evolution of the Missouri Company. Naturally, he could not vilify Carondelet or Trudeau; instead, he painted a picture of well-intentioned officials led astray by a glib talker. The project was "wisely conceived," and Robidoux had been persuaded to buy in, as had others. Clamorgan had taken them in with his "intriguing [and] great talking." Some investors pulled out when the first expedition ended in failure. Robidoux kept at it longer, and that decision cost him ten thousand dollars. No, he had no intention of suing to recoup his losses, but he wanted the Missouri Company reconstituted and Clamorgan barred from any role in its activities.[75]

Gayoso de Lemos told Trudeau to call Clamorgan to account, and

Trudeau was obliged to inform his superior that things did not look good. Clamorgan, Loisel and Co. had indeed managed to get their hands on all but one of the shares of the Missouri Company. With Todd's death, though, "the great project has gone to the four winds."[76] Clamorgan was still boasting about what he could achieve if the government gave him his ten thousand pesos a year. The company would drive back the British and "place . . . the standard of our empire in the midst of the most distant savage nations."[77] Trudeau was unimpressed: these were "the absurdities of a . . . madman." Of course Clamorgan wanted the ten thousand pesos, but by then it was a pittance compared to what he owed.[78]

Jacques Clamorgan's financial woes were not his alone. He had extended credit to scores of people in St. Louis itself and in outlying villages such as Marais des Liards and St. Ferdinand. To try to save himself, he began pressing them to pay up. Daniel Clark and Isaac Todd both appointed attorneys, and *they* began harassing anyone unfortunate enough to have become enmeshed in Jacques Clamorgan's financial web. Debtors were forced to pledge their farms, their cattle, everything they had. Farmers and small-scale traders did not know whom they were supposed to listen to: Clark's man, William Porter; or Todd's, John Hay; or Clamorgan himself. Most could not pay up anyway.

Tensions rose, and Jacques found himself on the receiving end of threats of bodily harm.[79] He tried everything he could think of to dig himself out, but it was only a matter of time before he was driven into bankruptcy. In the summer of 1798 he dispatched a pleading letter to Clark, declaring that he and Regis Loisel would willingly hand over to Clark's representative everything Clamorgan, Loisel and Co. had to liquidate the debt, but Isaac Todd's attorney had "embargoed" all their assets. That approach cut no ice with Clark, so Jacques traveled down to New Orleans to make a personal appeal. Would Clark give the firm more time? He was begging for mercy.[80]

This tactic did not work, so once he was back in St. Louis, he tried another. On the morning of September 27 he rushed to Trudeau with a tale of woe—one that involved selling out a friend. Jacques Clamorgan and John Hay had been acquainted for several years. Hay boarded with Clamorgan when business brought him over to St. Louis from his home base in Cahokia, and in 1797, when Hay married, Clamorgan presented him and his new bride with an elegant carriage by way of a wedding gift.[81] However, Hay's role as Isaac Todd's representative complicated the relationship between the two men, and Clamorgan was quite prepared to try to save himself by casting aspersions on Hay. He explained to Trudeau that Hay had skipped town the previous night. Clamorgan knew Hay had the books of Clamorgan, Loisel and Co. at his lodgings in St. Louis, so he had hurried over to retrieve them, only to discover that Hay had done some fancy bookkeeping with the intent of defrauding Clark for the benefit of Todd. Clamorgan asked for Trudeau's help in authenticating the accounts. According to Clamorgan, he and Loisel had bought the shares of three of the members of the Missouri Company on behalf of Andrew Todd, who had wanted to increase his holdings without having that fact generally known. There were other matters. Clamorgan, Loisel and Co. had paid to construct a storehouse in New Orleans for the furs that were to be sent downriver from St. Louis on Andrew Todd's account, and had outfitted a bateau to bring trade goods upriver from New Orleans to St. Louis for Todd. The point Clamorgan was anxious to make was that a large part of the debt he and Loisel owed had been incurred on instructions from and in the interests of Andrew Todd. Unfortunately, Hay had appropriated the correspondence proving that.[82]

Trudeau was understandably skeptical, as were Daniel Clark, Jr., and Auguste Chouteau, the man to whom Clark had given power of attorney. Figuring that William Porter needed help to bring Jacques Clamorgan to book, Clark had enlisted the aid of Chouteau, who was only too familiar with Jacques Clamorgan's penchant for playing fast and loose with the truth. Neither Chouteau nor Clark was inclined to buy the story of purloined papers or to see Jacques Clamorgan as an innocent victim of the machinations of John Hay and Isaac Todd. Clark wanted his money. On his behalf, Chouteau requested that Trudeau seize all of Clamorgan's property in St. Louis, and the property of Regis Loisel and John Hay (on the basis that everything Hay had recouped in Isaac Todd's name actually belonged to Clark).[83] Trudeau complied and began inventorying the assets of the three men. Trade goods of all kinds came to light in Clamorgan, Loisel and Co.'s warehouse—

fabrics, needles, razors, candle molds, snuff boxes, lancets, beaver traps, whistles, earrings, a small bugle, a large quantity of firearms, and "Four silver crosses for the Indians." Loisel and Hay had very little personal property in St. Louis. It did not take long to seize their assets. Trudeau then turned his attention to the contents of Jacques Clamorgan's home, noting down all his possessions, including his slaves, his furniture, and the contents of his library. He also demanded a list of Jacques's real estate. Jacques tried to hide everything he could by conniving with one or two trusted friends, but there was only so much he could do.[84]

Jacques Clamorgan was desperate. Once more he hastened down to New Orleans to plead his case. He ended up staying longer than he intended, for Clark used the power of the law to prevent him from absconding. Eventually, after much haggling, Jacques reached an agreement with Clark, and both Clark and Chouteau helped him with credit.[85] They awoke to the realization that if Jacques went under he would drag down many more people, not just in St. Louis but also throughout Upper Louisiana, with devastating repercussions for the financial life of the region. As for Isaac Todd, he was ultimately frustrated in his bid to get anything back from "that Rascal Clamorgan."[86]

Lesser men would have retired from business at this point. Not Jacques Clamorgan. He had his fortune to rebuild, and it was time to see what he could achieve with a new governor. Gayoso de Lemos died in 1799, and the Marqués de Casa Calvo replaced him. This called for yet another trip to New Orleans. Early in 1800, Clamorgan arrived in the city to present his case. He described to Casa Calvo all he had done, or wanted the governor to believe he had done, to promote trade and exploration, and he detailed the expenses he had incurred. Most unfairly, Zenon Trudeau had not given him (on behalf of the Missouri Company, of course) the trading licenses he should have received. The company had established posts among the Oto, Omaha, and Ponca, and Jacques needed those licenses. He got the privileges restored, but then he asked for exclusive rights to trade with the Kansa people. He would have done better to leave well enough alone. Casa Calvo, irritated by the incessant pleading, reversed himself on the Omaha and

Ponca.[87] No matter. Casa Calvo was soon replaced by Juan Manuel de Salcedo. Clamorgan tried his luck with him. He did not get everything he wanted, but he did secure exclusive trading rights with the peoples of the Kansas and Platte rivers for five years. With the licenses he already had from Casa Calvo, he had almost the entire trade of the Missouri, except for the Osage and some of the Pawnee.[88] Did he have these privileges on behalf of the Missouri Company or as a private trader? That was a matter of opinion.

Back in St. Louis, Trudeau had been replaced as lieutenant-governor by Charles Dehault Delassus, so Clamorgan took up with him the matter of the ten thousand pesos. Could Delassus get him the money, with arrears from June 1796, when the king had given his blessing to the Missouri Company? And would Delassus grant him the right to build forts along the Kansas and Platte rivers to protect a new route to the Mandan villages?[89] Delassus soon discovered what Trudeau could have told him after six long years of dealing with Jacques Clamorgan: Give the man anything, and he would be back for more. Refuse to grant his requests, and he would simply fire off another barrage of petitions.

Not surprisingly, Jacques Clamorgan had no shortage of enemies. Many of his fellow traders resented the monopolies he seemed to secure with relative ease, despite his past.[90] In 1800, Joseph Robidoux spearheaded a petition drive to wreck the Missouri Company (insofar as it was still functioning) by getting the governor to revoke its privileges. Failing in that attempt, he conspired against Clamorgan with another trader, Manuel Lisa, but Clamorgan won out.[91] Robidoux and Lisa were up against a consummate risk taker. In an era when travel entailed not only a huge expenditure of time but also considerable danger, Jacques Clamorgan was ready to drop everything and head off to New Orleans. Most of his enemies were content to send the governor a respectful letter or two when they wanted a favor. Jacques Clamorgan was far more likely to turn up on the governor's doorstep.

Despite the differences Clamorgan had with his brother merchants, his desire to make money resulted in interesting alliances. In 1801, he and Auguste Chouteau joined forces to equip Regis Loisel for an expedition to the Upper Missouri. And in 1803, Jacques Clamorgan and Joseph Robidoux, once sworn enemies, collaborated to outfit another expedition.[92] It was the same with Manuel Lisa. As Clamorgan knew from long experience, greed had a way of transforming rivals into partners. And given the changes that were about to overtake everyone who did business on the Missouri, the willingness to enter into alliances would prove crucial.

In the early weeks of 1802 the inhabitants of St. Louis learned of Spain's agreement to trade them, along with the rest of the Louisiana Territory, to France.[93] Actually, Spain had been trying to unload the province for several years, but cash-strapped France lacked the means to pay. Then, for reasons of his own, France's first consul decided it was time to talk. In 1800, in the supposedly secret Treaty of San Ildefonso, Napoleon pledged to make the king of Spain's brother-in-law the ruler of the Duchy of Tuscany in return for the Louisiana Territory and a pledge never to relinquish it to a third power and imperil Spain's far more valuable provinces of Mexico and Texas. Ultimately Napoleon reneged, but he still expected Spain to give up Louisiana, which he envisaged serving as the breadbasket for France's colony of Saint Domingue once his forces had crushed the slave rebellion there and restored French control.

The white citizens of St. Louis, many of them of French ancestry, may have welcomed the return to French rule, but they had little time to savor it. With the failure of his armies to retake "the jewel of the Antilles," the Louisiana Territory lost its strategic importance in Napoleon's grand design. It was at this juncture that Thomas Jefferson, getting wind of the transfer from Spain, dispatched negotiators to Paris to buy New Orleans. For years Midwestern farmers had been demanding that the government secure them unimpeded access to the Mississippi. Wrangling between Spain and the United States had ended in 1795 with the Treaty of San Lorenzo, but the treaty would be meaningless if the Mississippi and the great port at its mouth were no longer under Spanish control.[94] Jefferson's emissaries queried the asking price for New Orleans and were stunned to be offered all of Louisiana for a bargain.

Word of this second regime change broke upon St. Louis in August 1803.[95] In light of his trips to New Orleans and his habit of welcoming all manner of visitors to his home in St. Louis, Jacques Clamorgan may have gotten wind of it even before that. Little went on concerning the Louisiana Territory that he did not learn of from one or another of his sources. Even so, there was precious little he could do about the transition to American rule beyond preparing himself for momentous changes.

On November 30, 1803, in a formal ceremony at the Cabildo in New Orleans, prefect Pierre de Laussat took possession of the city and the entire Louisiana Territory from Spain. The transfer from France to the United States did not happen for another three weeks. Things were more casual in St. Louis. Napoleon saved money by not bothering to send anyone over from France to accept Upper Louisiana and then surrender it to the United States. The American commissioner, Amos Stoddard, agreed to handle things. On March 9, 1804, Stoddard crossed over from Illinois and headed for Government House. Delassus welcomed him, and the flag of Spain was lowered. The *tricoleur* flew for just one day before it was hauled down and the Stars and Stripes hoisted in its stead. In twenty-four hours the people of Upper Louisiana, Jacques Clamorgan among them, went from being subjects of His Catholic Majesty to citizens of the French republic to citizens of the United States of America.

Awaiting the formal transfer of sovereignty were the members of the Corps of Discovery, the scientific and military expeditionary force Thomas Jefferson had commissioned to explore the newly purchased territory. They were camped across the river from St. Louis in Illinois, mindful of the need to stay in what was indisputably U.S. territory until the handover had been completed. Finally, on May 14, William Clark set off. Meriwether Lewis left a week later, accompanied on the first leg of his journey by Auguste Chouteau and "many other respectable inhabitants of St. Louis," among them almost certainly Jacques Clamorgan, if he was in town.[96] Two years later the Corps made a triumphal return, having accomplished what Clamorgan had hoped an expedition in *his* employ would achieve.

When he took control of Upper Louisiana in the name of the United States, Amos Stoddard reported that the people of St. Louis seemed perfectly content with the new state of affairs. That happy situation changed as soon as the town's leading men found out what was to happen to the territory and its inhabitants. The Governance Act, technically the "Act erecting Louisiana into two Territories and providing for the Temporary Government thereof," signed into law by Jefferson on March 26, 1804, divided the vast chunk of real estate into two separate entities, the territory of Orleans and the district of Louisiana. The district of Louisiana, which included all the land above the southern border of present-day Arkansas, was placed temporarily under the governance of the Council of Indiana. This immediately raised concerns. Slavery was banned from the territory of Indiana. Would it now be outlawed in Missouri? Equally alarming was the issue of land claims. Congress had decreed that no Spanish grants made after the signing of the Treaty of San Ildefonso (October 1, 1800) and the formal handover to the United States in New Orleans on December 20, 1803, were to be recognized unless the claimants or their families actually lived on the land.[97] Many of the influential men in and around St. Louis felt ill-used and betrayed, and they made sure the president and Congress knew it.[98]

The uncertainty over slavery was soon ended. On October 1, 1804, the Council of Indiana introduced a Black Code for Missouri, modeled on those already in force in Kentucky and Virginia. Slavery was given the sanction of the law.[99] The matter of the Spanish land claims, however, proved far more contentious.

Those like Jacques Clamorgan who had invested heavily in real estate rejoiced when they received word in the spring of 1805 that the Governance Act had been modified. Their happiness was short-lived: once they had the chance to study the new act, they concluded that it was scarcely any better than the old one. Actual occupation of the land was still a prerequisite for confirmation. No claims larger than one square mile would be approved, and claimants had just twelve months to make their case.[100] Clamorgan was among a dozen or so large-scale landowners at a protest meeting at the St. Louis courthouse on February 1, 1806. Congress's latest effort, they argued, robbed honest men of their rights. Unfortunately, their contention that they were not speculators was undermined by the fact that that was exactly what they all were.[101]

For years Jacques Clamorgan had been amassing land titles. Once he learned of the cession of Louisiana to the United States, he snapped up as much land as he could, wherever he could find it—in St. Louis itself, in neighboring St. Charles, on the Meramec, and farther afield.[102] He even had a title to land in what is today South Dakota. His former business partner Regis Loisel held a concession from the Spanish for the huge Cedar Island tract on the upper reaches of the Missouri. Loisel died in 1804, and Clamorgan, who just happened to be one of his executors, purchased the claim for a trifling sum.[103]

The assumption on the part of speculators such as Jacques Clamorgan was that the U.S. government would make them rich by confirming their claims. New arrivals from the east—and Clamorgan and his friends anticipated there would be a flood of them—would have to buy land from the legal owners, namely them. That was not what Jefferson or the majority in Congress had in mind, however. They made it their business to be sure each claim was carefully scrutinized by a specially appointed board. Honest farmers trying to legitimize their titles to a couple of hundred acres had nothing to fear. However, "a set of covetous, rapacious land jobbers" wielding "false, antedated, counterfeited deeds" could expect very different treatment.[104]

The federally appointed Board of Land Commissioners had begun holding hearings in the summer of 1805, several months before Clamorgan and his friends met at the courthouse in February 1806 to register their displeasure. Claimants were instructed to come in with such documents as they had, and such witnesses as they could muster, and state their case. Almost immediately problems arose—problems beyond the obvious one that the majority of claimants and witnesses spoke French, most of the land concessions were written in Spanish, and the commissioners spoke and read English. The board could not help noticing that a remarkably large number of claims had been surveyed in the brief period since the Louisiana Purchase, and this prompted inquiries into the role of Antoine Soulard. He had held the post of surveyor-general during the last years of Spanish rule, and the American authorities had decided it would be politic to keep him on. They did not know what that would lead to. He devoted time and energy to concocting surveys for his friends (Clamorgan among them) and for those willing to pay for his help. When challenged by the board, he insisted he was not guilty of malfeasance; he had simply made a good-faith effort to put the records in order, a task complicated by the fact that few grants had actually been surveyed during the Spanish administration.[105]

The Board of Land Commissioners did not function as smoothly as the federal government had hoped. Quite apart from the problems over language and Surveyor-General Soulard's handiwork, there were bitter divisions among the commissioners. Clamorgan and his associates exploited those divisions for all they were worth. Meanwhile, many of the smaller landowners, who could not afford to wait around for months, even years, for the board to act, sold their claims for whatever they could get.[106] A good many of those claims ended up in the hands of Jacques Clamorgan and other well-heeled individuals. For those who had the luxury of being able to wait, things improved slightly. In 1806, Congress ruled that actual settlement for a ten-year period could be taken as proof that permission to settle had been granted by the Spanish. Another act the following year extended the period for presenting proof of ownership and allowed the board to confirm grants of up to two thousand arpents.[107]

Even with the changes in the law, Jacques Clamorgan did not get everything he wanted, any more than the likes of the Chouteaus and other substantial landowners did. Their smaller claims were confirmed, but the much larger claims they submitted raised eyebrows.[108]

Nevertheless, Jacques Clamorgan did not do badly under the new regime. The governor of the Indiana Territory, William Henry Harrison, had arrived in St. Louis in October 1804 eager to appease influential French inhabitants. Clamorgan secured an appointment as a judge, despite his lack of formal legal training. He even made money renting one of his houses (suitably reinforced) for use as a jail.[109]

Missouri did not remain under Harrison's jurisdiction for long. In the spring of 1805 it became a territory in its own right, and President Jefferson announced the appointment of General James Wilkinson as governor. On July 4 there was a gala Independence Day celebration to welcome him. On the organizing committee for the festivities was none other than Jacques Clamorgan, as eager to ingratiate himself with Wilkinson as he had been with Carondelet and Caso Calvo.[110] A different government, a different language, a different man at the helm—Clamorgan would make the best of the situation. Well disposed though

Clamorgan was to the general, there is nothing to suggest that he was in Wilkinson's inner circle, and certainly no indication that he met Wilkinson's good friend, the former vice-president Aaron Burr, when Burr visited St. Louis to plot the creation of an empire in the West. Co-conspirator Jacques Clamorgan might not have been, but he certainly approved of Wilkinson, and he was among those who petitioned Jefferson to retain the general when rumors began circulating that Wilkinson was not to be trusted.[111]

The pace of Jacques Clamorgan's business activities was as hectic as ever in the wake of the Louisiana Purchase. He made use of the newly created Court of Common Pleas and the Circuit Court, juggling dozens of cases involving everything from unpaid debts to the ownership of hogs and horses. His adversaries were a mix of old French inhabitants and newly arrived Americans. Sometimes he prevailed, and sometimes they did, but anyone he believed owed him a cent could expect to be hauled into court.[112] And of course he continued buying real estate in the expectation that sooner or later the commissioners would confirm his titles and make him rich.

He also tried his hand at diplomacy in a somewhat unlikely quarter. Since the Americans did not follow the Spanish example of giving exclusive trading rights, it was left to the traders themselves to reach informal agreements about who should do business with which Indian tribes or peoples. Jacques Clamorgan's old foe Manuel Lisa had a grudge against the Chouteaus that was poisoning the atmosphere and causing difficulties all around. Clamorgan helped arrange a rapprochement. In the early weeks of 1805 he hosted a couple of dinners to which he invited, among others, Lisa, his brother Joachim, and the Chouteaus. Plied with good food and good wine by an attentive host, the guests reached an amicable agreement: Lisa would focus his energies on the peoples of the Upper Missouri and not challenge the Chouteaus over trade with the Osage.[113]

In the months that followed, Clamorgan and Lisa, who had once been at each other's throats, joined forces, setting their sights not on the Upper Missouri but on the far more enticing prospect of Santa Fé. They had heard that trade goods were much in demand among the people of the Spanish borderlands and that the intrepid adventurer who could get to Santa Fé was assured of returning home a rich man. Clamorgan and Lisa made their preparations. They got the commercial licenses they would need—Clamorgan for the Republican Pawnee and Lisa for the Republican Osage.[114] As far as the American authorities understood it, the two were going to trade with these peoples. In reality, though, they intended simply to pass through their territory.

Jacques Clamorgan had no illusions about the risks he was taking. He was sixty-three years old, and the journey would tax him to the utmost. Hazards aplenty awaited him in the wilderness. Sluggish rivers unexpectedly became raging torrents. Storms sprang up out of nowhere. Native peoples resented incursions into their hunting grounds. And then there was the unpredictable attitude of Spanish officials toward traders from the United States. No matter. Clamorgan would trust to luck and to his powers of persuasion. In 1781 the Spanish authorities had forbidden him to go to St. Louis and he had defied them. Defiant still, he seldom backed down when money was to be made.[115]

Before leaving St. Louis, Jacques had certain family matters to attend to. Although in the eyes of the Church and the law he had no wife or children, the reality was very different. Cohabitation outside the bonds of marriage was commonplace among the merchants of St. Louis. A good many traders had wives and progeny in Indian country. Some of their brother merchants opted for long-term relationships with African American or West Indian women in St. Louis itself. Invariably, though, these men also took white wives and fathered legitimate as well as "natural" children. Jacques Clamorgan rejected monogamy in any form. More to the point, he did not trouble to hide his domestic arrangements. Over the years he lived openly with a succession of black women, all of them at some point his slaves, and several of these women bore him children. One of his final acts before he set off on his epic journey was to ensure that his family—the family so many of his contemporaries refused to recognize as a family—was in good hands.[116]

2

"Ester, a Free Woman of Color"

O F ALL THE WOMEN Jacques Clamorgan shared his St. Louis home with over the years, Ester was by far the best known. The passage of time tinged their relationship with romance, and it was remembered by later generations as a great love story. In one version, Jacques was a Spanish nobleman on his way to represent the king of Spain in the United States sometime around 1790. He stopped off in Cuba, fell in love with Ester, a beautiful slave of African and Spanish descent, married her, and brought her to St. Louis, where the two raised a family together. Another version had Ester arriving in St. Louis with her owners, who were fleeing the slave uprising in Saint Domingue. Jacques saw her, was entranced by her beauty, and begged to be allowed to buy her, after which he married her. Every version of the story—and there were many—agreed on certain points: Ester had borne Jacques's children, and he had cared deeply for her.[1] The former was untrue, the latter doubtful. If love ever factored into the tempestuous relationship of Ester and Jacques, so did the equally powerful emotions of greed, fear, and revenge.

Ester came into Jacques's life in the summer of 1784, not in Cuba, but in the settlement of Kaskaskia, across the river from St. Louis in

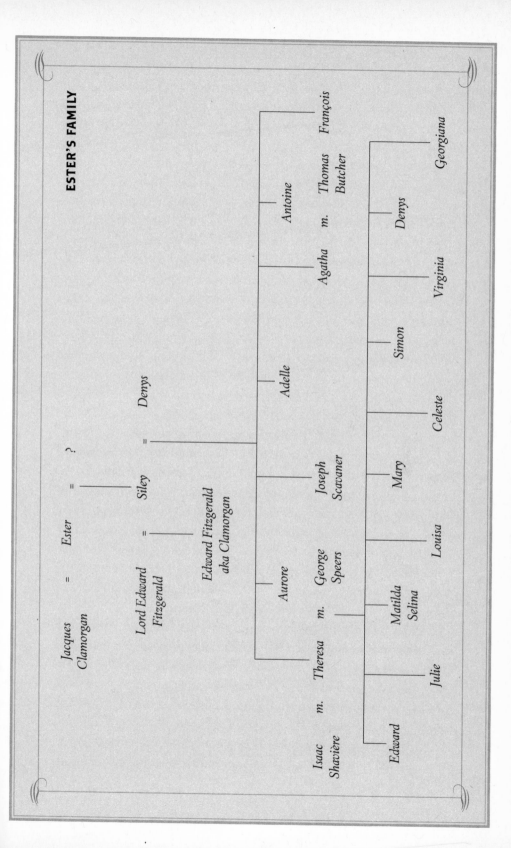

ESTER'S FAMILY

the Illinois Country. Jacques acquired her from frontier trader Ichabod Camp. Originally an Anglican minister, Camp had been for some years the incumbent of a parish in Amherst County, Virginia. He had prospered there, gaining land and slaves. One of those slaves was Ester.[2]

Although Camp endorsed the early protests against Britain, he could not stomach a permanent break with the mother country. Rather than make his peace with Virginia's Patriot gentry, he opted to move to British-controlled West Florida. In 1778, the entire Camp household, including their slaves, boarded flatboats for the journey down the Monongahela, Ohio, and Mississippi rivers to Natchez. But life in Natchez was not to Camp's liking, and the family soon headed back up the Mississippi to Kaskaskia. There, on a tract of land subsequently known as Camp's Creek, the minister's slaves were put to work to create a farm and trading post out of the wilderness.[3] One of the merchants with whom Ichabod Camp traded in the Illinois Country was Jacques Clamorgan, and one of the commodities he was willing to trade was Ester, who was then about thirty-one or thirty-two years of age. Ester had a young daughter, Siley, whose father was likely a slave owned by Camp. Ester's sale forced her to leave Siley behind, but in a matter of months she had persuaded Jacques to buy the girl. On June 17, 1785, Camp sold Siley, described as a twelve-year-old "creole of Virginia," to Jacques for $550.[4]

Becoming Jacques Clamorgan's property and living with him in his home in St. Louis spared Ester and Siley some of the suffering endured by the rest of Camp's slaves. Some died as a result of the rigors of frontier life. Others were abducted by Indians. And when one of his sons-in-law killed Camp in 1786 in a liquor-fueled fight, his surviving slaves, along with the rest of his estate, were parceled out to Camp's widow and children or auctioned off to settle his debts.[5]

Camp's death gained Ester a much-needed ally. His widow left Kaskaskia for St. Louis, where she bought a house not far from the one Ester shared with Jacques. Ann Camp's home provided a refuge for Ester. Louisa Wherry, one of Camp's daughters, recalled that at some point after Ester was sold to Jacques Clamorgan, she fled to Widow Camp's home "and asked permission to remain there a short time Complaining that her Master . . . had beat her and drove her out of his House." She had been sick as a result of the cruel treatment she had received.

Another of Camp's daughters, Catherine Dodge, bore out Wherry's account.[6] Ultimately, though, Ester had to return to Clamorgan. As his property, she had no choice in the matter.

Over the ensuing months the abuse lessened and the nature of Ester and Jacques's relationship evolved. They were still master and slave, but they were also lovers and, in a sense beyond the purely physical one, partners. Jacques relied on Ester to oversee his household during his frequent absences.[7] Although she never learned to read or write, she became fluent in French and may have acquired a smattering of Spanish. This allowed her to manage Jacques's other slaves, his various boarders, and the steady stream of callers who came to consult with him on everything from commercial prospects in distant markets to the politics of Upper Louisiana. Visitors commented that Ester "seemed to have the control within the premises when Clamorgan was absent and very much so when he was at home." They also observed that the couple "lived like man & wife."[8] Had he chosen, Jacques could have married Ester, since Spanish law permitted interracial unions.

On July 14, 1793, Ester became a free woman. Jacques claimed in his deed of emancipation that she had paid him back five hundred dollars of her original purchase price (although in fact she had been given to him to settle a debt). He stated that he was waiving the balance out of principles of religion and humanity and gratitude for what he described as her "faithful services." He also pledged to pay her fifty dollars each year she remained with him.[9]

Ester then negotiated Siley's freedom. Some weeks after he freed Ester, Jacques appeared before Lieutenant-Governor Zenon Trudeau and formally transferred ownership of Siley to Ester. Siley would get her freedom on her mother's death. That this was a purchase and not a deed of gift was carefully spelled out. Ester authorized Joseph Brazeau, a longtime friend of both hers and Jacques's, to hand over to Jacques the sum of four hundred dollars. Brazeau declared under oath that the money was not his, and hence he had no claim to Siley. It was "paid out of the earnings and industry alone of . . . Ester."[10]

Ester was also determined to free her grandchild. In 1790, Siley had borne a son. Her lover was Lord Edward Fitzgerald, a British army officer and a member of the Anglo-Irish nobility. In the summer of 1789, Fitzgerald and five companions were dispatched on an intelligence-gathering mission. With the very real possibility of war between Britain and Spain, Fitzgerald and his party were to travel the length of the Mississippi and check on the state of Spanish defenses. Along the way they called in at St. Louis for supplies and information. During his brief sojourn, Fitzgerald, then in his mid-twenties, met and seduced sixteen-year-old Siley. Fitzgerald probably had no idea when he parted from Siley that she was pregnant. Their child was born on June 11, 1790. One is left to wonder whether, in the years that followed, the little family Lord Edward left behind in St. Louis ever learned what had become of him. Siley's lover returned home to become one of the leaders of the United Irishmen and to die a martyr to the cause of Irish independence.[11]

Since Siley was Clamorgan's slave, the baby, named Edward after his father, inherited her status. He did not get his freedom until 1793, most likely through his grandmother's influence. Jacques provided well for Ester's grandson, even while he was still enslaved. Edward was baptized the day after his birth, with Joseph Brazeau as his godfather.[12] At this point, Jacques had no children of his own, and Ester may have entertained the hope that he would adopt Edward. As it was, he freed him just one day after he freed Ester. Two months later, on September 14, 1793, the boy became a slaveholder when Brazeau gave him two slaves: Ben, three and a half, and Charlotte, two and a half. Brazeau had purchased the slaves from Jacques, and now he entrusted them to Jacques in Jacques's capacity as Edward's guardian. Brazeau made it clear, though, that they were "an irrevocable gift" to Edward.[13]

In addition to slaves, Edward had real estate to call his own. On September 27, Brazeau petitioned Zenon Trudeau for a tract of land on the northern fringe of the town. The land was especially valuable because there was believed to be a rich seam of coal just below the surface. On the same day Brazeau received the land, he gave half to his godson. Like the two slaves, the land was entrusted to Jacques until Edward came of age.[14]

By the fall of 1793, prospects for Edward, Siley, and Ester seemed very bright. Grandmother and grandson had their freedom, and Siley, while not technically free, had passed from Jacques's ownership to that of her mother. Thanks to the gifts of land and slaves from Brazeau,

Edward could look forward to a prosperous future. As for Ester, she, too, would be a substantial landowner before the year was out. The only problem was that she would not know she owned any real estate, and Jacques did not intend for her to find out.

However later generations might refashion the story of Jacques and Ester, his freeing of her was not a grateful master's reward to the woman who had shared his bed and superintended his household. The subtle and manipulative Jacques saw Ester as someone he could exploit. As a slave, she was a chattel—a mere object in the eyes of the law. Bestowing personhood on her transformed her, making her legally competent to petition for, buy, and hold land. Of course, Jacques did not propose to involve Ester in any of the real estate transactions he was about to embark upon. He simply planned to make use of her new status. Her name would be on the various deeds, but Jacques would be the true owner. Should his assets be seized—and in his business affairs he frequently courted bankruptcy—he hoped to shield some of those assets from his creditors by claiming they were not legally his. Since Jacques was contemplating a major trade initiative in 1793, his actions with regard to Ester were eminently sensible.

Four days after Jacques freed her, Ester—or, rather, Jacques acting in her name—approached Zenon Trudeau with a request for land. Spain's colonial land policy was predicated on the assumption that Britain, France, and the aggressive new power to the east, the United States, were all eager to seize control of the Louisiana Territory. As an officer of the Crown, Trudeau wanted Spain's borderlands occupied by people who acknowledged Spanish rule, and he did not turn down any reasonable request for a land grant. Race and gender were immaterial. The petitioner simply had to be free. Ester's request was for a lot adjoining Jacques's home so she could plant a garden and build a barn for her livestock. Trudeau approved the grant the next day.[15]

On September 24, Trudeau received another petition, ostensibly from Ester, for a second lot next to Clamorgan's home. Ester wanted it for an orchard. Once more Trudeau granted the request. On October 5, responding to a third request, Trudeau awarded Ester eighty arpents (just over sixty-seven acres) north of the town, between an Indian mound known as La Grange de Terre and the Mississippi.[16]

There were also grants from private individuals. On November 4, Gabriel Dodier and Joseph Brazeau confirmed "to the free mulatto woman named Ester" a tract measuring one arpent by forty in the Little Prairie. According to the deed, Ester already owned the land, having paid eighty dollars for it. The deed merely spelled out her rights. Finally, on November 15, Clamorgan himself sold Ester a lot. She supposedly paid him one hundred dollars, and he took note of "the cultivation and labor she [had] bestowed" on it, implying she had been farming the land before she gained title to it.[17]

Joseph Brazeau could not recall exactly when the first rift between Ester and Jacques occurred. He just knew it was during the Spanish administration. Pascal Cerré, one of the many local merchants with whom Clamorgan did business, thought it happened around 1795, but John Hay put the estrangement between the two in 1797—the very time when Jacques's financial empire was crumbling. His partner Andrew Todd had died, and Clamorgan was deeply indebted to Todd's heirs. He was fighting for his economic survival, and his rage and frustration boiled over. Poor Ester was his target. Hay had been boarding with Clamorgan at the time. He recalled that one day Jacques had become enraged with Ester "and abused her by striking her and . . . turned her out of doors." Hay had also witnessed Clamorgan beating Ester on a previous occasion. He added that she frequently complained of the treatment she received. She declared that she was devoted to serving Clamorgan "as long as she lived," but she would not endure being ordered about by the "young negro wenches of the house." And Jacques had recently acquired two new "wenches"—Sophie and her teenage daughter, Hélène, whose insolent ways Ester found insufferable. The fact that Jacques allowed and maybe even encouraged Sophie and Hélène to defy Ester signaled to her that her reign as his "chief wife" was over. Was Ester at fault in any way? Hay thought not. She was an exemplary housekeeper, honest, hardworking, and very attentive to the needs of the entire household. After Clamorgan evicted Ester, in Hay's presence he beat and abused Siley before tossing her out into the street as well.[18]

Despite the cruel treatment she and Siley suffered at Jacques's hands, Ester did not turn against him. She quietly removed her family's belongings from Jacques's home. Unbeknownst to him, she also took with her certain papers—her own and Edward's manumissions, and the deed for Siley. Mixed in with those papers, as Jacques would later discover, were the documents giving Ester ownership of the land he had secured in her name. Ester did not know precisely what the different documents were, because she could not read them, but she understood that they were important to her and her family.

Once Ester was out of Jacques's house, she set about making herself financially independent. Over the years she had planted and harvested crops on Jacques's land (much of which, although she was unaware of it, was actually hers). She had also raised cattle, pasturing her herd with Jacques's on La Grange de Terre, or the Big Mound, tract. She was a better farmer than he, a fact that her neighbors and perhaps even Jacques himself recognized. The cows on Jacques's property "were always called Esther's [*sic*] cows," recalled one neighbor, implying that it was Ester who took care of the farming as well as overseeing the household while Jacques was off on his travels.[19]

After the break with Jacques, Ester used the money she had saved to buy a piece of real estate. On August 23, 1798, she paid Pierre Lord twenty dollars for a lot on Rue de l'Eglise (Church Street), on the same block where Ann Camp had her house. Widow Camp and her daughters had helped Ester in the past, and Ester's ties to the Camp family were strong. The same day that Ester bought the property on Church Street, she made a gift of it to Siley. Ester did not relinquish control of the land, however. Although there was nothing on the lot when Lord sold it to her, she soon had a house ready for her family to occupy.[20] With her kinfolk around her, and friends she could turn to in times of need, Ester felt reasonably secure in this new setting.

Things were eventually patched up between Ester and Jacques, and she went back to work for him from time to time, but she maintained her own home and developed her own circle of friends. Some were probably slaves; others were free people of color, of whom there were about seventy in the town by 1800. The African American miller Joseph Labadie and his wife, Geneviève Labuche, were neighbors of Ester's for many years.[21] Ester was also on good terms with her white neighbors. John Cooms arrived in the wake of the Louisiana Purchase. He recalled that Ester was living in the house next to his when he moved in, although she was "occasionally" at Clamorgan's house. His daughter, Rosanna, remembered fondly that in 1806 Ester had helped to bake her wedding cake. The two women stayed in touch after Rosanna left home to set up housekeeping with her new husband.[22]

An especially valuable ally of Ester's was Alexander McNair, the man who would become Missouri's first governor once statehood was achieved. They were neighbors, but in fact Ester's connection with his family went back decades. As a slave in Virginia, Ester had helped care for the Camps' daughter Stella. Stella eventually married merchant Antoine Reihle, and their daughter, Marguerite, wed McNair. Stella died in 1793, but Ester's link with her daughter, and eventually her daughter's husband, endured. Ester often turned to the McNairs for money and advice. And she needed both once she discovered that the man who, in her words, "had . . . been [her] friend and benefactor . . . had become her enemy."[23]

What eventually led to Ester and Jacques battling each other in court depends on whose version of events one believes. Once subpoenas were issued, people began remembering things in strikingly different ways. Some made sincere efforts to tell the truth and nothing but the truth. However, memories were hazy, and precise dates were difficult to pin down. And of course there were those who had very selective memories and recalled only what was to their advantage.

Some points were well established. Ester continued to work for Jacques Clamorgan when he had need of her. She never again reigned supreme over his household, though. After Ester moved out, Hélène, the "negro wench" whose insolent ways Ester found so insufferable, took her place. In the spring of 1799 she bore Jacques a son, St. Eutrope. But Hélène's tenure as Jacques's "chief wife" did not last as long as Ester's had. Jacques soon replaced her with another concubine, Susanne. In February 1803, Susanne gave birth to a daughter, Apoline. Susanne was Jacques's favorite for an even shorter period of time than Hélène. While Susanne was pregnant with Apoline, Jacques took another "wife," Julie. His child with her, Cyprian Martial, was born four months after Apoline.[24] As events would show, Julie was more to Jacques than a casual sex partner. In 1807, when Jacques began planning his trading expedition into Spanish territory, Julie had just given birth to another son, Maximin, and Jacques realized she needed help. He turned to Ester. She was in her early fifties by that time, had her own home, and did not need to battle Julie for control of Jacques's household. She was also genuinely fond of Jacques's children. It did not matter that she was not their birth mother. As Jacques made his final preparations, he asked Ester to move back into his house and take care of everything and everyone until he returned.[25] He may have promised to pay her for her time and trouble, but Ester was happy to watch over the children and assist Julie without demanding a cent. She may even have imagined that Jacques would be grateful and that he would do something for her and her family once he came back home. As far as she knew, he was still a rich and powerful man. For all of Ester's diligence, and all her efforts to keep the Clamorgan home in good order, something happened to precipitate a violent quarrel between her and Jacques on his return. Brazeau recounted how Ester had come to him to ask for the loan of his handcart because "Clamorgan had turned her out" and she needed to move her things from his house to her own. What had caused the rupture? John Cooms mentioned in his deposition that several members of Jacques's household had become sick while Ester was there, and that one woman, who turned out to be Julie, had died.[26]

When Jacques came back from Mexico and learned of Julie's death, he vented his grief and rage on Ester. Catherine Dodge explained why. Dodge recalled that Ester had come down with smallpox while caring for Jacques's children, and had unwittingly spread the infection.[27] As soon as she had been well enough to leave her bed, Ester had spared no effort to try to nurse everyone back to health. She had even called in one of the town's leading physicians, who had made almost daily visits to the Clamorgan home. All but one of those who had contracted the disease eventually recovered, but Julie had grown sicker and sicker. She had died while Jacques was hundreds of miles away, deep in Spanish territory.[28] When he returned home and learned how Julie had died, he turned on Ester. Adding to Jacques's grief were his fears about the future of his young, motherless children. They were likely to find themselves fatherless before too long, given that he was now in his mid-sixties.[29]

Aside from his sorrow over the loss of Julie and his concern for his children, Jacques Clamorgan was grappling with financial chaos that was threatening to bankrupt him. His foray into Spanish territory had been a risky one, and it could easily have cost him his life, as it had other adventurers.[30] He came home unscathed, but without the fortune he had hoped to make, and his lengthy absence had cost him dearly. His business interests had turned sour while he was away. Various people had secured judgments against him, and he owed thousands of dollars. Jacques's best hope of extricating himself from this quagmire was to realize what he could on the land he owned—land that was appreciating in value now that American settlers were pouring into Missouri. However, much of his real estate in and around St. Louis was in Ester's name, and he needed her consent to get clear title to it. It was how he went about getting her consent that would become the focus of her lawsuit.

Jacques had been treating Ester's land as his own for years. During his frequent appearances before the Board of Land Commissioners prior to his departure for Mexico he had tried to get some of Ester's claims confirmed to him. On July 25, 1806, for instance, he sought confirmation of the Little Prairie tract that Dodier and Brazeau had sold her. A month later he was back to try to get the Big Mound tract confirmed. He admitted that both pieces of land had originally been granted to Ester, but he maintained that she had since sold or given them to him. The board told him to come back with more convincing proof of ownership.[31] He needed to find a way to make Ester give up land she did not know she had—land that could make her a rich woman.

After Jacques's return, Ester learned for the first time, probably from Alexander McNair, about the transactions Jacques had engineered in her name back in 1793. She discovered that she had a legal right to several valuable properties. She could live out her life in comfort and see Siley and her children handsomely provided for. But Jacques was stepping up the pressure, demanding she give all the land to him and hinting at what he would do if she refused.

Jacques meant to use Ester's family as bargaining chips. As early as 1805 and without Ester's knowledge, he had a deed drawn up "proving" Ester had sold Siley back to him in 1794! The deed stated that the earlier transaction was null and void. The four hundred dollars Ester had promised to pay him had never been paid, and hence "Sieur Clamorgan is the . . . owner of . . . Silée," with full power to dispose of her as he wished. Ester had supposedly signed the document with her X, and Joseph Brazeau and another friend, Benito Vasquez, had witnessed it. Brazeau later stated under oath that Clamorgan had shown him the deed. He had been shocked to see himself listed as a witness, and had told Clamorgan the deed should have been approved by the new American commandant, or at the very least by a notary public. Clamorgan had ignored him.[32]

Ester's family had been growing steadily over the years, and Clamorgan was happy to exploit that fact. If Siley was his slave, as the spurious deed said, all of her children except Edward, whose freedom was a matter of record, were his slaves as well. After her brief liaison with Fitzgerald, Siley had children with a Frenchman by the name of Denys. The eldest was Theresa.[33] Another child, Aurore, was born in 1798. Joseph, who went by the last name Scavaner, was born around 1800. Adelle was born in 1802, and another daughter, Agatha, in 1804. Then there was Antoine, a year or so younger, and finally François, born in 1808 or 1809.[34] The birth of each child intensified the power Jacques Clamorgan could wield over Ester. To bolster the fake deed of sale for Siley, he got his hands on the baptismal register of the parish church and altered certain entries. For instance, the entry for Agatha said her mother, "Silas," was "a free Negro woman." Clamorgan wrote: "I declare that . . . Silé . . . is a slave." After the entry for Aurore, he angrily scrawled one comment, crossed it through, and then wrote "The negress is not free."[35]

Jacques had had other fraudulent deeds prepared besides the one giving him ownership of Siley. According to those deeds, Ester had traded him everything granted her in 1793: the Big Mound and Little Prairie tracts and the three town lots. All the deeds bore the same date, September 2, 1794.[36] Brazeau, whose name appeared as a witness on each, denied witnessing a single one. He also recounted how Clamorgan had tried to get him to sign off on the transfer of several pieces of property to Pierre Chouteau to settle some of his debts. Brazeau had refused because he knew the two back lots, those adjoining Clamorgan's dwelling, belonged to Ester. Clamorgan had snapped at him: "[T]hat wench . . . will take away . . . one half of my orchard."[37]

The lawyer Marie-Philippe Leduc's evidence confirmed Brazeau's account, and it is somewhat surprising that Leduc spoke up, because Jacques Clamorgan had been his client for some years and Leduc's testimony did not exactly help Jacques make his case. Leduc recalled that before his departure for Santa Fé, Jacques had asked him to draw up a deed from Ester granting him two of the lots next to his home. There was an orchard on the land, Leduc remembered. He went with Clamorgan to get Ester to sign the deed, but she refused to sign any document if she did not know what it said.[38] Jacques was obviously not going to read it to her and let her know what she would be giving up. Since Ester could not be browbeaten into putting her X on the deed, Jacques relied on forgery to carry the day.

Ester found out about the forgeries. She later described how she remonstrated with Jacques. His response was sadly predictable. He beat her, told her she had no rights to any property, and threatened to take Siley and her children downriver to New Orleans and sell them. Ester was painfully aware of how vulnerable she was. She was an illiterate woman of color who had spent the first four decades of her life in slavery. Jacques was a well-connected white man accustomed to getting his own way. When she thought of her weakness and his power, she was "almost in despair." Maybe the law really would allow him to take from her everything she had worked for and everyone she loved.[39]

In her distress, Ester turned to Alexander McNair and John Cooms. They told her to get a lawyer and recommended William C. Carr. They assured her he was "an able counselor and [an] honest man." He was also the U.S. attorney to the Board of Land Commissioners. Ester called on Carr and told him of her plight. Carr expressed great indignation and said he would protect her interests "as faithfully as . . . if he were acting for his mother." His price was one of her town lots, which she readily agreed to.[40] Carr then said he needed all her papers to prepare her case. Because she could not read, Ester did not know exactly what she was handing over. She gave him everything she had. Carr studied the documents and informed Ester that she and Edward had a great deal of land, and promised to see her vindicated in court. They would proceed against Jacques Clamorgan on two counts, the first for having used illegal tactics to deprive Ester of her property, and the second for withholding from her the fifty dollars a year he had promised to pay her when he freed her. She stood to gain a substantial sum of money, and of course her family would be safe. Once they defeated Jacques in court, he would not be able to carry out his threat to sell Siley and her children. Ester took Carr at his word, happy to think that all her difficulties would soon be over. She did not know he was planning to do exactly what Clamorgan had done—draw up fraudulent deeds showing she had given him virtually every piece of real estate she owned as payment for his legal services.[41]

Meanwhile, Jacques was beginning to feel uneasy. He had tried brutality and blackmail, and then resorted to forgery. Now, with Ester's two actions looming in Superior Court, one to have the forged deeds recognized for what they were, and the other to get her hundreds of dollars in unpaid wages, he hit upon a new tactic: he mixed an emotional appeal with veiled threats. Early in 1809 he went down to New Orleans on business, and from there he wrote to "Madame Ester," presumably through an intermediary, since she could not read. He began by saying he had heard she had been at his home attending to his family. He commended her, but insisted she had done no more than she ought, and had only performed the duties she owed him. As for her other actions toward him and his "house," he reproached her for her ingratitude when he had done so much for her in the past. He warned her that her friends "have not done you a service; on the contrary, they have done you more wrong than you can imagine." He denied threatening Siley. He was being very decent to Ester, even though he had it in his power to make her regret what he termed her "Independence." Did she not care that he was suffering? He had lost Julie. What would become of his "little innocent ones," who were too young to appreciate the magnitude of their loss? As he had so many times before, he was playing on her emotions to get her to do what he wanted.[42] But the welfare of her family came before his. Ester hesitated briefly and then told Carr to go ahead with her two lawsuits, saying "her friends had told her she would be a fool not to do so and that Clamorgan would probably make slaves of them all if she did not proceed."[43]

When he found he could not dissuade Ester from suing him, Jacques did his best to defend himself. He categorically denied the accusations of forgery. On the matter of her unpaid wages he said there had never been a contract between them. He represented himself as a kindly, even long-suffering, employer, and assembled a parade of witnesses who swore that Ester did not deserve a cent. James Mackay said she had often absented herself from Clamorgan's home, even though he had treated her and her family very well. Antoine Soulard said Clamorgan had clothed Ester when she lived with him, and Jacques even produced a dressmaker to corroborate Soulard's statement. Patrick Lee, one of Jacques Clamorgan's many business associates, testified that Jacques had given Ester whatever she wanted. Another man who said he had resided in Clamorgan's home supported his claims of "humanity and generosity."[44] And when he had a chance to speak in his own behalf, Jacques insisted that he, not Ester, was the aggrieved party. She had quit his home, obliging him to hire a servant in her stead. He even submitted a list of expenses incurred by her and her family dating back to 1794—everything from shoes to fine linen, calico gowns, handkerchiefs, and silk stockings. On his last trip to New Orleans she had plundered his wine cellar. She was, in short, a drain on his estate, and it was she who should compensate him![45]

Ester's friends rallied to her defense. Ann Camp was dead by the time Ester's two cases came to trial, but her daughters described the abuse Ester had suffered after she was traded to Clamorgan. John Hay spoke of the violence he had witnessed. Brazeau and others testified to the forgeries Clamorgan had perpetrated. All of them emphasized Ester's dutiful attendance on Jacques and his family despite his repeated acts of cruelty.[46]

In 1810, with both of her cases against Jacques Clamorgan dragging on in Superior Court, Ester begged to be allowed to sue as a pauper. She explained that she was elderly, impoverished, and in poor health. Her opponent had money. He could bear the costs of protracted lawsuits, but she could not. Moreover, she was well aware that, "from the circumstance of having been a slave or some prejudice existing in the minds of many persons against her," there were those who simply would not come forward voluntarily to testify on her behalf. That would oblige her attorney to take a large number of depositions in order to get at the truth, and she did not have the resources to cover the costs that would entail. The court granted her request.[47] The two cases would go ahead with Ester being spared many of the legal fees she would otherwise have incurred.

Despite the weight of the evidence, victory eluded Ester. Late in 1811, to her utter dismay, William C. Carr abandoned both of her suits. She could only guess why. For some time she had been hearing rumors that Carr and Clamorgan had become close. Had Carr been paid off? Some highly suspicious transactions had taken place while he was representing Ester. On November 6, 1810, for instance, Carr had sold Clamorgan one of Ester's town lots, which he claimed she had given him. Two days later, Clamorgan had conveyed a sizable piece of land to Carr for a bargain price. There had been other questionable transactions, a good number of which involved land that had at least at one time belonged to Ester. It looks very much as though, with Carr's connivance, Clamorgan was establishing his title to the lands he had already tried to get with the spurious deeds. Carr was helping Jacques Clamorgan clean up the paper trail and escape a forgery conviction. Clamorgan was understandably grateful and expressed his appreciation in a way the young lawyer found most acceptable: by putting some other choice pieces of land Carr's way.[48] Had Carr abused his position not only as Ester's lawyer but as U.S. attorney to the Board of Land Commissioners? A little digging on his part would have revealed why Clamorgan had been so anxious to produce proof of his ownership of Ester's lands. And in fact, on November 13, 1811, at the very time Ester was fighting him in court, Clamorgan went before the board and got the Little Prairie tract confirmed. Carr, in his official capacity, could have objected. He kept silent because he had been more than adequately compensated for doing so.[49] With no chance of getting her claims to her real estate or her wages upheld in court now that Carr had deserted her, Ester watched helplessly as Jacques Clamorgan disposed of even more of her land for his own benefit. As for the status of her family, she had not even been able to get that resolved, since Carr had all of her papers. Her only hope was that Jacques would not carry out his threat to sell Siley and her children now that he had what he wanted.

Over the next few years a number of significant changes took place in Ester's life. In November 1814, Jacques Clamorgan died. Whatever she may have felt at his passing, the only thing she knew for sure was that he could never again threaten her family. And almost immediately the size of that family increased. Jacques's executors approached her to ask if she would take in Jacques's children. She would be paid to house, feed, and clothe them, but given her genuine affection for them, money seems not to have been uppermost in her decision.[50]

Meanwhile, Siley's eldest child, the half-Irish Edward Fitzgerald, had struck out on his own and relocated to Louisville, Kentucky. Marie-Philippe Leduc tracked Edward down in Louisville and offered him a deal. In his capacity as Jacques Clamorgan's lawyer, Leduc had worked through Jacques's business papers after the old man's death and he saw an opportunity to profit from what he had learned. On January 20, 1816, Edward sold to Leduc for $250 and "divers good causes" the legal title to the land Brazeau had granted him back in 1793, land Edward believed Jacques Clamorgan had helped himself to. Along with the land, Edward sold Leduc his slaves, Ben and Charlotte, and any children Charlotte might bear. Clearly he was not averse to taking ready money for his slaves and for real estate he had little likelihood of reclaiming. And anyway he had no intention of returning to St. Louis. With money in his pocket, he aimed to seek his fortune elsewhere. Edward left Louisville. Making his way down the Ohio and Mississippi rivers, he headed to New Orleans. But his dream of a new life in the bustling metropolis came to an abrupt end. He fell ill soon after his arrival in New Orleans and within days he was dead. He was twenty-five, unmarried, and without issue.[51]

Eventually the news of Edward's death traveled back upriver to St. Louis. Ester knew she could do nothing more for her eldest grandchild, but she could take action to safeguard the rest of the family, especially since she could see no prospect of making Carr hand back her papers, and she had no idea what use the unscrupulous lawyer might make of them. Setting aside the deed Jacques had concocted giving him ownership of Siley, technically Siley was Ester's slave under the terms of the

1793 sale, and that made Siley's children Ester's property, too. And now there was another generation to worry about. Rather than marry a man from the admittedly small free community of color, Ester's granddaughter Theresa had embarked on a relationship with a Virginia-born slave, George Speers. Speers had already run afoul of the law. In the county jail in 1815 for some unspecified offense, he had helped stage a breakout. The sheriff had advertised Speers as someone who had lived in the city for several years as a free man, but who was in reality a slave.[52] Ester stepped in and purchased George, and he and Theresa were able to live together as man and wife. But George was still a slave, and so, on the face of it, were all the other members of Ester's family. Supposing she died and someone—Carr perhaps—made a claim against her estate. Without overwhelming proof of their freedom, they could all be judged to be her property and auctioned off to pay her debts. Ester had to act.

In May 1817, Ester had a deed drawn up freeing her family. She itemized them all—Siley; Siley's three surviving sons, Joseph, Antoine, and François; Siley's daughters, Agatha and Theresa (Adelle and Aurore had died young); Theresa's husband; and the couple's three children, Edward, Julie, and Matilda Selina.[53] In the years ahead, Ester's family would continue to grow, but she would not have to agonize about each member's legal status. Now that Theresa and Agatha were free, under Missouri law any children they bore would be free as well.

Once Ester had dealt with the most pressing matter, her family's freedom, she began putting her other affairs in order. She paid Siley ten dollars for her title to the lot Ester had bought from Pierre Lord back in 1798 and deeded to Siley.[54] She also provided for Theresa, who, as the mother of a growing family, was in much greater need than her younger unmarried sister. On March 29, 1820, Ester "Clamorgan," as she styled herself, "in consideration of the good will affection and maternal love" she had for Theresa, gave Alexander McNair, in trust for Theresa and her children, two town lots across the river in Alton, Illinois. Along with the real estate, she gave McNair, for Theresa's use, a wagon, a horse, several head of cattle, and some furniture. There was also in trust for Theresa a lot in St. Louis on the corner of Fifth and Myrtle streets. Ester had seen the wisdom of buying land in that part of the town. When she had acquired it, the lot had been relatively cheap and well within her means, since it was on the outskirts of St. Louis, but the surge in population enhanced its value. When she made it over to Theresa it was valued at $450, and that amount was sure to increase. The property was leased out, and Theresa would get the rental income. It was essentially an investment fund for Theresa and her children.[55] Ester understood the wisdom of putting Theresa's real estate in trust. Under the new "American" law, which now prevailed in Missouri, everything a wife had was considered her husband's, and could be taken to settle his debts. Ester did not want to see Theresa left penniless if George got into difficulties. Creating a trust was a way of guaranteeing that this would not happen.

Despite Ester's careful planning, life was far from easy for her and her family over the next few years. Siley died, and then Antoine. Ester soon lost another grandson, although not to the grave. After working briefly as a carpenter, Joseph Scavaner quit St. Louis and headed south to Baton Rouge, Louisiana.[56]

With Antoine dead and Joseph gone to seek his fortune, financial pressures mounted. As a consequence of either mental or physical incapacity, Ester's one remaining grandson, François, was unable to take care of himself, let alone contribute to the household income. Theresa's husband was a hardworking man, but he could not bear the burden alone. Ester did what she had to do. To raise money to meet her family's immediate needs, she sold part of the lot on which she lived.[57] However, she had her sights set on a more permanent solution to her family's money woes.

Despite all the setbacks she had encountered, Ester had never given up hope of recovering the land Clamorgan and Carr had swindled her out of. To do so, though, she knew she needed a good lawyer. Well aware she did not have the cash for lawyer's fees, Ester decided to use the claims themselves. On February 19, 1829, she made a deal with the attorney Isaac McGirk. He paid her a nominal sum of one dollar for a half share of the three grants she had received from Zenon Trudeau— the two town lots and the eighty-arpent Big Mound tract. Ester and McGirk agreed that he would bear all the expenses involved in establishing her rights to the land and do all the legal work without Ester having to pay anything more. If he was successful, he would keep one half of Ester's real estate and she would get the other half.[58] Alas, according to Ester, McGirk proved no more reliable than William C. Carr, and he did not pursue anything on her behalf. That was how Ester saw things, but a more likely explanation is that McGirk soon realized that the matter was far more complicated than he had at first supposed and backed out of a courtroom fight he was not sure he could win. Ester would have to find another lawyer.

Ester's friend Alexander McNair had died back in 1826, but she continued to turn to his widow, Marguerite, for help. She also found an ally in Charles De Ward, the man who was betrothed to the McNairs' daughter. Marguerite McNair and Charles De Ward supplied Ester with cash as well as advice. On November 9, 1831, when she wrote her will, Ester acknowledged her indebtedness to the pair for all their help and for various sums of money they had given her. She bequeathed them half her estate, with the exception of the lot on which her home stood and her household goods. The rest was to be divided into four equal parts: Theresa and Agatha would each receive a one-fourth share. Joseph was also entitled to a share, provided he returned to St. Louis to take possession. If he failed to come home, his share would go to Theresa's son Edward. The remaining share went to Marguerite McNair in trust for François. The Widow McNair was to arrange for François to board with one of François's sisters for a reasonable compensation. If that sister did not treat him well, McNair was to board him with the other sister. Ester also appointed McNair her executrix, "having the fullest confidence in her integrity."[59]

Ester, by now in her late seventies, was still not prepared to abandon the fight to get what she was owed. After giving up on McGirk, she hired another lawyer. In Gustavus A. Bird, Ester believed she had finally found a trustworthy advocate for her rights. Bird had a reputation for defending members of the African American community, and over the years he had helped a number of enslaved men and women sue for their freedom. Ester placed her faith in him, and he promised to see her and her family vindicated. True to his word, Bird wasted little time initiating an action against William C. Carr in the St. Louis Circuit Court. However, since Carr was now a judge in that circuit, the case was transferred to the St. Charles Circuit Court.[60]

Presumably some of the money McNair and De Ward had given Ester had been for legal expenses, but their resources were not limitless. Now that a change of venue had been ordered, the cost of prosecuting the case was rising. Ester had to find another way to pay Bird. On October 25, 1832, she, De Ward, and McNair entered into an agreement with him. In return for a one-fifth interest in Ester's land claims, Bird would bear some of the expenses that had already been incurred and all future expenses. To clarify their title, that same day Ester executed a conveyance to De Ward and McNair restating what she had already provided for in her will. In return for nine hundred dollars, part of which sum she conceded she owed them, and the balance of which they paid her, she made over to them half of all her claims and half of anything recovered at the trial.[61]

The trial got under way. Ester's case, as stated by Attorney Bird, was that she had gone to Carr in 1808 on the recommendation of her friends. Although she was unaware of it at the time, he either tricked her into selling him all of her land or faked deeds to that effect. Had she not in fact agreed to sell him one of her town lots? Yes, but that was to pay for his legal services, and far from protecting her interests, he had done everything in his power to undermine them. She had never intended to give him all of her real estate.[62]

Carr had told Ester he would handle everything, and he had indeed commenced two suits against Clamorgan, one for back wages and the other to have the fraudulent deeds set aside. Evidence had emerged in the one case that proved the deeds were forgeries, but Carr had kept both cases dragging on for two years and then abandoned them. Furthermore, Ester had reason to believe Carr had gotten money out of Clamorgan for her wages and kept it. She had also heard that Carr and Clamorgan "had been much together" while Carr was supposed to be fighting him on her behalf. She firmly believed they had conspired to rob her. When she employed Carr, he was struggling to get his law practice going. He had grown rich at her expense. He had betrayed her, and she wanted justice.[63]

Carr entered his reply to the "many falsehoods" in Ester's bill of complaint. She had come to him of her own accord. She had told him about Clamorgan's threats and, at his request, she had produced documents proving she and Edward were free and that Siley belonged not to Jacques Clamorgan but to her. Carr told her she had it in her power to stop Clamorgan, that he owed her back wages, and that she and her grandson owned various pieces of real estate. She said all she cared about was saving her family. She did not think there had ever been any contract between her and Clamorgan regarding wages, "and she did not wish to take any thing from him and his children." She had never asked Jacques for any land and she didn't want it if the Americans would tax her for it. Carr claimed that when he offered to take all of it as payment for his services, she agreed, "with great cheerfulness." He had disposed of the land, as he was legally entitled to, soon after he had acquired it. If Ester felt aggrieved, why hadn't she come forward then? As for her back wages, he had handed to her every cent he had gotten from Clamorgan.[64]

Attorney Bird fired back. The deeds in which his client supposedly transferred all her land to Carr had been witnessed by her neighbors, Joseph Labadie and John Cooms. But were their signatures genuine? In a deposition, Cooms, then in his seventies and in failing health, had insisted someone had forged his signature on the deeds. Unfortunately, he died before the matter came to trial. His son, William, said he thought the signatures were genuine, adding that his father's mental condition had deteriorated before his death. Countering his testimony was his sister, Ester's friend Rosanna Cooms Berry. She had been with her father when he was deposed and judged him to have been in full possession of his faculties.[65] Joseph Labadie had died some years earlier, but several people swore they recognized his signature. But here another point emerged. Witnesses recalled that Labadie had spoken no English, while Thomas Riddick, the justice of the peace before whom the deeds had supposedly been acknowledged, had spoken no French. How could the two have communicated? It also came out that Riddick and Carr were good friends.[66]

Bird rehashed the whole matter of Jacques Clamorgan's alleged forgeries as well as Carr's, and matters became very murky indeed. Marie-Philippe Leduc's testimony was somewhat at variance with his deposition back in 1809. He was asked by Bird whether he had called on Ester with Clamorgan before Clamorgan left for Mexico. He replied he had not. He did remember being in Clamorgan's place of business with two other gentlemen. Ester was doing housework in an adjoining room. Clamorgan was holding some kind of document and called to her to come and put her mark to it. She refused outright, threw down her scrubbing brush, "and went off in a rage cursing and swearing." Leduc denied knowing what the paper was. He also said he had seen more of Ester since Clamorgan's death than prior to it. She had come to him in his capacity as county recorder, asking to see various papers and complaining that Clamorgan and others had cheated her and her family. On her first visit, Leduc said he had read the papers to her, but she kept coming back, and he got so tired of her that he refused to speak with her.[67]

The testimony of Pierre Chouteau, Sr., also undermined Ester's case. He was asked if there was ever any difficulty between Clamorgan and Ester when she was required to execute a deed. Not to his recollection, he replied. Chouteau acknowledged he had claimed a great deal of land around 1808 or 1809 that had not yet been confirmed, and some of that land had at one time belonged to Ester, although it had been sold to him (Chouteau) by Jacques Clamorgan. And, yes, Judge Carr had been the U.S. attorney to the Board of Land Commissioners at the time and had confirmed a great many of Chouteau's titles. Obviously Chouteau was not about to admit any more than he had to about his dealings with Carr and Clamorgan two decades earlier—dealings that might cast doubt on the veracity of his statement that Clamorgan had never tried to coerce Ester into giving him her land.[68] If it emerged that Carr had connived with Clamorgan to cover up the latter's forgeries, where did that leave Chouteau, who had gotten parcels of land from Clamorgan that Ester had a legitimate claim to?

Ester's case dragged on for many months. Eventually, on May 15, 1833, the court dismissed it. Two days later, Bird filed a bill of exceptions, the technical term for a list of reasons why (according to him) the verdict should be thrown out and an appeal granted. On August 28, before any appeal could be pursued, Ester died at the age of eighty or eighty-one.[69] Her death came just as she was on the verge of a significant victory. Bird had made an application to the reconstituted Board of Land Commissioners to have her right to the Big Mound tract confirmed. He had produced several new witnesses, who spoke of her having owned the land, and on November 8, the Board recommended her claim for approval.[70] Of course, it remained to be seen whether the federal authorities would act on that recommendation.

When it came to settling Ester's estate, her grandchildren found they could not count on Marguerite McNair. She told the clerk of the County Court that she was unwilling to act as executrix; George Speers was appointed in her stead. The task confronting him was a daunting one, made all the more difficult because the sickly François had died a few days before his grandmother. Everything she had put in trust for him had to be divided among his siblings.[71]

Speers made a good-faith effort to fulfill his duty as administrator.[72] And it was not just Ester's estate that required settlement. It emerged that the affairs of the long-dead Edward Fitzgerald had never been properly wound up. There might be money coming to his heirs, and they could certainly use it. Back in 1821, Siley had been named administrator of her son's estate. However, nothing had been resolved before her death. Now, on Bird's advice, Speers took over. And a vexing business it proved to be. Bird, either unaware of Fitzgerald's deal with Leduc, or believing he had grounds for getting it overturned, commenced suit against Jean-Pierre Cabanné, one of Jacques Clamorgan's executors, alleging he had withheld from Edward and his heirs certain valuable items of property. What made the suit unusual, given the background of the litigants, was the nature of that property. George Speers, an ex-slave, sued Cabanné for depriving Edward, himself born into slavery, of one of the slaves Brazeau had given Edward back in 1793. Charlotte and her progeny, five children and two grandchildren, were appraised at four thousand dollars. Cabanné contested the suit; possession, as so often in such matters, was nine-tenths of the law.[73]

Complicating matters further was the pending issue of Ester's appeal in the case against Carr. Bird needed to make sure he would be paid for all the time and effort he was expending, and in 1836 he discovered he had lost a vital document. He could not find the deed promising him a one-fifth interest in Ester's lands. Ester's legatees, her granddaughters and their husbands, along with De Ward and McNair, agreed to have another conveyance drawn up. This time Bird took care to get it properly registered.[74]

Bird's anxiety regarding the deed is explained by another deed Ester's granddaughters Theresa and Agatha entered into later that year. The wealthy broker Daniel D. Page paid them $1,500 for their interest in the Big Mound tract. Since Congress had upheld the decision of the Board of Land Commissioners confirming Ester's claim, Page and Bird stood to gain a great deal of money.[75] Though Ester's granddaughters gave up that money when they sold their rights to Page, they also avoided the headache of sorting out who owned what. Theresa and Agatha needed cash, and cash now for a claim that might be worthless was more alluring than thousands of dollars for land to which they might never be able to secure clear title. The Big Mound tract remained the subject of litigation for decades. It had been awarded to Ester or her "legal representatives," and who exactly they were—her grandchildren, Jacques Clamorgan's descendants, or the people to whom he had disposed of the land—remained to be fought over.[76]

Supporting themselves and their growing family was a constant struggle for George and Theresa Speers. George was not without resources. Although listed in the city directory as a common laborer, he was actually a skilled craftsman, and he undertook various construction projects around the city, sometimes assisted by his son Edward.[77] There was also the rental income from the real estate held in trust for Theresa. Even so, the family could hardly be described as financially secure. Life would have been so much easier if they could have established their right to even one of Ester's properties.

Besides dishonest lawyers, George and Theresa had a greedy son-in-law to contend with. On December 29, 1831, Matilda Selina Speers, not yet fifteen, had wed Gabriel Helms, a much older ex-slave from South Carolina.[78] Helms proved to be shrewd and rapacious. He was eager to get his hands on Ester's undisputed town lot—the one she had purchased from Pierre Lord, deeded to Siley, and then bought back from her. In 1839 Helms bought out Ester's grandchildren Joseph Scavaner and Agatha and her husband, Thomas Butcher. Then his in-laws somewhat rashly pledged a portion of their interest in the lot as security for a loan Helms made to them. When they failed to repay

him, he sued. And when they fell behind on their taxes and the sheriff
sold off another part of their interest in the lot, Helms got it at a bargain price.[79] Theresa and George were not destitute, but they needed
to recoup whatever they could if they were to provide for themselves
in their old age.[80] They had to get their appeal reinstated. They had to
make good their title to Ester's lands.

Down in Louisiana, Joseph Scavaner had given up waiting for his
inheritance. He would take what he could get. In 1841, Scavaner sold
his share of Ester's estate and whatever was due to him from François's
share to a land speculator for four thousand dollars.[81] Meanwhile, back
in St. Louis, Agatha was still hoping to get her legacy from her grandmother. Like Theresa, she was greatly in need of money. She had married Thomas Butcher, an unskilled free man of color, and husband and
wife worked hard to support themselves. Agatha toiled away as a washerwoman, and Thomas as a common laborer. However, they had been trying to elevate their status. In 1841 the couple had bought some farmland
in the area of St. Louis County known as Chouteau's Pond. Their dreams
of achieving modest prosperity as truck farmers were dashed the following year when Thomas fell ill and died. The sale of the farm and everything on it netted just under $560, but there were significant claims
against the estate. When everything was settled, Agatha had less than
$150 to her name.[82] She needed Ester's claims recognized and a cash
settlement made if she were not to spend the rest of her days living on
the charity of her already overburdened sister and brother-in-law.

Even before Thomas Butcher's death and his widow's pleas that he
have Ester's claims reopened, George Speers had lost confidence in
Bird. He had learned that Bird had sold part of his stake in Ester's property to various people, and fairly obviously those people did not want
to see Ester's heirs emerge victorious in their case against Carr, because it might undermine their own rights. Disgusted and disheart-
ened, Speers began hunting for another lawyer. There was no money
to pay legal fees, but in what was an all-too-familiar pattern, a share of
Ester's claims served in lieu of cash. George and Theresa reached an
agreement with Thomas M. Knox. For ten dollars and his professional
services, they promised him a fifth of all the disputed real estate. They
contended that the agreements with Knox's predecessors for a stake in

the property as payment for legal services had been rendered null and void because neither McGirk nor Bird had accomplished anything.[83] Feeling secure that he would be paid for his efforts, Knox set to work.

The case brought by Knox on behalf of his clients in the Missouri Supreme Court in 1842 began with a recapitulation of the earlier action against Carr. Knox pointed out that Ester had filed a notice of appeal but had died before any further action could be taken. Time had been lost when McNair refused to act as executrix. After Ester's death, Bird and Speers had agreed to keep the matter alive, and Bird had obtained more money from the overly trusting Speers. Speers had frequently urged Bird to pursue Ester's claims. All he had received were empty promises. Admittedly, Speers should have followed up on the appeal much earlier, but he was "illiterate . . . and totally unacquainted with the rules & forms of proceeding in such cases." And anyway he thought Bird was taking the appropriate action. He had finally lost all hope and applied to Knox. If the appeal was not reinstated, Ester's heirs would be deprived of any hope of redress. Moreover, Carr was very much alive and in a position to state his side of the case.[84]

As might have been expected, the case went nowhere. The appeal was not reinstated. Carr, now a very wealthy and influential man, was safe. He would not have to stand trial a second time for tricking Ester out of her lands and conniving with her adversary. Knox would not get his fee, since it was contingent on his establishing Ester's rights. Apart from Carr, the victors were the individuals who had bought the different pieces of property granted to Ester back in 1793. In fairness to them, they had purchased their land from people they believed had clear title. But even with the refusal of the state's highest court to grant an appeal, the "Ester claims" would not die. For her heirs, it was fortunate they would not. Even unproven, those claims were marketable.

On November 27, 1848, George and Theresa, the widowed Agatha, and Joseph Scavaner accepted ten thousand dollars from the speculator William C. McElroy for all their rights to Ester's claims. They also conveyed to him their interest in the land deeded to Edward Fitzgerald by Joseph Brazeau. The understanding was that McElroy would pursue their claims at his own expense and, within ten days of securing any money for those claims, would pay half to them.[85] Perhaps they still clung to a forlorn hope that victory was just around the corner. Still, ten thousand dollars split three ways was enough to keep the specter of poverty away from their doors.

What finally became of Ester's heirs? Joseph spent the rest of his days in Louisiana.[86] Agatha vanished after the deal with McElroy. She may have died; she may have remarried and changed her name. She was, after all, only in her early forties in 1848, and with her share of the ten thousand dollars, she would have been an attractive marriage prospect. George Speers died of consumption in 1855 at the age of sixty-five, having outlived four of his daughters and three of his sons.[87] Theresa survived her husband by more than three decades and weathered many more losses. Back in 1842, her daughter Julie (who often went by the less French-sounding name of Julia), had wed Robert Jerome Wilkinson, a well-to-do free black barber from Pennsylvania. In 1862 diphtheria carried off two of Julie's children, and then she herself fell victim to congestive fever.[88] Two years later, the youngest of Theresa's children, Georgiana, died of complications in childbirth. Her husband's family took in her daughter, but she soon followed her mother to the grave.[89]

The death of yet another daughter left Theresa, by then nearly seventy, to raise three orphaned grandchildren. Mary Speers Cox died when an epidemic of cholera struck the city in the fall of 1866. Mary's husband had died three years earlier, so there was no one else to care for the couple's children, the eldest of them just eight years old. Unable to bear the thought of seeing them bundled off to an orphanage, Theresa took them in.[90]

Theresa was not rich, but she had her rents and whatever she had managed to save from the sale of her grandmother's land claims. In 1867, with the needs of her grandchildren uppermost in her mind, she used most of the capital she had available and paid $1,600 outright for a sizable lot on Jules Street.[91] This would be the children's inheritance, and Theresa probably hoped that her new home, not exactly in the suburbs, but certainly some distance away from the increasingly congested downtown area of St. Louis, would prove a healthier setting for the youngsters to grow up in. She also provided them with a step-grandfather. On

August 15, 1868, thirteen years after George's death, she married again. Her new husband was Isaac Roger Shavière, a white craftsman who was a relative newcomer to St. Louis. Without any connections of his own in the city, Shavière might have been happy to find a home and an instant family.[92] He certainly fulfilled the role of father figure to Theresa's young charges.

The census takers had difficulty correctly identifying the Shavière family. They could not cope with Isaac's last name. In 1870, Isaac "Schuvier," a French-born gunsmith, owned real estate worth $1,600. His Missouri-born wife, Theresa, had real estate worth much more. Most significant, husband and wife were listed as white, but with them lived two "mulatto" girls, Mary and Theresa, both of whom attended school. Of course, the "mulatto" girls were the "white" Theresa's granddaughters. A decade later the census taker still had trouble with their race. All except Isaac were mulatto, but there was a blot after his name, suggesting that the official was confused and wrote one thing before trying to correct it and write something else over it.[93]

By 1880, Isaac and Theresa had taken in yet another member of Theresa's extended family, her orphaned great-granddaughter Geneva Creveling. The teenage girl had been bounced from home to home, as one relative after another died. Finally there was no one left except her irascible grandfather, Gabriel Helms, or an aunt in another state whom Geneva hardly knew. Unwilling to trust the young orphan to either of them, Theresa stepped in. Geneva would live with her.[94]

On March 11, 1881, when she wrote her will, Theresa acknowledged that she was "advanced in years beyond the allotted duration of human life." Lest any questions be raised about her mental competency, though, she insisted she was "of sound and disposing mind and memory." She wanted her husband, Isaac, to have a life interest in her real estate—the land on Jules Street on which he had his lock- and gunsmith's shop, and the building itself. All of her children were dead, and so were many of her grandchildren. She did what she could for those who remained. Matilda Selina's children, Theresa Helms Sawyer, Joseph Helms, and Louis Gabriel Helms, were to get five dollars apiece. All three were well into middle age, and had inherited property from their father when he died in 1879. Daughter Mary's children would be tenants in common of the Jules Street property. They would also divide among them the rest of her estate. The Wilkinson grandchildren, daughter Julie's children, got nothing, but they were presumably well enough provided for. Geneva Creveling was left to make her own way in the world, but like her aunt and uncles, she had a share in Gabriel Helms's estate.[95]

Theresa Speers Shavière died on July 24, 1881, of malaria, at the age of eighty-five or eighty-six. Her nursing care and funeral costs swallowed up much of the cash on hand. Even so, her heirs reaped the benefit of her foresight, and the thrift and hard work of Theresa's grandmother, for Theresa's estate included the lot on Fifth and Myrtle streets that Ester had put in trust for her almost six decades earlier.[96]

The number of heirs who shared Theresa's estate dwindled by the day. Theresa's granddaughter Theresa Helms Sawyer outlived her by only a matter of a few months, and the Sawyer children all died young.[97] Another of Theresa Speers Shavière's grandchildren, Joseph Helms, died of tuberculosis in the spring of 1885. His cousin George Cox died a month or so later of the same affliction. The following year, Louis Gabriel Helms succumbed. As for those who did survive, one or two would venture off in search of opportunities elsewhere, but most of Theresa's—and Ester's—kin lived on in St. Louis, firmly entrenched in the African American community.[98] None would ever see the wealth Ester had hoped so fervently to be able to pass on to them. The lands she had claimed, though, would continue to be fought over. This time the battle would be waged not by her family but by the children she had raised as tenderly as if they had been her own. Jacques Clamorgan's children and his grandchildren would prove as litigious as Ester's heirs. In so many respects, though, their outlook was unlike that of Ester and her family. She and her grandchildren had trusted in the law, and it had failed them. Jacques's heirs were far more cynical when it came to believing in the impartiality of the legal system. Like Jacques, they saw the law as an instrument to be used, not trusted. Like him, they would bend the law to their advantage—and if they had to, they would simply break it.

3

Natural Children

THE SUMMONS was an urgent one, but in his capacity as a lawyer, Marie-Philippe Leduc had received such summonses before. Someone was dying and wanted to settle their earthly affairs while there was still time to do so. Given his community's rapid growth in the wake of the Louisiana Purchase, sometimes such calls came from virtual strangers, anxious to do what they could for loved ones back east. That was not the case on this occasion, though. The message Leduc received on the last day of October in 1814 was from a man he had known for years. Jacques Clamorgan was one of the most celebrated, and notorious, individuals in St. Louis. Leduc took up the tools of his trade—quill pens, ink pot, and paper—and hurried to the Clamorgan residence. He found the elderly merchant bedridden but most definitely in full possession of his faculties. Jacques Clamorgan knew exactly what he wanted done with his estate. Leduc sat down and began writing. As a first item of business, the dying man directed that "his debts . . . be paid and wrongs redressed, if any there be found." Then he moved on to specifics. He bequeathed the sum of $150 for the relief of the poor of St. Louis. Everything else he owned—all his land, his claims to land, the contents of his home, and his stock as a merchant—

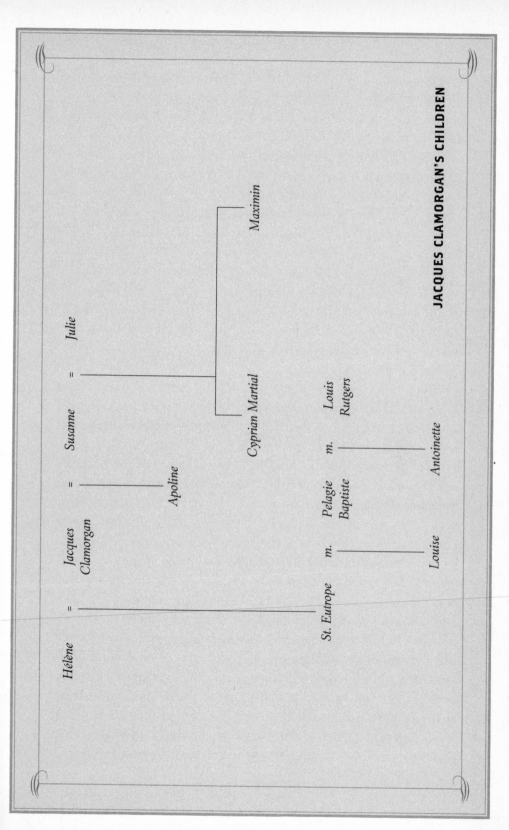

Hélène = Jacques Clamorgan = Susanne = Julie

Apoline

Cyprian Martial   Maximin

St. Eutrope m. Louise   Pelagie   Antoinette m. Louis
                                Baptiste   Rutgers

JACQUES CLAMORGAN'S CHILDREN

was to go to his four "natural children." His executors, fellow merchant Jean-Pierre Cabanné and former surveyor-general Antoine Soulard, were instructed to divide his estate into five equal parts. St. Eutrope, Apoline, and Cyprian Martial would get one share apiece, and Maximin two. Leduc made notes of what exactly Clamorgan wanted done and then drew up the will in proper legal form. Clamorgan signed it, and so did the three men hovering around his bed, Soulard, Cabanné, and another old friend, Charles Gratiot.[1] Like Leduc, all were French speakers. Even on his deathbed, Jacques Clamorgan distanced himself from the "Americans." He had had many business dealings with them and he spoke their language—since English was fast becoming the language of trade in St. Louis—but he had never liked them, did not care to associate with them any more than he had to, and was not about to entrust to them the welfare of his children. Jacques Clamorgan also appreciated where the power still resided in St. Louis. It was no coincidence that all four of the men at his bedside were members of the Chouteau clan—Gratiot and Soulard were brothers-in-law of Auguste and Pierre Chouteau, and Leduc and Cabanné were nephews by marriage. Jacques knew his children would need all the influential friends he could muster to protect them once he was gone.[2]

His will was a deathbed will, but Jacques Clamorgan was not quite ready to leave this world. The old adventurer was tough and he was stubborn. Mentally alert to the last, he had ample time for reflection.

In 1807, the year after the triumphal return of the Corps of Discovery to St. Louis, Jacques Clamorgan had set out with such high hopes to forge a path to Spanish lands in the Southwest. What Lewis and Clark had achieved with their foray to the Pacific, he was sure he could emulate with his venture to Santa Fé. He would open up new commercial possibilities, make himself rich, and win all kinds of favors from a grateful U.S. government. Of course, it was supposed to be a joint undertaking with Manuel Lisa. Clamorgan and Lisa had bound themselves to the Philadelphia firm of Geisse, Snyder and Co. to get the trade goods they planned to exchange for gold and silver in Spanish territory, and they were indebted to the company for almost $6,500. By the end of July, Jacques was champing at the bit, eager to start. His boatmen had everything loaded, ready for the signal to depart, when Jacques discovered that Manuel Lisa was nowhere to be found. He contacted Madame Lisa, anxious to know what instructions her husband had left. She and Hiacinthe Egliz, the man to whom Lisa had given power of attorney, responded that Lisa had already told Clamorgan to his face that he wanted nothing to do with the project, so why was Clamorgan pestering them?[3]

Jacques was puzzled and angry. Manuel Lisa had told him nothing of the sort, but if he wanted out of the arrangement, then Jacques would reap all the profits. And he was confident there would be profits. He left St. Louis almost immediately after the exchange of letters and made his way with his companions—three other white merchants and a slave. They traveled by river most of the way, west along the Missouri, and then down its various tributaries, taking to dry land only when they had to. It was a hazardous trek, as they were only too well aware. Others had made the journey before them, some, such as Zebulon Pike, with most unpleasant consequences. (The Spanish were very suspicious about the motives of Pike and his party. They seized them and held them in captivity for a while before taking them to the U.S. border and unceremoniously ordering them out of Spanish territory.) Jacques Clamorgan and his little band had no hostile encounters with the Indian nations whose territories they passed through, and when they reached their destination they met with a cordial reception from the Spanish. There were good reasons for this. While Jacques might have been a U.S. citizen, it was by default. For many years he had been a Spanish subject, and he had a good command of the Spanish language. He was also blessed with the power to charm and cajole. The Spanish authorities warmed to him. He and his friends were in Santa Fé before Christmas. From there they rode under escort six hundred miles to Chihuahua. When Pike and his group had made the same trip they had been under arrest. Clamorgan's group was merely escorted for reasons of safety, and when they reached Chihuahua, the governor welcomed them and gave them permission to sell their goods. Jacques Clamorgan returned to his home base via Texas unmolested, with cash and a fund of knowledge.[4]

Once he returned to St. Louis, Jacques wasted little time in publicizing his success and sharing his thoughts about what it might lead to. In a letter to the press, he observed that the United States "enjoy[ed] the benefit of the manufactures of the whole world." Its neighbor to the south had an ample population and large reserves of mineral wealth, but no manufacturing capacity. Bold adventurers such as he, who took to New Spain the kinds of goods its inhabitants craved, would reap "the most abundant harvest." And who better to advise merchants and statesmen on such matters than he? "I shall be abundantly remunerated if I can render myself beneficial to my countrymen."[5] Unfortunately, while his fellow Americans were enthralled with the exploits of Lewis and Clark, they ignored Jacques Clamorgan's discoveries.

Despite the positive spin he put on his exploits, times were tough for Jacques after his return from Santa Fé. Apart from his personal tragedy, the loss of Julie, he found himself confronting the reality of financial ruin. Again and again he was on the receiving end of writs and judgments for debt. Back in the summer of 1807, before he set off for Santa Fé, he had borrowed money from Pierre Petrimoulx over in St. Charles. He had not been able to pay off the debt, which mounted inexorably with interest, and Petrimoulx, eager to recover something, traded the debt to Edward Hempstead, a rapacious and well-connected lawyer intent upon amassing as many land claims as he could. Hempstead had his eye on Jacques Clamorgan's real estate, and eventually some of that land was auctioned off by court order to satisfy the debt. Precisely what lands were seized and sold would remain at issue, and would trouble Jacques's heirs (and the courts) for decades. Hempstead bided his time and got his hands on yet more Clamorgan land as the old adventurer fell deeper and deeper into debt.[6] The vultures were gathering, and Jacques's real estate empire was their prey.

Manuel Lisa also ended up with some of Jacques's real estate . . . at least for a while.[7] In Lisa, Jacques Clamorgan had met his match, for Jacques's on-again, off-again partner was as unscrupulous as he was. Lisa wanted a share of the profits of the Santa Fé project. On the surface it seemed he had no claim. He had reneged on the deal with Jacques.

That was not how the courts saw it, though, especially in light of the fact that Geisse, Snyder and Co. wanted their money and did not care who paid up, Lisa or Clamorgan.[8] Things dragged on interminably, and Jacques Clamorgan's financial position became hopelessly tangled. Lisa sued Clamorgan, who returned the favor. Geisse, Snyder and Co. sued them both, failed to get what was due them, and sold the debt to a speculator, who kept the whole matter tied up in litigation for years.[9]

There were other debts that Jacques Clamorgan could not pay off. In the summer of 1808, while Clamorgan was probably somewhere in the wilds of Texas on his way home from Santa Fé, the General Court in Missouri awarded Gregoire Sarpy, Antoine Reihle's executor, over twenty-three hundred dollars for the benefit of the powerful Detroit trading concern of Meldrum and Park. Reihle, one of the traders whom Jacques had persuaded to buy into the ill-fated Missouri Company, had died back in 1802, and Sarpy had been trying for several years to wrap up his estate. Upon going through Reihle's papers, Sarpy had discovered that while Reihle was indebted to Meldrum and Park, Jacques Clamorgan was indebted to Reihle. Jacques was in serious trouble. He had had dealings with George Meldrum and William Park before, and there had been hard feelings. If they wanted their money, as there was every reason to believe they did, they would spare no effort to get it. In execution of the judgment, the sheriff seized a 320-arpent tract in the Meramec district that Clamorgan owned and sold it at auction. Eager to snap it up at a bargain price was none other than Edward Hempstead.[10]

In November 1808, a few months after Sarpy sued Jacques Clamorgan in the Missouri General Court, Pierre Chouteau got a judgment against Clamorgan in the Court of Common Pleas. The amount at issue was almost twenty-seven hundred dollars, and the court wasted little time issuing a writ for the seizure of sufficient property to settle the debt. In March 1809 the sheriff auctioned off a large tract on Gingras Creek belonging to Jacques. Chouteau bid one hundred dollars for it.[11] Before too long, however, the relationship between Jacques Clamorgan and Pierre Chouteau became less adversarial. Rather than have the sheriff take piece after piece of Jacques's land and offer it for sale, Chouteau let Clamorgan sell it to him directly. According to Pierre Chouteau, Jr., his father acted as he did "to prevent a sacrifice of Clamorgan's property." Chouteau Sr. intended to help Jacques Clamorgan by buying his real estate and then allowing him to buy it back piecemeal—in effect becoming his banker and extending credit to him.[12] Why was an old rival prepared to be so benevolent? Because Pierre Chouteau understood that Jacques Clamorgan was too big to fail. It was a repetition of the events of the 1790s when Andrew Todd's death had left Clamorgan high and dry. Financial disaster for Jacques Clamorgan meant financial disaster for all those, great and small, with whom he did business. Clamorgan's failure would have destabilized the economy of St. Louis and much of the surrounding region at the very time Chouteau and a bunch of other traders, among them Manuel Lisa, were trying to get their new Missouri Fur Company off the ground. If the enterprise was to succeed, there had to be capital available within the business community to invest in the company, but with Jacques Clamorgan on the verge of bankruptcy, there was the very real possibility that he would bring down other traders and cause capital to dry up, at least in some quarters. Pierre Chouteau *had* to intervene, for his own good.[13]

To settle the debt to Pierre Chouteau, Jacques Clamorgan did indeed begin trading chunks of real estate to him. On May 2, 1809, four separate transactions took place. In one, Chouteau bought from Jacques a one-by-forty-arpent tract in the Marais Croche area of St. Charles County. In another, Chouteau acquired all or part of the enormous St. Charles tract. In a third he got the Cedar Island tract. The fourth was even more complex. On paper at least, Pierre Chouteau pledged to pay Jacques four thousand dollars in return for six properties: a forty-arpent tract in the Little Prairie, three enormous grants in the Tête de Boeuf area on the Meramec, complete with salines and saltworks, a nine-hundred-arpent tract on Little Rock Creek, and another large parcel in the Creve Coeur district that Jacques had bought from Pierre Chouteau's half-brother, Auguste. On June 13, 1809, Pierre Chouteau undertook to pay Jacques five hundred dollars for another piece of land in St. Louis.[14]

Over the next year or so, Jacques Clamorgan regained his property—or most of it. Confusion ensued about precisely what he had purchased from Pierre Chouteau, when exactly he had purchased it, and what

Chouteau had disposed of to other people. In the summer of 1810, for instance, Jacques sold half of what was subsequently known as the Baden claim to Chouteau, who had been awarded all of it by the Court of Common Pleas in 1808. The full extent of the tract was eight hundred arpents. While he was in possession of the land, Chouteau had sold four hundred arpents to various individuals. He and Jacques eventually agreed that eight hundred arpents exceeded the amount of the court judgment, and Chouteau sold the entire tract back to Jacques, who then gave Chouteau a deed for the half Chouteau had sold, so there would be no difficulties with the purchasers. Jacques kept the other half. The arrangement seemed to satisfy everyone concerned in 1810, but in the long run it played havoc with the paper trail.[15] In three more vaguely worded deeds drawn up a few months later, Pierre Chouteau sold back to Clamorgan some properties in St. Charles and St. Louis counties, but the deeds neglected to spell out *which* properties. Clamorgan and Chouteau knew, and so did their lawyers, but when they were no longer on the scene, their heirs would clash over precisely what land had changed hands, and a new generation of lawyers would reap fat fees arguing the matter in court.[16]

It was not only the Clamorgan and Chouteau heirs who would find themselves in court. As Jacques redeemed his property piece by piece from Pierre Chouteau, he sold some of it to raise additional funds. The purchasers, their heirs, and the individuals and entities who bought Jacques's lands from them would have a difficult time establishing who owned what. Jacques's sale of some of his St. Louis real estate to Samuel Bridge in 1811 was typical. Bridge bought land that had belonged to Jacques before Jacques sold it to Chouteau, who then sold it back to him. Bridge would have been well advised to ask some searching questions before he parted with any money, but he was eager to make what he believed would be a profitable investment, and Jacques was keen to get his hands on some hard cash.[17] Just what Jacques Clamorgan was prepared to do for money should also have injected a certain amount of caution into any purchase made from him. For example, the lot he sold to Thomas Brady in 1812—and received a handsome price for—actually belonged to the unfortunate Ester, granted to her back in 1793 by Zenon Trudeau. Without the connivance of her lawyer

William C. Carr, Jacques would not have been able to push the deal through.[18] No wonder Ester considered herself ill-used. What should have been hers to pass on to her daughter and her daughter's children had been gobbled up by greedy men. Her lawyer had enriched himself, and so, in a roundabout way, had Pierre Chouteau, but the true villain was Jacques Clamorgan, the man whose bed she had shared, whose home she had overseen, and whose children she had helped raise.

As Jacques Clamorgan, Pierre Chouteau, and the other members of the fraternity of land speculators knew, when it came to real estate sales, it wasn't just a question of negotiating a good price or deceiving a gullible buyer. They needed to get the Board of Land Commissioners to confirm their land claims before they could exploit those claims. Unfortunately, the commissioners, and ultimately the lawmakers back in Washington, were not especially sympathetic. They demanded to know how this band of opportunists had gotten so much land. Had the king of Spain made *that* many grants, or were these men trying to appropriate land that belonged to the United States under the terms of the Louisiana Purchase? Was it actually public domain? The tenaciousness of Clamorgan, the Chouteaus, and their associates did not help matters. They never gave up. They were constantly appearing before the land commissioners trying to get every last acre or arpent confirmed, and often producing "evidence" that would not stand up to close scrutiny. When the board was finally dissolved, the claimants turned to harassing the Recorder of Land Claims.[19] On the eve of the War of 1812, Congress enacted a new law regarding land claims, and it was one that the likes of Clamorgan and the Chouteaus considered most unjust. Claims in Missouri that did not exceed eight hundred arpents would be honored if the people living on the land had been occupying it in 1803.[20] Obviously this protected farmers, but not large-scale investors. Jacques, for one, had claims all over the place. He could not possibly demonstrate that he had lived on every single one of them. While the smaller ones, such as his town lots, and his properties in the Great and Little Prairies, were safe—provided he could outwit Ester—

the much larger claims in St. Charles and along the Meramec were in danger of being declared invalid.[21]

Jacques Clamorgan did not try to raise money only by trading in land. He was a merchant, and he sold every item on which he fancied he could make a profit, from a female slave, "good for all sort[s] of work," to barrels of tar, window sashes, glassware, and "a fine stove and pipe" he had imported from Canada.[22] He kept the courts busy, suing people for debt, foreclosing on mortgages, and trying to enforce various contracts for goods and services.[23] He went after the assets of people who had died owing him money.[24] Although he did not usually stoop to airing disputes in the press, in the case of the heirs of François Vallé he made an exception. The man's widow had the temerity to proceed against him, claiming that he actually owed money to her late husband's estate, rather than the other way around. Jacques Clamorgan publicly chastised her, telling her that her actions were "provoking to the ghost of [her] spouse" and bringing ignominy upon her.[25] He also had his say about a new law he considered too lenient on those who owed sixty dollars or less. It is easy to see why he was so exercised about the law. Buried under a mountain of debt, Clamorgan needed to be able to force the scores of people who owed modest amounts of money to him to pay up. It did not seem fair that the law protected those individuals but not him.[26]

Obsessed though he was with making and holding on to money and land, Jacques Clamorgan found time for a few other matters. Civic affairs interested him, although it is fair to say that politics and finance invariably went hand in hand as far as he was concerned. With rumors swirling about his loyalty to the United States, General James Wilkinson had been replaced as governor of the Missouri Territory by Meriwether Lewis before Jacques set off for Spanish territory. In the fall of 1809, when news of Lewis's "melancholy and premature death" reached St. Louis, Jacques Clamorgan joined in lobbying—unsuccessfully, as it turned out—for the appointment of a man he and his fellow speculators hoped would be accommodating when it came to land claims.[27]

Advancing age slowed Jacques down, but not much. Toward the end of 1811, with Ester's lawsuits wrapped up to his satisfaction, he headed down to New Orleans with the intention of stopping several months, doing some business, and no doubt politicking with the authorities there, just as he had back in the days when the Spanish had been in control. He had probably already set out before the mid-December New Madrid earthquake rattled buildings and nerves in St. Louis.[28]

What unsettled people as much, if not more, than the aftershocks were the rumors that another war with Britain was imminent. Jacques had his sources of information, and he mulled over what they were telling him. Open warfare would disrupt international trade even more than Royal Navy harassment in the form of blockades and impressments was already disrupting it. War might bring an American incursion into Canada . . . or a British advance from Canada into Missouri and the surrounding territories. And for a time, after the outbreak of war, it did indeed look as though the British and their Indian allies might consolidate their hold on the trade in the upper Missouri and even threaten St. Louis. There was panic in the early weeks of 1813, as rumors spread that an attack was impending, but those rumors soon subsided.[29] In the autumn of 1814, as Jacques lay dying, peace negotiations were under way in Europe that would determine geographically, economically, and politically the shape of the country his children would grow up in.

Increasingly, Jacques Clamorgan's thoughts turned to the fate of those he would leave behind. The death of Julie, the woman he had come to care for more than he had any of his other "wives," had been a bitter blow. When he threw Ester out of his house, and more especially when the ungrateful hussy dared to drag him into court, he had searched around for a reliable woman to run his home and care for his children. His only daughter, Apoline, was not yet in her teens when he returned from Santa Fé; she was far too young to assume the role of housekeeper. Jacques had turned instead to someone he had known for years. Catherine Crevier had been his slave. Back in the early 1790s he had had no compunction about selling her and her then husband, Charles, or separating her from her children. But things were different now. Catherine had succeeded in working her way out of slavery. With the help of her new husband, Antoine Crevier, a free man of color, she was determined to extricate her children from bondage. If Jacques could make her situation attractive enough, she might consent to return to manage his home. And the fact that she was originally from Virginia and spoke English and French with equal fluency, as Ester had done, added to her value. No, he was not searching for a concubine. He had other women much younger than Catherine Crevier at his beck and call. He wanted a reliable housekeeper, and the lure for Catherine was land. Jacques Clamorgan was prepared to sell her some real estate on uncharacteristically generous terms. Land would give her and her family a measure of security. So it was that Catherine returned as a free woman to oversee the household in which she had once lived as a slave.[30]

Unlike so many of Catherine Crevier's children, Jacques Clamorgan's children would never be slaves. He had made certain of that. At each of their baptisms he had had the priest enter into the register a short note stating categorically that they had been free from the moment of their birth.[31] A couple of years after Maximin's baptism, though, Clamorgan had thought it prudent to take another step, one he hoped would do away with any lingering doubts. If there was any ambiguity about his children's status, his creditors might claim them as assets of his estate and sell them as slaves—the very fate with which he had threatened Ester's family. He was also unsure about the impact of the transition to American rule. Believing it better not to leave anything to chance, on September 6, 1809, Jacques put his signature to formal deeds of emancipation. Each was based on a legal fiction—that their mothers had paid him for their children as soon as they were born. Anxious to comply fully with the laws and customs of the United States, Jacques was compelled to go on record as stating explicitly that the children were not and never had been "property" belonging to his estate. And in making sure that his children would always be treated as free persons, Jacques enlisted the help not only of his lawyer but of the son of his principal creditor. Witnessing each of the deeds were Marie-Philippe Leduc and Pierre Chouteau, Jr. The Chouteaus were slave owners. They had no hesitation about buying and selling people, meting out harsh discipline to recalcitrant slaves, and splitting up families. However, they were prepared to be merciful when it came to Jacques's children.[32]

Jacques being Jacques, though, he could not leave well enough alone. He took one more step after executing deeds of emancipation for his children. He got hold of the baptismal registers from the parish church and doctored them. In the case of Ester's grandchildren, his handiwork had rendered them slaves. He amended the entries for his own children to prove just the opposite. St. Eutrope's passed muster with Jacques, and he left it alone, but not the entries for his younger children. He blotted the words "slave" and "belonging to" after the names of Susanne and Julie, hopeful that he could make his children free by obscuring any reference to the fact that their mothers had been enslaved.

While Jacques Clamorgan could use all of his cunning to make his children free, what no amount of manipulation of the law could do was to make them white. The new body of laws introduced into Missouri in 1804 defined as a mulatto anyone with one black grandparent. Every one of Jacques's children would have to live with that legal disability and somehow work their way around it.

Jacques Clamorgan wanted to leave his offspring more than their freedom, and he had started planning how best to do that several years before the birth of his youngest child. On November 8, 1803, in the waning weeks of Spanish rule, Jacques and his friend Joseph Brazeau had appeared before the lieutenant-governor of Upper Louisiana. Jacques declared he had that day sold Brazeau two adjoining parcels of land close to his (Jacques's) own home. On one of the lots there stood a stone house divided in two with a double chimney that Jacques had had built to his specifications back in 1799.[33] Clamorgan also sold to Brazeau two slaves, twelve-year-old Francisca, and her father, Luis. For the land and slaves, Brazeau supposedly paid Clamorgan fifteen hundred dollars. As soon as the sale was completed, Brazeau made a gift of the land and the slaves to four-year-old St. Eutrope, who was his godson, and to Jacques Clamorgan's other two children, nine-month-old Apoline and five-month-old Cyprian Martial. They could not dispose of the land and slaves until the youngest of them turned twenty-five. If any one of them died without issue, their siblings would inherit their share. And in 1803, Jacques, who was obviously dictating the terms of the arrangement, trusted Ester well enough to stipulate that she was to live rent-free in the house and look after the children.[34] The deed of gift was almost identical to the one Clamorgan had helped Brazeau engineer a decade earlier for another of Brazeau's godchildren, Ester's grandson Edward Fitzgerald. It seems unlikely that Brazeau ever paid Clamorgan a cent for the land or the slaves, but by laying out the details of a fictitious sale, Jacques Clamorgan was ensuring that his creditors could not get their hands on the property, because it had not come directly from him to his children. However briefly, it had belonged to Brazeau.

Presumably when he and Brazeau made this arrangement, Jacques Clamorgan did not anticipate that he would have any more children to provide for. And then, quite unexpectedly, Julie gave birth to Maximin. Jacques could not alter the deed of gift, but he could try to pressure his three older children to be generous to Maximin. He added an endorsement on the deeds of emancipation he had had drawn up for St. Eutrope, Apoline, and Cyprian Martial. They were to remember when the time came that they should share the Brazeau property equally with Maximin. If they did not do so, "I will be angry with you." On Cyprian Martial's deed there was an especially poignant plea. His mother's dying wish had been, "Remember Cyprian never to abandon your brother Maximin."[35]

A decade after the Brazeau transfer, Jacques Clamorgan arranged for more property to be set aside for Cyprian Martial and Maximin. First he sought out an ally, in this case an ambitious young trader, Jean-Eli Tholozan. Looking to the future, it made sense to partner with someone who would be around for a good many years. Brazeau was not much younger than Clamorgan, and Clamorgan had doubts about his loyalty after Brazeau had given evidence against him in Ester's two lawsuits.

What Jacques conjured up, with the connivance of Tholozan, was a masterpiece of legalese, and a shrewd appeal to human greed. At various times in 1813, according to the deed Jacques's lawyer prepared, Tholozan had bought from Jacques four enormous parcels of land. Now,

in consideration of $1,800 paid to Tholozan by one Jean-Baptiste Pelis-
sier, Tholozan was conveying to Cyprian Martial and Maximin all four
tracts. Who was the mysterious Monsieur Pelissier? According to the
deed, he was Cyprian and Maximin's maternal uncle. Supposedly, long
before her death, the boys' mother, Julie, had given her brother $1,800
to buy property for her sons' benefit. It is hardly likely that Julie could
have accumulated such a substantial sum of money, given that she was
still a slave when she died. Almost certainly Jacques was playing fast
and loose with the truth again, wrapping the property transfer in so
many layers that it would be impossible for anyone with a claim against
his estate to persuade the courts to attach the land. He was also doing
away with any legal argument anyone might try to make that his sons
could not inherit from him because they were illegitimate. This was not
a straightforward gift from Jacques to his sons; it was a sale from him to
Tholozan, and from Tholozan to Pelissier, who very well may have been
a figment of Jacques Clamorgan's fertile imagination.[36]

The four parcels of land Jacques Clamorgan sold to Tholozan were
ones he had tried and failed to get the Board of Land Commissioners
to confirm. Three were Spanish grants—the St. Charles tract, the New
Madrid grant, and the Meramec grant. The fourth was the Cedar Island claim that Jacques had acquired from the estate of Regis Loisel.
That particular piece of land Jacques had likely never seen, given that
it was far up the Missouri in what is today South Dakota.[37] All told, the
claims were for almost a million acres.

Through Tholozan, Jacques stipulated that the transfer was made
on the condition that Cyprian Martial divided with his younger brother
his share of the property Brazeau had settled on him and his siblings
back in 1803. If Cyprian refused to do so, Maximin would get all the
land. Tholozan acknowledged that none of the four grants had been
confirmed. It was his job to see that they were. In the case of three of
the grants, if he could get them confirmed, he could keep half of the
land for himself. The only tract that was to go to the Clamorgan sons
in its entirety was the eight-thousand-arpent parcel on the Meramec.
Tholozan agreed that if he did not take steps to have the lands confirmed within twelve years, he could not retain any part of the property.

Neither of the Clamorgan brothers could sell or lease the real estate until the twelve years were up. Jacques Clamorgan—for this property deal was so obviously his handiwork—was realistic enough to know that Tholozan might be able to get one or two of the claims confirmed, but not all four. A partial victory was better than none at all, and Tholozan would still get his share as long as he acted.[38]

While Jacques Clamorgan had left his four children well provided for, he did not provide for each equally well. Why he arranged matters as he did he never explained, at least not on paper. Perhaps he assumed St. Eutrope, as the eldest, was more capable than either Cyprian Martial or Maximin of making his way in the world. In Apoline's case, he could well have reasoned that she had enough for a good dowry and that was all a daughter had a right to expect. Or perhaps he had felt a deeper attachment to Julie, and hence to the sons she had borne him, than to Hélène and Susanne and their children. Whatever the case, he had settled his affairs as he wanted them settled. There was no need in those last few days to call Leduc back to rework his will or add a codicil.

After holding death at bay for so long, Jacques finally succumbed. On November 11, 1814, the parish priest wrote in the burial register that he had that day laid to rest, according to the rites of the Catholic Church, Jacques Clamorgan, "formerly a merchant," aged (he believed) about eighty years. The deceased might have quibbled about having "formerly" been a merchant. He was a merchant to the end. He was also closer to seventy than to eighty. The priest did not mention whether the Clamorgan children or any other members of his household were in attendance at the funeral. The only people whose presence he noted were the two men Clamorgan had named as his executors.[39]

Immediately after the funeral, Jean-Pierre Cabanné and Antoine Soulard began the onerous business of settling Jacques Clamorgan's estate. The most pressing problem was where and with whom to place his children. Into the breach stepped Ester. Of course, the property settlement back in 1803 had authorized her to move into the home Clamorgan and Brazeau had set aside for her, live there for the rest of her days, and raise the children. But much had happened since 1803, and Ester, with a home and family of her own, no longer needed the inducement of a rent-free house. The fact was that Jacques's erstwhile mistress was prepared to care for his children regardless, as Jacques himself might have told his executors. She had known them all their lives and was deeply attached to them. It says much for her generous nature that she took them in fully understanding that they had inherited from their father titles to numerous pieces of land in and around St. Louis that she considered her own.

In the years ahead, Cabanné and Soulard made regular payments to Ester for the children's board and lodging. They also settled the bills that various merchants submitted to them for everything from bearskins to shoes, socks, handkerchiefs, suspenders, buttons, and thread—all itemized and delivered to "Esther Mulattoe woman."[40]

Having made arrangements for the care of their old friend's children, Cabanné and Soulard turned their attention to his estate. They paid Marie-Philippe Leduc twelve dollars for preparing the inventory, and judging by its length and complexity, the lawyer earned his money. It must have taken days to compile, as Leduc took note of everything, from soup spoons to chandeliers to livestock to the works of classical literature in Jacques's study and the fashionable attire in his wardrobe.[41] Jacques's slaves, however, went unmentioned. He may have traded away most of them as his financial situation worsened. He had owned at least one young woman, though, at the time of his death. Taking advantage of the confusion after the old man's passing, Aimée had made a bid for freedom, only to be captured by the town constable, whom the executors had to pay for his time and trouble. Her fate is unknown. Possibly, as one of the assets of Jacques's estate, she was sent to wait upon his children. She was not auctioned off with the rest of his property.[42]

All manner of people, male and female, white and "free colored," turned up to see what they could buy at the Clamorgan estate sale, which Cabanné and Soulard held bright and early on the morning of November 14. There were merchants looking to stock their stores, and individuals buying things for themselves and their homes. Charles Gratiot bid successfully for five pairs of pantaloons, a coat, and several other items of clothing, while the future governor Alexander McNair joined

Sally Datchuret, a free woman of color, in picking over Jacques Clamorgan's household goods, the stock of his store, and the contents of his wardrobe. The sale realized almost $1,150. Cabanné and Soulard were eventually able to raise several hundred dollars more by selling off some real estate.[43]

The vendue and the land sale hardly wrapped matters up, though. The executors still had a daunting task before them, one that necessitated frequent court appearances in the months and years following Jacques's death. There were mortgages to be foreclosed upon.[44] There were various claims against the estate that needed settling. Those claims totaled almost $1,950 as of November 1816, and they kept climbing as more people came forward with unpaid bills and promissory notes. Some suits Cabanné and Soulard challenged, but others they chose not to, knowing they would lose.[45]

There was one complication after another. A seemingly endless cast of characters came out of the woodwork, each laying claim to some bit of the estate. The executors found themselves dealing with the Missouri Supreme Court, as well as the local courts.[46] The business dragged on and on, and the bonds the two men had entered into in the St. Louis Probate Court obligated them to perform their duties faithfully and in full.

Getting the Clamorgan heirs everything due them entailed getting Jacques's various land claims recognized, and that meant prevailing on the U.S. Congress to act. In this regard, Jean-Eli Tholozan was ahead of Cabanné and Soulard, for he had a great deal to gain personally. He wanted his share of a million arpents of land—land that was becoming more valuable by the day as settlers surged across the Mississippi looking to buy farm land for themselves and their families. To make his (and the Clamorgans') case before Congress, in 1816, Tholozan reached an agreement with attorneys Risdon H. Price and Charles Frimon Delaurière. On the face of it, this was a wise decision. Between them they had a command of English, French, and Spanish—vital given the nature of the documents they were dealing with—and a grasp of the complexities of the laws relating to land tenure under the Spanish and

American jurisdictions. Tholozan made Price and Delaurière in effect his partners, since the deal the three men hammered out gave the attorneys a share of the proceeds if they could get the Clamorgan titles recognized.[47] Unfortunately, Tholozan had also done his best to complicate things. He made the deal with Price and Delaurière in October 1816 regarding all four of the Clamorgan claims, but in May of that year he had sold his interest in the Cedar Island tract and the St. Charles grant to businessman Louis Lebeaume for two thousand dollars. For Tholozan it meant cash for land he had never really owned. For Cyprian Martial and Maximin Clamorgan, it was a trade that could potentially weaken their rights.[48]

On January 15, 1818, in the House of Representatives, future vice-president Richard Mentor Johnson, then a member of Congress from Kentucky, presented Price and Delaurière's petition. Through his attorneys, Tholozan was making his first move. He was going after the St. Charles grant. Unbeknownst to the two lawyers, Tholozan had already disposed of his stake in that particular property, but the sale to Labeaume could well be rendered invalid if Tholozan could not establish his own and the Clamorgan brothers' title. Just sixty miles from St. Louis, the St. Charles grant was arguably the most valuable of the four tracts Jacques Clamorgan had entrusted to Tholozan.[49] In their petition, Price and Delaurière made the case that back in the mid-1790s Jacques Clamorgan had rendered "great and eminent services" to the Spanish Crown, for which he had been promised ten thousand dollars a year. However, the Spanish treasury was empty, and he had been recompensed with land instead. The treaty that had secured the Louisiana Territory for the United States said nothing about depriving people of land they rightfully owned, and the petitioners could demonstrate that Clamorgan had indeed owned the real estate in question. The king of Spain had given it to him, and no treaty, no change of administration, could justly deprive him of it.[50] Despite the best efforts of Price and Delaurière, the matter of confirmation went absolutely nowhere. Yes, Jacques Clamorgan had once been granted a large piece of land by the Spanish Crown, but how much land, precisely where it was, and who now had legal title to it no one knew for sure.

In their capacity as Jacques Clamorgan's executors and the guardians of his children, Cabanné and Soulard pursued more of the Clamorgan claims in the same session of Congress. There were at least a dozen in addition to the four Jacques had conveyed to Tholozan. In fact, with statehood for Missouri looming, lawmakers found themselves wading through a flood of petitions regarding Spanish land grants. The government had announced it was about to start selling off what it considered public domain. Claimants had to get their ownership rights recognized or risk the situation becoming far more complex. Once the land was opened up for settlement, they would have to do battle with the government and with the people who had purchased the land fair and square from the government. On February 11, 1818, the House proceeded with a bill to settle a whole series of claims, Jacques Clamorgan's among them. But if any of the claimants thought they were about to get what was due them, they were sadly disappointed. The bill was stalled in committee for years.[51]

Antoine Soulard did not live long enough to fulfill his obligations as Jacques Clamorgan's executor. He died in 1824. Not until the summer of 1826 was the surviving executor, Jean-Pierre Cabanné, able to give notice that his guardianship of the Clamorgan children had ended and to call on anyone who believed their father's estate still owed them anything to come forward before he made a final settlement.[52] The Clamorgan offspring were on their own now, judged competent to manage their own affairs. Ester had proved to be loving and attentive, and they had adjusted well to life in her household. But they had had to make other adjustments. The community in which they grew to adulthood was undergoing a momentous transformation—one that affected them in many different ways.

St. Louis in the 1810s and early 1820s fluctuated between rapid growth and equally rapid decline, between boundless optimism and dire predictions of disaster. Settlers arrived in droves before 1819, pushing up land values and bringing new opportunities for many in the Mound City, but deadly outbreaks of malarial fever in St. Louis over the next

few years deterred many from making their homes there. The financial
instability that characterized the nationwide Panic of 1819 also hit the
town especially hard. Not until 1823 did the first signs of recovery become apparent.[53]

The young Clamorgans were better prepared than many natives of
St. Louis to weather these changes. They were bilingual. Their father,
although a Frenchman, could converse with relative ease in English
and Spanish, and he had encouraged his children to master French
and English as basic survival tools. Catherine Crevier, who superintended Clamorgan's household after Julie's death, was a native speaker
of English who had become proficient in French. The children's exposure to both languages continued after they moved in with Ester. Her
mother tongue was English, and she had had to learn French once
Jacques Clamorgan had acquired her. Although in the late 1810s French
was still the first language of many St. Louis residents—a future mayor
recalled that the prevailing language on the streets was French—the
influx of "Americans" was bringing about a change.[54] Not to be able to
converse with the newcomers, most of whom showed no inclination to
learn French, was to isolate oneself from a host of opportunities. And
the Clamorgans were, in their different ways, alive to opportunity in
whatever form it presented itself.

Ester might have helped the Clamorgan children perfect their English, but neither she nor any other member of her household could
help them in matters of literacy. She never learned to read or write, and
nor, for that matter, did her daughter. The only one of her grandchildren who could sign his name was Edward Fitzgerald, since Ester had
cajoled Jacques into paying for his schooling, but Edward had most
likely ventured off on his own long before the young Clamorgans took
up residence with Ester.[55]

The Clamorgans could at least sign their names, and may well have
been able to do more than that. Jacques himself had encouraged, and
probably schooled, them, and by their sixth birthdays, Cyprian Martial
and Apoline were practicing their writing.[56] In that, as in so much else,
they were at a distinct advantage over most members of the free community of color in St. Louis, and a good number of white residents, who
remained illiterate their entire lives.

St. Eutrope was not of age when his father died. The gossip in the community was that if Jacques's first-born son had been a few years older, Jacques would have made over his entire business to St. Eutrope and retired. This was not to be. When Jacques died, St. Eutrope was only fifteen. Cabanné and Soulard packed him off to live with Ester while they figured out whom to indenture him to. Eventually, St. Eutrope was set up to become a barber. Since he could not dispose of his share of the Brazeau property until his half-brother Cyprian Martial turned twenty-five, he pursued the trade with vigor.[57]

On April 20, 1820, at the parish church in St. Louis, St. Eutrope married Pelagie Antoine Baptiste, a former slave. He was just a few days short of his twenty-first birthday (and the formal ending of his indenture), and Pelagie was a couple of years younger. Among the witnesses at the wedding was St. Eutrope's half-brother, who signed himself Cyprian "Morgan." The following year, when St. Eutrope and Pelagie's infant daughter, Louise, was baptized, St. Eutrope's half-sister, Apoline, was her godmother.[58]

The young father needed money to provide for his family. Shortly after Louise's birth, St. Eutrope took his barbering tools and headed to Missouri's new capital, St. Charles, in search of a means to support his wife and child.[59] White men of the class who gathered in and around the legislature as lawmakers or lobbyists were not in the habit of grooming themselves, and St. Eutrope no doubt hoped to make his skill with razors, scissors, and combs pay off.

But no sooner had he left than his infant daughter fell ill and died, and he returned home to St. Louis to mourn with Pelagie—as well as to try to extricate himself from his mounting debts. His principal creditor was Elias T. Langham, and Langham had given up waiting for his money. He brought suit against St. Eutrope in the St. Louis Circuit Court. On October 18, 1822, both plaintiff and defendant appeared in court, and St. Eutrope was ordered to pay Langham more than a hundred dollars.[60] He could not, of course, sell or lease the land in St. Louis that he and his half-siblings had been deeded by Joseph Brazeau. That was tied up until 1828, when Cyprian Martial turned twenty-five. But Langham would not wait another six years. In the summer of 1823, probably in an effort to dig himself out of the financial mess, St. Eutrope boarded a steamboat bound for New Orleans, which promised more opportunities to make money than St. Louis or St. Charles. His decision had fatal consequences. While working on board ship, the young barber contracted yellow fever. He never made it back home, and word of his death reached his wife and the rest of his family by early October. On October 11, Horatio Cozens, the attorney representing St. Eutrope in the Langham suit, informed the court that his client was dead.[61]

Eager to recover what he could, Langham applied to be appointed the administrator of St. Eutrope's estate. On January 14, 1824, he and his two securities pledged themselves in the amount of three hundred dollars to execute the duty conferred upon them by the Probate Court in an honest and timely manner. Langham swore that, to the best of his knowledge, St. Eutrope had died intestate, and there is certainly no evidence of a will. Nor is there any mention of Pelagie Clamorgan having relinquished her right to administer her husband's estate. Neither her race nor her illiteracy would have barred her from acting, but she already knew how financially overburdened St. Eutrope had been. Langham was unlikely to cheat her, because there was precious little coming to her anyway.[62]

Langham hunted high and low for hidden assets, but he was eventually forced to report that no one owed St. Eutrope any money and he had owned no real estate that could be attached. His rights to the Brazeau property and to his father's numerous land claims had died with him. Since he died childless, his siblings were entitled to everything; his widow received nothing beyond his personal effects. It was a meager inheritance—a cherrywood bureau and tea table, a walnut bedstead, a straw mattress, a glass decanter and two tumblers, a pair of iron tongs, a "small waiter," one brass candlestick, and three split-bottom chairs. All told, the estate was worth just over twenty dollars.[63]

Unlike his elder brothers, Maximin Clamorgan was not sent out to work as an apprentice and learn a trade. He was a sickly youth, and seems to have spent much of his time at home. While Ester received generous sums from Soulard and Cabanné for Maximin's board and care, she looked after him as diligently as she did her own family. But there was only so much she could do for him, and in June 1825, at the age of eighteen, Maximin died. After a funeral Mass, he was laid to rest in the parish cemetery.[64]

When Maximin passed, so did his inheritance. Everything left to him by his father, all the land and all the land claims, went to his siblings. To one of those siblings, Cyprian Martial, went Maximin's quarter share of the claims the two brothers divided with Tholozan. Cyprian was now the heir to an enormous amount of land—if Tholozan could ever get his claims confirmed. The rest of Maximin's estate, which comprised two-fifths of all the lands his father had not otherwise disposed of, in addition to whatever fraction of the Clamorgan estate had come to him when St. Eutrope died, went to Cyprian Martial and to Apoline. Figuring out just what each was entitled to required a command of mathematics and a firm grasp of the intricacies of land and inheritance laws. The fact that those laws had changed as the Louisiana Territory had been traded from Spain to France and then to the United States made matters even more involved.

Complicating the situation still further was the action of the federal government. On May 26, 1824, Congress finally passed a law giving the claimants of land in the new state of Missouri and the adjoining territory of Arkansas the right to have those claims tried in a court of law. The legislation covered any claim that "might have been perfected into a complete title" by "the government under which the same originated" had the change to U.S. sovereignty not occurred. In other words, it did not matter whether the French or the Spanish had been in control at the time of the original concession. Claimants or their representatives had to submit petitions to the District Court of Missouri. Each would then receive a formal hearing. If a decision went against a claimant, the land in question would become the property of the United States. If it emerged that the land had been sold by the United States, "or otherwise disposed of," the claimant was entitled to compensation. None of this was going to help Cyprian Martial Clamorgan, though, at least as regarded the huge St. Charles tract. The act stipulated that none of its provisions "shall be applied to a claim of the representatives . . . of Jacques Clamorgan, deceased, lying between the Missouri and Mississippi rivers, and covering parts of the counties of St. Charles and Lincoln, in the state of Missouri."[65] Somehow, a member of Congress, or someone with influence over a member, had managed to get this rider inserted. It was an insuperable barrier—or so it seemed. But Cyprian Martial was resourceful and he would not give up without a fight.

Unlike his half-brother, St. Eutrope, Cyprian Martial did not take to the trade, or to the circumstances, that Soulard and Cabanné had arranged for him following Jacques's death. After being removed from Ester's care, Cyprian was sent to work for a carpenter, James Irwin. But Irwin was not just a carpenter; he was also a slave owner, and Cyprian may have seen his own status as coming unpleasantly close to that of the slaves in the Irwin home.[66] His opportunity to escape came in the spring of 1821 when he made the acquaintance of Senator Thomas Hart Benton, one of the principal architects of Missouri's statehood—and incidentally the man who would pressure Congress in 1824 to reopen the old Spanish land claims. Benton likely offered Cyprian not simply escape but also patronage. An offer of employment from someone as powerful as Senator Benton was not to be rejected out of hand. As Cyprian knew if he read the newspapers and listened to conversations in the streets, Benton was no abolitionist. He was, in fact, a staunch advocate of Missouri's admission to the Union as a slave state. But, then, Cyprian was not a slave. He was free and he could prove it. And he was astute enough to realize Benton could do far more for him than James Irwin ever could. In company with Benton, and in the capacity of a personal attendant, Cyprian set off for Washington.[67]

There is nothing to indicate how Cyprian fared in Benton's service, but the trip was surely eye-opening—traveling by riverboat and on horseback many hundreds of miles to arrive at the half-finished city that Washington still was in the early 1820s. Slavery existed there, as it did in all the states Cyprian passed through, but the capital was also home to an emerging free black community. And then there were the political figures of note Cyprian would have read about and heard about back home.[68]

Eventually Cyprian and Benton parted company and the young man branched out on his own. Not surprisingly he was eager to capitalize on his land claims. By the end of 1825, the twelve years allowed Tholozan, under the terms of the deal with Jacques Clamorgan, to seek confirmation of Cyprian and Maximin's titles had expired. Tholozan had tried, and he had expended a considerable amount of money, but he and his lawyers had been unable to bring matters to a successful conclusion. With Maximin's death, Cyprian was now the sole owner of the claims, just under a million acres. Of course, he had to get his father's titles confirmed first. He began considering how best to proceed. He needed a lawyer, but he had no money to pay legal fees. What could he use? Like Ester, he decided to use the claims themselves. He talked to attorney George French Strother. Originally from Virginia, Strother had twice represented that state in Congress. Cyprian obviously believed Strother had the power to get things done. A shrewd and well-connected lawyer might find ways around the clause in the 1824 Act barring claims to the St. Charles grant. And there were the other pieces of land to be confirmed: the Meramec grant, the half-million-acre New Madrid tract, and the claim hundreds of miles up the Missouri at Cedar Island. On February 9, 1826, Cyprian and Strother reached an agreement. In return for one dollar and his professional services, Strother would acquire "one full Moiety or undivided half" of the four tracts if and when he could secure confirmation of them.[69] Galling though it was to Cyprian Martial Clamorgan to have to give up half of his inheritance, without the services of a competent lawyer, or a means of paying that lawyer, he could not secure any of it. Attorney Strother did his best for his client, given the fortune that was at stake, but his best turned out to be just not good enough.

At some point Jacques Clamorgan's two surviving children moved into the adjoining houses that their father had built and Joseph Brazeau had set aside for them. Apoline and her children occupied one, and Cyprian Martial the other. Cyprian did not live lavishly, but neither was he poverty-stricken. His house was furnished modestly, with a trunk, a cupboard, a work table, a four-poster bed, and a feather mattress. He also owned a horse and a gold watch.[70]

Although it caused Cyprian Martial and his heirs no end of trouble, the fuss over one of his prized possessions helps illuminate his life-style, his circle of acquaintances, and the realities of doing business at a time when banking was in its infancy and personal credit bound people together. In January 1826, Cyprian visited the store of saddler William R. Grimsley and took a fancy to a bureau Grimsley had on consignment from one John Anderson. What Cyprian offered by way of payment was not cash but a note he held from attorney Horatio Cozens. Cozens was happy to sign the note over to Grimsley. Cyprian got the bureau. Grimsley paid Anderson, and prepared to collect from Cozens. Then disaster struck. Cyprian's lawyer, George French Strother, had a hotheaded nephew who was also an attorney. One day the younger Strother found himself losing to Horatio Cozens in a courtroom battle. There was bad blood between the two because, among other things, Strother saw Cozens as a political enemy of his esteemed uncle. A heated "conference" during a recess ended with Strother stabbing Cozens to death. He was immediately arrested, and then compounded his initial offense by staging a spectacular jailbreak.[71] Grimsley entered a claim against Cozens's estate, only to discover he had died bankrupt. Unable to get his money, Grimsley went after Cyprian, and then after his estate. It was a protracted affair. Grimsley was pushing his luck, as he probably knew from the start, and the courts eventually dismissed his suit.[72]

In the case of Horatio Cozens, Cyprian Martial had extended a loan, but in other instances he had persuaded various people to lend him money, presumably on the strength of his land claims. After all, whether or not his lawyer got his four large claims confirmed, Cyprian still had his half share of the Brazeau land coming to him when he turned twenty-five. Sullivan Blood, a constable and later deputy sheriff of St. Louis, was induced to advance him eighteen dollars in March 1826.[73] A few months later, Cyprian talked Jeremiah Clever or Cleaver, a man of color, into lending him fifty dollars. The loan was not repaid, and

Cleaver eventually had recourse to the courts, as did white traders Ephraim Town and Samuel Kearney.[74]

One of Cyprian's most intriguing connections was with ex-slave Armstead Lawless, a Kentucky native who more than lived up to his last name. Lawless was frequently hauled into court to answer for his wrongdoings, real and alleged.[75] In the spring of 1826 the two men bought a bunch of lottery tickets and drew as a prize a considerable quantity of silverware. Lawless picked up the silverware and seemed inclined to hang on to all of it. Cyprian sent him a terse note telling him to turn over a half share to a white friend of his, Charles Collins, apparently for the benefit of Apoline's son Henry, who was Cyprian's godson. Lawless neglected to do so, and the matter ended up in court.[76]

Like his father before him, Cyprian Martial Clamorgan knew a good deal about the workings of the law and the marketplace. In his early twenties he was already proving himself adept and resourceful. Quick-witted and personable, literate and bilingual, he was on the brink of a promising career. And once he got his hands on his father's land claims and had significant amounts of money at his disposal, he would cut an impressive figure in St. Louis, even with the growing body of restrictions being placed on free people of color.

On November 15, 1826, Cyprian Martial and his half-sister reached an agreement to partition the real estate they held in common. Of course, the terms of Brazeau's deed of gift meant neither could dispose of the property until June 10, 1828, Cyprian's twenty-fifth birthday. Still, it made sense to divide it. St. Eutrope was dead, so his share had passed to Cyprian and Apoline. The Tholozan transfer would have required Cyprian to divide his share with Maximin, but *he* was dead. Under the deed of partition their lawyers drew up, Cyprian got three pieces of land and one of the two houses, and Apoline two pieces and the second house. With St. Louis prospering again after the downturn in trade in the early 1820s, land values were rising steadily. The Clamorgan property in what was now Block 25 was assessed at $1,200 in 1824, $1,800 in 1825, and $3,000 just two years later. Jacques Clamorgan and Joseph Brazeau had created for Jacques's children an excellent investment fund.[77]

Unfortunately, what Jacques Clamorgan and Joseph Brazeau could not do was to guarantee how long Jacques's children would be around to reap the benefits of their foresight. St. Eutrope had died young, and so had Maximin. By the fall of 1826, Cyprian Martial's health was in a precarious state, and a legal division of the property with Apoline was a wise move. He was ailing for many months before his death, likely suffering from the scourge of the nineteenth century: tuberculosis. On February 2, 1827, "being sensible that my final dissolution is at hand and wishing to settle all my temporal affairs as far as is now in my power," Cyprian summoned lawyer Isaac McGirk—he had given up on Strother—and made his will. He named as his principal legatee five-year-old Henry, the younger of Apoline's two sons. Henry was to inherit one of Cyprian's pieces of land in Block 25, his house on the same block, and the small piece of ground adjoining the house. Cyprian's executors, Apoline and his friend Charles Collins, were empowered to lease out the property to pay for Henry's support and schooling until he turned twenty-one. Then Henry could dispose of it as he wished. Apoline's other two children, Louis and Louisa, would be tenants in common of the third lot Cyprian owned on the same block. This property was to be leased out until Louisa married or turned twenty-one, at which point she and Louis would divide it between them. If either died without issue before that time, the survivor would take the whole parcel. Apoline and her children were also to inherit all the land Cyprian Martial was entitled to anywhere in Missouri, a provision that encompassed most of what had come to Cyprian from his brother Maximin and from Jacques Clamorgan's estate, although neither Cyprian nor McGirk picked up on one vital fact: the Cedar Island property was outside the bounds of Missouri. Cyprian also bequeathed to Apoline all the debts due him, together with his horse and cart. "Lastly I bequeath my soul to God my maker [and] my body to the earth & bid an eternal adieu to the world whenever it shall please God to call me hence to another world."[78]

Cyprian Martial wrote his will on February 2. Before the month was out he was dead. One of his last acts had been to commission artist John J. Douberman to paint his portrait so his family would have a lasting image of him, but he died before the picture was finished.[79] His funeral took place at the parish church on February 27, and he was buried in the adjoining churchyard. At the time of his death he was just twenty-three years old.[80]

In little more than a decade all three of Jacques Clamorgan's sons had died. Jacques had lived into his seventieth year. Not one of his sons reached his twenty-fifth birthday, and none left children to carry on the family name. The Clamorgan line would continue, though. Apoline had already made sure of that. And since she never married, her children would bear her name. She and her offspring would also inherit everything Jacques Clamorgan had left—every parcel of land, every title to land. But they would have to fight each step of the way to secure their inheritance.

4

"In Them Days Everything Was Free and Easy"

APOLINE CLAMORGAN was a charming and vivacious young woman at a time when the population of St. Louis was overwhelmingly male, and as her brothers set out on their respective paths, she sought her own way in the world. Not a slave, and not without friends, she was less vulnerable to sexual coercion than were the scores of enslaved women who toiled in white households throughout the town. She had options denied them. But even as a free woman, Apoline understood that those options were limited by her race. She could choose the conventional path: allow a free man of color to court her and eventually make her an offer of marriage. What could she expect from such a marriage, though, other than a lifetime of drudgery and financial hardship? Growing up in Ester's household, she had witnessed firsthand the struggles of Ester's granddaughter Theresa and her husband to stave off poverty. As each year passed, the employment opportunities available to free men of color declined. If she married someone from her own circle, Apoline knew she would find herself working as a washerwoman or a domestic to help pay the rent and put food on the table. By the time she was fourteen she had made up her mind to take a different path. White men she encountered let her know they

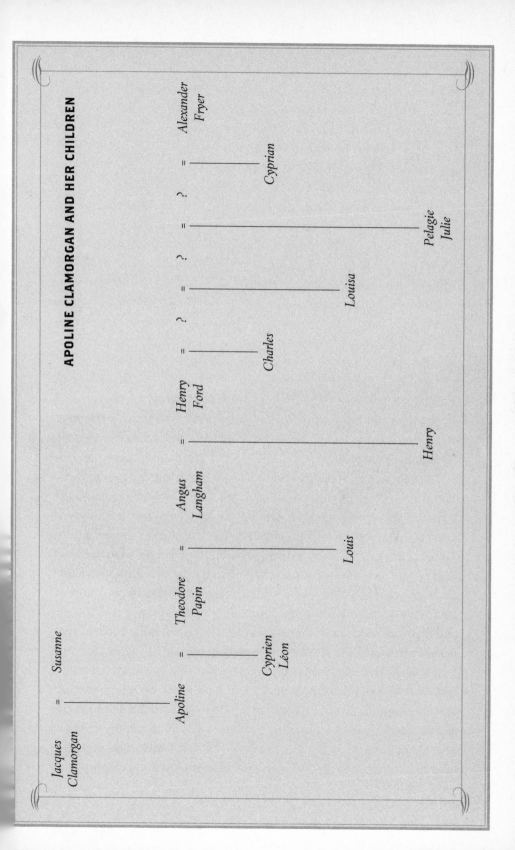

APOLINE CLAMORGAN AND HER CHILDREN

Jacques Clamorgan = Susanne

Apoline = Theodore Papin = Angus Langham = Henry Ford = ? = ? = ? = Alexander Fryer

Cyprien Léon

Louis

Henry

Charles

Louisa

Pelagie Julie

Cyprian

found her attractive. She could reject their advances or she could encourage them. She decided to do the latter. She would seek out a lover, a well-placed individual who would support her and who might come to care enough for her that they would be husband and wife in all but name. Eschewing marriage to a free man of color, Apoline chose instead to be the mistress of a white man—or, rather, men.

Arrangements in which white men and African American women cohabited for years and raised children together were hardly unusual in St. Louis, or, for that matter, in virtually every Southern community. Such liaisons occasioned little comment among either blacks or whites. They were simply a fact of life. As one of her contemporaries from the free community of color observed, "in them days"—he was reminiscing about the St. Louis of the 1810s and '20s—"everything was free and easy."[1] None of her friends or family members would judge Apoline harshly for the path she was embarking upon. A rich lover could make a young woman's life pleasant and comfortable, as long as she was not foolish enough to believe he would marry her. She also had to be prepared for him to abandon her and take a white wife, although there were plenty of men who kept both a wife and a mistress. Apoline Clamorgan was realistic.

Of course, she might not have been so cold-blooded about Theodore Papin, the first of her lovers. She and Theodore had a great deal in common. They were close in age—he was only four years her senior—and they were both orphans. Theodore's guardian was Marie-Philippe Leduc, his sister's husband (and, incidentally, Jacques Clamorgan's lawyer.)[2] Leduc was just one of the associates of the Papin family who had done business with Jacques Clamorgan over the years, knew about his "Negro wives," and had probably met his children. Their ancestry defined Apoline and Theodore as racially different, but both were French-speaking Catholics in a community that was rapidly being transformed by an influx of English-speaking Protestants.

Regardless of her attraction to him, Apoline was aware she had much to gain from an affair with Theodore Papin. He was one of the many grandchildren of Marie-Thérèse Chouteau and Pierre Laclède. There was a certain irony in their relationship. Apoline Clamorgan, the biracial daughter of another of the "founding fathers" of St. Louis, had managed to find herself a lover who was both wealthy and well connected. The Chouteau and Clamorgan clans were linked by the union of these two young people, although surely not in a way their respective families had ever intended. Pierre Chouteau, Jr., and Marie-Philippe Leduc had no idea back in 1809, when they witnessed for Jacques Clamorgan the deed emancipating Apoline, that his daughter would become their young kinsman's mistress.

Apoline Clamorgan and Theodore Papin became lovers while she was living under Ester's roof. Ester did nothing to keep the two apart. She may even have encouraged the affair, reasoning that her young charge had done very well for herself. Theodore had lost both of his parents when he was in his mid-teens, and with older siblings preoccupied with raising families of their own, he could easily escape their supervision, and that of his guardian, and visit Apoline. In fact, given prevailing attitudes about white male sexuality, it was unlikely Leduc or anyone in Theodore's extended family would have raised serious objections. Of course, had Theodore rejected marriage to a member of his own social class in favor of a long-term commitment to Apoline, they would undoubtedly have reminded him that he needed to fulfill his familial obligations. He could continue to keep a mistress as long as he also took a white wife and produced legitimate offspring. Had he sought to marry Apoline—and at the time there were, strictly speaking, no legal barriers to such a union—his Papin and Chouteau kinfolk would have howled in protest. Theodore, though, did not need to be reminded of his duty to his kin. Whatever the depth of their mutual affection at the start of their affair, Apoline and Theodore soon went their separate ways. Even the birth of a child could not keep them together.

The couple's son was born on May 8, 1818, when Apoline was fifteen and Theodore nineteen. When the baby was five months old, his mother took him to the parish church to be baptized, and he was given the name Cyprien Léon Clamorgan. The priest noted in the register that the child's mother, "Pauline" Clamorgan, was a free mulatto woman. He made no mention of the father, simply writing "unknown." Still, at least a few of Theodore Papin's relatives knew the identity of the baby's father. Cyprien Léon's godfather was Jean Pierre Gratiot, one of Theodore's cousins. The godmother, Marianne Labbadie, may have been another cousin, but the blurring of racial lines that had been going on for decades in St. Louis often complicated lineages. The variations in spelling did not help either. Labadie, Labbadie, and occasionally Labady was the name borne in St. Louis by dozens of men and women, some of them white and others of mixed race. Marianne could have been another of Theodore's cousins or a "free colored" friend of Apoline's.[3]

Cyprien Léon Clamorgan did not survive infancy. On July 2, 1819, the parish priest recorded that he had that day buried the fourteen-month-old son of Apoline "Morgan" and Theodore Papin. The baby's father, "unknown" at his baptism, had belatedly stepped forward to acknowledge paternity.[4]

Apoline's second child, Louis, was born on July 25, 1820, and baptized six days later, with his uncle, St. Eutrope, as one of his sponsors. The French-speaking priest had no trouble with the name of the baby's mother, but he struggled with the father's name, finally writing it down as "Auguste Langom."[5] By the time Louis was born, Apoline and Theodore's affair was a thing of the past, and judging by the timing, it was Apoline who had ended it. Theodore did take a white wife. In October 1820 he wed Marie Celeste Duchouquet, who came from a family much like his own.[6] However, many months before Theodore and his bride headed to the altar, Apoline had left him for another man.

Apoline's new lover, whose name the French-speaking priest recorded as Auguste Langom, was actually Major Angus Lewis Langham. He was appreciably older than Apoline, and he was an English-speaking "American." Raised in Virginia and Ohio, by the time he was eighteen he had shown a marked preference for soldiering over farming, and his parents had used their influence to get him a commission in the U.S. Army. Promotion came swiftly during the War of 1812, and Langham served with distinction in the campaigns in the Midwest. Apoline might even have read about his exploits, for they were widely reported.[7] After the war, Langham spent some time in Ohio and then made his way to St. Louis. His brother Elias, who eventually became the administrator of St. Eutrope Clamorgan's estate, had already relocated there, as had another brother and a sister. Angus's siblings soon married into local families and settled down. He, on the other hand, seldom stayed put for any length of time. In certain respects his career mirrored that of Jacques Clamorgan. Angus was always promoting get-rich-quick schemes. Like Jacques Clamorgan, he gambled on the real estate market, and, just like Clamorgan, he was wealthy one minute and deep in debt the next.[8] Absent from St. Louis for months at a time—overseeing his various landholdings, negotiating treaties with Indian nations in his capacity as an officer of the U.S. Army, and investigating prospects in distant communities—he had neither the time nor the inclination to establish a permanent home. An attractive and compliant mistress with whom he would live when he was in town suited him well.

While Apoline generally went by the name of "Mrs. Langham," she did not feel bound by the monogamy that such a title implied.[9] Nor did Angus expect his mistress to be scrupulously faithful to him. During at least one of his lengthy absences Apoline took another lover. Her son Henry, born on October 8, 1822, was fathered by Irishman Henry Ford, who seems to have shown no interest whatsoever in the child. Fortunately for young Henry, his uncle, Cyprian Martial, who was also his godfather, took him under his wing and eventually made him his heir.[10]

Two years after Henry's birth, Apoline presented another son to the parish priest to be baptized. No father was listed in the register for Charles Clamorgan. If he was Angus Langham's son there was no reason why Langham should not have acknowledged paternity, as he had in the case of Louis, but the issue was moot anyway, since Charles died in infancy.[11] A daughter, Louisa, was born to Apoline in the spring of 1826. She was not Langham's child. He was away for many months on a military expedition up the Missouri River. At some point after he left, Apoline took another lover.[12] Angus may have been back in St. Louis in time to have fathered Apoline's sixth child, Pelagie Julie. Apoline's daughter was born on February 6, 1828, and baptized the following June. Again, no father was listed in the baptismal register.[13] Whether or not Langham was Pelagie Julie's father—and she, too, died in infancy—he and Apoline ended their relationship around the time the baby was born. Angus left on a surveying trip to Ohio and Illinois, and Apoline caught the eye of another man.

At some point during her liaison with Angus Langham, Apoline moved out of Ester's home and took possession of the house and lot that Joseph Brazeau and her father had set aside for her and her half-brothers back in 1803. Langham was generous with his money, when he *had* money, and he afforded Apoline the means to furnish her home tastefully. The house the couple shared when Angus was in town boasted many of the trappings of refinement—a bureau, an assortment of tables and chairs, a workstand, a cupboard, a bedstead complete with bed hangings, beds for Apoline's children, and numerous quilts and sets of cotton sheets. Apoline covered the floors with "India Carpeting" and adorned the walls with looking glasses and framed pictures. Her windows were curtained, not merely covered with wooden shutters. When she entertained she set her dinner table with a salver and an array of glasses, cutlery, and fine "Queensware." She lived far more comfortably than she would have done had she wed a free man of color. She lived, in fact, surrounded by more luxuries than most white women in St. Louis could boast of.[14]

A shrewd businesswoman, enmeshed in the market economy of the growing town, Apoline understood that one did not let one's money sit idle. She was familiar with the complexities of the system of informal banking that flourished in an era when individuals in search of short-term credit were as likely to approach a neighbor as they were a bank, and when money loaned at interest could yield a savvy investor a good return. She extended loans, and when those loans were not repaid, she did not hesitate to haul a debtor into court. In 1826, for instance, she brought suit against her half-brother Cyprian Martial's friend, the wily ex-slave Armstead Lawless, alleging that he had talked her into lending him one hundred dollars and then neglected to pay her back. She wanted her money, plus damages for nonpayment, and she insisted the magistrate make Lawless post a substantial bond, since she had doubts about whether he would turn up for his trial.[15]

Apoline's sound business sense stood her in good stead when her half-brother died in 1827 and she was called upon to help settle his estate. Immediately after Cyprian Martial's funeral, she and the other executor, white land speculator Charles Collins, set to work. Once Cyprian's possessions had been inventoried and appraised, they sold off whatever they could. His clothes, his furniture, and his horse fetched over sixty-five dollars, an amount that would have been greater had they discovered the whereabouts of his gold watch, which they were forced to enter on the official accounting of his estate as "lost or stolen."[16]

They quickly found that Cyprian had been delinquent on his taxes, and that matter needed to be attended to lest the various parcels of land he had owned be confiscated and sold off by the sheriff.[17] They went through Cyprian's papers, learned there was almost three hundred dollars due his estate, and took the necessary steps to collect the money. They also dealt with the debts Cyprian had incurred. He owed various sums for everything from legal services to clothing and household repairs.[18] They began discussing how best to pay off those debts, and that was when they had a falling-out.

In the spring of 1828 the St. Louis County Court received a petition, ostensibly from both executors, asking for permission to sell enough of Cyprian's land to satisfy his debts. The court decreed that a sale could go ahead.[19] The usual practice after the court approved a request by executors or administrators to liquidate an individual's assets was to put an advertisement in the newspapers and hold a public auction. When Apoline learned of the petition, she was furious: Collins had petitioned the court without her knowledge. He had also delivered a stinging insult. The petition bore his signature and what purported to be her mark, implying that, as a woman of color, she was naturally incapable of "signing" with anything other than an X. Not only had Collins treated her with contempt and acted without her consent, but, Apoline contended, he had also disposed of some of Cyprian's land for less than she had offered to pay for it. In fact, she had protested against any sale of real estate to settle Cyprian's debts, since she had gone ahead and paid most of them herself. Her son Henry was Cyprian's principal heir. Cyprian had set aside one of his town lots for him. He had left the rest of his land to Apoline and her two other surviving children, Louis and Louisa. She, not Collins, should decide how Cyprian's estate was to be handled, and she was adamant that not an inch of land should be sold.[20]

Apoline found a way to even the score. Back in the fall of 1827, when the two were on fairly good terms, she had agreed to sell to Collins a sizable piece of land adjoining Cyprian's property for three hundred dollars. At the time, she maintained she had every right to sell it, since it had been awarded to her in the deed of partition she had entered into with Cyprian a few months before he died. Not long after Apoline conveyed the land to him, Collins resold it to one Xavier Dougal.[21]

Collins was understandably outraged when he learned that Apoline planned to sell the same piece of land to someone else. He told her she had no right to do so. She snapped right back at him. She had learned that the land was worth a good deal more than he had undertaken to pay her for it, and bent on getting what she felt was her due, she concocted an excuse: she had been underage at the time of the original sale, and this fact therefore rendered the transaction null and void. The original grant from Joseph Brazeau stipulated that none of the Clamorgan children could dispose of any part of the property until the youngest turned twenty-five. She was the sole survivor, and at the time she had agreed to sell Collins the land, she was only twenty-four.[22] Collins fumed and raged, but Apoline defied him, confident she had the law on her side. On July 9, 1828, four months after her twenty-fifth birthday, she sold the parcel of land to Alexander Fryer, the man who was, or would shortly become, her lover. He paid her ten dollars down, and pledged to pay an additional six hundred dollars, double what Collins had agreed to pay, within a year.[23] Collins seethed, but he was powerless to act.

The age restriction in Brazeau's deed of gift raised another issue. When Cyprian Martial had bequeathed one of his lots to young Henry, had he the legal authority to do so? He had been only twenty-three when he made his will. Surely, under the terms of the original deed of gift from Brazeau, all the real estate that Cyprian Martial claimed as his should have passed to Apoline on his death. She and her lawyers prepared to challenge in court the validity of Cyprian's bequest. Admittedly Apoline was proposing to deprive her own son of his inheritance, but she had Louis and Louisa, and any more children born to her in the future, to think of. The land was not Henry's. It belonged to her, and she intended to divide it more equitably.

Apoline's lawsuit complicated any arrangements made regarding the land in the Brazeau gift. On March 24, 1829, she and Collins sank their differences long enough to negotiate a lease. For sixty dollars, business-man Thomas J. Miller bought the use of the land Cyprian Martial had earmarked for Henry for one year. By the time the year was up, all the parties concerned anticipated that the court would have rendered a verdict in Apoline's case. If it ruled in her favor, she would pay Miller for any improvements he had made and regain possession of the land. If the verdict went against her, the lease could continue from year to year until Henry's twenty-first birthday.[24]

Apoline Clamorgan was turning out to be just as litigious as her father, and just as ingenious when it came to manipulating the law. In a sense she was even bolder, for she understood only too well that her gender and her race were against her. On the other hand, she realized she had advantages few in her situation enjoyed. She was literate, flu-ent in both French and English, and more conversant with commerce and the law than most women, black or white, in St. Louis at that time. She was intent on having what she believed she was entitled to, namely a valuable parcel of real estate in the heart of the rapidly growing town. St. Louis was in the midst of a building boom. The land Brazeau and her father had deeded to her and her half-brothers was increasing in value by the day, and she wanted to get her hands on it.

Much as she would have liked to wrest control of her half-brother's estate from Charles Collins, Apoline could not sever her ties with him. Cyprian Martial had made sure she could not when he named them as joint executors. Apoline was also eager to advance her children's inter-ests, and that forced her to work with Collins, even as she accused him of double-dealing. On May 15, 1828, Apoline appeared before the St. Louis Probate Court and gave her formal consent to Collins's being named as the legal guardian of Louis and Henry.[25] She even let him send the boys out of the state. Collins boarded them with a respectable white family, the Thomases, in Lebanon, Illinois. Obviously this meant Apoline did not get to see her sons very often, but that was a sacrifice she was willing to make, because Collins had promised to enroll them in school in Lebanon and use some of the money from Cyprian Martial's estate to see to it that they got a sound education.[26] As Apoline appreci-ated, arranging for their formal instruction required ingenuity as well as cash. Increasingly unnerved by the prospect of free people of color, and ultimately slaves, becoming literate, the authorities in St. Louis did their best to curtail African Americans' access to education. By the mid-1840s there would be stringent laws in place to ensure this, but for years before that there were informal restrictions on the teaching of free people as well as slaves. Under the circumstances, Apoline and Collins agreed that the most sensible course of action was to send Louis and Henry across the state line to Illinois. Apoline was adamant, though: Collins must not think for a moment that he could do as he pleased with every cent her half-brother had left her and her children. Schooling her boys was one thing; selling real estate without her consent, lying to her, and treating her as if she had no right to express an opinion was another thing entirely. She would drag Collins into court if she had to, and she would let him know that, female and of mixed race though she might be, he would have to respect her rights.

What ultimately defeated Apoline was neither the capricious nature of the legal system in Missouri nor her uncertain status as a woman of color, but her failing health. In the autumn of 1829 she discovered she was expecting Alexander Fryer's child. This would be her seventh pregnancy in eleven years, and six or seven months into the pregnancy she became ill—sicker than she had been during any of her earlier pregnancies.[27] It seems likely that she was suffering from some underlying ailment, perhaps tuberculosis, and that the strain on her body of bearing yet another child exacerbated the condition. As her health deteriorated, she began to fear not only for herself but for her children.

On April 11, 1830, with the ordeal of childbirth less than a month away, Apoline dispatched an urgent message to her lawyer. He must come to her home without delay and draw up her will. It was time to abandon her bid to overturn Cyprian Martial's will and accept that Henry, at least, was provided for. She intended to frame her own will in such a way as to "place [her] several children on [an] equal footing . . . as regards their worldly advancement." Because Henry already had his uncle's share of the Brazeau tract, he would not inherit her share of it. That would go to Louis, Louisa, and her unborn child.[28]

Apoline named her latest lover, Alexander Fryer, as her executor and trusted him to see to it that her wishes were carried out. She reiterated that the property she had sold him, and on which she had given him a mortgage when he had failed to pay her the full purchase price by the agreed-upon date, was indeed his.[29] She acknowledged that he was embroiled in a court battle over the parcel of land with Xavier Dougal. If Dougal prevailed, Fryer was to make sure her estate was not burdened with a huge bill for damages. She knew what could happen when the courts got hold of something, and she did not want her children left penniless.

In addition to making Fryer her executor, Apoline appointed him to be her children's guardian. Fearing she did not have long to live, and no longer willing to place her confidence in Charles Collins, she explicitly revoked her consent to his continuing to be their guardian. All of her children, including Henry, were to share in any land she might be entitled to as a result of her father's as-yet-unresolved claims. Aware how much it cost to hire competent lawyers, and familiar with deals such as the one Cyprian Martial had entered into with attorney George French Strother—namely, 50 percent of his claims in return for legal services to secure recognition of those claims—Apoline authorized Fryer to negotiate whatever agreements he felt were needed to get her children what was due them. As their guardian he was also instructed to make suitable provisions for them. She wanted Louisa placed in a home where she would "be educated and reared in a decent & becoming manner," and Louis and Henry brought back to St. Louis, removed from Collins's care, and bound "to some useful trade." Apoline signed her will, and two neighbors witnessed it.[30] Then she steeled herself to endure yet another confinement.

Either the ministrations of her doctors, who called on her almost daily, or her own resilience kept Apoline alive long enough to deliver her child. A boy, he was born on April 27. She named him Cyprian, after her half-brother, Cyprian Martial, and Cyprien Léon, the son she had lost a decade earlier. (The same first name could be spelled either way. It all depended on the whim of the priest or the parish clerk who was recording it.) Apoline chose her baby's name (however *she* wanted it spelled), but she did not live to see him baptized. She died when he was just a few days old.[31]

Apoline's funeral took place on May 1 at the parish church. It was an

elegant affair, in keeping with her lifestyle. For grave clothes and mourning apparel, merchants Alexander Scott and William K. Rule furnished
six yards of fine cotton "jaconet," lengths of black and white crepe, a
pair of stockings, white silk gloves, and six yards of ribbon. A neighbor,
Sarah Tobin, charged Apoline's estate eight dollars "For Shrouding the
Corpse." The firm of Finch and Whitehill received twenty-five dollars
for "1 Coffin trim[m]ed & finished in the Best manner." Another five
dollars went to the sexton for digging Apoline's grave. Jess Colburn supplied the hearse that bore her coffin to the church and from thence to
the graveyard. Both the funeral Mass and the burial were well attended,
as her stricken family and friends came to mourn the death of one who
had been so young and so vibrant.[32]

Apoline Clamorgan was barely twenty-seven when she died. History
seemed to be repeating itself. Just as Jacques had left three young sons
and a daughter when he died in 1814, Apoline now left four children
parentless. Her eldest, Louis, was not quite ten; Henry was six; Louisa
was four; and Cyprian was just two or three days old. In 1814, the competent and caring Ester had stepped forward to offer a home to Jacques's
offspring. In 1830, Ester was close to eighty and weighed down by the
needs of her own large family. Nor could the youngsters count on their
fathers to take their mother's place. Angus Langham, Louis's father,
had relocated to Arkansas before Apoline's death. If he did anything to
provide for his son there is no evidence of it, and he died in 1834 without leaving a will. His brother, Elias, had to wrap up his estate, which
was heavily encumbered, and Elias was not about to go inquiring after
Angus's biracial offspring.[33] There was no word of Henry's father, the
mysterious Henry Ford, and the unnamed man who had fathered Louisa had long since disappeared. As for Alexander Fryer, Cyprian's father,
it soon became apparent that Apoline had overestimated his administrative abilities.

   Jacques Clamorgan's children were fortunate in that they had been
entrusted to two shrewd and experienced men of business who had
worked together to protect their interests. Apoline's children were turned
over to two individuals who despised each other and agreed on nothing.

When she wrote her will, Apoline had expressed herself as clearly as she could about her children's future. She wanted Alexander Fryer to be their guardian. There was no question about whether Fryer should take charge of Cyprian, who was, after all, his own son. But who would be the guardian of the older children? Apoline's will named Fryer. But the order of the Probate Court—an order Apoline had freely consented to—made Collins their guardian. Could she overturn the court's order by simply stating that she wanted to make a different arrangement, or would her executor need to get the court to act? It was a situation ripe for confusion. Apoline had meant to safeguard her children from exploitation and do what she believed was in their best interest. Instead, she had put them in the middle of a power struggle.

Within days of Apoline's funeral, Alexander Fryer arranged to have her will probated and himself recognized as her executor. Two white neighbors of Apoline's inventoried her estate. They put the value of her furniture and other household goods at over $185, a far-from-negligible sum in St. Louis in 1830. Neither they nor Fryer were in a position to report to the Probate Court on the land Apoline had owned in the town, because they did not have the title papers. Evidently Charles Collins had taken possession of them. Fryer added that he understood there were "Other Lands, tenements, &c." that could legally be considered part of Apoline's estate, but again he did not have any papers showing where that property might be.[34]

Fryer took care of a number of other items of business. He paid Apoline's state and county taxes for 1830. He sold the contents of her home and then began going through the claims of her various creditors. There were bills for everything from firewood to shoes, tableware to fabrics. As Cyprian Martial had done when he knew he was dying, Apoline had commissioned a portrait of herself for her family to remember her by. Cabinetmaker Robert Hall wanted eight dollars for fashioning an ornate frame for it. Her physicians wanted payment for the visits they had made to Apoline and for the medicines that had either prolonged her life or perhaps hastened her demise. Fryer was left struggling to determine which bills were legitimate and which were not.[35]

The ongoing dispute between Apoline and Collins over Cyprian Martial's estate did not end with her death, and Fryer picked up where

Apoline left off. On March 9, 1831, he penned a strongly worded note to Collins advising him that he intended to apply to have him removed as executor because he had mismanaged the estate. When Fryer had his day in court, he alleged that Collins had abused his trust by selling pieces of Cyprian Martial's real estate on the pretext of needing to pay the debts of the deceased. In fact, according to Fryer, the largest of the debts Collins paid off with the sale's proceeds was one to the blacksmith Lewis Newell that Collins himself had incurred, and he had compounded his initial act of dishonesty by permitting Newell to occupy some of Cyprian Martial's land rent-free. There should have been substantial amounts of rent money coming to the estate, but Collins hadn't made any return regarding those rents and had neglected to pay the taxes due on the real estate, risking its forfeiture and forced sale.[36]

Actually, Collins *had* paid the taxes, and he presented receipts proving he had done so. He had also paid for repairs to the house Cyprian Martial had occupied, and he had had other much-needed bits of maintenance attended to. As for providing for Apoline's children, he produced his accounts showing that he had furnished Louis and Henry with everything from fur caps to silverware. He had paid for their schooling and purchased for them a dictionary, a grammar book, an English reader, and a bottle of ink.[37] Fryer was not exactly in a position of strength when he challenged Collins's performance as executor and guardian: he had been digging himself deeper and deeper into debt, and by 1832 he was bankrupt. When he failed to make his annual report to the court on his administration of Apoline's estate, the presiding judge issued an order to seize some of his property. The sheriff went in search of Fryer and discovered that not only did he not have any assets, but also that he had fled St. Louis to escape his creditors. A public administrator was appointed to oversee the estate.[38]

Free at last from Fryer's interference, Charles Collins went ahead with administering Cyprian Martial's estate as he saw fit. In 1832 he petitioned the St. Louis County Court, explaining that Henry, Louis, and Louisa had inherited parcels of land from their uncle. The land could be leased for their maintenance, but it could not be disposed of until, in the case of the property left to Henry, he reached the age of twenty-one, and in the case of the property left to Louis and Louisa as tenants-in-common, until Louisa married or turned twenty-one. Collins had negotiated leases, but the money they generated was insufficient to cover the state and local taxes and the children's living expenses, which he had already dipped into his own pocket to pay. He asked permission to sell some of the land. The court granted his request, and an auction was held which raised more than eleven hundred dollars.[39]

The wrangling over Apoline's sale of the same piece of property to Collins and to Fryer continued for years. The unfortunate Xavier Dougal, who had bought the land from Collins, had been harassed by Fryer, who had insisted it was his. In 1831, the matter had ended up in the Missouri Supreme Court, which had found in Fryer's favor. Dougal had to vacate the land, and not unreasonably he had insisted that Collins buy it back from him, since obviously Collins had not had clear title when he sold it.[40] Collins had then waged war against Fryer. And after Fryer had absconded and been replaced as Apoline's executor, Collins battled the court-appointed administrator, since his adversary was not technically any one individual but Apoline's estate.

Collins realized he had no hope of getting the land back. In 1832 the impecunious Fryer had pledged it as security for a mortgage, on which he had promptly defaulted.[41] The land was gone, but Collins wanted to be compensated. And what he demanded was not the sum of money he had paid Apoline at the time of the original sale, but what he judged the land to be worth at the time of his suit. In 1836 he demanded twelve thousand dollars. Where did he imagine such a huge sum would come from? Perhaps he believed he could get his hands on some of Jacques Clamorgan's unconfirmed claims. Collins fought in the St. Louis Circuit Court for the twelve thousand dollars he insisted he should receive, with interest, and when he did not like the verdict he appealed to the Missouri Supreme Court. In the end, his persistence got him nowhere. Apoline, or at least her estate, prevailed. Even so, when the dust settled and Collins was told he was entitled to just under five hundred dollars, not the thousands he had sued for, the public administrator was left wondering how he could come up with even that amount from Apoline's much-depleted estate.[42] There would have to be another land sale, which would further diminish her children's inheritance.

And where in this welter of litigation and charges of double-dealing were Apoline's children? How had they fared at the hands of their warring guardians? The most vulnerable of the four was obviously Cyprian, who was deprived almost from the moment of his birth of his mother's care. It was his father, inept as he was in so many other matters, who had ensured his survival. Fryer located a wet nurse, and Cyprian spent the first year of his life in her care.[43] Then he was placed with an African American couple, the Chenies, and he lived with them until he turned five. Perhaps it was Philip Chenie and his wife who remembered somewhat belatedly that there was an important spiritual matter that needed attending to. On November 24, 1834, at the newly built cathedral, which had replaced the old parish church where two generations of Clamorgans had been baptized, married, and laid to rest, Cyprian, identified in the register as the son of "Pauline Clamorgan" and one "Freyor," was received into the Catholic faith.[44]

In compliance with Apoline's will, Fryer had seen to it that her daughter Louisa was placed in a respectable household. He entrusted her to Isabel Jeanette, a free woman of color, and paid her for Louisa's care. After Fryer's abrupt disappearance, Collins took over as the girl's guardian, and he placed her in the care of one Eliza, another free woman of color. He also arranged for Louisa to receive some schooling. (In her case, he did not think it necessary to send her out of state.) But soon thereafter she fell ill, and in August 1834 she died: the cathedral register on August 19 recorded the burial of one "Louisa, aged eight years." The priest omitted her last name and noted down nothing at all about her parentage or race. That the young girl buried in the churchyard that August day was in fact Louisa Clamorgan emerged only in subsequent court actions, because her death as a minor meant her property claims passed to her brothers.[45]

As for Louis and Henry, although the loss of their mother was undoubtedly traumatic for them, they had not actually been living with Apoline at the time of her death. They had been boarding with the Thomases in Illinois.[46] Charles Collins might not even have sent for them to attend Apoline's funeral. At some point in the mid-1830s, however, he did bring the boys back to St. Louis. He could see that they had been well cared for in the Thomas household and that their education had been attended to. They could read and write, and they had a grasp of mathematics. With no children of their own, Collins and his wife, now that the dust had settled with regard to the matter of guardianship, decided to take Louis and Henry into their home and raise them. There was still some of their inheritance money left, so the Collinses would not be out of pocket as regarded housing, feeding, and clothing the boys. And Collins anticipated that in a few years he could put them to work.

Louis Clamorgan learned the fundamentals of business from Collins, and so, in time, did Henry. As a teenager, Louis worked in the store Collins owned. Collins found him to be unusually intelligent and quick to master new skills. He showed him how to keep accounts. And since Collins bought and sold land, he also instructed his young clerk in the art of surveying and in the complexities of the real estate market.[47]

Clerking did not suit Louis for long, though. When he was eighteen he declared his independence by leaving Collins and setting up for himself. Like so many young men of color in search of some way to make a living, he gravitated to the "tonsorial profession." But cutting hair and trimming beards was not how Louis envisaged spending the rest of his life. As soon as he could he would claim his inheritance. Over the years, taxes of one sort or another, legal fees, court-ordered sales, and the cost of raising him and his siblings had nibbled away at the property his mother and uncle had left. Even so, Louis was confident there was enough left to give him, Henry, and young Cyprian a measure of financial security. And beyond what Apoline and Cyprian Martial had left, there was the enticing prospect of one day being able to assert his own and his half-brothers' rights to the land their grandfather had acquired from the Spanish Crown back when Missouri had been part of Upper Louisiana.

Anyone who read the newspapers and kept their ears open when men of business gossiped knew that Jacques Clamorgan's claims had gained immensely in value as wave after wave of settlers from the east surged into Missouri. Louis was literate. Moreover, when he left Collins's employ he had gone to work in a barbershop that catered to an elite white clientele. The merchants and politicians he waited on liked to talk with one another and occasionally even with him, especially when they discovered that the young African American barber was a Clamorgan.

Louis was certainly aware of developments regarding his grandfather's lands. A consortium of speculators in Washington and New York was hoping to grow rich by exploiting the enormous New Madrid claim. They contended the land was one of the pieces of real estate that Jacques Clamorgan had traded to Pierre Chouteau in 1809 and that they had acquired it from the men Chouteau had sold it to. The officers of the Clamorgan Land Association were powerful individuals—a bank president, a former state governor, a couple of members of Congress, and a bevy of jurists, led by none other than Daniel Webster. They were busy telling investors on both sides of the Atlantic about the wonderful prospects offered by the so-called Clamorgan Tract. It boasted superb farming land, vast stocks of timber, and ready access to that admirable highway, the Mississippi, for conveying the agricultural wealth of the region to market. All that was needed was cash for some minor improvements, such as reinforcing riverbanks and building levees. They dismissed out of hand any suggestion that the land was part of the public domain, or that Jacques Clamorgan had regained possession of it—or never surrendered it to Chouteau in the first place. It was *theirs*, and they offered a raft of legal opinions to prove it. Buy shares now, investors were told, or lose out on a once-in-a-lifetime opportunity.[48] If Webster and company ever had any inkling that Jacques Clamorgan had left descendants, that fact would hardly have disrupted their grand money-making scheme. Elsewhere, moves were afoot to have the Cedar Island tract confirmed. Closer to home, Judge William C. Carr, Ester's nemesis, and William Clark of Lewis and Clark fame had managed to get the reconstituted Board of Land Commissioners to confirm to them a three-thousand-acre claim in St. Louis County, even though the land had been granted to Jacques Clamorgan back in the 1790s.[49] Other people were sniffing around after the St. Charles grant and hiring legal muscle to validate Jacques's title, and hence their own.[50] Everyone, it seemed, was endeavoring to grow rich from Jacques Clamorgan's lands. No one even appeared to acknowledge the heirs' existence, much less to see they got what was rightfully theirs. Louis was determined to change that. As a first step, on September 12, 1840, he applied to the St. Louis County Court for letters of administration for his grandfather's estate. The court ordered the surviving executor, Jean-Pierre Cabanné, to say why Louis's petition should not be granted.[51] Cabanné did not bother to challenge it. After a quarter century he was happy to be relieved of the burden of managing Jacques Clamorgan's estate.

Before he attained his majority, Apoline's eldest son was intent on proving that he was a Clamorgan. He knew he had land and he wanted it, or at least what it was worth in hard currency. Like his mother, he resolved to make the law work for him. As they grew to manhood, Henry and Cyprian would prove equally determined to get what they believed was theirs by right. However, they would have to confront not only rival claimants but a legal system increasingly restrictive to people of African descent as having rights. The Clamorgan brothers refused to back down. Men of color they might be, but they were Jacques Clamorgan's grandsons. They would have the vast estate he had amassed, and they would fight any claimant, even the U.S. government if they had to, in order to get it.

5

The Aristocracy of Color

O N SEPTEMBER 17, 1840, the "colored aristocracy" of St. Louis gathered at the cathedral to celebrate the marriage of two of its own, Louis Clamorgan and Julia McNight. Members of the bride's and groom's extended families were there, as were a host of acquaintances, some of them longtime residents with French names and ties of blood to prominent white families, and others who were relative newcomers to St. Louis.[1] Most of the guests knew the bride's background as well as the groom's. Julia McNight's ancestry, like her husband's, was rooted in the free colored community. Her grandmother was Catherine Crevier, who had kept house for Jacques Clamorgan during his last years. Her mother, Matilda Bertrand, was a light-skinned freeborn woman who owned a piece or two of real estate. Her father was a well-to-do Irish merchant.[2] If Julia did not have the prospects Louis did—her family had no claims to a million acres of western lands—she was hardly poor.

The couple's first child was born on June 20, 1841, a respectable nine months after their wedding. With a nod to both grandmothers, the baby was christened Matilda Apoline. Two years later Julia gave birth to a son, Louis St. Eutrope.[3]

Louis Clamorgan married young, and so did his half-brother Henry.

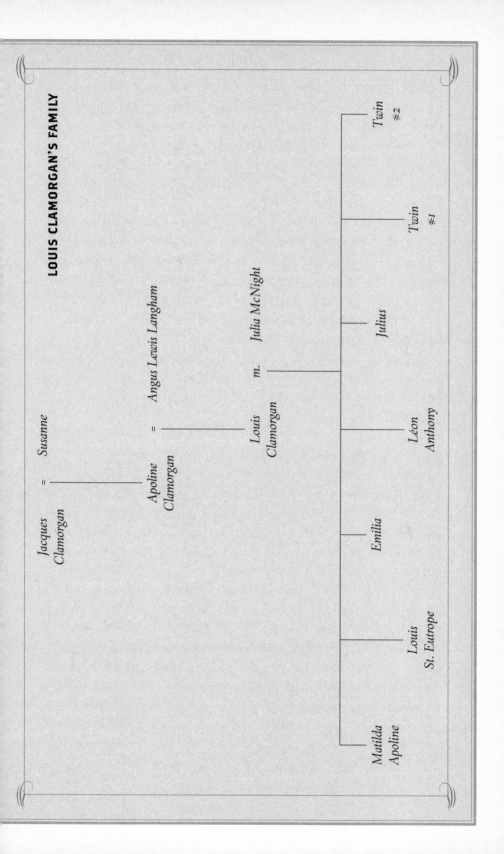

LOUIS CLAMORGAN'S FAMILY

Jacques Clamorgan = Susanne

Apoline Clamorgan = Angus Lewis Langham

Louis Clamorgan m. Julia McNight

Matilda Apoline

Louis St. Eutrope

Emilia

Léon Anthony

Julius

Twin #1

Twin #2

Henry was not quite twenty years of age on May 18, 1842, when he wed seventeen-year-old Harriet Eagleson. Although she was a member of the city's colored aristocracy by adoption, Harriet had not been born in St. Louis. And technically her name was not Eagleson but Thompson.[4]

Harriet grew up in Harrisburg, Pennsylvania, with her parents, James and Hannah Thompson, who were members of that town's small free community of color. But like the Clamorgans, the Thompsons had European roots as well, and they were so light-skinned that some considered them white.[5] While the Thompsons thrived in Harrisburg, they knew that the opportunities there for Harriet and her sister, Mary, were limited. So when Hannah's brother, William Eagleson, offered them a home in St. Louis, they graciously accepted.[6] The girls settled in well, worshipping at the cathedral with their aunt and uncle and cousins and forging links with other free people of color. In 1840 they attended the wedding of Louis Clamorgan and Julia McNight, signing the register as witnesses. Less than two years later Harriet wed the bridegroom's brother, and her own married life began in the home Henry shared with Louis and Julia.

Only two years apart in age, as children Louis and Henry had been boarded together by their guardian and schooled together. They might have had different fathers, but that did not matter. The bond between the two was close. Once Louis had a home of his own, he took in Henry and the much younger Cyprian. The year he married, Louis headed a boisterous household of six: himself, his wife, her mother, his two half-brothers, and perhaps another of Julia's relatives. After a year or two, Cyprian left, but Henry, now a married man, continued to board with Louis and Julia. When he and Harriet eventually set up housekeeping on their own, they did not move far away, and their children grew up with Louis and Julia's children.[7]

The arrival of a new generation of Clamorgans cemented the bonds between the brothers. Henry and Harriet's first child, Henry Jacques, was baptized on the Feast of the Epiphany, January 6, 1844, with his aunt Julia as his godmother. Julia and Louis's own son was baptized the same day, with Harriet acting as *his* godmother. Henry and Harriet's second child, Fanny Louise, was born in 1847. Two years later Harriet gave birth to another daughter, Kate.[8]

Henry and Harriet watched their children grow and thrive. Louis and Julia were not so fortunate. A third child, Emilia, was born to them in 1845, but over the next few years the couple endured a series of losses. In the fall of 1846, Louis St. Eutrope sickened and died. Just over a year later Emilia died. If the grief they felt was eased slightly by the birth of a fourth child, Léon Anthony, a short time after Emilia's passing, Julia and Louis were soon mourning yet another of their children. Their eldest, Matilda Apoline, died in 1849, three months short of her eighth birthday. Remarkably, their fifth child, Julius, born later that same year in the midst of a deadly outbreak of cholera, defied the odds and survived.[9]

In their choice of spouses and friends, Louis and Henry Clamorgan clearly identified themselves as "colored," but their situation was far better than that of many people in St. Louis who shared their racial heritage. They were free, and they had the documentation to prove it. They obviously felt safe enough to ignore the 1835 law requiring "free Negroes and mulattoes" to register and post a bond, because it was unclear whether the law applied to native-born Missourians as well as new arrivals. Even so, people they knew who had been born and raised in St. Louis sought licenses, preferring to leave nothing to chance. A decade later, the Missouri General Assembly passed An Act Concerning Free Negroes and Mulattoes that removed the ambiguities of the earlier law. Free people of color born in Missouri were supposed to get licenses, but those licenses would automatically be granted to all who could furnish proof that they were natives of the state. Out-of-staters, however, had to convince the courts that they should be allowed to stay. Louis, Henry, and Julia never did request licenses, but Harriet did. When the St. Louis County Court met on December 30, 1846, the justices reviewed a number of applications, including one from Harriet and another from her sister, Mary. Henry stood surety for his sister-in-law; his barber friend James D. Bonner did the same for Harriet; and Henry returned the favor by acting for Bonner's wife. All three applications were approved.[10]

The penalties for falling foul of any of the laws relating to free people of color could range from a fine, imprisonment, and expulsion from the state, to something a great deal worse. Seared into the collective memory of the Clamorgans and their friends was the horrific punishment meted out to Francis McIntosh. For an assault that had killed one city constable and badly injured another, McIntosh was burned alive by an enraged mob in the spring of 1836.[11] Even if one did not share the dreadful fate of McIntosh, every free person of color knew that he or she was in St. Louis under sufferance. One of the guests at Louis Clamorgan's wedding, Robert J. Wilkinson, discovered that this was the case when he was thrown in jail for not having a license. It cut no ice with the authorities that he was born free in another state and hence entitled under the U.S. Constitution to all the rights and immunities of a citizen in any other state of the Union. He could rot in jail, he was told, until he obeyed the laws of Missouri, humbled himself before the court, and found someone to stand surety for him.[12] Wilkinson was not the only acquaintance of the Clamorgans to have it made clear to him that "freedom" did not mean the same for people of color as it did for whites.

Indeed, the authorities were far from happy that a free community of color existed at all. Officials charged with maintaining good order in St. Louis saw little difference between the free and the enslaved, and roundly condemned "the saucy and insolent air of the free Negroes" as being "most dangerous to the slave population." By 1840, when Louis and Julia wed, there were 531 free people in the city. All told, the African American population of St. Louis, free and slave, comprised just over 2,600 men, women, and children, 12.5 percent of the city's total head count. Slaveholding was not a major social or economic factor in the life of St. Louis by the early 1840s. Only a handful of citizens owned more than 20 slaves. The average white family had a slave or two who worked around the house or was hired out to work in various capacities about the city. Relatively low numbers of slaves, compared to other Southern cities, did not translate into a burgeoning antislavery sentiment, though. White newspaper editor Elijah P. Lovejoy had several printing presses destroyed by angry mobs because he had the temerity to speak out against slavery, and he was ultimately obliged to move across the river to Alton, Illinois (where he died in a clash with proslavery elements). And lest any doubt remain about the city's commitment to slavery, in 1846 a group of citizens troubled by the growth of opposition to the "peculiar institution" in certain quarters formed the St. Louis Anti-Abolition Society.[13]

The Clamorgans could hardly blind themselves to the pervasiveness of slavery. Because of the peculiar history of their family, Louis and Henry did not have any kinfolk held in bondage, but they knew free people of color who did and who agonized over their relatives' plight. The two brothers could not read a newspaper without seeing advertisements for slaves to be sold or hired out, or notices for runaways. If they ventured down to the courthouse on business they could find themselves reluctant witnesses to the auctioning off of adults and children, since one of the busiest slave marts was located just outside the building's eastern door. White St. Louisans might not have a great need for gangs of slaves, but the city's role as a major transportation hub made it a thriving market for the sale of slaves. On the levees along the Mississippi, Henry and Louis encountered bondmen and -women, some as light-complexioned as they, waiting to be herded aboard steamboats for the trip south. Slavery was everywhere in the city they called home, and plenty of their white neighbors were comfortable with this.[14]

Regardless of his status as a man of color—in the eyes of his fellow St. Louisans or the eyes of the law—when it came to having his day in court, Louis expected a fair hearing. He did not relish being taken advantage of, and in 1841 he sued several white men who refused to make payment on a promissory note. He wanted justice, and that is what he got. The court took the view that a deal was a deal, no matter the race of the parties involved.[15] Three years later, Louis was the defendant in an action in the Circuit Court. A white couple, James and Catherine Madden, alleged he had cheated Catherine out of her dower right when he bought a piece of land her first husband had owned. The Maddens harped on Louis's status as a man of color, obviously hoping to prejudice the court against him. That tactic got them nowhere. The court was more concerned with land titles than with extraneous issues such as an individual's ancestry.[16] Whether this would continue to be the attitude of the courts, though, Louis had no way of knowing. Constant vigilance was required, but at the same time it did not hurt to cultivate a few influen-

tial white men who might come to his aid if and when the situation required it. Because of their education, their family name, their freeborn
status, and their network of contacts, Louis and Henry Clamorgan enjoyed a modicum of security. However, it was a security that could easily
erode if they angered the wrong people or transgressed too openly in any
respect. But as true descendants of the rascally Jacques, that consummate risk taker, transgress they did, again and again.

Land! It was the Clamorgan brothers' key to prosperity. It was the equivalent of money in the bank, and Louis and Henry wasted no time making withdrawals. Wherever it was, and by whatever means it had come
to them, they were happy to take hard cash for their real estate. Unfortunately, few of their deals were straightforward. A good many wound up
in court, and anyone who bought land from them could expect to pay
hundreds of dollars over the purchase price in lawyers' fees.

Individually and in partnership, the brothers engaged in so many
land deals over the years that it is impossible to keep track of them all.
Collectively those deals demonstrate, beyond the Clamorgans' obvious
desire to make money, how deeply involved they were in the waves of
land speculation that swept the rapidly growing city. Like so many residents of St. Louis with even a modest amount of capital at their disposal, they were always on the lookout for the next big investment.

Louis had begun dabbling in real estate as soon as he had the means
(or the credit) to do so. In 1840 he bought a small parcel of land from the
administrator of his mother's estate. Later that same year, he acquired
another tract on which he eventually made a 300 percent profit.[17]

Those were relatively minor transactions. His first major foray into
the real estate market was vintage Jacques Clamorgan. In the late summer of 1840, Louis decided to sell his rights to the lot in Block 25 he
had inherited from his mother. His marriage to Julia was fast approach-
ing, and a decent sum of money would be welcome. He had a buyer,
physician Hardage Lane, and the two settled on a price of five thousand dollars, but Lane's lawyer cautioned that Louis must prove he
was of age before any cash changed hands. Louis lied about the year of
his birth, and Lane paid up. When it emerged that Louis had not in

fact attained his majority, he was blasé about the matter, promising to show up on his birthday and confirm the sale. Lane trusted him, but the minute Louis turned twenty-one, he sold the land to Murry McConnell, a friend of his guardian, Charles Collins. Although Louis repudiated the first sale on the grounds that he had been a minor at the time and therefore not responsible for his actions, he kept Lane's money. When Lane and his lawyer charged him with perpetrating "a rascally piece of business," Louis said it really wasn't his fault and that Collins had coerced him into making the deal with McConnell. Moreover, he was too young and uneducated to understand such matters.[18]

Endless complications ensued. McConnell wasted little time selling the land to someone else, and that buyer wanted to know where *he* stood. Back in 1832, another man, Samuel Gaty, had bought part of the disputed lot from Charles Collins in Collins's capacity as the guardian of Louis and Louisa Clamorgan. Gaty and his partners had built a foundry on the site, and they feared the loss of their investment. Sometime after Louis sold his parcel of Block 25, Henry sold his, and that involved still more people.[19]

The whole mess wound up in the Missouri Supreme Court. It soon emerged that Collins and McConnell had been trying to cheat Louis, but he was no innocent either, as his lies to Lane demonstrated.[20] The justices characterized Louis as "a complete knave . . . an absolute rascal," and Louis, Collins, and McConnell collectively as "a triad of scoundrels" who were happy to sell out one another, and anyone else, for their own advantage.[21]

Lane eventually got what he had paid for, and he bought out most of the other claimants. Gaty and his partners managed to safeguard their foundry. Louis and Henry walked away with several thousand dollars apiece, money was set aside for Cyprian, and an unrepentant Louis went on to yet more dubious land deals.[22]

Louis was adept at moving money around. Back before he was of age, he had purchased a prime piece of real estate a couple of blocks from the Mississippi for seven hundred dollars. It had potential because of its location, and that was what Louis counted on. Of course, he didn't have the cash to pay for it outright, but he had *some* cash, and he pledged the land itself as security for the rest.[23] Louis was gambling that he would be able to meet his obligations when the loan came due. His gamble paid off, and eventually he sold the land to someone else. That buyer paid him with promissory notes and then defaulted. Louis regained possession of the land after a year or two, traded most of it back to the people he had bought it from, and made a nice profit on the sliver of it he kept for himself. A true descendant of Jacques, Louis Clamorgan proved that he was a shrewd operator in the game of real estate speculation.[24]

There *were* occasional missteps. Ester's old nemesis Judge William C. Carr had an excellent nose for a bargain. In 1843 he snapped up one piece of Clamorgan land when Louis and his brothers neglected to pay the taxes on it. Frustratingly, it was a tract their grandfather had managed to get confirmed by the Board of Land Commissioners, and Charles Collins should have settled the tax bill, because the problem arose when all three half-brothers were minors. Louis could have prevented the sheriff's sale had he learned about the problem once he came of age, but he did not. Carr saw his chance and took it.[25] Four years later ignorance again cost Louis dearly. He lost two tracts in the township of St. Ferdinand in St. Louis County because he was delinquent on the taxes.[26] Such oversights were rare, however. Louis knew the real estate market and the areas ripe for development. A couple of deals in 1845, for instance, netted him a nice profit. In the space of six months he sold one property for more than double what he paid for it, and then bought another he anticipated doing equally well with.[27]

Once acquired, property needed to be protected. In an increasingly congested city, with all sorts of workshops and factories cheek by jowl with private residences, fire was an ever-present danger. On May 17, 1849, a fire broke out on the steamboat *White Cloud*, moored at one of the wharves along the Mississippi. The vessel was set adrift, but it was too late. The flames leaped from boat to boat, then to the levees, and then to the warehouses, where all sorts of combustible materials were stored. The volunteer fire companies responded to the clanging fire bells. They fought the flames as best they could, but a combination of high winds and narrow, congested streets lined with wooden buildings defeated them. For a while it seemed the entire city might go up in flames, but the authorities ordered the use of gunpowder to create firebreaks, and then the wind changed. When the fire was out, the waterfront and much of the commercial heart of the Mound City lay in ruins—fifteen blocks in all—and the costs were in excess of six million dollars.[28] Louis and his family were safe. He and Henry lived out on Fifteenth Street, beyond the reach of the fire. Still, he took heed of the staggering financial losses and purchased fire insurance. It was a sensible move. Later that same year one of his rental properties came under threat. A fire began in Henry Taylor Blow's white lead and oil factory at the corner of Tenth and Clark, and the workers could not stop it spreading. The conflagration destroyed a two-story frame house Louis owned across the alley from the factory, and high winds blew burning embers to neighboring homes, several more of which burned to the ground. His foresight meant that the fire cost Louis very little in the end, although it took every stick of furniture his hapless tenants owned.[29]

By the time he was in his mid-twenties, Louis Clamorgan was a man of prominence within the free community of color. He was a vital member of a complex network of kinship and friendship that knit the community together. If not old enough to be counted as an elder statesman in colored St. Louis, he could realistically expect to achieve that status in the not-too-distant future. He was literate and he had a flair for business. In a modest way he had patronage to give, since he was both an employer and a landlord. He knew a good bit about the law and about the managing of money. He could also dispense that most invaluable commodity, advice. People sought him out, and if he could assist them he generally did.

In the late 1840s, Louis devoted a good deal of his time to handling the affairs of Louis Rutgers, an ex-slave he had known for years. It was a huge endeavor, but old established loyalties were involved, as was the chance to make money. Louis Clamorgan and Louis Rutgers moved in the same circles, and Rutgers had married Pelagie Clamorgan, the widow of Louis's uncle St. Eutrope. Before he died, Louis Rutgers's white father, Arend, had settled on him and his family thirty-three arpents of land (about twenty-eight acres) on the outskirts of the city. Arend was as explicit as he could be. The land was for Louis Rutgers and his heirs, and no one else had a right to it, but the loss of valuable real estate did not sit well with Arend's white heirs, and they fought it. Louis Clamorgan helped Louis and Pelagie Rutgers protect their interests by engaging in a complex swapping of land titles, and he became the titular owner of much of their real estate in a bid to block any claim from Arend's white family.[30] Nevertheless, the legal wrangling continued unabated, with Louis Clamorgan now drawn into the mess. The quarrelling claimants finally agreed to compromise. Some of the land was given up, but Louis Rutgers, with Louis Clamorgan's aid, succeeded in creating a trust for his daughter Antoinette, with the two of them as trustees. Louis Rutgers's death in 1847 complicated things, but Louis Clamorgan remained the trustee. On behalf of Antoinette and her mother, he negotiated leases that would ensure them a very good income for the rest of their lives. Thanks, in part, to his hard work and financial know-how, mother and daughter lived in style in a handsomely furnished mansion, and Pelagie reigned supreme as the grand duchess of colored St. Louis.[31]

Under the tutelage of his elder half-brother, Henry Clamorgan soon mastered the art of trading real estate. Sometimes the two pooled their money to acquire land, and sometimes they bought land from and sold land to each other.[32] Back and forth went money and credit between Louis and Henry, within their extended family and with various friends in the free community of color. White men and women borrowed from the Clamorgans and they also gave them loans. A loan at interest, with the right kind of security, was worth making, no matter whether the borrower was white, black, or of mixed racial ancestry. Money was money. As for real estate, there were deals with Julia Clamorgan's mother and with Harriet's sister and her husband. There were other transactions with members of the Clamorgans' social circle. And inevitably, in the boomtown that St. Louis was in the 1840s, there were dozens of land deals with white people—old friends, casual acquaintances, and total strangers simply intent, as the Clamorgans themselves were, on turning a healthy profit.[33]

A healthy profit was one thing, and the brothers were as keen to prosper as anyone else. But untold riches, rather than a good deal here or
there, were within their grasp if they could exploit their inheritance from
Jacques Clamorgan. And they set about doing that as soon as they were
able. On July 30, 1841, Louis Clamorgan, who had turned twenty-one
just five days earlier, and Henry, who was still not of age, authorized
Charles Collins to sell for them on terms that "shall seem most to our
advantage and profit" one-half of the various properties that had come
to them from their grandfather.[34] These were the tracts Jacques Clamorgan had set aside for Maximin and Cyprian Martial back in 1813.
With the deaths of their uncles, unmarried and without issue, the lands
(so the family maintained) had passed to Louis and his brothers through
Apoline. Although Apoline's sons were not actually in possession of a
single acre of the real estate, they hoped to induce investors to part with
money to buy their legal claims. Of course, the purchasers would then
have to fight in the courts to oust the people who were occupying the
land. Frankly, the situation was murky and complex, especially since the
U.S. government had not in fact recognized Jacques Clamorgan's titles
to any of the four land grants. Still, his grandsons intended to try to
profit from the very uncertainty over who owned what.

Charles Collins was well aware of the potential value of his wards'
land claims. In 1833 he had advised the Probate Court that Louis and
his siblings had inherited the right to vast tracts of real estate. He explained that getting those claims confirmed would require someone to
make representation to Congress. There were "conflicting interests" out
to prevent their being confirmed, and he pointed to "the absolute necessity of employing counsel competent to the task." It might be necessary, Collins explained, to offer a good lawyer a share of the claims as
his fee, but he insisted he wanted to see the Clamorgan children righted.
Collins let the matter drop after that. His own business interests were
in bad shape, and the crisis in the national economy resulting from the
Panic of 1837 had caused land values to plummet. But things looked
much brighter as a new decade dawned, and Louis's coming-of-age
prompted Collins to action.[35]

A New Yorker by birth, Charles Collins kept up his business contacts in the city, and he was confident that it was in his hometown that

the largest number of well-heeled land speculators was to be found. Once the Clamorgans authorized him to act for them, he headed east and went to work. By mid-September 1841 he had brokered a deal to sell more than eight thousand acres in St. Charles and Lincoln Counties to one investor for almost twenty-two thousand dollars. Two more sales the following month netted more than ninety thousand.[36] Two additional sales a couple of months later increased that total by another ten and a half thousand dollars, and another the next year brought in two thousand more. By the summer of 1843, Louis and Henry felt confident enough to handle the sales themselves without trusting to Collins or trekking off to New York. St. Louis County farmer Warrick Tunstall paid them sixteen thousand dollars for a quarter share of the half-million-acre St. Charles grant. They were also able to arrange a sale of another part of the tract to the area businessman John Stacker. Of course, there were stipulations. The purchasers, all of them astute investors, were not about to hand over any cash until the sellers could furnish them with clear title, and that meant the Clamorgans and Collins would have to go to court to eject the various individuals who had appropriated the land.[37] But, in true Clamorgan fashion, the brothers weren't put off by the prospect of a courtroom tussle. While it would have suited them much better if the purchasers had simply paid them for their land claims and borne the costs of the lawsuits, they were prepared to do the fighting themselves if they had to. When they won—and they were confident they would—they would be very wealthy indeed. They might never be in quite the same league as the members of the super-rich Chouteau clan, but they would come close.

The work of getting back what the brothers claimed was rightfully theirs began while Collins was wrapping up the land transactions in New York City. In 1842, Louis hired attorney Gustavus A. Bird (the same man who had represented Ester's family in their bid to regain her lands) to bring actions in the St. Charles Circuit Court against four local farmers who had occupied 1,066 arpents (just over 900 acres) on the Missouri River. It was not the St. Charles grant, but it was in the vicinity. Jacques Clamorgan had bought the title to this piece of property from the estate of fellow trader Jacques D'Eglise, and in 1811 he had succeeded in persuading the land commissioners to confirm it to him. He left it to his children, and via Apoline it had come down to Louis and his brothers, although there was some debate as to whether the land had actually ended up in the hands of lawyer Edward Hempstead when Jacques had fallen into debt after his return from Santa Fé. Louis Clamorgan and his attorney pressed ahead anyway. The cases dragged on, and Bird asked for a change of venue, pointing out that his client's adversaries were wealthy and well connected and had exerted undue influence to ensure that Louis could not get a fair hearing. The defendants insisted there was no case to answer. One of the four, John Seigle, mounted the most spirited defense. His lawyer did not deny that Jacques had once owned the land, but he maintained Jacques had lost it as a result of a judgment against him. As soon as he got back to St. Louis, Charles Collins weighed in, but too much time had elapsed and the titles were too muddied to sort out. Seigle and the others had bought the land in good faith, and that was sufficient for the court to decide in their favor.[38]

Louis and Henry encountered even more problems with the St. Charles grant, since their grandfather had never managed to get it confirmed. When they could not convey clear title to the New York speculators, the sales were voided. Local investor Warrick Tunstall was in the deal for the long haul, however, and he and Henry joined forces. Tunstall would underwrite a bid to get Congress to act on the claim, but it would be done in Henry's name as Jacques's grandson. Should they win, Tunstall would walk away with a quarter of the proceeds, while Henry, Louis, and Cyprian pocketed the rest.

Representations soon got under way in Washington. Tunstall's attorneys adroitly avoided any mention of the fact that Henry and the other heirs were persons of color. They had no wish to prejudice their case. Again the proofs were laid out. Jacques Clamorgan had been given land for his services by a cash-strapped Spanish Crown, but he had been unable to get his title confirmed, and the land had been declared public domain. Had his heirs been able to bring suit under the 1824 Act for the adjudication of Spanish land claims, many of the people who had settled on the land would have been evicted. However, with the passage of time, those settlers had regularized their titles, and they were eager to have the matter resolved. There was always the nagging fear that the heirs might be able to bring suit at some future date and they would see their ownership rights compromised. The federal government should admit its mistake in appropriating Jacques Clamorgan's land, compensate his heirs, and ensure that the settlers were left in peace. It was a novel argument: Henry Clamorgan was not so much petitioning for himself, the lawyers implied, as for the honest and industrious men and women who were farming his grandfather's land. Some members of Congress accepted that argument and urged a compensation package for the Clamorgans that would make everyone happy, but that was not how things worked out in the long run. The petition bounced back and forth from one congressional committee to another during the latter half of the 1840s, until it simply died. Henry and his brothers were no nearer to getting the St. Charles grant confirmed, and Warrick Tunstall was stuck with a sheaf of bills for legal services.[39]

In the case of the St. Charles grant, the Clamorgans placed their hopes in the federal government and were disappointed. However, in the matter of another of their claims, it did seem that they might get partial vindication. In 1811, the Board of Land Commissioners had confirmed to Jacques Clamorgan a one-by-forty-arpent parcel of land in the Little Prairie. What had once been on the fringes of St. Louis was now close to the heart of the city. The boundary line ran right down the middle of Washington Avenue. The land had been confirmed to Jacques, but nothing more happened until 1845, when the federal government awoke to its past oversight and lumbered into action. In the intervening years, though, people other than the Clamorgan heirs had taken chunks of the land for themselves. The tract had been carved up into city blocks, subdivided into lots, and sold off piecemeal. Roads had been constructed and homes and businesses built. In a sense, while that complicated the rights of Jacques Clamorgan's grandsons, the fact that the area had been developed vastly increased its value. It was now just a matter of getting the federal government to issue a patent. Then Jacques's heirs could start pressuring people to pay up if they wanted to have their titles validated.

On February 10, 1845, the Government Land Office did indeed issue a patent for the land. In due course the patent found its way to President Polk's desk and he signed it. That did not necessarily mean the government was authorizing Jacques's grandsons to take back their land. The patent simply said that Jacques had had a good title to it in 1811. What had happened after that date would have to be the subject of litigation. Even so, the news that a patent was to be issued stirred up considerable interest in St. Louis and beyond. John Stacker knew the nature of the Clamorgan claims well enough to take a chance on them. He had already bought into the brothers' St. Charles claim, and he was willing to make an investment in their St. Louis title. He handed over fifteen hundred dollars for a stake. The law partners Isaac Taylor and Edwin R. Mason were not far behind Stacker, but they were a little more cautious—or had less money at their disposal. They bought a smaller stake for three hundred dollars.[40] Two speculators from Kentucky, Isaac Landes and Fidelio C. Sharp, waited until the patent was on its way to the White House for the presidential signature before they negotiated with Jacques's heirs. They put up ten thousand dollars for a share.[41] All the parties understood that they were buying the brothers' *interest*, and technically not their *title*. Firstly, Louis and Henry were not in possession of the land, so they could not sell *that*. Secondly, some of the people who *were* in possession were likely to mount legal challenges to try to uphold their own rights. Thirdly, the patent the president had signed simply said that at some point in the past Jacques Clamorgan had been the lawful owner of the land. It said nothing about *current* rights and titles. Inevitably, there would be legal battles ahead, as the Clamorgans and their backers fought and those who believed they were themselves the true owners fought back. Of course, there was always the possibility of compromising and settling out of court.

The threat of litigation was enough for some of those individuals who held land in the disputed area. They had bought their various pieces of real estate from (as they thought) the rightful owners. Now they discovered that the sellers might have misled them, and they rushed to see how much the Clamorgans and their partners, Messrs. Stacker, Taylor, Mason and company, would take to convey to them clear title. Thomas T. January settled with Louis and Henry Clamorgan even before Landes and Sharp entered the picture. Martin Lepore came on board soon afterward. Edward Hale was more of a gambler. He waited until the Clamorgans and their backers brought suit against him in the Circuit Court, and then he cut a deal. If they won, or if they lost but then won on appeal, he would pay them a thousand dollars. It was a neat arrangement. He was handing over nothing while limiting his future liability.[42] These small victories, and the possibility of more to come, attracted another investor. The New York businessman Frederick Norcum paid nine hundred dollars for a share in the Clamorgan claim. The local real estate dealer Isaac T. Greene was equally optimistic. His stake was for five thousand dollars.[43]

It was only to be expected that some of the people who believed their titles were legitimate would fight. Landes and Sharp bankrolled Louis, Henry, and Charles Collins, who was acting as Cyprian's guardian, when the trio sued speculators John O'Fallon and Jesse G. Lindell in the St. Louis Circuit Court in July 1845. The plaintiffs told a tale of ineptitude and double-dealing on the part of certain officials in St. Louis. Back in 1820, one Rufus Easton had won a judgment against Jacques Clamorgan's estate. It was settled with the sale of a piece of land Jacques owned, but the sheriff wrote down that the land sold for less than it actually did. As a result, another sale took place, in 1826. The sheriff unlawfully seized the entire Washington Avenue tract, and O'Fallon and Lindell gobbled it up for a fraction of its true worth.

The plaintiffs had no shortage of reasons why the 1826 sale should be voided. The first sale six years earlier had netted enough to settle the debt. And what about the rights of minors? When Jacques died, he left all his real estate, including the piece in question, to his children, all of whom were underage. They had been entitled to challenge the sale once they came of age. Moreover, the next generation of heirs had only just reached the age at which *they* could act for themselves. Surely they should have some latitude granted them. Of course, one matter that both the plaintiffs and the defendants were happy to keep silent about was how Jacques had acquired the land in dispute. What had once been the Little Prairie tract had originally belonged to Ester, and it was one of the properties she and her heirs claimed she had been swindled out of.

The attorneys for O'Fallon and Lindell countered with an argument based on a technicality: the plaintiffs had neglected to give notice of the impending legal action to the hundred or so individuals to whom the pair had sold pieces of the disputed tract over the previous two decades. Tracking down all the various sales in the rapidly growing

Washington Avenue corridor would be a superhuman task, and it was enough to undermine the Clamorgans' case.[44]

The whitewasher Enoch P. Perkins proved as tough an opponent as O'Fallon and Lindell. He had bought his Washington Avenue land fair and square: he would not budge, nor would he hand over a cent for quiet possession. On August 20, 1845, battle commenced in the Court of Common Pleas. Round and round the arguments went. This time the so-called Ester claims *did* feature. Perkins's lawyer contended the land had never belonged to Jacques. It had belonged to Ester, and she had sold it to William C. Carr. Judge Carr was called to testify and he trod delicately, since he knew some of his legal maneuverings were highly dubious. He swore that Ester had given him her land as payment for his legal services. He also said that Jacques had acknowledged to him that he had forged a deed of conveyance from Ester. Jacques Clamorgan, although "a remarkable man" in many respects, was most definitely not to be trusted when it came to any transaction involving real estate. Carr had been warned when he arrived in St. Louis to "have nothing to do with property which comes through" Clamorgan. While the question of the Clamorgan heirs' status as people of color was raised briefly in this case, it does not appear to have been of much importance. Other considerations, principally the chain of possession, weighed far more heavily with the jurors.

The verdict that came down in the summer of 1847 was hardly to the plaintiffs' liking. After days of deliberation, a sympathetic and doubtless exhausted jury found for Perkins. The claimants promptly appealed to the Missouri Supreme Court. As the Perkins case moved through the courts, the waters became murkier and murkier. The attorneys in the O'Fallon and Lindell case had argued over the 1820 judgment against Jacques Clamorgan's estate. Perkins's lawyers pointed to an even earlier judgment against Jacques himself. That judgment, in 1808, had resulted in the sale of part of his land, possibly the very tract in dispute. Inevitably that led to more questions. Was the 1808 judgment lawful, given that Jacques had been out of the country at the time—he had been on his trek to Santa Fé—and hence unable to defend himself? And when the commissioners confirmed his claim in 1811, had they been confirming it to *him* or to whoever had owned the land at that point?[45]

Perkins scored a victory in the Missouri Supreme Court, but the question of who owned what in the Little Prairie–Washington Avenue tract refused to die. Another case concerning the Clamorgans' title to this immensely valuable chunk of real estate ended up in the nation's highest court. It began in the St. Louis Circuit Court as a suit brought by Isaac Landes against Joshua B. Brant. Brant admitted he owned land in the Little Prairie tract, but he insisted he had acquired it in a legitimate sale. The jurors stumbled over the questions that had confused their counterparts in the Perkins case: Which tract of land was which? When had Jacques obtained title, if in fact he ever had? Had Ester been the true owner, and what had she traded to Carr? What about the sale to O'Fallon and Lindell? And so on. In this action, unlike the earlier ones, searching questions *were* raised about the Clamorgan heirs' illegitimacy and their status as people of color. If Jacques's children and grandchildren were "natural" progeny, were they entitled under Missouri's inheritance laws to anything? And if, into the bargain, they were people of color, did that not further weaken any property rights they might have? It was their right to inherit and then dispose of property that was at the heart of the matter. The jurors never went on record as stating whether they were swayed by the arguments about legitimacy and race. They simply rendered a verdict in Brant's favor. Isaac Landes pursued the matter all the way to the U.S. Supreme Court. Once more Brant and his lawyers brought the status of the Clamorgan heirs into the case, but the justices seemed more interested in whether Jacques had owned the land at the time he made his will. They decided he had not. His heirs could not inherit what he did not have to leave them.[46]

Even though the various cases ended in defeat for the Clamorgans and their ever-growing number of partners, they were time-consuming and expensive for everyone involved, and there was always the specter of an appeal. Numerous people and institutions along the Washington Avenue corridor decided the wisest course was to pay up and be done with it. As a lawyer in one of the Clamorgan actions observed, "Are not men daily buying titles adverse to those under which they hold . . . merely to remove specks or shadows from their titles which may affect the price of their lands in market."[47] Payments for clear title varied according to the amount of real estate at issue. Sometimes less than a hundred dollars to the Clamorgans and their fellow title-holders sufficed. Sometimes the price was several hundred dollars. And then there were the payouts from the likes of speculators John and William Finney, who forked over five thousand dollars, and the trustees of St. Louis University, who paid more than sixteen hundred dollars to cleanse the title to the land on which the school's famous Medical Hall stood.[48]

Some landholders refused outright to make payment, and they were served with writs to encourage them to reconsider. Obviously the threat of legal action was intended to yield a cash return. The claimants might never get the land itself, but they were resolved to get what they believed it was worth. Louis and Henry Clamorgan joined forces with Landes and Sharp and hired the law firm of Crockett and Briggs. Anticipating a flurry of actions, the lawyers had forms printed detailing the nature of the title and the consequences (five hundred dollars in damages, plus court costs) of not vacating the premises. All the clerk of the Circuit Court had to fill in was the name of the defendant. In January 1847 the writs went out.[49] This prompted a few more of the holdouts to strike a bargain. As a goodwill gesture, the claimants gave the trustees of the Fourth Street Methodist Episcopal Church a grant of clear title for ten dollars. Private citizens were expected to pay the market rate.[50] Finally, in September 1851, the sixteen cases that did actually go to trial were dismissed. By then the U.S. Supreme Court had ruled against the Clamorgan claim in *Landes v. Brant*. The plaintiffs knew they would lose at the local level and so did not bother to pursue the matter.[51]

Henry and Louis Clamorgan had done well to sell their claim when they did and induce nervous landholders to pay up. When the dust settled, the brothers had gained thousands of dollars for their interest in the Little Prairie tract, while Landes, Sharp, et al. had nothing except legal bills. Even the victors had a price to pay. Lindell, O'Fallon, and other interested parties had banded together to defend the Landes case, and they soon fell to bickering over how much they should pay.[52] The lawyers grew rich, and the Clamorgans had money. Ester's heirs got nothing at all.

For the Clamorgan brothers, the dream of getting untold riches from their grandfather's lands was merely a dream deferred. They would not give up on it, but until that dream was realized they had to make a living for themselves and their families.

Louis Clamorgan's first commercial venture was in partnership with William Johnson. Johnson, like Louis, was a native of Missouri. Although of English stock, if his name is anything to go by, he had cemented his ties to the old "French" community through his marriage to Marie Larivière, the teenage daughter of the African American barber Pierre Larivière and Marie Labadie. Johnson was fourteen years Louis Clamorgan's senior, a trusted friend, and possibly a father figure. A business partnership of some sort would, he and Louis hoped, prove mutually beneficial. They pooled their resources and, in 1840, opened a grocery store. It did not prosper, and the two soon returned full-time to a trade they knew well, namely, barbering. They parted amicably, though. In the years ahead they traded real estate back and forth, made loans to each other, and continued to interact socially.[53]

After the arrangement with Johnson ended, Louis went into business with William Henry Moses. Theirs was an interesting collaboration. Moses already had a barbershop, but Louis had cash. In 1841, Moses pledged almost everything he owned, the contents of his shop and most of his household furniture, as security for a debt he owed Louis. Louis got access to the fittings and fixtures needed to start up a barbershop—everything from barber's chairs and looking glasses to a caged mockingbird to entertain customers—while Moses gained some much-needed capital and a partner.[54]

Louis and Moses worked together until 1844, and Louis may have retained a partial interest in Moses's barbershop for some time after that, but in 1845 he branched out and joined forces with Jeffrey G. Iredell. Originally from North Carolina, Iredell was some years older than Louis, and he had operated a barbershop, on his own and with other partners, for several years before he and Louis teamed up.[55] Initially the duo offered the usual services, but then they hit upon the idea of bathing their customers as well as attending to their hair and beards. Conveniently located across from the post office on Chestnut Street, the "Italian Baths" was a novelty in St. Louis. For twenty-five cents, a gentleman could luxuriate in "water clear as crystal" in a tub "of the finest marble," after which he could take a seat in one of the barber's chairs for "an easy shave" and a fashionable haircut.[56]

Not everything went smoothly. Louis Clamorgan and Jeffrey Iredell leased the premises from dentist John S. Clark. As they began getting the Italian Baths ready for their new customers, the partners had an unpleasant confrontation with Alexander Foster and James S. Temple, who were also tenants of Dr. Clark. Foster and Temple alleged that the barbers had unlawfully entered their premises and broken the roof of their icehouse. The cistern Clamorgan and Iredell had installed to supply their bathtubs had done even more damage, allowing rainwater to pour in, destroying Foster and Temple's ice. Understandably aggrieved, Foster and Temple sued the barbers and their landlord. Happily for Clamorgan and Iredell, the court dismissed the charges against them, although it did find Dr. Clark liable.[57]

More problems over water and ice ensued. Italian confectioner Joseph Lamalfa specialized in making ice cream, and he, too, had an icehouse under the cistern that supplied the Italian Baths. One day in the summer of 1845, when his customers were clamoring for ice cream, the cistern overflowed and the resulting deluge put Lamalfa out of business. Once more the barbers' attorney prevailed, arguing that the flood was the result of an unfortunate accident, and not, as Lamalfa contended, gross negligence.[58]

After those initial setbacks, the enterprise thrived. Although, according to the editor of the St. Louis *Reveille*, the Italian Baths was not quite up to the standard of the baths at the famed St. Charles Hotel in New Orleans: Clamorgan and Iredell's operation "has just about the nicest arrangement in the shape of a bath that an up-river man can desire." And that was the editor's judgment when the business had been running for only a year.[59]

There was a downside to having it generally known that one was prospering, as Louis discovered in the fall of 1848 when thieves broke into his home and robbed him of a thousand dollars. However, the culprits were arrested, and he may have gotten some of his hard-earned money back.[60] The robbery had shaken him, but he and Iredell forged ahead. By the spring of 1849 they had increased the array of services the Italian Baths offered. One could get a shampoo and scalp massage to stave off hair loss (and deal with the all-too-common infestations of head lice). The establishment was "unsurpassed by any in the Union, either in the skill of its operators or elegance of operation." A single "luxurious bath" still cost a quarter, with regular customers having the option of buying a book of two dozen tickets for five dollars. And for those with even more money to spend, a soak in a "salt bath" could be had for thirty-five cents.[61]

By 1849, Jeffrey Iredell had struck out on his own and Louis had taken on his younger brother as his partner. Soon after his marriage, Henry had tried making a living as a riverman. He quickly gave that up, and in 1844 he and Harriet and their young son trekked off to Milwaukee, where Louis Clamorgan and Harriet's uncle William Eagleson had both made modest purchases of land. As it turned out, though, Milwaukee offered fewer opportunities than St. Louis. It did not take Henry long to realize that he could most easily make a living for his family by pooling his resources with Louis's and entering the "tonsorial profession." What had been Clamorgan and Iredell became, in 1849, L. and H. Clamorgan.[62]

The brothers' joint enterprise could have ended in financial disaster. The year 1849 witnessed crisis after crisis in St. Louis. The fire that destroyed so much of the city was followed by pestilence. An epidemic of Asiatic cholera took the lives of at least six thousand residents and sent many times that number fleeing in a bid to escape the scourge, while, at the same time, excitement over California's gold rush sent men, and capital, even farther west.[63] But what could have spelled disaster for the Clamorgan brothers in fact brought opportunity. St. Louis grew at a phenomenal rate. New brick buildings went up to replace the wooden structures lost to the flames in the great fire. Streets were widened, and the city began to take on a whole new look. The overgrown village that Jacques Clamorgan had known, with its timber-frame houses and its drying racks festooned with furs, was gone forever. In its place was what boosters referred to as "the great western metropolis."[64] Wealth poured into St. Louis as Forty-niners opting to take the overland route, as opposed to venturing around Cape Horn or across the isthmus of Panama, equipped themselves for the trek westward. Although few found the riches they sought, some did, and California wealth flowed back into St. Louis. For Louis and Henry Clamorgan, these were boom years as bathing was touted as a surefire preventative for cholera, and California gold paid for everything from haircuts and baths to pomades and hair dye. The city was also a military base, and officers and men wanted the goods and services the Clamorgans provided.[65] The new establishment functioned as baths, a barbershop, and a fancy goods store. Louis and Henry experimented, stocking a few items to catch the eyes of their clients. Soap and perfume sold well, so they added a few more things. Soon they were stocking costume jewelry, umbrellas, and all manner of goods. Before long the front of the store, where customers could browse for "must-have" items, was generating as much revenue as the area set aside for barbering and bathing.[66] Louis and Henry soon discovered they were victims of their own success: They had patrons lining up for a bath or a shave, and they were anxious to accommodate them, but they could not do so with their existing facilities. And customers inspecting their stock kept asking for more items than they had on hand. They knew if they had the space, they could bring in an even wider range of goods, and those goods would sell. However, without more spacious premises to move into, and the capital to cover the cost of relocating, they were stuck—until their younger brother offered them a way out of their difficulties.

In the spring of 1851, Cyprian had turned twenty-one and had come into his inheritance. On June 6, the same day his guardian finally handed over all the money due him, Cyprian loaned Louis and Henry four thousand dollars. In return, they took him into partnership.[67] One week later the three brothers took a ten-year lease on part of a new building going up on the corner of Fourth and Pine, in the heart of the commercial district. They pledged to pay the developers, lawyer Thomas T. Gantt and architect George J. Barnett, $2,600 per annum for the first five years and $2,800 for the second five years. It was a very considerable sum, but they offset it by subleasing the basement as a bowling alley.[68] It made perfect sense. A gentleman could work up a sweat with a vigorous game of bowls and then adjourn to the brothers' establishment for a bath, or round out a shopping trip with some healthy exercise. In short, nothing could have been better calculated to ensure that

L. Clamorgan and Brothers, generally referred to simply as Clamorgans, prospered. And prosper it did.

Customers flocked to Clamorgans, but it is worth noting that there was one segment of the community the brothers did not welcome in their establishment except as employees. Like so many other African Americans with their own businesses, they could not afford to cater to other people of color. To permit a black or "colored" man, however wealthy or refined, to occupy a barber's chair or enjoy any of the other amenities Clamorgans had to offer would spell ruin. White clients would leave en masse. That was simply the reality of life in antebellum St. Louis—and much of the rest of the nation. The Clamorgan brothers could not change it. If they wanted to survive and make money, they knew what they had to do. And survive and prosper they certainly did.

Everything that the fastidious white St. Louisan could possibly want was to be found at Clamorgans. The establishment boasted one of the choicest arrays of shaving accessories in the West. Hair preparations constituted a major stock in trade. Bottles of Bogle's Hyperion Fluid jostled for space on the shelves with containers of scented bandoline, a gummy preparation used by both sexes in an era before hairspray and hair gels.[69] For the bath there were "flesh gloves," sponges, and mounds of delicately scented soaps. There were brushes for the hair, the nails, for hats and clothes. For patrons keen to avoid the dentist's chair in an age before anesthesia, the brothers sold toothbrushes, toothpicks, and various "dentifrices." Mirrors of every kind were to be had at Clamorgans, from expensive looking glasses and "stand mirrors" with their own cases to the common or garden variety. Louis and his partners stocked perfumes, creams, and lotions imported from London, and no fewer than thirty different "odours" from the famed Lubin Perfume House of Paris.[70]

The establishment catered to many other needs beyond those of personal hygiene. Clamorgans carried a wide array of change purses in modestly priced fabrics and leather and in more expensive silver and mother-of-pearl. There were boxes of every kind (scenery boxes, bridal boxes, ladies' work boxes), and for everything from bonbons to powder puffs. There were ink stands and desk sets, portable writing desks, portfolios, pen wipers, and fancy inks. There were dressing cases and traveling cases, eye glasses and opera glasses. For the well-appointed home there were tea services, candlesticks, wax tapers, napkin rings, and baskets and trays for the receipt of visiting cards.

Ladies could purchase hairpins, shoes, reticules, crochet needles, vinaigrettes, and aromatic vinegars. They could also find at Clamorgans a choice assortment of fans, from ornate Spanish fans for the salon and ballroom to black-edged mourning fans for more somber settings. Gentlemen had their pick of an impressive array of canes: canes made of whalebone, canes with ivory heads and canes with silver heads, canes that concealed swords and others that hid opera glasses. Well aware that a cane was an essential accoutrement for every white male with any pretension to gentility, the Clamorgan brothers even stocked canes for young boys. Doting fathers could outfit their sons as well as themselves, and teach them the walk and the gestures of a man about town.

A half-century earlier, Jacques had stocked buffalo robes, bolts of cloth, and farming implements for his customers. Now his grandsons sold luxuries the old trader could not even have imagined in a setting that was startlingly different from the frontier trading post that was the St. Louis Jacques had known. The dozen French crystal glasses with bronze and mahogany handles that the brothers had in one of their display cases, for example, cost more than a laboring man could earn in a month.

Ladies were welcome in the front part of the premises. They could browse the "fancy items" and seek the advice of Julia and Harriet Clamorgan about hair ornaments and shoes. However, delicacy and propriety kept them out of the male part of the establishment. One whole section of Clamorgans was a "bathing saloon." Gentlemen could request a bath in one of the ten Italian marble tubs purchased at the unheard-of cost of almost eight hundred dollars. Those with a taste for the more traditional copper bathtub could be catered to, as could the hardy souls who preferred a shower. Two great cisterns held the water that was channeled through a network of copper pipes into the huge steam boiler. No matter how brisk business might be, there was always an ample supply of hot water. In the privacy of one of the eighteen well-equipped bathrooms, a gentleman who came to Clamorgans could enjoy a massage, be toweled dry by one of the many attendants the brothers employed, admire himself in the strategically placed mirrors each bathroom was furnished with, and emerge refreshed to face the world again.

Some clients came not for a bath but for a shave, a fashionable hair-cut, and perhaps a discreet coloring of their graying locks. There was no shortage of barbers to wait upon them. Almost anyone in the free community of color who reckoned himself a competent barber worked for the Clamorgans at some point. On occasion a white man might be hired, although, as one of the Clamorgans' black barbers observed, white customers were suspicious of their skill level. With a more than adequate workforce the Clamorgans tried to make sure no one had to wait too long, but in the event that the establishment was exceptionally busy, their clients could find a comfortable "setting chair," relax with a news-paper, and pass the time in conversation with one another.

Presiding over the establishment, making sure everything ran smoothly, and occasionally coming forward to attend personally to a particularly valued and well-connected client was senior partner Louis Clamorgan. He was a fastidious dresser, with impeccable taste (and he had the tailor's bills to prove it). Louis understood the importance of presentation, in his person and in his establishment. He and his brothers also appreciated the power of publicity. Clamorgans had running advertisements in the *Missouri Republican*, the *St. Louis Intelligencer*, and the *Organ and Reveille*.[71]

With the move to Fourth and Pine, and all three of the Clamorgan brothers in partnership together, their future seemed assured. They were making money, and they were making influential contacts. The white elite of St. Louis patronized their establishment. The brothers were well known in the city. They could not escape their status as men of color, but they could mitigate the consequences of being second-class citizens—or noncitizens. And who knew? With friends in high places—and scores of lawyers and high-ranking political figures came to Clamorgans to be pampered and to purchase its luxuries—the brothers *might* even be able to get one or two of their grandfather's land claims recognized. If, of course, their luck held.

6

A Settling of Scores

N O EXPENSE WAS SPARED to give Louis Clamorgan a funeral worthy of a man who had made his mark on the city. When the consumption that had been sapping his strength for months finally claimed him in the fall of 1851, his grieving widow and half-brothers had him carefully dressed. Louis, who had always been so attentive to his appearance, would go to his grave attired in a fine suit of clothes, complete with a white silk scarf and matching gloves, and shrouded in the finest cambric. His coffin was the best that the undertakers William and George Lynch could furnish—"extra fine," with silk and velvet lining, silver-plated handles, and a silver cross on the lid. After a funeral Mass at the cathedral, a host of mourners followed the hearse to Rock Spring Cemetery. Some walked, but dozens rode. The undertakers supplied no fewer than fifteen carriages, and some mourners had their own. The "colored aristocracy" turned out in force, just as they had at Louis's wedding a decade earlier, but in a testimony to his racially ambiguous status—and Louis was described as a white man in the official death register—a number of white citizens came to pay their respects.[1]

Just how many heirs Louis Clamorgan left remained uncertain as he

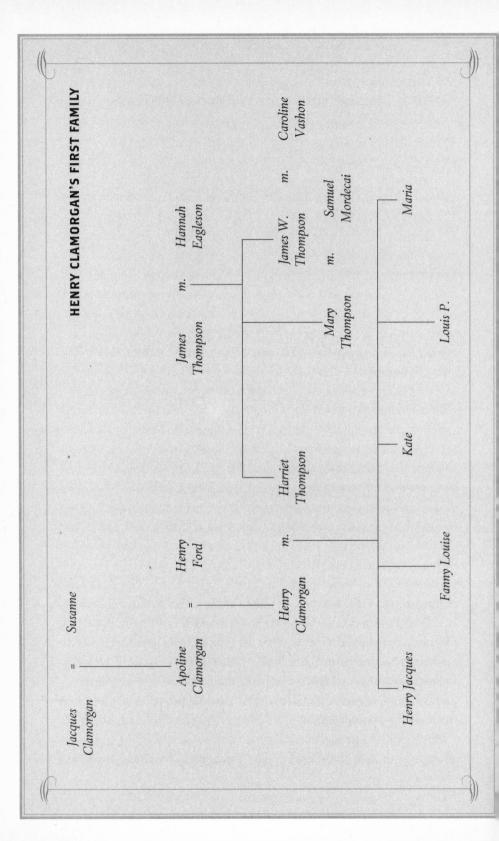

HENRY CLAMORGAN'S FIRST FAMILY

Jacques Clamorgan = Susanne

Apoline Clamorgan

Henry Clamorgan = Henry Ford

James Thompson m. Hannah Eagleson

Harriet Thompson

James W. Thompson m. Caroline Vashon

Mary Thompson m. Samuel Mordecai

Henry Clamorgan m. Kate

Henry Jacques   Fanny Louise   Maria   Louis P.

was laid to rest, for Julia was nearing yet another confinement. As it turned out, Léon and Julius came perilously close to losing their mother within weeks of burying their father. The tragedy of her husband's death, combined with the toll that repeated pregnancies had taken on her, brought on premature labor. Louis's funeral took place on October 15. Just over a month later Julia gave birth to stillborn twins, and there was another sad procession, albeit a more private one, to Rock Spring.[2] In ten years Julia had borne seven children and lost five of them.

Things would have been so much easier if Louis had left a will, but at no point during his illness did he call in his lawyer and give instructions regarding his affairs, although he knew as well as anyone that tuberculosis, once it had a grip on a victim, invariably proved fatal. In the absence of a will, Henry and Cyprian could simply have agreed with the court-appointed administrator—Julia renounced her right to handle her husband's estate—to buy out Louis's share of the business. But Cyprian was adamant: he wanted the money he had put into the brothers' joint venture, and he let Henry know he was prepared to make his life miserable until he got it.[3]

First, though, all the interested parties needed to ascertain just how much the business was worth. The public administrator, Du Bouffay Frémon, recruited three white neighbors of the Clamorgans', a druggist, a real estate agent, and a saddler, to take an inventory. The keys were handed to them and they moved methodically through the establishment, identifying every bottle of hair tonic, every "fancy item," every fitting and fixture. They got fifteen dollars apiece for their services, and the magnitude of the task—it took three days to catalogue and appraise every item—indicates that they earned their money. With their reports in hand, Frémon approached the St. Louis Probate Court and explained the situation. Henry and Cyprian had categorically "declined to undertake the management of the goods and chattels, rights and credits and other partnership estate" belonging to the firm. He asked for permission to sell the stock of the business privately, fearing the prices he would get at a public auction would be lower than the real worth of the various items.[4]

Once the court agreed to Frémon's request, he turned over the actual handling of the sale to Henry. Obviously Henry wanted to buy as much as he could and keep Clamorgans going, but he did not have the cash or the credit to purchase the entire contents of the store and all the fixtures. He accepted the reality of the situation. The business must be liquidated, the profits and losses calculated, Louis's one-third share handed over to Frémon for the benefit of Julia and her sons, and Cyprian paid off as soon as possible. Other store owners in St. Louis would have the chance to replenish their shelves as everything from jars of pomade to sword canes was sold off. Frémon and Henry were probably right in insisting that items would fetch more money in these private arrangements than in the kind of public vendue that had followed Jacques Clamorgan's death. There was also a greater likelihood of getting people to pay up. Auctions attracted plenty of bidders, but they could not always pay for what they bid on, and that could involve the administrator in no end of difficulties.

There was enough money already owed the firm without more debts to worry about. Some people owed just a dollar or two, while others owed a great deal more. Frémon had to chase them down and get what he could. Some debts he was obliged to write off as uncollectible. When the business's inventory had been sold, and all the debts that could be collected had been called in, the firm's assets amounted to almost fourteen thousand dollars.[5]

From that sum various amounts had to be paid out to individuals and companies that had furnished everything from shaving soap to legal services. There were stacks of bills, and Frémon needed to figure out what was owed by Louis Clamorgan as an individual and what by the partnership. In some cases this was easy. Funeral costs, medical bills, bills for clothing, house rent, and the like were obviously due from Louis's estate. But what about bills for wallpaper? Had the paper been for the business premises or for Louis and Julia's home? Which of the lawyers who submitted bills was demanding payment for defending the firm and which for representing the litigious Louis in one or another of his personal actions? Wrapping up the estate took months.

How much money did Julia and her sons derive from the family firm? Frémon waded through Louis's personal papers and the firm's accounts to see just what the family was entitled to. In addition to whatever cash came her way from the business, Julia inherited the household property she and Louis had accumulated. The catalogue of that property conveys a sense of the genteel middle-class lifestyle the couple had enjoyed. There were sofas, worktables, a carved wooden bedstead, mirrors, and so forth. The most expensive item, a bookcase and a number of books valued at forty dollars, indicates that Louis was not merely literate but enjoyed reading. Much of the money Frémon turned over to Julia she earmarked for living expenses, but she had enough left over to dabble in real estate. She invested judiciously. Her property appreciated over the years, and she pledged it as security for various loans before eventually selling it at a profit. While she and her sons might not be rich (unless, of course, the Clamorgan claims were settled), they would not starve.[6]

The 1850s was a tumultuous decade for the Clamorgans, and not just because of Louis's death or the rift between Henry and Cyprian. Julia was trying to raise her sons, and Henry to salvage his business, in a setting in which the twin issues of slavery and race were tearing at the fabric of St. Louis. Thanks in large measure to white immigration from Germany, and to a lesser extent from Ireland, the African American population was declining. In 1850, black people accounted for slightly less than 5.25 percent of the total population of St. Louis County. All told, some four thousand black men, women, and children lived in the county, and for every one who was free, two more were enslaved. By 1860, African Americans accounted for just 2 percent of the county's residents. Even more startling was the shifting balance between enslaved and free. There were more than seventeen hundred free people of color and just over fifteen hundred slaves. Slavery was not dead, but it was waning in importance in the social and economic life of St. Louis.[7] Where that shift left them the Clamorgans and their friends and neighbors within the free community of color were trying to work out for themselves.

To begin with, when it came to determining race, census takers and other officials were often swayed by wealth. In St. Louis, as in so many communities, the old saying that money whitened held true. A dark-skinned individual with money often made the transition from "black" to "mulatto." The Clamorgans and other mixed-race people sometimes took the next step, moving from "mulatto" to "white." It was not necessarily the case that they sought to move from one category to the other. Quite often the white men gathering data were genuinely perplexed by an individual's appearance or by their last name. White and free colored Labadies, Cabannés, Chouteaus, and Charlevilles abounded in St. Louis. It was safer when confronted with the scion of a prominent family whose race one could not readily determine to declare that person white.

St. Louis was truly the Gateway to the West during the early 1850s, and the city's rapid growth brought opportunities for free people of color, as it did for whites. River commerce boomed. African Americans labored at the most menial and onerous tasks on board the hundreds of riverboats that steamed into and out of the port. Often their condition was little better than that of the slaves who worked alongside them, and white bosses generally treated them with the same callous disregard they did a slave hireling. Despite what the law said, many St. Louis slaveowners not only hired out their slaves by the day, the week, or the month to anyone, including riverboat captains, looking for additional labor, but allowed their slaves to hire their own time. The practice of slave hiring blurred the distinctions between free and enslaved.[8]

But if there were those free men of color who toiled for a pittance on the river as lowly deckhands and firemen, there were others who prospered as stewards, earning tips from passengers and kickbacks from suppliers. They decided whom to patronize when it came to ordering food and drink for the dining saloon. They could send business the way of friends and family in the free community. African American "boat furnishers" such as Henry Alexander McGee and butchers such as the Charlevilles and the Labadies did well thanks to the increase in river traffic.[9]

As for other business endeavors, although the law was clear enough, the authorities often turned a blind eye to violations. No man of color was supposed to work as a drayman, but plenty did. They were not supposed to receive licenses to sell liquor. Marshall Starks, a friend of Henry Clamorgan's, got around this by calling his establishment a coffeehouse, while Robert Smith didn't even bother with such subterfuges. He kept a saloon, and that was exactly how he described it.[10]

An increasingly sophisticated and variegated free community of color was spawning its own institutions. The Clamorgans, of course, were Catholics, but they knew men and women who attended one or another of the city's black Protestant churches. There was also a Prince Hall Lodge. While Henry Clamorgan probably adhered to his church's anti-Masonic stance, he had kinfolk who were active in the Brotherhood. If the presence of the "peculiar institution" and the oppressiveness of the legal code that governed the lives of free blacks made it impossible to organize the array of social and self-improvement organizations that enlivened the existence of African Americans in New York or Philadelphia or Boston, black St. Louisans were not without a rich communal life. Ties of family and friendship mattered. People who had grown up together, worshipped at the same churches, and traced their lineage back to the early French and Spanish settlers interacted and intermarried with newcomers from the North and the East with decidedly Anglo names and very different perceptions of racial dynamics. Migration from Tennessee and Virginia, Pennsylvania and Kentucky, was reshaping the free community. Try as they might to restrict the numbers of free black newcomers, city authorities were losing control of this segment of the population, and they knew it.[11]

Overall, the picture was mixed. As a group, free blacks were not welcome and not wanted in St. Louis, but they were everywhere in the city, and they contributed in myriad ways. Running afoul of the laws that regulated the day-to-day existence of free people of color could have dire consequences. African Americans were vulnerable in so many aspects of their lives, long before the Supreme Court ruled in the *Dred Scott* case—a case that had originated in St. Louis—that black men had no rights white men were bound to respect. At the individual level, though, the security of a person of color was often determined by who that person's white friends or enemies were. A powerful white ally—and the Clamorgans had a number of them—could insulate someone from the restrictions that successive acts of the General Assembly had imposed to keep free people in check. A vindictive and influential white foe, however, could expose one to the full rigor of the law.

This, then, was the setting in which Louis and Julia's young sons Julius and Léon Clamorgan grew up. This was the city Henry and Harriet's children were raised in, and it was in this atmosphere of mixed opportunities and limitations that Henry sought to make his mark as a businessman.

In the months following Louis's death, Henry struggled to salvage what he could of the family business and buy Cyprian out. On March 1, 1852, Robert J. Wilkinson leased part of the premises at Fourth and Pine for five hundred dollars a year as a barbershop. Henry undertook to provide "a full complement of sitting chairs mirrors wash stands oil cloths gas & gas fixtures & fuel and six barber chairs." It was Wilkinson's responsibility to keep the place clean and in good repair.[12] The agreement with Wilkinson was a temporary expedient. Henry needed a reliable long-term partner. He could not turn to the men Louis had been in business with. William Henry Moses was dead, and Jeffrey Iredell had moved to Philadelphia. Henry's old friend James D. Bonner had also forsaken St. Louis, to open an employment exchange in Chicago.[13] But Henry knew one man who was still in town and in whom he had the utmost confidence. While Henry's relationship with Cyprian soured, his ties to his brother-in-law became stronger.

Samuel Mordecai was from Frankfort, Kentucky, the son of a free man of color, Harry Mordecai, who ran a successful plastering business, and a white woman. Harry Mordecai subsequently married a slave, and had to negotiate to free from bondage the children of that union, but *Samuel's* mother's status meant Samuel had been free from the moment of his birth.[14] He arrived in St. Louis sometime in the late 1830s, probably in the company of a powerful white friend. Lawyer and up-and-coming politician Montgomery Blair was a few years older than Samuel Mordecai. Born and raised in Frankfort, he was well aware of Samuel's history. Blair stepped forward, testified to the St. Louis County Court that Samuel was "a man of good moral character and of industrious and sober habits," and got him his license to reside in Missouri. On June 8, 1843, Samuel Mordecai, then twenty-three years of age, wed seventeen-year-old Mary Thompson, Harriet Clamorgan's younger sister.[15]

Before Louis Clamorgan's death Samuel Mordecai had been putting money into the Clamorgans' business. In the summer of 1851, as the brothers moved into their new, much larger premises, he furnished them with five hundred dollars' worth of merchandise, and as they got settled, he made the firm a loan of one thousand dollars.[16] Now, with Louis gone and Cyprian eager to branch out on his own, Henry and Samuel joined forces as equal partners. In the short term their priority was to buy out Cyprian, pay off their suppliers, and cover the rent. They soon discovered that their combined resources were not sufficient to do all that, and they reached out to fellow barber James Ford.

On April 1, 1852, Henry Clamorgan, Samuel Mordecai, and James Ford pledged to African American cattle dealer Louis Charleville, an old friend of the Clamorgan family, the entire contents of the baths, barbershop, and adjoining store as security for a promissory note of seven thousand dollars payable in ten years to Cyprian at 6 percent per annum interest. Then they scraped together whatever they could and paid Cyprian back in just a matter of a few months.[17] With Cyprian no longer hounding them, it was time to consolidate and expand. The partners negotiated another loan on better terms. On the day after Cyprian had been paid off, they once more pledged to Charleville everything "belonging to the Bathing Saloon known as the Clamorgan Baths"—ten marble bathtubs and eight copper ones, two shower baths, two "Douse" baths, the marble slabs the masseurs used, mirrors, chairs, washstands, the chandeliers and paintings that brightened the barbershop, the marble-top counter, the heating apparatus, the two great cisterns, and everything down to the lead piping and faucets, the oilcloth and carpeting, and the iron safe in which they kept the day's takings. Combined, their stock in trade was the security for a loan of $5,400 from Emma Powell White, a woman with a nose for a good investment. The gamble paid off for everyone. White had her money back in two years, not the nine she had agreed to. Henry Clamorgan, Samuel Mordecai, and James Ford still had everything they had pledged as security, and they had the money they needed to consolidate and expand.[18]

The partners did face one or two setbacks, though. Somewhat rashly, as they struggled to pay off the loan to White ahead of time, they branched out and began selling lottery tickets. Many other folks did the same. Unfortunately, it was against the law to do so without a license, and the authorities cracked down. In January 1854, with business booming and the loan close to being paid, the threesome suddenly found themselves facing criminal charges. Eventually the matter was dropped, perhaps with some behind-the-scenes help from one or two of their well-placed white clients, and Henry and his partners went back to work.[19]

Clamorgans again became the byword for elegance and impeccable service. Once the partners had refitted it, it boasted mahogany chairs, Italian marble tubs, "and the finest of tonsorial paraphernalia."[20] It also featured as a part of the social scene: A wit in the *Missouri Republican*, for instance, wrote a fanciful piece about a fashionable young man who, among other signs of elegance and good breeding, always took care to be shaved at Clamorgans.[21] (The name endured, even though Henry was the only Clamorgan now overseeing the establishment.) The same paper recommended that its male readers treat themselves to a bath at Clamorgans during a particularly steamy summer. They could cool off, relax, and, suitably refreshed after the heat and toil of the day, enjoy a good night's rest. Clamorgans was "the model bath rooms of the West"—conveniently located, scrupulously clean, and admirably well run.[22] Such press notices were welcome advertising. At most Henry and his partners might have had to bribe the editor with the offer of a bath or two gratis.

Even though the economy of St. Louis was not as buoyant as it had been in the heady gold rush days, business was good at Clamorgans through at least the first half of the 1850s. Ulysses S. Grant was one of Clamorgans' regulars. He would ride into town from the farm on the outskirts of St. Louis that he managed for his father-in-law, and whatever other matters he had to see to, he would invariably stop by Clamorgans. Visitors to the city were advised that *the* premier barbershop and baths was Clamorgans. The Little Giant, Senator Stephen Douglas, also came in, as did Thomas Hart Benton and his son-in-law John C. Frémont (although, given the bad blood between them, probably not at the same time).[23] In short, Clamorgans' clientele was exactly the kind Henry and his partners had hoped to attract.

Henry renegotiated the lease for the premises at Fourth and Pine in

1854. The previous one was with all three half-brothers. With Louis dead and Cyprian out of the partnership, Henry became the sole tenant on the same terms and for the same amount he and his brothers had agreed to pay.[24] It was not always easy to scrape together the money to make the quarterly payments, especially when the Panic of 1857 set in. Men cut back on their expenses, and for a good number of them, visits to Clamorgans became less frequent. Then James Ford dropped out of the partnership. Henry and Samuel did what they had to. On July 15, 1857, they rented to Albert White for four and a half years the barbershop that Robert J. Wilkinson had once operated. White agreed to pay them six hundred dollars a year for the first two years and seven hundred a year for the remaining two and a half years. The lease stipulated that White "shall conduct the business of the Shaving department and have the entire control of the same and . . . employ and discharge such men as he . . . may consider necessary." From his profits he would buy all the supplies and pay the men their wages. Each week he would split the remainder with Henry and Samuel, handing half to them and keeping the other half.[25] Henry and Samuel knew they need have no anxiety about White's ability to pay his share of the rent. He and his wife were Forty-niners. Unlike most of those who trekked off to the goldfields of California, the Whites had come back with plenty of money in their pockets.[26] Plus Albert White knew his trade. With him in charge of the barbershop and Henry and Samuel running the baths, Clamorgans weathered the financial crisis of the late 1850s, surviving, and indeed flourishing, as other businesses foundered.

A steady stream of people passed through Henry Clamorgan's employ in the 1850s. Dozens of practitioners of the "tonsorial art" worked for him and Samuel Mordecai, some for a week or two, and others for years. One of the most dashing was James P. Thomas. Born in Nashville, the son of white jurist John Catron (eventually a U.S. Supreme Court justice), and Sally Thomas, a slave who hired her own time and ran a laundry, Thomas owed his freedom not to his wealthy father but to his mother, who labored at the washtub to earn the money to buy him. Literate and well traveled, Thomas had had his own barbershop in Nashville. By 1857, when he moved to St. Louis, he had already toured the free states as a valet to a well-heeled white Southerner, and had gone filibustering in Nicaragua with the infamous William Walker. In St. Louis, Thomas got himself hired by Henry Clamorgan and Samuel Mordecai while he adjusted to his new setting. It was at Clamorgans that Thomas received a "compliment" from "a gentleman occupying the front rank of the statesmen of the West." The unidentified gentleman (possibly Thomas Hart Benton or Stephen Douglas) remarked that "all that prevented [Thomas] from becoming one of the greatest men of the age was his color." Thomas doubtless responded to the compliment in the way that was expected of him, and anyway he had other matters to attend to. He had met Antoinette Rutgers and won her heart. Unfortunately, he hadn't reckoned on her mother, who had other ideas about the man she wanted for a son-in-law. Thomas was busy, no doubt with the benefit of Henry Clamorgan's advice, finding ways to soften Pelagie and induce her to consent to her daughter's marriage. Henry and Samuel knew Thomas had capital and excellent business sense. A close bond developed among the three men, and Thomas eventually joined their partnership.[27]

There were other demands on Henry's time and energy besides overseeing the barbershop and baths. Just as he had when Louis was alive, he bought and sold real estate at a frantic pace. In that he was hardly unusual. Land speculation was how many St. Louisans imagined they would become rich. With the Clamorgans, of course, the belief that it would bring them great wealth was not just a fond hope but an obsession.

First and foremost, his various transactions enmeshed Henry firmly in the free community of color. Many of his dealings were with his relatives. He and Harriet often bought real estate from Mary and Samuel Mordecai and sold property to them.[28] That tight-knit network expanded in the early 1850s, when Harriet and Mary's brother James W. Thompson moved to St. Louis. Once he found work as a riverboat steward and barber, probably with help from his in-laws, he sent back to Pennsylvania for his fiancée, Caroline Vashon, and the two were married in November 1853.[29] Before long, James and Caroline were trading real estate with the Clamorgans and the Mordecais.

Some of the deals among the members of this intermarried clan were carefully choreographed to circumvent the law. This was the case, for example, with a valuable tract on Fifteenth and Spruce. The Mordecais bought it from Louis Charleville and then sold it to James Thompson. He sold it back to Mary Mordecai, but he did so through Henry Clamorgan. Henry would hold the property as Mary's trustee. If Samuel experienced any financial setbacks, his creditors could not touch the property, since it was technically not his. Henry and his relatives knew how the law stood with regard to the rights of married women. Any property a wife owned was considered her husband's, and liable for his debts, unless the couple took care to provide otherwise. Setting up a trust was a neat way of ensuring a family would not be left without any resources.[30]

Henry and his in-laws did many deals with Pelagie and Antoinette Rutgers. Louis Clamorgan had helped Louis Rutgers handle his affairs until the older man's death in 1847. Thanks to Arend Rutgers's provisions for his son's family, Pelagie was a very rich widow, with land worth hundreds of thousands of dollars, and Antoinette, her only surviving child, was set to inherit everything. Small wonder that Pelagie spent her time chasing away fortune-hunting suitors! Pelagie trusted the Clamorgan brothers, who were, in a roundabout way, "family," since her first husband had been their uncle St. Eutrope Clamorgan. Louis had helped her and her daughter, and when Louis died, Pelagie turned to Henry, and by extension his in-laws. Henry wrapped up deals for Pelagie and Antoinette that his brother had begun. He witnessed deeds for them. He held property in trust for them. Throughout the 1850s, money and real estate changed hands among the Rutgers women and Henry and his kin with dizzying frequency, and some of those deals also involved the Charlevilles and the Labadies.[31]

Plenty of Henry's friends benefited from his financial know-how. For instance, a complex series of dealings involving one piece of land enabled him to make some money for himself and help Sarah Haslett, the young wife of riverman Monroe Haslett, in much the same way he had helped his sister-in-law.[32] The Clamorgans and the Hasletts were well acquainted. Henry had known Monroe's first wife, and the ties with Sarah would endure after Monroe's death, with the Haslett daughters marrying into other free families of color in the Clamorgans' circle.

Favors were conferred and also returned. Louis Charleville, Louise Labadie Charleville, and their son, Louis Jr., helped Henry and Harriet make a deal similar to those Henry had brokered for the Mordecais and the Hasletts. Real estate was purchased from Louis Sr. and his family and vested in Harriet separate from her husband. The fact that the Clamorgans did not have the funds to buy the property outright from the Charlevilles did not matter: the latter were happy to accept the Clamorgans' promissory notes.[33] Henry had known Louis and Louise since childhood. They shared the same status, racially and economically, and they were prepared to stand by one another.

When it came to business contacts, Henry's circle was an extensive one, although it is probably more accurate to say that he moved in many circles. His most frequent contacts were with members of his family. Then came his old friends, people such as the Rutgers, the Hasletts, the Charlevilles, and the Labadies. Beyond them were the likes of Albert White and Robert J. Wilkinson, who rented from him or supplied him with goods and services.[34] Then there was the wider free community of color. Letitia Sebastian, for example, was not a close friend, nor was she a relative, but her late husband, riverman Charles Sebastian, had left her a considerable amount of money, and she was alive to the need to put that money to work. When Henry Clamorgan went looking for some additional capital, Letitia saw the advantage of making him a loan at interest and accepting his land as collateral.[35]

Beyond the free community of color, Henry and his partners did deals with dozens of white people. Especially when they were getting their business back on a firm footing after Cyprian's defection, Henry and Samuel needed loans, and they found plenty of white investors willing to lend to them.[36] Back when Louis was alive, he and Henry had collaborated with Edwin R. Mason and Isaac W. Taylor in the matter of Jacques Clamorgan's lands. Taylor and Mason knew Henry, and during the 1850s they did further business with him. Some of the deals Henry entered into with white St. Louisans concerned simply the buying and selling of land, but others enabled him to get short-term credit for his business so he could pay the rent and buy the supplies he needed.[37]

Race mattered in St. Louis, as it did in every community, but at least for some individuals the chance to make a profit mattered more.

Henry, like the rest of the family, had never given up hope of getting the Clamorgan land claims confirmed. It vexed him greatly that other people were pursuing at least a few of those claims.

Funding a bid to have the huge New Madrid claim validated was the same consortium that had organized itself back in the mid-1830s as the Clamorgan Land Association. Daniel Webster had been involved in the association from the start, and in 1851, on behalf of himself and his partners, the aging jurist did battle in the nation's highest court with no less an entity than the federal government. He contended that the tract should not have been seized and opened for settlement because it was not public land. It had belonged to Jacques Clamorgan, who had sold it to Pierre Chouteau, and it was through Chouteau that the association derived its title to it.[38] Never presented to the justices, though, were *all* the links in the chain of possession. Jacques might have sold some claims to Chouteau, but not the New Madrid one. That claim he conveyed to Jean-Eli Tholozan in trust for his two youngest sons. On Maximin's death it passed to Cyprian Martial, and he bequeathed it to his half-sister, who left it to her children. Henry Clamorgan considered that he, his half-brother, and his nephews were the rightful owners of the land, and not some bunch of white businessmen who had manufactured a title and assembled a team of high-priced lawyers. Not that Webster and his colleagues achieved much with their arguments anyway, for the Supreme Court ruled against them.[39] Proving that the New Madrid claim belonged to Jacques Clamorgan's lineal descendants would take a great deal of money and influence, and the Clamorgan heirs did not have enough of either to induce the court to reconsider its ruling—but Henry did see an opportunity to get another claim upheld.

On February 16, 1852, Henry and Cyprian sank their differences long enough to conclude a deal with speculator Isaac T. Greene. Greene offered to bear the expense of the battle to have Jacques's Cedar Island claim confirmed. Because it lay outside the boundaries of Missouri, the land commissioners had rejected it back in 1834, but Greene was confident he could get that ruling reversed. He pledged that if he prevailed he would pay Henry and Cyprian $6,000—the equivalent of $150,000 today—for the claim he and they believed they had inherited from their grandfather. The brothers would get nothing now, but there was the enticing prospect of money in the near future. Of course, having the claim confirmed did not mean Greene would ever get an inch of the land, but that was his lookout. What Henry and Cyprian were selling was intangible—a ruling that Congress might or might not make in favor of the long-dead Regis Loisel, and by extension Jacques Clamorgan, who had supposedly purchased from Loisel's estate the original grant to Loisel from the king of Spain. Intangible or not, the claim was worth cold, hard cash. Greene pledged that he would pay them for their interest in the claim, and Henry and Cyprian took him at his word.[40]

Greene may not have known what he was getting into. Progress in Washington to secure confirmation was painfully slow, and of course the claim itself was anything but straightforward. After failing in his attempts to have it confirmed by the land commissioners, Jacques Clamorgan had conveyed it to Jean-Eli Tholozan, just as he had done the New Madrid claim, in trust for Cyprian Martial and Maximin. In 1816, however, Tholozan sold the claim to Louis Labeaume, even though he had no legal right to do so, since he really did not own it. Tholozan's ownership was contingent on his getting the claim confirmed, and if he managed to do so he was to split everything he got with Cyprian Martial and Maximin. Of course, Labeaume did not know that when he paid Tholozan for the claim. Now, in addition to Greene and the Clamorgans, Labeaume's heirs wanted the claim confirmed to them. Loisel's heirs also chimed in, challenging the legality of the sale to Clamorgan. Sorting out all of the competing claims and determining whether the Loisel grant had been a legitimate one in the first place could take years. It was quite possible that none of the people who thought they had a claim would win, and even if they did, they might never get possession of the land, since the U.S. government had long since declared the land public domain. Greene wasted no time getting to work, but as the months dragged on he grew frustrated. He needed someone to move things along on Capitol Hill. In the summer of 1856, without consulting the Clamorgans, he approached attorney James E. Mumford. According to Mumford, Greene represented himself as the sole owner of the Spanish concession to Loisel. Greene contracted with Mumford to get the claim confirmed, but he did not offer him money for his services. Instead, Greene offered Mumford a quarter of whatever he was able to recover. Mumford subsequently insisted that he had expended a great deal of time and effort tracking down documents, preparing arguments, and traveling to Washington to appear before the Committee on Private Land Claims. He maintained that he was the person responsible for securing confirmation . . . and that's when the trouble began.[41]

Who exactly had done what, and what did Congress finally decide? Those two questions were at the heart of the suits and countersuits Henry Clamorgan found himself embroiled in. On May 24, 1858, Congress passed An Act for the Relief of Regis Loisel or His Legal Representatives.[42] A few days later, on June 2, in a bid to wrap up a whole series of claims, including the Cedar Island one, lawmakers approved An Act to Provide for the Location of Certain Confirmed Private Land Claims in the State of Missouri. Basically, all the claimants covered by the second act were to get their lands, but if the tract in question was unavailable because the government had already opened it for settlement, the claimants were entitled to an equivalent piece of public land in one of the western territories.[43] In the case of the Cedar Island claim, confirmation was granted to the "legal representatives" of Regis Loisel, the original holder of the concession from the Spanish Crown. It was no business of Congress to determine who those individuals were. That was the task of officials in the area where the claim had originated. The surveyor-general of Missouri and Illinois established fairly quickly that Loisel's legal representatives were entitled to 38,411 acres of public land in the Kansas territory.[44] What he found it less easy to establish was who precisely those people were.

That was good enough for Henry Clamorgan. He and Cyprian had contracted with Greene, and Greene had agreed to pay them six thousand dollars upon confirmation of the claim. The claim had been confirmed, and it was time for Greene to pay up. Henry pressed him on the matter. Greene refused to hand over a cent. Henry knew what his next step should be. In February 1859, when Greene had had ample time to fulfill his contractual obligation, Henry commenced suit against him in the St. Louis Circuit Court. He did so in his own name, in Cyprian's, and in the names of his nephews. Henry had already undertaken to turn over to Julia her sons' share of whatever he recovered: either the land itself or the money. At his urging, and with the help of a white friend, she petitioned the Probate Court to be named the legal guardian of Léon and Julius so she could administer any funds that came to them.[45] Henry was careful to leave no loose ends that could in any way compromise the family's case against Greene.

Henry and his attorneys asked the court to order Greene to hand over the six thousand dollars and the interest that had accrued on it since May 24, 1858, when Congress had approved the Cedar Island claim. Greene's response was that Henry and Cyprian had tried to defraud him. They had represented themselves as Jacques Clamorgan's grandchildren and the rightful owners of the claim. They had hidden the fact that there were other heirs, namely their deceased brother's children. They had also lied when they asserted that Jacques had died possessed of the claim. Back in 1809 he had bargained it away to Pierre Chouteau. Yes, a bill did eventually pass Congress, but in light of Jacques's alienation of the claim, Greene was not at all sure he himself could benefit.[46]

Over Greene's objections Henry's lawyers had several key items read into evidence. The court had before it a sworn statement from Congressman Francis P. Blair. He recounted how Greene, Mumford, and rival claimant Theophile Papin (ironically a nephew of Theodore Papin, the first of Apoline Clamorgan's lovers) had enlisted his aid in late 1857 or early 1858 to secure the passage of an act of confirmation. All three had declared they had some kind of interest in the claim. Obviously Greene had had no qualms about whether he would benefit if an act were passed. He believed he would, and now he was simply casting around for excuses to withhold from the Clamorgans what he legitimately owed them.

The court heard next from John Loughborough, surveyor-general of Illinois and Missouri. He explained that on the instructions of the commissioner of the General Land Office, he had put notices in the news-papers in September 1858 about the Cedar Island claim and several individuals had laid claim to the certificate of relocation. Some did so under Regis Loisel and some under Jacques Clamorgan. Among the claimants was Greene, who claimed it under his agreement with the Clamorgan heirs. Loughborough had not yet decided who was entitled to the certificate, but his testimony was clear enough. The claim had been confirmed and Greene considered himself justified in asking that the certificate be handed over to him. If he felt confident enough to make that request, he was conceding that the terms of his agreement with Henry and Cyprian had been fulfilled.[47] Whether he intended to sell the certificate or take possession of the land was immaterial. The issue before the court was whether or not Greene was obliged to make good on his deal with the Clamorgans—and it looked very much as though he was. When he was called to testify, James E. Mumford took credit for getting the claim confirmed. He had drafted the bill (so he said) that Congress finally passed. By now, though, Mumford had his own quarrel with Greene, and he shot holes in Greene's case against the Clamorgans. No, there had been no attempt to conceal the exis-tence of a third Clamorgan brother, or that brother's children. He (Mumford) had been well aware that Henry and Cyprian had an older brother, and so had Greene.

When Isaac Greene did his best to confuse the court about how many heirs there were, even going as far as to invent a sister who was still alive, attorney Thomas T. Gantt demolished Greene's argument. He testified that he had known the three Clamorgan brothers since 1840, and they had no sister living then. Moreover, no attempt had been made to hide from Greene the existence of Louis's two sons. (And although it was never brought up in the trial, Greene knew there was a third Cla-morgan brother. In 1846 he had paid Louis five thousand dollars in a real estate deal.)[48] Gantt explained that he had drafted the agreement be-tween Greene and the Clamorgans at Greene's request and had made absolutely certain that Greene understood there were two brothers liv-ing and a third who had died, leaving children. Gantt had spelled out that the six thousand dollars was to be split three ways—a third for Henry, a third for Cyprian, and a third for Louis's sons.[49]

Given the weight of the evidence, the jury found for the plaintiffs. Greene was ordered to pay the debt, an additional $120 in damages, and the Clamorgans' legal bills. He promptly moved for a new trial. This was overruled, and he appealed to the Missouri Supreme Court.[50] But Greene was not the only individual intent on withholding from Henry Clamorgan and his family what they considered rightfully theirs. Someone else was hoping to enrich himself at their expense. Mumford considered that Greene had cheated him, and he wanted someone—Greene, the Clamorgans, Theophile Papin, or anyone else who thought they had a claim to the Cedar Island tract—to compensate him for his services.

On March 12, 1859, the Missouri General Assembly approved An Act Authorizing the Sale of Certificates of Relocation by Executors, Administrators, and Guardians. This was Mumford's handiwork. The research he had done for Greene had acquainted him with the peculiar history of the Clamorgan family, and he had seen an opportunity to appropriate the land certificate. According to Missouri law, Cyprian Martial and Maximin had died without heirs. Apoline was only their half-sister, and state law did not recognize that relationship as conferring inheritance rights. Moreover, all three were illegitimate. It did not matter that Jacques had acknowledged them as his natural children, nor did it matter that Cyprian Martial had written a will naming Apoline and her children as his heirs. They were not his heirs in the eyes of the law. If there were no heirs under the law, and yet there was property to be administered, that property would pass to the state, but first someone would have to be named to administer it, and that administrator would have a great deal of latitude when it came to selling off the assets of the estate.[51]

Mumford approached the St. Louis Probate Court and explained the situation. The court might hear from people who *said* they were heirs, but the law disqualified them because of the chain of descent through a half-sibling. For good measure Mumford made sure the court knew that all four of Jacques Clamorgan's children had been born to "Negro mothers." Since Apoline, the only one of the four who had left children, was a person of color, so were her offspring. That certainly cast doubt, as Mumford meant it should, on their standing. And anyway, so he advised the court, they had shown no inclination to act. Louis was dead, and his sons were minors. Cyprian, so Mumford had been told, lived in New Orleans and was out of the picture. According to Mumford, Henry Clamorgan, the only family member who was of age and lived locally, was not interested. (Obviously the court had no way of knowing that was an outright lie. Henry was *very* much interested in his family's land claims.) Mumford went on to explain that some small amount of property had come the way of the two estates and needed to be administered. The Probate Court did exactly as he had hoped, naming him the administrator of both estates.[52]

Less than a month later, Mumford submitted his preliminary inventory—and lo and behold, he learned that Maximin and Cyprian Martial were entitled to a valuable relocation certificate! Mumford had done his homework. Jacques Clamorgan's will left all of his children (yet again Mumford reminded the court that they were people of color and not lawful heirs anyway) shares of his land, but some years prior to his death Jacques had set portions of that land aside for his two youngest children. On Maximin's death, his share had passed to his brother. Although Cyprian Martial had left a will specifying that his half-sister's children were to inherit his real estate "lying & being in the State of Missouri," the Cedar Island claim was patently not in Missouri. It was a nice piece of legal maneuvering. Mumford insisted the relocation certificate belonged to no one in particular, and he, as administrator, was duty bound to take charge of it.[53]

Henry Clamorgan got wind of what was going on. Mumford advertised in the *Missouri Republican* that he would auction off the certificate of relocation on December 13, 1859. (He did not have it in his possession, but he did not mean to let a technicality like that stand in his way.) On December 1, Henry and Julia, in her role as her sons' guardian, served notice on Mumford that they intended to challenge him in court, have his appointment as administrator revoked, and halt the sale.

The Clamorgans' attorneys gave a brief history of the claim. After the passage of the act of Congress on June 2, 1858, confirming, among other claims, that of Regis Loisel and his legal representatives, the commissioner of the General Land Office had directed the surveyor-general of Missouri and Illinois to find out who those legal representatives were. He did so, reported back to Washington, and relocation certificate number 232 was issued, with an endorsement on the back listing the representatives. The Clamorgans presented a copy of the certificate to support their claims. In fact, neither Cyprian Martial nor Maximin was named on the certificate, but Henry, Cyprian, and Louis's sons did derive claims, as, apparently, did Theophile Papin and his brother Sylvester Vilray Papin. The Papins were descended from one of Regis Loisel's daughters, both of whom had married into the Papin clan. The various endorsees opted to take land in the Kansas territory. Once the land was technically "located," as it had been, in legal terms the certificate had no further existence. In essence, there was no longer any certificate for Mumford to sell. As for Mumford's motives, he "has made repeated . . . efforts to obtain from said endorsees . . . a conveyance of a large part of said certificate . . . by way of quieting his claim." Since he had failed to get anything from the Clamorgans or the Papins, he was advertising the sale in order to cast doubt on their title. If he had done any work to get the claim validated—and they questioned whether he had—it was certainly not at *their* request. And as for his contention that someone had to administer the estates of Cyprian Martial and Maximin because there were debts owed by the two, how could they have incurred debts when they had been dead many years? It was a specious argument, and he should be removed as administrator forthwith.[54]

Mumford mounted a vigorous counterattack. Once more he brought up the issue of race. Henry Clamorgan was "a mulatto & incompetent in law to testify or make affidavit against" him. The allegations about his (Mumford's) motives were assumptions only. The petition to have him removed as administrator was not the work of the Clamorgans but of "other persons" hoping to advance their own interests and secure the relocation certificate for themselves. He strenuously denied attempts to coerce the various endorsees into paying him, either in land or in money. He himself had been wronged. He had expended an enormous amount of effort in rendering valuable what had previously been worthless. He had done the work of getting the claim confirmed, only to learn that Greene intended to cheat him out of his fee: the one-quarter share he had been promised. In fact, Greene had turned over to some or all of the people whose names were endorsed on the certificate a large part of his "assumed right." More important, so Mumford asserted, during his investigation he had come to doubt whether any persons except Cyprian Martial and Maximin were Regis Loisel's legal representatives. That was why he had asked to be appointed to administer their estates. He was acting in the name of justice!

In the short term, Henry and his legal team were unable to stop the sale. Mumford auctioned off something purporting to be the certificate. They also failed in their attempt to get the Probate Court to remove him as administrator. It was a legal nightmare, rendered even worse by the intervention of the Papins.[55] They were offshoots of the immensely powerful Chouteau clan. Not only did they press their claim as Loisel's lineal descendants, but they were prepared to argue that Jacques Clamorgan, shady businessman that he had been, had never actually paid Loisel's estate for the concession from the king of Spain. Apparently Greene caved in when the Papins threatened him and he made over to them whatever rights he had. The Clamorgans knew when they were beaten. They seethed, but they understood it was better not to contest the matter, given the power of their opponents.[56] It did not do to provoke the likes of the Papins. Isaac Greene, though, was a far less formidable adversary. Henry and the rest of the Clamorgans were determined to have their six thousand dollars from him, with interest. And they had no intention of letting Mumford outwit them either. However, for Henry Clamorgan there were issues other than land, money, and titles that demanded his attention during the course of what were a tumultuous few years for him and his family.

Within months of his elder brother's death, and in the midst of his wrangling with Cyprian over the family business, Henry had to bear the severest of personal misfortunes. So far he and Harriet had been spared the losses that had befallen Louis and Julia. That happy situation was not to last. As 1851 drew to a close, so did the life of their eldest daughter, five-year-old Fanny Louise. They buried her on New Year's Day. The day after the funeral, two-year-old Kate succumbed to the same ailment that had killed her sister, "disease of the nerves."[57]

A measure of consolation came with the birth of a son barely a

month after the funerals.[58] (Harriet and Henry gave him the first name
Louis, after Henry's recently deceased half-brother. Louis had a middle
name, and as an adult he generally went by Louis P. Clamorgan, but
the available records reveal nothing about what his middle name was.)
Although the newborn child thrived, the family was not done grieving.
On October 25, 1854, eleven-year-old Henry Jacques died of "inflammation of the brain," probably meningitis. Within a month of his death,
Henry and Harriet lost another child, three-day-old Maria.[59] Even
worse was to follow. Worn down by grief, Harriet began to sicken, and
on May 13, 1855, she died. She was just thirty-two years old. Henry
buried her beside their children at Rock Spring. Several years later,
when he and the Mordecais bought a lot in the new Catholic cemetery,
Calvary, he had them all reinterred there and a monument erected.[60]

   With Harriet gone, and one lone child left to his care, Henry needed
his relatives as he had never needed them before. Mary and Samuel
Mordecai did whatever they could for him. The two families had shared
a home for several years, and Mary and Harriet had helped raise each
other's children. Now Henry's in-laws took charge of little Louis for
him while he tried to adjust to widowerhood. For a while Henry had
other kinfolk he could turn to. James and Caroline Thompson lived
nearby and may well have come to his assistance, even if it was only to
offer what solace they could as he mourned for Harriet and the children.[61] Yet another bond was broken, though, when James contracted
tuberculosis. Before the decade was out, Caroline found herself in
much the same role as Henry: a widowed parent with (in her case) two
children to bring up alone.[62]

   On March 18, 1859, almost four years after Harriet's death, Henry
married again. His new wife, nineteen-year-old Amanda Woodside, was
half his age. Although she had been raised in St. Louis, she was originally from Illinois.[63] She sometimes used Vandine as her last name,
but that was actually the name of her stepfather. Her father's identity
is a mystery. Given the fact that she and her sisters, Adeline and Jane,
could "pass" with ease, the elusive Mr. Woodside was almost certainly
white. Amanda's mother, Lucinda, who hailed from Virginia, was invariably identified as a woman of color. Lucinda eventually married George
Henry Vandine, an African American who made his living on the river.

Henry Clamorgan and George Vandine moved in the same circles, so it was hardly surprising that Henry should have been introduced to George's stepdaughter.[64]

By 1860, when the federal census was taken, Henry and Amanda had an infant daughter, Clara. They shared their home with Lucinda, now a widow, and her two children by George Vandine, Sophia and Charles Henry. All were classified as mulattoes by the census taker. Henry was doing well financially: combined, his real estate and personal property was worth thirteen thousand dollars. Although the census taker had no way of knowing it, Henry had kinfolk living close by. He owned the empty house adjoining the one he and his family occupied, but next door to that was the home of the barber Washington Smith. With the Smiths lived Henry's sister-in-law Caroline Vashon Thompson and her children. Like Henry, Caroline would marry again and produce a second family with her new spouse, making even more intricate the web of kinship that connected the members of St. Louis's colored aristocracy.[65]

One step at a time, Henry was rebuilding his life. After losing almost his entire family, he had found happiness with his new wife and their baby daughter. His priorities in the years ahead would once more center on his family. Amanda was so much younger than he, and he wanted to see her, Clara, and the other children they would surely have well provided for if he was not around. He had no intention of forgetting about the Clamorgan land claims. Greene and Mumford, villains that they were, must be made to pay up. And so must everyone who had taken Clamorgan land, from individual speculators and farmers on up to the federal government. He and his family would have what was rightfully theirs.

After the lean years following Cyprian's departure, Clamorgans, the mainstay of the family, was flourishing. For the time being, there was only one Clamorgan in charge of the business, but in the years to come there would be other Clamorgans to keep it going. Perhaps young Louis, being brought up by his aunt and uncle, would take it over, or maybe Clamorgan sons yet unborn would join Henry in supervising a small army of barbers and bath attendants. Henry had no shortage of distinguished customers. Senators, generals, and visiting dignitaries all knew that Clamorgans was the only place where a gentleman could be properly taken care of. And then, in the fall of 1860, Clamorgans received the supreme accolade. A young Englishman who styled himself Baron Renfrew dropped by for a bath. He was barely out of his teens, but he had several older gentlemen with him who treated him with marked deference. Henry rushed forward to wait upon his client. He would not dream of handing him over to an underling. Henry followed the news and knew what virtually everyone else in St. Louis knew: "Baron Renfrew" was none other than Edward, Prince of Wales, heir to the British throne. He was touring the United States incognito, but the secret of his identity had long since leaked out. Although the prince was staying at St. Louis's premier hotel, the Planters' House, he was appalled at the bathing facilities there, which he found to be positively "primeval." What could he do? There was only one bathing establishment in St. Louis for those of truly refined tastes, he was told.[66] When it became known that such an exalted personage had judged Clamorgans worthy of his patronage, Henry gained for his establishment the kind of publicity no amount of money could buy. If Clamorgans was highly regarded before, the royal seal of approval meant it had no rivals now.

7

An Independent Man

FATE, or the vagaries of genetics, had dealt the youngest of Apoline Clamorgan's sons a trump card. To all but the keenest of white observers, Cyprian looked to be of unmixed European ancestry. Henry was often taken for white, but he was generally known to be a man of color. The same had been true of Louis. Cyprian, though, could "pass" with ease, and that gave him a degree of freedom many of his kinfolk never had. Once beyond the confines of St. Louis, where people might take note of the Clamorgan name and make certain associations, Cyprian could reinvent himself as a white man and be reasonably confident that no one would question him about his antecedents. And even in St. Louis . . . well, Cyprian was a gambler: he would trust to his luck, and hope it never ran out on him.

To appreciate why Cyprian Clamorgan took the chances he did, and why he learned early on to live by his wits, one needs to understand the chaotic upbringing he had. He never knew his birth mother. His father was a hazy presence who soon faded from his life. Once he was removed from his wet nurse, he was placed in the Chenie household, and there he stayed until he turned five. Free people of color they might have been, but Philip Chenie and his wife hardly ranked as

CYPRIAN CLAMORGAN'S FAMILY

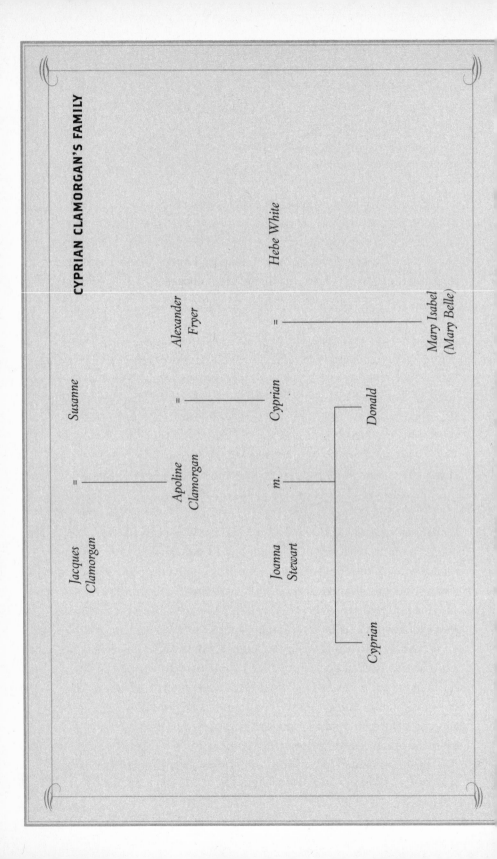

members of the city's colored aristocracy. They were poor, illiterate, and undoubtedly glad of the money they earned for Cyprian's keep, but they provided the only stability he was to experience for many years. What happened to him after that arrangement ended is anyone's guess. Charles Collins, who took over from Cyprian's father as his legal guardian, did not spend the time or money on his care and education that he did on Louis's and Henry's. The boy was passed from one home to another, boarded with whoever could be induced to take him in and feed him for the least amount of money.[1] The reason for that neglect was simple. Compared with Louis and Henry, Cyprian was a pauper. He had inherited nothing from his uncle and namesake, Cyprian Martial, and very little from his mother, unless and until the family's elusive land claims could be confirmed.

When Cyprian was ten or eleven, Louis offered him a home. Ten years Cyprian's senior, and virtually a stranger to the boy, he was still willing to shoulder what he regarded as his family responsibility. Charles Collins was delighted to be rid of his young ward, whom he obviously regarded as a burden at this point. When Collins submitted his accounts to the Probate Court in December 1841, he reported that Louis had charge of Cyprian "and pays all his expenses." Collins also noted that Cyprian had no estate that needed looking after and asked to be relieved of his responsibilities.

Cyprian did not, however, stay with Louis and Julia and grow up with their children. In the summer of 1843 the boy was sent off to Philadelphia and then to New York City. Why remains a mystery. He was not employed by anyone. His guardian, apparently still the reluctant Charles Collins, footed the bill for his travel expenses, his board, lodging, and clothing.[2] Had Cyprian's long-absent father, living perhaps in New York with a new family, finally expressed a wish to see his son? Possibly. One explanation that does not fit the facts, though, is that Cyprian was sent north for an education. To his intense annoyance, his schooling went neglected. His brothers could read, write, and keep accounts while he could not even sign his name. To an ambitious and intellectually gifted youth, this was galling indeed. A wider world was closed to him, and he bitterly resented it.

Toward the end of 1846, Charles Collins suddenly interested himself once more in Cyprian's affairs. He petitioned the Probate Court to authorize him to take charge of the boy's assets. The court complied and ordered Collins bound in the amount of twelve thousand dollars. This amount indicates the very mercenary reason for Collins's change of heart. A court-appointed guardian or administrator was expected to offer as security for faithful performance of his duties double the value of the estate in his charge. Cyprian had no money back in 1841, and Collins was glad to be rid of him. However, the various real estate sales his half-brothers had negotiated since then meant the youngster now had money. The proceeds from the sale of Clamorgan land and titles had been split three ways. Louis and Henry took their shares at once. The much younger Cyprian would not get his until he came of age, and in the meantime, Collins was eager to look after it for him.

Cyprian was furious. With Louis's help as his "next friend," since Cyprian was a minor and illiterate, he lost no time petitioning the Probate Court. He explained that he had essentially had no guardian for the past few years, and he certainly did not want Collins to act for him now. The wealthy and influential businessman Henry P. Chouteau, son of St. Louis's "Founding Father" Auguste Chouteau, had agreed to watch over Cyprian's affairs, and Cyprian insisted on exercising his right, now that he was old enough to do so, to have Collins removed and Chouteau appointed in his place.[3]

Chouteau proved every bit as calculating and self-interested as Collins. By the spring of 1849, Cyprian was back before the Probate Court. He claimed that Chouteau had kept him in "entire ignorance . . . of his state and condition." He had discovered that when he attained his majority he stood to inherit at least $10,000. He needed money now, though. Barbering was "the one vocation he is able to follow," but "his employment is not certain and regular." In a good month he earned $25. However, his rent alone—he obviously was not living with Louis any longer—came to ten or twelve dollars. Chouteau should be ordered to hand over to him $150 a year for basic living expenses. The court considered the request a reasonable one, and Chouteau was told to comply.

With that battle won, Cyprian decided to tackle the matter of his long-delayed education. He found a teacher, Joseph B. Hortiz, a self-described "professor of penmanship," and arranged to take lessons, for which he insisted his guardian pay. Cyprian proved an apt pupil, and within a few weeks he was able to put his signature on documents. It was not a particularly neat signature, but it represented a tremendous victory. And it whetted his appetite. Soon he was back before the court asking that Chouteau be made to hand over fifty dollars to cover his expenses while he attended school. (No one questioned the violation of Missouri law: free people of color were not supposed to be educated, but maybe the white men on the Probate Court did not see the light-skinned young man as being anything other than white.) Cyprian's schooling was a great success, in large measure because of his sheer determination. In a matter of months he had learned to read and write.[4] In the years to come he would polish those basic skills, not merely achieving functional literacy but also emerging as a witty and entertaining author.

Tracking Cyprian's movements as he grew to manhood presents certain challenges. Some facts emerge, though. He traveled extensively from the time he was in his mid-teens. His writings indicate that he ventured down the Mississippi to New Orleans, probably as a barber on a riverboat. At age sixteen he referred in one of his petitions to the Probate Court to having been "frequently absent . . . elsewhere," but never having been a resident of anywhere other than St. Louis. Occasionally he returned to the city of his birth. He was in town in April 1848 when Louis and Julia invited him to act as godfather to their son Léon. That same year he made his first appearance in the city directory as a barber at the fashionable American Hotel. Presumably that was where he considered he was so poorly paid.[5] That was the last time for several years he featured in the directory. In the fall of 1850, though, he was back living with Louis and Julia. Louis advised the Probate Court that Cyprian "is now staying with us to see how [he] will Conduct himself." Louis's statement also indicated that Cyprian was working for him and Henry.[6]

In the spring of 1851, Cyprian turned twenty-one, and this enabled him to get his hands on the small amount of money from his mother's estate, as well as other, much larger sums held in trust for him as a result of the various Clamorgan land sales. On May 22, with his legal guardianship of Cyprian now at an end, Henry P. Chouteau handed over to him two thousand dollars and on June 6 the balance: more than sixty-five hundred dollars. Cyprian immediately made a loan to his half-brothers and bought a stake in their firm. His investment in the barbershop and baths was a substantial one, and he expected a good return. However, within days of Louis's death, Cyprian broke with Henry and demanded that the business be liquidated. Financially it would have made much more sense to have carried on as before. If they had pooled their resources and used the stock and fixtures of the business as collateral, Cyprian and Henry could have paid their widowed sister-in-law for Louis's share and continued making money. Clamorgans was doing well. There was no need to sell up. But Cyprian was adamant. He had lived with Louis, and quite possibly his emotional ties to the business ended with Louis's death. Maybe the split with Henry was rooted in long-simmering anger that Henry could have done more for him had he chosen. Those lonely years of being shunted from home to home, untaught and unwanted, may have eroded any fraternal feeling. Whatever the case, Cyprian wanted his money. Eventually, of course, he got it. On April 19, 1852, he acknowledged payment of a promissory note for seven thousand dollars from Henry and his new partners.[7]

Cyprian was in funds again, and the money came none too soon. He had been doing some financial juggling, and it had not been very successful. Toward the end of 1851 he had borrowed a couple of hundred dollars from Robert M. O'Blenis, a partner in an omnibus company. Before the note matured, O'Blenis signed it over to jeweler Joseph L. Papin. When the time came to pay up, Cyprian defaulted. Papin wanted his money, plus interest. On April 8, 1852, he informed the St. Louis Circuit Court that he had good reason to believe Cyprian had "absented himself from his usual place of abode . . . so that the ordinary process of law cannot be served upon him." The case was eventually dismissed. Presumably, once Henry settled with him, Cyprian paid off the debt.[8]

Now that he had his money, Cyprian had great plans. Not content with forcing Henry to dissolve their partnership, he meant to poach his customers. He did so in a typically devious manner. He capitalized on the Clamorgan name and the years of hard work Henry and Louis had put into building up their business. Cyprian recruited fellow barber James F. Nash, formed the firm of Clamorgan and Nash, and rented space at 88 Chestnut Street, the self-same building where Henry and Louis had worked before the move to Fourth and Pine. He also appropriated the name his half-brothers had once used, the Italian Baths.[9] There was little Henry could do except get the word out that his establishment was far superior to Cyprian's.

For all of Cyprian's scheming, and all his self-promotion, his and his partner's operation simply did not have the opulence of Henry's luxurious "bathing saloon." Whereas Henry had marble tubs, the best they could manage were six lead tubs and six copper ones. Henry's premises were lavishly decorated. They had the basics of the barber's trade, some pictures on the wall, an oilcloth on the floor, and a carpet or two. And anyway, the entire contents of the Italian Baths were pledged to plumber Thomas G. Thomas to pay for the work he had done.[10] Cyprian dreamed big, but Henry won in the end. Cyprian's partner, Nash, was left in the lurch as Cyprian devoted less time and energy to what was supposed to be a joint enterprise. The Italian Baths appeared only once in the city directory before it was eclipsed by Clamorgans, and James Nash was back plying his trade as a barber on a riverboat. Happily, he married well, and Cyprian's desertion did not condemn him to penury.[11] It also turned out just as well the partners had vacated 88 Chestnut, since the building proved structurally unsound. It eventually collapsed, the gas pipes ruptured, and there was considerable loss of life among the remaining tenants.[12]

Cyprian Clamorgan's approach to marriage was a somewhat casual one. On November 28, 1850, before Justice of the Peace Frederick Kretschmar, he wed one Joanna E. Stewart.[13] Joanna, like Cyprian, was a Catholic, so why not go to the cathedral and be married by a priest, with friends and family in attendance? One reason was that the couple had already been to the cathedral to have their firstborn baptized. They had told the priest they were man and wife, and hence Cyprian Jr., born on April 6, 1849, was legitimate. This was a lie. And it was a lie that obliged Cyprian and Joanna to ask casual acquaintances, rather than relatives or close friends, to act as the baby's godparents.[14]

If Cyprian kept quiet about his family ties and did not trouble to share too much information with his brothers and his friends, he had his reasons. Not only had the birth of their child occurred months before Cyprian and Joanna wed, but there was also the vexed matter of race. Cyprian was a man of color, albeit one who could "pass." Joanna was white. Louis had chosen a wife from St. Louis's free community of color. Henry had wed a woman from another state, but Harriet Thompson was indisputably a woman of color. Cyprian, though, had crossed the often imperceptible line that, at least in theory, kept "black" men away from "white" women. At some point in his meanderings, perhaps in New Orleans, or perhaps in one of the northern states, he had met Joanna, an Irish immigrant. For several years they lived together as husband and wife, and Cyprian's half-brothers and their families apparently had no idea that Joanna even existed, let alone that she and Cyprian had a child together.

By the time Cyprian and Joanna *did* marry, their first child was a year and a half old and Joanna was pregnant again. Frederick Kretschmar, an officer of the court rather than a priest, was unlikely to be inquisitive. In a rapidly growing city like St. Louis, he was used to having virtual strangers turn up and ask to be married. And in a number of cases the bride was visibly pregnant. As for matters of race, Kretschmar took Cyprian and Joanna for what they claimed to be: white.[15] The couple was married, and their second child, another son, "Don," was born in the summer of 1851.

If Don (presumably Donald) Clamorgan was baptized, it was not at the cathedral, although it was there on September 26, 1852, that his funeral took place. He was just fourteen months old and had succumbed to "inflammation." The officiating priest (not the same man who had baptized Don's elder brother) identified the baby's parents as "Peppin Claymorgan" and "Johanna Steward." The entry in the city's official register of deaths adds one or two more details. When it came to "place of nativity," the official wrote down not where Don had been born but where his parents were from. Joanna was Irish, and Cyprian supposedly from Pennsylvania. That was not the first time, and it would certainly not be the last, that Cyprian would be less than honest about his personal history.[16]

Given the emotional crisis he was facing, a lie or two to an official probably did not greatly trouble Cyprian. By the time he buried his son he was almost certainly a widower. Joanna may even have died giving birth to Don. There is no record of her burial, but there is the next best thing: in February 1852, Cyprian and Henry set aside their differences long enough to conclude the deal with Isaac T. Greene over their grandfather's Cedar Island claim. The law in Missouri, as in many other states, required that a married man involve his wife in any sale of land or property rights. Without her consent—and she was to be questioned by the recorder in a setting where her husband could not overhear her—the deal was invalid. Henry brought Harriet along, and she formally agreed to the transaction. Cyprian appeared alone. Of course, he might have been flouting the law for reasons of his own, but a few years later, Greene and his lawyer were casting around for irregularities that would enable Greene to walk away from the deal. The existence of a wife whose consent had never been sought would have made Greene's case for him. While Joanna may still have been alive in 1852, it seems unlikely. She was never called to consent to the deal with Greene.[17] Nor did she make an appearance when Cyprian closed another deal later that same year, and it was one in which the purchasers were anxious to do everything they could to secure clear title. Samuel Gaty and his partners in the Mississippi Foundry had had their ownership of the parcel of property in Block 25 tied up in court for years, thanks to Louis Clamorgan's dubious dealings with Hardage Lane. Louis's sale of his portion of Block 25 to Lane, his lies to Lane about being legally entitled to sell the land, and his subsequent sale of the same piece of land to someone else, without any attempt to refund Lane's money, had led to a series of courtroom battles and much confusion about who owned what. That confusion only intensified when Henry Clamorgan decided to sell some of *his* land in the same block. Now, with the youngest of the Clamorgan heirs having attained his majority, Gaty and his associates wanted things resolved once and for all. They knew this was Clamorgan land, however convoluted the title, and they were prepared to offer Cyprian a token payment for any interest in the property he might have.[18] Once more, a wife whose consent was not a matter of record was a legal impediment. If Joanna had been alive she would surely have been obliged to show up. Cyprian might have taken a somewhat cavalier approach to his marital status: those who were doing business with him and parting with hard cash could not afford to. Joanna had simply faded out of the picture, and so, for that matter, had Cyprian Jr. With Don's death in the fall of 1852, Cyprian Clamorgan, an orphan almost since birth, bereft of one brother and estranged from the other, was in all likelihood a childless widower.

He was not on his own for very long, however. Hebe White was a relative newcomer to St. Louis and several years older than Cyprian when the two met. Joanna Stewart's life is shrouded in mystery, but Hebe White's is not, and her story contrasts strikingly with Cyprian's for reasons other than race. Hebe was the youngest of six children of Thomas White, an English merchant, and his wife, Catherine Parry. Thomas did a great deal of business in the Low Countries, and when he traveled, Catherine accompanied him, as a consequence of which Hebe and at least two of her siblings were born in what is today Belgium. Wherever they were born, all of the White children were brought up in the Whites' hometown of Liverpool. Thomas and Catherine gave them a sound English education, and this stood Hebe in good stead. After her father's death she took up one of the few occupations open to a genteel young woman with limited financial means: she became a governess.

What eventually brought Hebe to St. Louis were her ties to two of her sisters, Caroline and Emma. Mallet Case Jackson, an enterprising man of business, had courted Caroline back in England. He sailed to America in 1849 and set himself up as a whiskey distiller, a profitable trade in St. Louis, a city teeming with thirsty men. Once he had a home to offer her, he sent for Caroline, who made the journey from Liverpool with Emma. Caroline Kate White and Mallet Case Jackson were married in St. Louis in September 1851, with Emma as one of the witnesses; Hebe arrived somewhat later. Although she was still in England when Caroline and Mallet wed, she may have come over in time to attend Emma's wedding to the Virginia-born carpenter William Silcot. By the spring of 1853, Hebe had not only arrived in St. Louis but also met Cyprian Clamorgan and persuaded herself that he would marry her. The proof of this lies an ocean away, in the records of a church in Liverpool. Hebe's brother, Thomas Jr., and his wife made a habit of giving their children the names of various in-laws. Their son Ashlin received the name "Mallet" as a token of respect for Caroline's husband. And baby Sophia, baptized on April 20, 1853, received the middle name "Clamorgan." Clearly, Thomas believed Cyprian Clamorgan either was or would soon become his brother-in-law. Just what the Whites back in England knew of Hebe's "husband" is anybody's guess.[19]

Cyprian's business ventures are as frustratingly difficult to trace as the facts of his personal life. Something—perhaps brighter financial prospects or the need to escape his money woes in St. Louis—took him to Louisiana soon after he and Hebe met. But perhaps it was not financial concerns that prompted the move. Perhaps Hebe's sisters and their husbands were beginning to question Cyprian's intentions and just possibly his racial identity. St. Louis might have been growing into a crowded metropolis where secrets could be hidden, but those secrets did not always remain hidden. Money, race, sex—any and all of those factors could have made a move to a new home far away from St. Louis attractive.

New Orleans's multiracial and polyglot society offered Hebe and Cyprian a chance to blend in and lose themselves amid the mix of peoples who had made the city their home. And yet it was not the great river port that they chose, but the smaller and far less cosmopolitan community of New Iberia. Cyprian ventured to New Orleans now and again. He knew the city like the back of his hand, and knew there was money to be made there. But New Iberia became his home, insofar as he had one, for the next few years.

New Iberia was not without its advantages. The town was situated on one of the loops of Bayou Teche, the watercourse that had developed over millennia as the great Mississippi Delta had been formed. Bayou Teche (the name meant "snake" in the language of the Chitimacha, the native people of the area) wound its way through the southwestern region of Louisiana, effectively separating that part of the state from the area around New Orleans, nearly a hundred miles to the east. It did not take merchants doing business with western Louisiana and Texas long to figure out that they could save a lot of aggravation by unloading their vessels in New Iberia and transshipping their cargo by land. Navigating twenty-five miles of waterway was tedious and time-consuming, but it was just two miles overland from the point at which the great loop began to where it ended and one could take to the bayou again. Before the railroads came to the region in the 1880s, the meanderings of Bayou Teche made New Iberia a flourishing commercial center.[20]

Out of sight of their relatives back in St. Louis, Hebe and Cyprian continued their affair. Presumably everyone in New Iberia took them for what they pretended to be, a white married couple. Admittedly, Cyprian was absent from the matrimonial home for extended periods of time, leaving Hebe to support herself by teaching, as she had back in England. Was he in New Iberia on March 7, 1855, when their child was born? Possibly, but it was Hebe who decided where the baby should be christened. Cyprian, a Catholic, would have opted for St. Peter's Church. Hebe, though, had been raised a member of the Church of England, and she took the baby to New Iberia's recently established Church of the Epiphany. There, on April 18, Mary Isabel Clamorgan was baptized. The minister gave no hint as to the irregularities of the situation, and he may well not have known that the child's parents were not married. Undoubtedly he was ignorant of the racial dynamics of their relationship.[21] Had the situation of the parents been reversed, had a white man fathered a child with a free woman of color . . . well, that was simply the way of the world in antebellum Louisiana. But a liaison between a man of color and a white woman was a different matter entirely.

In 1858, Cyprian judged the time was right to publish an extraordinary series of vignettes he titled *The Colored Aristocracy of St. Louis*. For a man who had been unable to sign his name a decade earlier, the authorship of this wickedly funny little book was a remarkable achievement. Replete with literary allusions and well-turned phrases, poignant and vicious by turns, *The Colored Aristocracy* was and is a tour de force. If one did not know better, one would assume the author had had the benefit of a thorough education beginning at an early age. The reality, of course, was far different, and this in itself casts a new light on Cyprian's relationship with Hebe. A vital element in that relationship was a mutual love of learning. Hebe had had the advantages Cyprian craved. Without her tutoring and her encouragement, Cyprian could not have ventured into print. This is not to suggest that Hebe wrote all or even part of *The Colored Aristocracy*. She did not have an intimate knowledge of St. Louis and its free community of color. However, she helped Cyprian develop the intellectual background and the mechanics of writing that made it possible for him to put his thoughts down on paper. Whatever Cyprian's indebtedness to Hebe, though, the ideas in *The Colored Aristocracy* were his alone.

Cyprian almost certainly paid out of his own pocket to have his book printed. If he expected to get rich as a writer he was disappointed. *The Colored Aristocracy* was the kind of ephemeral piece that people bought for a few cents, read, and then consigned to the trash. But perhaps Cyprian anticipated making money from his handiwork in other, less direct ways. Decades later, when Cyprian was dead and buried, one St. Louis newspaper reported that "it is a matter of tradition that one family for whom streets and parks are named" was omitted from the book "at the urgent request of members of that generation."[22] Did the members of that family pay Cyprian for his silence about their African antecedents? Cyprian indicated he had potentially unsettling disclosures to make if he chose. He could, so he said, point to people in St. Louis who "are separated from the white race by a line of division so faint that it can be traced only by the keen eye of prejudice." Although he declared it his intention to focus only on those men and women "who have the mark [of blackness] unmistakably fixed upon their brows," he claimed to know of others firmly entrenched in the white community who were "passing." "We, who know the history of all the old families of St. Louis, might readily point to the scions of some of our 'first families,' and trace their genealogy back to the swarthy tribes of Congo or Guinea."[23] Quite possibly he was holding over people's heads the threat that, if not adequately compensated, he could put together a far more revealing work.

Beyond any veiled threat, what Cyprian offered his white readers was a glimpse into a world few of them knew much about. In the midst of the national heart-searching about slavery, the status of free people of color, particularly wealthy and well-connected people, was generally ignored. It was far easier to focus on the bondman or -woman, whatever one's perspective on the burning question of the day, than have to contemplate the existence of people who challenged the neat racial divide that held "white" to be synonymous with "citizen" and "black" with "property." As for Cyprian's African American readers, who could resist seeing what one of their own had to say about them in print?

On the origins of the colored aristocracy, Cyprian waxed lyrical. Back in the 1700s, scores of French and Spanish adventurers had "left their families in peaceful security" at home to venture into the wilds of North America. "But man without woman . . . becomes a . . . morose and discontented being. He longs for the endearments of a wife, and sighs for the prattle of children in the solitude of his forest home." While some of those intrepid explorers "sought wives among the sylvan maids of the forest," others allied themselves with women of African descent, and it was those extra-legal unions that had produced what Cyprian termed "the colored aristocracy."[24] However, some of those individuals he highlighted were relative newcomers to St. Louis who hailed from regions that had never been under French or Spanish rule. The truth was that, for all his flowery language about the offspring of heroic *voyageurs* and their beautiful concubines, Cyprian was not overly precise when it came to identifying aristocratic status. In Philadelphia another man of color writing about the African American "higher classes" had agonized over whom to include and whom to leave out. Joseph Willson had finally settled upon "that portion of colored society whose incomes, from their pursuits or otherwise, (immoralities or criminalities . . . excepted,) enables them to maintain the position of house-holders, and their families in comparative ease and comfort."[25] Cyprian Clamorgan was less worried about precise definitions. One simply *knew* who belonged. To qualify as an aristocrat, at least as he understood the term, one needed wealth, education, or "natural ability." As for "immoralities or criminalities," in *his* opinion it did not do to be too squeamish about such things. But then Joseph Willson was a sociologist at heart, anxious to send a serious message to his readers, black and white. Cyprian Clamorgan? He intended to display his erudition, settle some old scores, make a few dollars, and just perhaps enlighten the public in the process.

The aristocracy Cyprian described was variegated as regards origin, complexion, and ethnicity. Virginians rubbed shoulders with Tennesseans. Scions of old "French" families intermarried with newcomers. Some bore French names and others English names. Some could "pass" anytime they chose, but others were unmistakably of African descent. Not surprisingly, Cyprian was fascinated by the whole question of racial identity. Again and again he drew attention to physical indicators of race among his aristocrats. Barber Allen Gunnell had straight hair, while James Williams was a "yellow man." Richard Merrin "resembles a Moor." Nancy Lyons, the keeper of a genteel boardinghouse, "resembles an Indian, and may possibly have the blood of Pontiac in her veins." The barkeeper Robert Smith was "nearly dark in color," but still "a large, fine-looking man." Antoine Labadie "is nearly white and looks more like a Mexican than anything else."[26] One did not have to be light-skinned to be classed as an aristocrat, but mixed racial ancestry often accounted for an individual's wealth and freedom.

Cyprian admired the talent to make and hold on to money. He recounted how William Johnson had started out in a small way as a barber. By dint of hard work and thrift, he accumulated enough money to enter the real estate market, a fact Cyprian knew because both of his brothers had had dealings with Johnson. At exactly the right time, when property prices were low but when a sagacious investor could see good times coming, Johnson bought a block of land on one of the major thoroughfares in St. Louis. When land values rose to spectacular heights, he sold, and promptly retired on the proceeds. Cyprian could not help but observe to his white readers: "Not so bad a speculation for a colored man!" Although somewhat haughty, and "excessively proud of his family," Johnson merited Cyprian's approval.[27]

Cyprian, a barber himself, was not above poking fun at his profession. Men of color who made their living with razor and soap had, so he observed, certain privileges because of the role reversal that barbering entailed. One way a white man could challenge an adversary to a duel was to seize his opponent's nose and tweak it. The action inflicted both pain and humiliation. Naturally, no white man would deign to challenge a black man. One only dueled with one's equals. And yet, every day in the course of their work, African American barbers "take white men by the nose without giving offense, and without causing an effusion of blood."[28] There was also the racial protocol of not voicing one's opinion to a white man. Cyprian described how the "talking barber" would scrupulously observe the conventions, keeping deathly silent as he soaped a client's chin. Then, with his patron lathered up, he would let loose as he plied his straight-edge razor, showering upon his customer "a perfect Niagara of words." The white man was powerless. "Like a prisoner chained to the stake, he is compelled to listen to the 'sentiments' of his tormenter; for if he dares to open his mouth . . . down his throat rushes a torrent of lather."[29]

Some of Cyprian's portraits were benign enough. Fellow barbers and stewards Allen and Thomas Gunnell he liked. Frank Roberson was a busybody, a "knight of the razor" who came close to talking his clients to death. James Nash, William Johnson's son-in-law, and Cyprian's erstwhile business partner, had a reputation for kindness and generosity. Albert White, who sublet part of Henry Clamorgan's establishment, was a great talker but had a good head for business. He and his "excellent and thrifty wife," Charlotte, had made their fortunes in California. James P. Thomas earned Cyprian's warm approbation as "a man of mark—one who has seen the world . . . genteel in his manners, attentive to business, and . . . a remarkably fine looking man." His filibustering in Central America with the celebrated William Walker made him a man worth watching. Saloon owner Marshall Starks was a devotee of the "code of honor" who had engaged in duels in New Orleans and California (presumably with other men of color) and lived to tell of them. With Starks being a good man of business and a skilled card player, the worst Cyprian could find to say of him was that he was tightfisted. Samuel Mordecai (Cyprian neglected to mention that he was a relative by marriage) was "the most inveterate gambler we have ever met with," but he was "strictly honest, and his word is as good as his bond."[30] And so on.

A few of Cyprian's sketches were downright venomous, though. His aunt by marriage, Pelagie Rutgers, might not have been able to read, but her daughter surely got hold of a copy of Cyprian's book and read aloud to Pelagie what he had written. And what he had said about her was uncharitable in the extreme. He condemned Pelagie as ignorant, ungrateful, and concerned only with outward show. "She makes a fine appearance in society, but exposes her ignorance when she attempts to converse." Her marriage to Louis Rutgers had made her very rich indeed, but she was too cheap to give poor Antoinette a decent education. Worse than denying her daughter a genteel education, Pelagie was busy trying to ruin Antoinette's emotional life by separating her from the man she loved. Although she made a pretense of being a devout Catholic, Pelagie "worships the almighty dollar more than Almighty God." In brief, she was cheap, hypocritical, and selfish: how such a woman could hold up her head in good society Cyprian had no idea.[31]

Rivaling the sketch of Pelagie Rutgers in viciousness was that of the woman Cyprian identified as Pelagie Foreman, although she had been born Marie Lacroix, and by the time *The Colored Aristocracy* went to press she was actually Mary Holland. Whatever he called her, Cyprian supplied more than enough clues to the identity of St. Louis's "yellow Delilah."[32]

Preston G. Wells was another of the villains of Cyprian's book, on a par with Pelagie Foreman, and worse than Madame Rutgers. The Kentuckian had "led the life of a spy and a dog" and had been at one point "an informer against his own race." His wife was "too good for such a fellow."[33] What offense had Wells committed that raised Cyprian's ire? A little digging reveals the answer. Back when Cyprian and his brothers were in business together, Wells had operated the Nonpareil Hair Dressing Saloon and Baths. He had had the temerity to boast of his establishment's fine marble tubs and inexhaustible supply of hot water. He was "competition," and Cyprian held a grudge.[34]

Not quite as harshly treated by Cyprian, but still exposed to censure, was the barber Robert J. Wilkinson. When he started out, most of his customers were rivermen, but as he rose in the world he turned his back on them and was heard to utter disparaging remarks about "that noble class." He was a relative newcomer to St. Louis, having fled Cincinnati after seducing an innocent young woman and incurring the fury of her male relatives. Only a fortunate marriage helped him establish himself among the colored aristocrats of St. Louis.[35]

A sexual double standard permeated *The Colored Aristocracy*. What were serious moral failings in women were peccadilloes in the case of a man. Barber George Carey, for instance, was "excessively fond of the fair sex." The same went for William Johnson, although whether his roving eye ever caused a rift between him and his wife Cyprian did not say. Still, his was "a fault . . . which men censure lightly, and women are apt to forgive." This man had a taste for strong drink. That man drove his buggy too fast and terrorized the neighborhood.[36] The female members of the aristocracy Cyprian divided into belles, shrews, and virtuous matrons. Woe betide the gossiping female aristocrat or the one who was too proud of her family or too showy in her dress, for she could expect to see herself pilloried by Cyprian. And should she ever have been suspected of any sexual impropriety . . . well, Cyprian was not above making sly innuendos.

Despite reveling in the occasional lurid detail, Cyprian insisted that the free colored women of his acquaintance were generally chaste before they wed and faithful to their marriage vows thereafter. That was what their community expected of them, and transgressors were shunned, as were their families. For example, Henry Alexander McGee was excluded from "the first circles" because of "certain reports in regard to the character of his wife before marriage." But Cyprian did not stop once he had praised the strict moral standards of St. Louis's free people of color. He ventured into dangerous territory by asserting that the city's upper-class white women were less chaste, but that wealth and whiteness combined to gloss over conduct that would have caused them to be ostracized had they been "tinctured with the blood of Ham."[37] His assertion that people of color lived by a stricter moral code than whites was bold indeed in 1850s America. If not as shocking as the aspersions Ida B. Wells cast on white women's chastity a generation later—assertions that forced her to flee the South in fear for her life—his statement was risky, to say the least!

Where Cyprian stood as regards the issue of the day, abolition, it is difficult to know. In one breath he assailed Harriet Beecher Stowe as the possessor of a "morbid and diseased brain," but in the next he condemned slavery, acknowledging that the outlawing of the "peculiar institution" would immeasurably improve his own life and the lives of people of color in general. St. Louis's "colored aristocrats," he observed, were using their wealth to promote what he called the Emancipation Party. They were astute enough to know that the end of slavery in Missouri, which they anticipated a Republican victory would bring about, would benefit them as well as the enslaved. Do away with human bondage and no political party will "dare to erect a platform on which the black man cannot stand side by side with his white brother."[38]

Just what, though, did freedom mean for people of color? And to whom was Cyprian appealing when he launched into criticism of those states that claimed to have done away with all the vestiges of slavery? He maintained that people of color from the supposedly free states generally brought with them "more faults and vices" than were possessed by those raised in St. Louis. Was this the chauvinism of one whose own roots ran deep in St. Louis? Whatever the case, he asserted that people from those states "where the laws make all men literally equal" were not as honest, virtuous, or intelligent as "those who have always lived among those whom they have been taught to regard as belonging to a superior race." Why that should be was for "abolition philosophers" to figure out.[39]

After working one's way through *The Colored Aristocracy* one is left wondering how well the peripatetic Cyprian actually knew some of the folks he wrote about. Sometimes he got people's names wrong, and he was not always aware of the intricate network of kinship that linked families within the aristocracy. And if Cyprian had only a passing acquaintance with some of his subjects, how much did he know about their economic standing? In over two-thirds of his thumbnail sketches he mentioned an individual's wealth. If he is to be believed, collectively the women and men he wrote about commanded resources totaling more than $1.5 million (which translates to $36 million today). Pelagie Rutgers may have been worth the $500,000 he said she was, but Cyprian's other estimations of wealth are highly suspect. Samuel Mor-

decai and Pelagie Foreman had far less than the $100,000 apiece he
credited them with. William Johnson might have had an excellent nose
for real estate, but he did not have anything like $150,000. Granted,
census takers were biased when it came to recording the property free
families of color were possessed of, and people routinely lied about
their assets to avoid being taxed heavily. Even so, Cyprian's totals are
vastly inflated. The colored aristocrats were an affluent bunch of people, but collectively they were not as rich as he maintained they were.

Why, then, did Cyprian harp on wealth? He did so because it was
central to his argument. If they were not citizens, as the nation's highest
court had declared in the *Dred Scott* decision, what power could people
of color exert? His answer was the power of the purse. In St. Louis and,
by implication, many other communities, the colored aristocracy had
money. They owned real estate, and in an era when the secret ballot was
unheard of, they could "suggest" to white people who rented from them
which candidate to vote for. They did business with white merchants
and shippers. They purchased goods and services. They had patronage
to give or withhold. They could also help fill the campaign coffers of
politicians who promised to ameliorate their conditions and advance
their rights. "Wealth is power, and there is not a colored man . . . who
would not cheerfully part with his last dollar to effect the elevation of
his race. They know who are their friends, and when the opportunity
arrives they exhibit their gratitude in a manner most acceptable to the
recipient."[40] Disfranchised though they might be, people of color, at
least in Cyprian's reading of the state of things in America, had a political voice, and white people would do well to take note of that.

Wickedly funny and perceptive, *The Colored Aristocracy* remains a
stimulating read. Cyprian had a way with words that could prove quite
devastating. The state of Virginia he hails as "the mother of Presidents
and mullatos [sic]." Roger B. Taney, the chief justice who handed down
the opinion of the U.S. Supreme Court that black men had no rights
that white men were bound to respect, "has in this state kindred of a
darker hue."[41] And so on. Cyprian aimed to shock, and he certainly managed to do so.

As was so often the case with Cyprian, though, he promised more
than he delivered. There was a second class of colored society in St.

Louis, he observed, not equal in taste or breeding to the true aristocracy, but worthy of note nevertheless. Who constituted this second class? When he had more time, Cyprian declared, he would author another book and tell all. The facts contained in *that* book would "startle many of our white friends." Indeed, "The romantic incidents connected with this subject surpass the wildest dreams of fiction."[42] Sadly, that second book remained unwritten.

What was the response to Cyprian's revelations? Some of those in the aristocracy were obviously delighted to see themselves praised for their wit, their industry, their neighborliness. Others who had been dealt with less generously were probably furious. As for white readers, some were amused. Others were just as likely outraged, or deeply apprehensive about the secrets Cyprian had to tell . . . and the secrets he was quite capable of inventing should he feel so inclined. Who was this man of color who was so patently well traveled, who could quote Shakespeare and Byron with ease, and who was conversant with the great political debates of the day? Was it safe to have such a man in their midst? Under the circumstances, it is to be wondered at that Cyprian stayed put in St. Louis after his book appeared in print. A hasty trip downriver to Louisiana would have seemed in order. But Cyprian had other matters to attend to, and he was, after all, the quintessential gambler.

Samuel Mordecai was aghast! He knew he did not owe Cyprian Clamorgan a cent, but Cyprian was flourishing in his face a promissory note with Samuel's signature on it. Yes, the signature was genuine, but Samuel would hardly have forgotten contracting a debt of three thousand dollars payable in six months. Was this some kind of joke? But Cyprian was in deadly earnest. He wanted his money, and he told Mordecai in no uncertain terms that he was prepared to go to court to get it. And that was exactly what Cyprian did. He got a lawyer and, in the St. Louis Circuit Court in February 1858, a matter of a month or two perhaps before *The Colored Aristocracy* went to the printer, filed suit against Mordecai. Cyprian testified under oath that a couple of years earlier Mordecai had borrowed the sum in question and had repeatedly refused payment.

Samuel Mordecai racked his brains. How could Cyprian have gotten hold of his signature? The handwriting of the note was not his, but he recognized his own signature when he saw it. Then he remembered a peculiar little episode that explained everything. Cyprian had tried to perpetrate a swindle worthy of his illustrious grandfather, that arch trickster Jacques Clamorgan, but if Cyprian thought Samuel Mordecai was an easy mark, he could think again.

Through his attorney Mordecai struck back, asking the court to make Cyprian give security for court costs, since he was not a resident of the state, was insolvent, and had no property the court could attach. Mordecai's lawyer also brought to light some facts that cast doubt on the authenticity of the note. Mordecai was a steward on the riverboat the *Morning Star* and his job entailed keeping careful accounts. Sometime previously he had purchased a book in which to record his various expenses and receipts. To identify the book as his he had written his name on the flyleaf, and someone—he and his lawyer suspected they knew who—had gotten their hands on the book and ripped out that page. Cyprian must have come across the book, appropriated the front page, written the bogus agreement above the signature, and tried to extort a huge sum of money from the unwitting steward. In short order, Cyprian found his case against Mordecai dismissed and himself under indictment for forgery.

The evidence against Cyprian was damning. Samuel Mordecai was in no mood to forgive and forget. And Julia Clamorgan gave testimony against her brother-in-law. She explained that Cyprian had loaned a considerable amount of money to the firm her late husband and his brother had operated. Cyprian had long since been paid back, but he had been far from happy about the way in which repayment had been made. He had apparently sold the note Henry Clamorgan and Samuel Mordecai had given him for less than its face value, and Henry and Samuel had paid him the lesser amount. Julia deposed that Cyprian had said in her hearing that he intended to get his revenge on the two of them by "giv[ing] them all the trouble he could." When she first heard about his suit against Mordecai she thought it was a joke. Once the suit got under way, she had asked Cyprian point-blank about the alleged debt. He told her Mordecai had lost three thousand dollars to him in a card game.

She didn't believe that version of events and she repeated the rumor going the rounds about his theft of the flyleaf. "I told him that it was a forged note, and he said no one could prove that unless they stood over his shoulder when he done [*sic*] it." She knew for a fact that Cyprian could not have loaned Mordecai anything like three thousand dollars back in 1856, because he simply didn't have that kind of money.[43] His inheritance was long gone. Julia's testimony against him, coupled with Samuel Mordecai's vehement denial that he owed Cyprian any money, made a conviction likely when the case finally came before the court in May 1860. Cyprian secured continuances, and things dragged on until mid-September. Under the circumstances, a plea bargain might have been in order. Ever the gambler, Cyprian refused to consider anything of the sort. He proclaimed his innocence. Cyprian Clamorgan, a man of color with a highly dubious reputation, was willing to let a dozen white men determine his fate. The nation's highest court had already declared that black men had no rights that white men were bound to respect. No matter. Cyprian would take his chances. The jury retired to deliberate and returned with a verdict of not guilty. Cyprian had prevailed. It turned out that he (and happily the members of the jury) understood the law better than the county attorney. The charge should not have been forgery, since Mordecai's signature was perfectly genuine, but attempted fraud! Cyprian walked from the court a free man.[44]

Once the verdict was in, Cyprian wisely put a lot of distance between himself and the city of his birth. He could not return to New Iberia and resume his relationship with Hebe, though, for she had given up waiting for him to come back to her.[45] In his absence she had found another man who was prepared to make her his wife and help her raise her daughter. Merchant Emile Soulier, a recent immigrant from France, was a far better prospect than the peripatetic and perennially unreliable Cyprian. Hebe and Emile were married on February 28, 1859.[46] When the census taker called the following year, he naturally assumed young Mary Isabel was Emile's child, and in a sense, of course, she was.[47] Emile was the only father she knew.

There was no warm welcome awaiting Cyprian in New Iberia. Hebe did not want him, and his daughter did not know who he was. He kept

going, this time to New Orleans, once more searching out the ano-
nymity that came from big-city life. In the Crescent City he would
reinvent himself and start over.[48]

In the early spring of 1861 the nation was holding its collective breath.
Would the "erring sisters," those states that had made it clear they could
not stomach the election of Abraham Lincoln as president, be allowed
to depart in peace, or would war ensue? Louisiana was among the first
of the states to secede. Like their counterparts in the other member
states of the fledgling Confederacy, her lawmakers turned quickly to
the issue of internal security. The slave population must be prevented
at all costs from rising up and toppling the "peculiar institution." And
who were more to be feared as agents provocateurs than free people of
color, who would, it was supposed, make common cause with friends
and family still enslaved? They must be controlled. Only the most trustworthy could be permitted to retain the tenuous grasp on freedom they
enjoyed. They must find white people of unimpeachable respectability
to vouch for them. So it was that in New Orleans on March 13, 1861,
James A. Humphrey, a twenty-eight-year-old man of color whose occupation was "steamboating," presented himself to justices of the peace
Arthur Saucier and D. F. Mitchell with his brother, Washington Humphrey, and two white gentlemen who were prepared to testify under
oath to James's good character. Saucier and Mitchell had no notion that
one of those "white" gentlemen was not what he seemed. Perjuring
himself for the sake of the Humphrey brothers was none other than
Cyprian Clamorgan.[49] Literate, urbane, well traveled, sophisticated to
a degree the justices could not begin to comprehend, Cyprian, a man of
color who could "pass" with ease wherever and whenever he chose,
posed a far greater threat to the slave system than a humble boatman.
A consummate risk taker, who lived by his wits and defied the conventions of race, Cyprian Clamorgan was truly the "enemy within."

8

Thickets of the Law

I N HIS LATER YEARS, Henry Clamorgan's friend and former partner
James P. Thomas was fond of reminiscing about the people he had
known and the tumultuous times he had lived through. One of his
most vivid recollections was of the tension-filled months leading up to
the Civil War. A deep sense of unease had pervaded St. Louis in the
wake of Abraham Lincoln's election. While Missouri as a whole had
gone for Stephen Douglas and the Democrats, St. Louis was in the
Republican camp. Through the winter of 1860 and into the following
spring, as one state after another left the Union, the people of St. Louis
agonized over what it would mean for the nation and for them. Trade
stagnated and land values plummeted. Class and ethnic tensions bubbled to the surface. "The old and wealthy families . . . were all southern in sentiment," Thomas recalled, while the immigrant population
was polarized, with the Irish solidly Democratic and the Germans
staunchly Republican and pro-Union.[1]

Where did that leave the members of the free community of color?
They were understandably fearful, especially when they learned of a
move in the Missouri legislature to oust them from the state. However,
lawmakers did not have the chance to act before the session ended, and

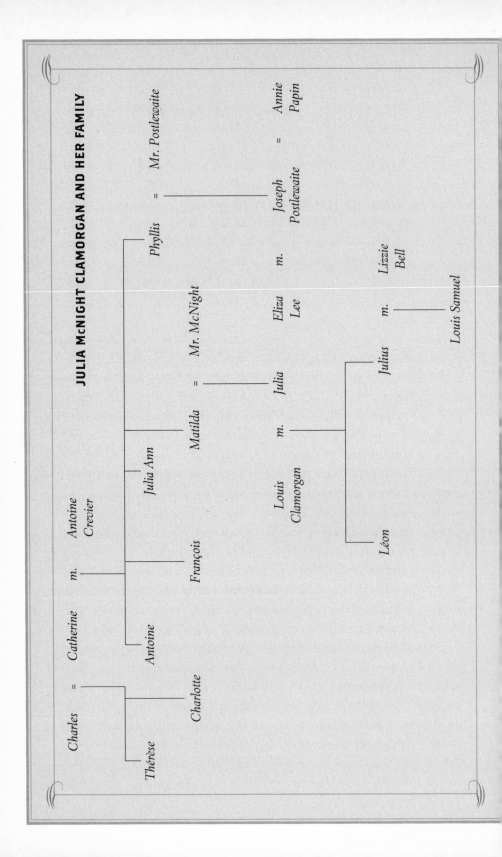

JULIA McNIGHT CLAMORGAN AND HER FAMILY

the St. Louis County Court adopted a relatively benign approach. There was a roundup, and questions were asked about people's identities, occupations, and general standing in the community, but after that everyone was given permission to remain. Thomas observed that the scions of the "old families" were treated pretty well, and "not called upon to prove nothing." Even so, the "old colored Catholics," whose ranks Thomas aspired to join, wanted "to see Federal bayonets brought in."[2]

Their wish was granted. The federal government could not afford to ignore St. Louis. Missouri's governor, Claiborne Jackson, was known to be a friend of secession, and he did his best to induce his state to join the Confederacy. Although the special convention that met in the early weeks of 1861 to weigh the matter handed Jackson a humiliating defeat, there were plenty of Missourians who felt as he did. Confederate sympathizers seized the federal arsenal in one town. The same could not be allowed to happen to the much larger arsenal in St. Louis, and the government in Washington ordered in "Federal bayonets." The presence of troops was the catalyst for bloody street clashes between groups of armed civilians, and innocent bystanders were often caught up in the fray. In the worst outbreak, the Camp Jackson Affair, twenty-eight people lost their lives and dozens more were hurt.[3]

Julia Clamorgan was not comforted by the sight of several regiments of Union soldiers or by the arrival of General John C. Frémont to take charge of the city and impose martial law. She deemed it "a duty devolving upon her for the benefit of [her] children" to leave the scene of so much unrest. Although born and raised in St. Louis, she had a network of kinfolk in Ohio, Illinois, and Canada. Where should she go? Reviewing her options, she chose London, Ontario. She was there by the fall of 1861. Not until the summer of 1864 would she and her sons return home.[4]

Henry and Amanda Clamorgan stayed put, watching with growing trepidation as Missouri came apart at the seams. Politically divided, pulled in different directions economically, and polarized over the issue of slavery, it was truly a border state in 1861, and the uncertainty about its people's commitment to the Union plagued Lincoln's administration for virtually the entire war. That sense of a community rent by bitterly contested loyalties was evident in the state's largest urban center. The very landscape of St. Louis changed. The old Berthold mansion, just a block away from Clamorgans, became a hub of secessionist activity, while Bernard M. Lynch's infamous slave mart was used to imprison disloyal whites. The authorities took over buildings to house the thousands of Union soldiers converging on the city. They closed down all kinds of establishments, from taverns to newspaper offices, believed to be gathering places for the friends of the Confederacy. Freedom of movement was restricted, as was freedom of expression.[5] Of course, such limits on personal liberty had no real impact on the likes of the Clamorgans and James P. Thomas: as people of color, they had never enjoyed very many legal rights anyway.

Henry Clamorgan continued doing what he had always done: he focused on making money. In the tense weeks before the start of the war, as Thomas observed, the real estate market was down, but Henry gambled that it would come back up and he snapped up a prime piece of downtown property. His shop could also use an infusion of cash. He did a deal with a local craftsman, William B. Betts, to get a loan, pledging as security a one-half stake in the furniture and fixtures of the barbershop and baths.[6] Once the federal authorities took control, Henry scouted around for more ways to make money. Some of his old customers had fled to Confederate lines or been thrown in jail, but surely Union men would appreciate a good bath and shave just as much as anyone else.

In wartime St. Louis, it helped to have well-placed friends, and Henry welcomed the appointment of his landlord, Thomas T. Gantt, as provost marshal.[7] Still, he understood that even the staunchest white Unionists were not necessarily champions of civil and political rights for people of color. It did not do to speak out on controversial issues. Security lay in keeping quiet and getting on with business. Not that Henry was ready to shirk a fight: he had a war to win, and the right kind of allies could help him. The nation might be disintegrating. Men might be dying by the thousand every day on battlefields from Pennsylvania to the Gulf of Mexico. No matter. Henry's gaze was fixed unwaveringly upon his family's land claims. The war to get the Clamorgans what was rightfully theirs was the only war that truly mattered to him.

————

The Missouri Supreme Court had begun hearing the Clamorgans' suit against Isaac T. Greene in the matter of the Cedar Island tract back in 1860. Although the family had eventually been maneuvered out of the claim itself by the Papin brothers, they were surely entitled to the six thousand dollars Greene had originally promised them for it. In light of the unprecedented circumstances of wartime, the justices did not convene to render their decision until March 1862, but it was worth the wait as far as Henry was concerned. The court threw out all of Greene's arguments, ruling that it was irrelevant whether or not the Clamorgans were the legal representatives of the original grantee, Regis Loisel, whose title Jacques Clamorgan had purchased. They had offered to sell to Greene any claim they might have to that title, and he had promised to pay them for it. The principle of caveat emptor prevailed. The transaction between Greene and Jacques's heirs was valid in the eyes of the law, and Greene was told in no uncertain terms that he must pay what he owed. At long last the Clamorgans got their money.[8]

With that victory in hand, Henry mapped out his next campaign, the undoing of the rascally James Mumford. On January 16, 1863, Senator Felix Coste introduced in the upper house of the Missouri legislature An Act for the Relief of Henry Clamorgan, Cyprian Clamorgan and the Heirs of Louis Clamorgan, Deceased. It had its first and second reading, and then, in a night session on March 18, it came before the lower house.[9] R. F. Wingate, one of the St. Louis delegates, was decidedly unsympathetic: the claimants "were not as white as they should be," and since they were illegitimate, he presumed "the old common law maxim would hold that they were the children of nobody."[10] His colleague E. J. Bennett begged to differ. He explained the background of the case. In March 1859, Messrs. Greene and Mumford had secured the passage of an act authorizing them to sell the government-issued certificate of relocation for the Cedar Island tract. Mumford then double-crossed Greene by having himself appointed administrator of the estates of the two uncles from whom the present generation of Clamorgans derived their title. He claimed the certificate and promptly sold it. Greene got nothing, but, more to the point, neither did the Clamorgans. The state of Missouri had inadvertently done the family a grave wrong in 1859, and it was time to correct it. Other lawmakers chimed in. If the mother of the claimants had been free, that was good enough, declared one. That she had not been white was immaterial. Although maintaining he was no abolitionist, another insisted that right was right: "God was the father of us all," and "these innocents" deserved to be treated honestly and fairly.[11]

A few days later the bill passed the last of its legislative hurdles. Lawmakers agreed that although Cyprian Martial and Maximin had left no *legal* heirs, because Apoline was only their half-sister, and under Missouri law a half-sibling could not inherit, it was possible they had left *natural* heirs. The St. Louis Probate Court would take testimony to determine if such natural heirs existed and who they might be. Once they were identified, they would inherit just as if they had been heirs in law.[12]

Mumford was not ready to give up without a fight. He told the St. Louis Probate Court he expected to be reimbursed for all sorts of expenses, including hundreds of dollars in attorney's fees. The man to whom he had sold the certificate had defaulted. Mumford had accepted a promissory note but could not get his money because the purchaser was now "in the lines of the so called Southern confederacy." Another man was suing Mumford because he thought the certificate should have been sold to *him*. And so on. The court was unmoved. Mumford protested. He pleaded that he had been ill used. He appealed to the St. Louis Circuit Court. Eventually he exhausted his legal options. Of course, the sixteen hundred dollars he was forced to hand over to the Clamorgans constituted a tiny fraction of what they should have had, and lawyers' fees gobbled up a good portion of it, but something was better than nothing.[13]

By the time the court acted, Henry needed whatever cash he could scrape together. Although the federal government put him in that class of St. Louisans earning enough to pay taxes, the war was hurting his business. He managed to pay off the loan to Betts, but he defaulted on another and forfeited the property he had pledged. Just to keep their heads above water, he and Amanda had to sell some of their real estate.[14] The situation looked grim, and the couple was concerned about the welfare of their growing family. In addition to Clara, they had a son, Peter Howard, born in January 1862.[15] Before long, Amanda was pregnant again. No, the long-overdue payment from Mumford was not the thousands Henry had hoped for, but it was not to be sneered at.

A glance at the city by the midpoint in the war makes it easy to see why the Clamorgans were faring so badly: they were enduring the same hardships as most of the other residents. Prices for essentials were soaring and business was down. Many hundreds of white refugees were flocking to St. Louis from Missouri's western fringes, where the fighting was raging. Adding to the general misery was the plight of the ex-slaves, who arrived in droves, some fleeing their masters and others brought in by the military as "contraband of war." Hunger, poverty, and the ever-present fear of disease stalked the city. Then labor unrest broke out, as workers accused employers of exploiting the wartime crisis to force down wages.[16] Slowly, though, things began to turn around. Henry's fortunes improved to the point that he could start buying real estate again and begin to recoup his losses.[17]

If Henry helped recruit black troops, as did other African Americans in St. Louis, there is no evidence of it, nor is there any indication that Amanda or Julia (once she returned from her self-imposed exile) joined other women of color in assisting black soldiers and their families.[18] And yet, although the Clamorgans did not immerse themselves in advancing the Union cause with the enthusiasm that some of their friends and neighbors did, that does not necessarily mean they did not care about the war's final outcome. Admittedly Henry and Amanda did not take part in the celebrations on January 14, 1865, when Missouri's abolition law went into effect, but there was a reason for their absence. Their young son was gravely ill. While others were rejoicing in the streets, they were hovering around the boy's bedside. Little Peter Howard Clamorgan died just three days after slavery ended in the state.[19]

The end of the war, and the final defeat of the Confederacy, left the Clamorgans to reflect on just what those four years of conflict and turmoil had meant for them. Julia and her sons had abandoned their home. Henry and Amanda had endured financial hardship and, in the death of their son, a loss far more grievous than money or land. Collectively, though, the Clamorgans had weathered the storm. Now it was time to see what they could make of their lives as the city and the nation rebuilt.

The home Henry and Amanda and their children occupied in down-town St. Louis by the mid-1860s had many of the trappings of gentil-ity, including that hallmark of middle-class status, a piano.[20] Shortly after Peter's death, Amanda gave birth to another daughter, Lettie. Two years later Henry Jr. came along. Within a matter of months Amanda was pregnant again.[21] Henry knew it was high time to provide for his fam-ily's future. While he never despaired of getting his share of the Clamor-gan fortune, he and Amanda needed to consider what was, rather than what might be. The safest investment was land, but caution was called for. Henry had suffered reverses in the past, and he and Amanda saw the sense of putting any land they bought in her name. If she survived him, as there was every reason to expect she would, that would enable her to avoid the complex process of probate. More important, it would prevent any creditors Henry might have at the time of his death from getting their hands on the property.

To accomplish what they intended, Henry and Amanda needed capital. On October 17, 1867, they did a deal with shoe manufacturer James Hale. For one dollar they conveyed their home to Hale's attorney, Leicester Babcock, as security for a three-thousand-dollar loan. When they paid off Hale, regained their home, and put it up for sale, they net-ted a modest profit, but that was just a minor part of the arrangement. Hale's loan gave them the cash to underwrite a complex series of ven-tures.[22] Once they had the money, the couple bought a sizable chunk of land from developer Jacob Fritschle. They agreed to pay him $3,450 for six lots at the intersection of Chippewa Street and Iowa Avenue, an area on the edge of the city ripe for development. The deed stipulated that the whole should be in trust for Amanda. The Clamorgans did not intend to pay the full purchase price outright. Some of Hale's money would go to construct a new home for them. They paid one thousand dollars down, and Fritschle gave them credit for the rest, with the land itself as security.[23]

In a little more than a year, Henry and Amanda had built their home. That and the land on which it stood provided the security for a loan to build additional houses on their adjoining lots.[24] They planned to rent out those properties and use the income to pay off the various loans. As long as land values kept rising and the city's population kept growing, they were in good shape. To keep building, they disposed of more of their land downtown. They even let one of their Chippewa Street properties go when they had a good offer, but they promptly used the cash to buy another lot.[25] They were juggling loans and land with considerable success. By 1870, Henry's net worth was $21,000. That was the figure the census taker jotted down, but it was probably an underestimate. The following year an article in the *New York Daily Tribune* on "The Freedmen of Missouri" made mention of Henry, who, "with his razor and brush, has made $40,000."[26]

Keeping Clamorgans going required the same astuteness Henry put into building his real estate empire. (Although Henry had a number of different partners over the years, the barbershop and "bathing saloon" was still generally referred to as Clamorgans.) A series of events in 1867 and 1868 obliged him to think seriously about the future of the business. Those events concerned people who had been as close to him as family. For years he had overseen the interests of Pelagie and Antoinette Rutgers, serving as a combination of financial adviser and property manager. When Pelagie died early in 1867, Henry was one of the appraisers of her estate. He helped Antoinette with funeral arrangements, and even supervised the removal of her father's remains and those of her adopted sister from Rock Spring Cemetery to the lot she had purchased at Calvary.[27]

To her last breath Pelagie had bitterly opposed her daughter's marriage to James Thomas. When she knew she was dying and that the union would inevitably take place once she was gone, she sent for her lawyer to make sure Antoinette's fortune was tied up in such a way that Thomas could not make free with it.[28] Antoinette mourned a full year for her mother before she sent out wedding invitations. The ceremony took place at the Church of St. Vincent de Paul on February 12, 1868. The Clamorgans were not in the wedding party because Amanda was due to give birth any day, but Henry put in a brief appearance. His link to the groom was commented upon in the press, which reported extensively on the elegant nuptials: Thomas was "a partner of Clamorgan, whose baths are well known."[29]

Henry understood that with an heiress for a wife, his old friend James Thomas would want his own establishment and might even abandon barbering altogether. As the newlyweds set off on their honeymoon, Henry began the task of reorganizing his business. His first move was to renegotiate the lease on the premises on Fourth and Pine. Gantt and the other landlords agreed on a ten-year lease at $14,500 a year. It was a huge sum, but the property was extensive and there were already sitting tenants whose rents Henry hoped would help him meet his obligations.[30]

The basement was fitted up as a restaurant and leased to John W. Bame and Jacob Stoutenburg. Since Bame was the chief engineer for the Fire Department, and a budding restaurateur, and he planned to live on the premises, Henry congratulated himself on having such good tenants. All went well at first, but then the pair stopped paying the rent. Fearing they were going to skip town, Henry brought suit in the Circuit Court. The court seized, among other items, two stoves, eighteen marble-top tables, a couple of water coolers, and a barrel of vinegar. Henry did not want Bame and Stoutenburg's property; he wanted his money. Eventually the partners paid up, and he dropped the suit and evicted them.[31] He did no better with their successors, William Sever and John Kavanagh. Somewhere along the line, Sever faded out of the picture and Kavanagh defaulted. Once more Henry turned to the courts, but Kavanagh had already absconded, and Henry ended up with a quantity of furniture and cookware, a barrel of whiskey, and some sweet potatoes. No doubt he realized what he could on the assorted goods, grumbling all the while about the trials and tribulations of being a landlord.[32]

It was not only the operators of restaurants with whom Henry had difficulties. Albright and Son sold items much in demand by Henry's customers: firearms. The gun dealers dutifully paid their rent for a couple of years, became delinquent, paid something on account, and defaulted again. Henry finally gave up making polite requests. He sent for his lawyer and swore out a writ. Once the Albrights realized Henry was not bluffing, they made up the arrears and the case was dropped.[33]

Henry did have one exemplary tenant. Andrew Donaldson had been a junior partner of clothier Cyrus G. Helferstein. Helferstein leased space from Henry, and when he retired he sublet the premises to Donaldson, who renegotiated directly with Henry. The arrangement was a mutually beneficial one. Donaldson sold "Gentlemen's Furnishing Goods," and customers who stopped by to inspect his inventory might well decide to get a bath or a shave at Clamorgans, while Henry's clients could be induced to call at his tenant's store before they ventured off about their business freshly bathed and shaved.[34] In the old days, Henry and his brothers would have sold such goods as Donaldson carried, but elegant though Clamorgans still was, it was no longer the great emporium of all that fashionable St. Louisans might require for their persons or their homes.

Without James Thomas, Henry needed a new partner, and as he had in the past, he reached out to his brother-in-law Samuel Mordecai. Through thick and thin the ties to his first wife's family had endured. On February 1, 1870, the two men negotiated a series of loans with Henry's landlords to help pay the rent. As security they pledged the entire contents of the building. The movables in the upper stories, where some of the barbers and bath attendants boarded, consisted of furniture, washstands, bed linens, chamber pots, and a laundry stove. The barbershop and baths on the first floor were what generated the revenue. There were marble tubs and copper ones, barber's chairs, mirrors, washstands, a water tank, and all the plumbing fixtures, along with brass chandeliers and an assortment of pictures.[35] Even with the loans, Henry and Samuel found it prudent to take on another partner. Henry's half-brother Cyprian described Barriteer Hickman as a "descendant of 'one of the first families of Virginia.'"[36] Henry and Samuel were less interested in his lineage than in his business know-how. Hickman soon proved that he was an excellent man to have on board. Henry could feel good about the arrangements he had made. After a few upheavals, Clamorgans was doing well, and his real estate investments were working out just as he and Amanda had hoped.

Across town, Julia and her sons were not doing as well. To supplement the family's income, Julia took in sewing and at one point ran a small notions store.[37] When the elder of her two sons, Léon, finished school, he went to work as a clerk for his uncle. A couple of years later he was hired by another African American barber, William Roberson, as his cashier. By 1871 he was a riverboat steward, but he was quick to see the writing on the wall. Railroads were eclipsing steamboats, and wages for river workers were taking a nose dive. The railroads offered opportunities that the river did not. In 1873, Léon listed his occupation as "conductor." Julia's younger son, Julius, was less adventurous: he never had any trade other than barbering.[38]

Could Léon and Julius have done better for themselves? Possibly, had they been more financially astute. Thanks to the judgments their uncle had secured against Greene and Mumford, they had some savings. As their guardian, Julia had taken charge of their share of the court-ordered payments. Once they were of age, though, the money was theirs to do with as they chose. They did not choose wisely. They sank their savings into two lots on the outskirts of the city. The seller was none other than James Mumford, and his involvement should have been warning enough. The brothers purchased the land anyway.[39] In 1870, Léon used his property as security for a loan. He paid that off by the expedient of borrowing money from someone else and using the same land as collateral. His gamble failed and the County Court ordered the lot sold for back taxes.[40] Julius did no better: he pledged his property to get a loan, defaulted, and lost everything.[41]

In Julius's case a certain inattention to business was understandable, for his emotional life was all-consuming. In late 1871 or early 1872 he wed a young woman of color, Lizzie Bell. On February 3, 1873, Lizzie gave birth to a son. Less than a week later she was dead of puerperal fever, the killer of so many new mothers in the era before antisepsis. On February 12, two days after Lizzie's funeral, Julius brought their baby to church to be baptized. Louis Samuel may well have been a sickly infant, deprived as he was of his mother's care. Before the end of the month, Julius was bereft of both his wife and his son. Devastated by the double tragedy, he headed off to St. Paul, Minnesota, a community, interestingly enough, where other men and women of French Creole heritage had made new lives for themselves. Either Julius did not find a warm welcome in St. Paul or he grew homesick. Within a year he was back living with his mother and working as a barber.[42]

Although Henry was doing fairly well financially by the early 1870s, he aimed to do far better. While Julia and her sons were not exactly destitute, they were struggling financially, and they were hardly likely to reject the chance to join the ranks of the truly wealthy. That was the lure Henry held out. The settlements they had secured from Greene and Mumford over the Cedar Island tract? As Jacques Clamorgan's descendants, they had deserved the money for their title, even if they had lost the actual claim to the Papins. But what about all the other unresolved Clamorgan claims? It was a travesty that so much real estate had been stolen from the rightful heirs. Yes, Henry acknowledged, they had been to court before and had little to show for it, but times were different now. It was surely worth renewing their efforts. There was just one catch: the price of victory would be the full disclosure of their complex racial history.

If they wanted their inheritance, the Clamorgans would need to prove to the satisfaction of the courts that they were Jacques's descendants. They had had a taste of what that entailed when Henry led the charge to get the state legislature to do right by his family, and the likes of Mr. Wingate were vocal on the matter of their mixed-race ancestry. It would be no different now. They would have to furnish evidence of identity, and that evidence would speak to the undeniable fact that Jacques Clamorgan had cohabited exclusively with women of color.[43]

Try as they might, the Clamorgans could not erase their African ancestry. It was not a matter of appearance; they were often taken for white. It was a question of reputation. Missouri law defined people such as them as "colored," and in the St. Louis of the 1870s, as in so much of the nation, that had a devastating impact. White St. Louisans vilified poor and illiterate African Americans fresh out of slavery. Nor were the well-to-do spared, as Henry had good reason to know. The elegant Rutgers-Thomas wedding had been ridiculed in the press. Who did "colored folks" think they were to make such a display? It was all sadly reminiscent of the coverage of another wedding Henry attended just before the war. When Monroe Haslett's daughter, Theodosia, the "colored belle" of St. Louis, married Felix Dora in the summer of 1860, reporters stooped to the use of vulgar racial epithets to describe bride, groom, and guests, and when the Dora and Haslett families dared to protest, the press derided them, and by extension the whole community of color, as "sassy" and "arrogant."[44] Four years of war and the ending of slavery had failed to change most white hearts and minds.

Where did that leave the Clamorgans? They could deny their descent and forgo their inheritance, or they could admit it and hope for the best. A fortune was within their grasp, but it came with strings attached. They thought long and hard about the consequences of making their ancestry a matter of gossip and opted to proceed. If they prevailed, they would join the ranks of the nation's millionaires and test the truth of the old maxim that wealth whitened.

Their campaign began modestly. On August 4, 1873, no doubt after a little prodding from the family's attorneys, the U.S. government issued a patent to Jacques Clamorgan or his "legal representatives" for approximately six acres in downtown St. Louis that the Board of Land Commissioners had confirmed to Jacques back in 1810.[45] He had been dead for almost sixty years, and inevitably, after such an interval, the chain of possession was a twisted one. It was a question of what land was what and who had clear title. This was a game at which the Clamorgan heirs were old and accomplished hands.

George and Washington Todd saw the wisdom of handing over several hundred dollars to cleanse the title to their real estate. It might be cheaper in the long run than facing off against the Clamorgans in court.[46] Others required a little more pressure, and one of the most subtle and sophisticated members of the Clamorgan clan was on hand to supply it. From his base of operations in Calhoun County, Illinois, Cyprian worked with three members of the St. Louis legal fraternity, Edward P. Johnson, John B. Henderson, and George W. Hall, to coerce Johanna Gibbons into paying for her title to what they insisted was land in the Clamorgan patent. The land and the buildings on it earned Gibbons over a thousand dollars a year, and it was just one piece of her large real estate empire. Faced with the specter of a lawsuit, she paid. When all was said and done, the $275 that Cyprian and his lawyer cronies wanted was a pittance.[47]

Taking on Fanny Deaver proved a tougher proposition, for the elderly widow was wealthy and well connected: on her father's side she was a Chouteau and through her mother she was linked to Jacques Clamorgan's old ally Joseph Brazeau. In the St. Louis Circuit Court's June 1874 term, Cyprian filed suit against her and one John Burke. Messrs. Hall and Johnson did not do a competent job. Deaver's lawyers proved far more adept. They acknowledged that the land commissioners had confirmed Jacques's claim, but they contended that there was a distinct possibility he had subsequently traded some of the land—their client's parcel—to William C. Carr. The case dragged on for two and a half years until the court dismissed it.[48]

Unwilling to accept defeat, Cyprian hired a new legal team, George and William R. Walker. In 1877, Walker and Walker sued Deaver and Burke for three thousand dollars in damages and one hundred dollars per month in rent. The defendants' lawyers rejected this outright, maintaining their clients had acquired the property in a legitimate sale. They also pointed out that the case had been dismissed once. Cyprian lost a second time and was ordered to pay costs. Actually, it was William Walker who had to pay up. Before the case went to court, lawyer and client agreed to split anything Walker recovered, but Cyprian was cautious enough to insist that Walker bear the costs if the suit failed.[49]

Cutting deals with lawyers was an established Clamorgan custom. For decades Jacques's heirs had been recruiting attorneys to help them pursue their claims with the promise of great wealth, and they would continue to do so as long as they could find anyone willing to wager his time and expenses on what they always insisted was a safe bet. On November 11, 1873, Henry, Cyprian, and their nephews sold to Alexander D. Anderson for a dollar, "and . . . professional services heretofore rendered and to be rendered," half of the so-called Meramec claim: the 8,000 arpents (6,700 acres) Jacques had been granted by Zenon Trudeau in 1796 to supply wood for his saltworks on the Meramec River. The land commissioners had rejected the claim in 1810, but it had been confirmed in 1843, and now it seemed there was money to be made, since Congress was revisiting these old titles.[50] All that was required was a little more pressure from a good lawyer.

Victory seemed enticingly close. On February 24, 1874, the Meramec claim was approved by the U.S. Land Office. The matter bounced around in Congress for a while, only to end up, as so many Clamorgan claims had before, with the Committee on Private Land Claims. Despite Anderson's best efforts, nothing came of it. The Clamorgans returned his dollar and regained such title as they had.[51] It was disappointing, but like the contest with Widow Deaver, it was a side action. The family was anxiously watching two major battles play out, one in the Missouri Supreme Court and another in the U.S. Supreme Court. A victory in either could net them a fortune.

The first action was one the Clamorgans had been itching to fight for decades. In 1873 they were sure their time had finally come. An act of Congress passed the previous year allowed "dilatory or unfortunate claimants" to pursue in the district courts cases in which they believed land had been mistakenly sold by the federal government.[52] Did the Clamorgans fall into that class of "unfortunate claimants"? They believed they did, and they persuaded several attorneys to help them prove it. What they set their sights on was a prize that had eluded them in the past: the massive St. Charles grant. If the case they intended to bring in the District Court went their way, they did not propose to dispossess the current landholders. They would, however, expect to be compensated with the same acreage in public lands, at the rate of $1.25 an acre. Given the extent of the St. Charles grant, the Clamorgans stood to become very rich indeed.[53]

The case attracted a lot of attention. It was one that, according to the *Globe-Democrat*, "will carry judges and lawyers back to days and events which, to us . . . seem almost mythical." Briefly, in 1797, Jacques had petitioned Zenon Trudeau for a grant between the Dardenne and Cuivre rivers so he could erect saw- and gristmills, and build slaughterhouses to supply New Orleans with salted meat. In 1811, Jacques presented his claim to the land commissioners, only to have them reject it outright. Two years later he conveyed the St. Charles grant, along with three other claims, to Jean-Eli Tholozan, who was to get them confirmed on behalf of Maximin and Cyprian Martial. However, in 1816, Tholozan sold the St. Charles grant to Louis Labeaume. Clamorgan's "representatives," apparently the Labeaume heirs, submitted the claim to the reconstituted Board of Land Commissioners in 1833, but the board voted it down, insisting that Jacques Clamorgan had never complied with the terms of the grant and that the Spanish authorities had therefore disregarded it and given the land to other claimants.[54] Almost two decades later, in 1852, a bid was made to get Congress to act. The result was Senate Bill number 551. The report from the Committee on Private Land Claims accompanying the bill stated outright that the members judged the title a valid one. However, bills and committee reports meant nothing without action. The bill languished for two years, resurfaced briefly, and then was simply forgotten.[55] There matters rested until Congress made it possible to reopen the case, by which time the land had been declared public domain and sold off.

The case proceeded with agonizing slowness. Matters were not helped by the intervention of the powerful Blow family, who alleged that they were Labeaume's heirs and the St. Charles grant belonged to *them*.[56] In June 1876 the court finally took the matter under advisement, and on the twenty-second of that month, the *Globe-Democrat* told its readers a decision was imminent. That very day, in fact, the court decided in favor of the Clamorgans.[57] How much land would they get? Based on the county surveyor's calculations, the court made an award of 94,136 acres, or the cash equivalent. The assistant U.S. attorney appealed against any award whatsoever, and it became clear that the next round would have to be fought in the U.S. Supreme Court.[58]

"If the decree is confirmed . . . the lawyers will get the lion's share of the land," the *Globe-Democrat* predicted, "but the Clamorgans will have enough for a good chunk of a farm for each of them." Rather than revel in their victory, the Clamorgans seethed with rage. A "good chunk"! Just over 94,000 acres! It was outrageous. At $1.25 an acre, that would net them less than $120,000. Henry held out for 675,000 acres, or compensation of almost $1 million—with inflation, about $20 million today.[59] Cyprian insisted that figure was far too low. By his reckoning, the grant was more than double that. Henry should step aside and let *him* handle the matter. Cyprian left Illinois and took up residence in St. Louis, vowing "to stay . . . till the end is reached." He knew he would have a fight on his hands. The Blow family claimed the land in question was *theirs*, and they charged Cyprian with trying to rob them of it by fraud and deceit. His response was that if they wanted a fight, he would give them one.[60] Nor was he deterred by the prospect of taking on the U.S. government. Although he and Henry differed over how much the family was entitled to, they were of one mind when it came to believing they deserved far more than the District Court had awarded them.

Reporters were fascinated by the sheer complexity of the case. And yes, the Clamorgans' race featured in reports of the court battle. It was well known that Jacques had purchased "a quadroon woman of great beauty" and the two had lived as man and wife. It "has been pretty generally stated that the heirs . . . derive their blood, in part, from this same Esther"—it was Ester people remembered, not Susanne—"but some . . . stoutly deny this. They claim that they are of French and Spanish blood, and that no taint of the negro runs in their veins."[61] They might have claimed that, but if it had come to a choice between being white or being rich, the Clamorgans would have taken the cash every time.

Three separate but related actions ended up on the docket of the U.S. Supreme Court. In the first, the government contested any award whatsoever. The other two were bids by Henry and Cyprian to get more than the lower court had given them. When the justices handed down their ruling in January 1880 it was a crushing blow to the family. They overturned the decree of the District Court, citing the passage of time and the fact that neither the claimants nor Jacques himself had ever actually been in possession of the land. Moreover, it was impossible to work out from Zenon Trudeau's original concession where the land was located, and the court was of the opinion that when he submitted his petition in 1797, Jacques himself had had no firm idea where it was: he just wanted land, and Trudeau had obligingly given it to him. Why had the claimants not had a survey done for the full amount of land they believed they were entitled to? Because they knew such a survey would disprove their claim. In essence, they and their lawyers were endeavoring to cheat the United States out of two million dollars' worth of land scrip. Further weakening the Clamorgans' case was the indisputable fact that Jacques had never complied with the conditions upon which the land had been promised him. The government had been justified in declaring the St. Charles grant public land and selling it off piece by piece.[62]

The outcome of the case was reported in newspapers from coast to coast. So much land and so much money had been at stake. Could the Clamorgans have walked away with something? Perhaps. Reportedly, the government had offered them $375,000 (by today's reckoning well over $8 million) to let the whole matter drop, and they had rejected it.[63] They had missed their chance. Still, although their bid to get one claim validated had ended in defeat, they had another immensely valuable claim to pursue. They were pinning their hopes on that.

The residents of the area of St. Louis known as Baden had ample reason to feel aggrieved. For decades development in their neighborhood had been stalled. People were reluctant to buy or build in Baden. And what was the blight on that section of the city? It was another of the seemingly endless Clamorgan claims.[64] This particular claim originated in a grant from Trudeau to Jacques in 1793 of 800 arpents (around 670 acres) of land. Where was the grant? For the people of Baden and for the Clamorgan heirs, this was a crucial issue. It was outside the town of St. Louis as it had existed in 1793, at a small stream or spring which emptied into the Gingras Creek. There was a reference in the original grant to "the hills," but nothing to indicate *which* hills. Still, in 1806 the surveyor of the territory had provided a plat (a scale map showing the major physical features) of the chunk of real estate in question.[65] Nothing could have been clearer—but nothing about the claim was clear at all.

When the land commissioners took up Jacques's claim in 1807, questions had arisen over the boundaries of other people's claims. The board had ruled that Jacques would get his eight hundred arpents, "provided so much may be found vacant," but there was some doubt as to whether what he actually laid claim to conformed to what Trudeau had granted him. In 1811 a certificate for a survey was issued by the board, but the claim itself was turned down. In 1822 a second plat was filed with the General Land Office.[66] There the matter rested for half a century. No wonder confusion reigned about the validity of the Baden title.

On February 12, 1874, in a general cleanup of a host of ancient claims, the United States issued a patent to Jacques Clamorgan "or his legal representatives." Henry and his kinfolk stepped forward.[67] They and their attorneys, Messrs. Edward P. Johnson and George W. Hall, the same team that had represented them in some of their other actions, wasted no time getting the patent filed and unleashing a barrage of lawsuits in the St. Louis Circuit Court.[68] The Clamorgans were demanding thousands of dollars in damages, and substantial monthly payments for lost rents.[69] They did not expect the targets of their lawsuits to vacate the land: they merely wanted them to pay for peaceful possession. If the attack over the Baden lands was carefully coordinated, complete with preprinted forms on which the clerk of the court had only to fill in the name of each defendant, the collective defense was equally well organized. Messrs. Krum and Madill had their own forms drawn up rebutting the plaintiffs' case point by point.[70]

Virtually any individual or entity occupying land in Baden was served with a writ, courtesy of Johnson and Hall. The flood of cases, and the implications of a Clamorgan victory, generated considerable excitement.[71] Naturally, the Clamorgans followed each twist and turn. Henry was particularly zealous. Every motion for appeal approved or overruled, every judgment affirmed, every continuance granted, he tallied them all. And there was hardly a session of the court in which one or other of the Clamorgan cases did not appear on the docket.[72]

From the start the prime targets were two railroad companies, the Bellefontaine and the Baden and St. Louis, since the Clamorgans and their attorneys reasoned that railroad companies occupied far more land than any private citizen and had much deeper pockets.[73] Eventually the case against the Bellefontaine Company was dropped, but the suit against the Baden and St. Louis wound up in the Missouri Supreme Court, where it took on the nature of a test case. If the Clamorgans prevailed, the company would have to pay up, and so would all the other defendants, great and small. If they lost . . . well, Henry and the rest of the family would not entertain the thought of losing. They and their lawyers had laid the groundwork with such care.

They knew they needed to establish the chain of descent from the original grantee, and they located two venerable residents of St. Louis to help them. Thérèse Crevier, a former slave of Jacques's, and incidentally one of Julia Clamorgan's aunts (lineages were very complicated indeed among the city's old families of color), testified that she had known all of Jacques's children and their mothers, although, at almost ninety years of age, she was a little vague on some points. Johnson and Hall lost no time taking her testimony and having her swear to it. It was just as well they did, for Thérèse died shortly after she was deposed. Also called to give evidence was Gabriel Helms. He had not known Jacques or his "wives," but he had known every one of the children, and *their* children.[74]

So much for questions of identity, but at the time of his death, had Jacques owned the land his descendants were laying claim to? That was a source of much contention. In 1808, Pierre Chouteau had won a massive judgment against him, and had acquired some of his land, including, so the railroad company's lawyers maintained, the Baden tract. In 1810, Chouteau had sold some land back to Jacques. Did *that* include the Baden claim? Some months earlier, Jacques had voluntarily sold four hundred arpents to Chouteau, who had resold it. The Clamorgans' lawyers did not dispute that. Their version of events was that Chouteau had agreed with Jacques that the sheriff had confiscated too much land: just four hundred arpents would have satisfied the judgment, and Chouteau had already received that much and sold it to other people. Jacques made him a deed for that amount, and Chouteau conveyed the remainder back to him. Then there was the matter of a deed from Clamorgan to William Clark (of Lewis and Clark fame) and William C. Carr, and another deed from Jacques's executors that disposed of yet more land. Johnson and Hall insisted none of those deeds had been for the Baden tract.[75] Frankly, though, it was enough to make anyone's head spin.

The Clamorgans lost the first round in 1878 and promptly appealed. The attorneys for the railroad company pulled out all the stops. They asserted, among other things, that Chouteau's deed to Jacques was so vague that it could not be construed as conveying the land at issue, and it was not technically a deed anyway. Even if it was valid, it was for land Chouteau had already sold to other people. They attacked Jacques's will as invalid because it lacked a signature. Moreover, by the time he made the will, he no longer owned the land, so his heirs could not have inherited it. They blasted Cyprian: he claimed to be "the last catch of Appoline's brood of naturals," but his identity had not been sufficiently proven, and he should not be a party in this case. And they shot holes in the 1863 act of the Missouri legislature that Henry had fought so hard to secure. Maximin and Cyprian Martial had left no "natural" heirs because no such persons could exist in law. The Clamorgans were all illegitimate and hence barred from inheriting.[76]

The Clamorgans' lawyers insisted that the land at issue was not the land Chouteau had traded away. As for Jacques's will, it *was* valid according to the law in force at the time of his death. He died before the introduction of common law into Missouri. Common law and civil law conflicted on certain vital points, among them the rights of children born out of wedlock and inheritance by half-siblings. The Clamorgans' rights, derived from their mother and by her from her half-brothers, were legally sound.[77]

If, as was later asserted, the Clamorgans had been offered $40,000 (equal to almost $880,000 today) to abandon their claim, they should have taken it.[78] They pushed ahead and got nothing. By the fall of 1880 the case against the Baden and St. Louis Railway Company was settled, and with it all the other suits relating to the Baden tract. In terms of their land claims, 1880 had been a disastrous year for the Clamorgan clan. Whether they would accept their multiple defeats remained to be seen.[79] In 1882 two bills were introduced into the U.S. Senate confirming certain claims in St. Louis to the "legal representatives" of Jacques Clamorgan and others.[80] Might *they* not be the prelude to a financial windfall? And just because the case against the Baden and St. Louis Railway Company had gone down to defeat, might there not still be grounds for reopening one of the other Baden cases?[81] Henry never gave up believing he would be a very rich man one day. In the meantime, though, he had a family to support and a business to run.[82]

Clamorgans remained a fixture in downtown St. Louis. Henry's lease was set to expire on March 1, 1878. On December 31, 1877, he renegotiated with his landlords for another six years. The rent was considerably less than under the earlier lease and it was for much less real estate, but Henry was tired of having to find reliable tenants for the various shops and the trouble-plagued basement eatery, and preferred to rent only the space he needed for his barbershop and baths. Where he had once held sway over the entire premises at Fourth and Pine, he now occupied just part of it. There were other businesses in the building: Gerardi and Stickney stocked cigars, which presumably Henry's customers appreciated; and George F. Duenckel sold firearms, but they rented directly from Gantt and Co., rather than from Henry.[83]

Henry also changed the nature of his partnership. Barriteer Hickman had left to open his own establishment, and even though he kept his stake in Clamorgans, Samuel Mordecai seemed more interested in working as a plasterer, the trade he had learned long ago in Kentucky from his father.[84] A new partner was needed, and Henry and Samuel joined forces with a much younger German-born recruit to the "tonsorial profession." Joseph Roeser was hardly a stranger, at least to Henry. Back in 1868, he and his wife, Josephine, had purchased from Henry and Amanda one of their properties on Chippewa Street. How cordial were relations between the two families? Cordial enough that Henry and Amanda named one of their own children Josephine.[85] Although the Roesers eventually sold up and moved away, the ties with the Clamorgans endured. Joseph became Henry's junior partner just around the time Henry renegotiated the lease on Fourth and Pine. He provided much-needed capital and ran the barbershop while Henry and Samuel concentrated on operating the "bathing saloon."[86]

By 1880, Henry and his family were living quietly on Chippewa Street. Amanda kept house, assisted by Clara. Lettie, Henry Jr., and Thomas were in school, while the two youngest children, Oliver and Josephine, were at home. The Clamorgans were listed twice in that year's census. The first census taker, Pitcairn M. Rector, reported that Henry spent his days "at home," but his fellow enumerator, Otto Friede, categorized Henry as a "speculator." Unlike Rector, Friede lived in the same neighborhood as Henry and knew how extensive the latter's real estate holdings were. That he was a speculator Friede had no doubt. On one fact, though, Rector and Friede were in agreement: everyone in Henry's household was white. Although they were by no means as rich as Henry had hoped they would be, the family's lifestyle conformed to the census takers' notions of white middle-class norms. The Clamorgan name meant nothing to Friede: he was a German immigrant, and anyway he thought the name was Morgan. Rector had been born and bred in St. Louis, but he was ignorant of the intimate history of one of the city's more notorious founders. The Clamorgans looked white to him, and that was good enough.[87]

Henry and his family did not intentionally "pass." They kept alive their bonds of friendship within the old free community of color, some of whose members were as light-skinned as they.[88] Henry maintained his friendships, but what he did not do was engage in advancing the cause of civil rights. This was an era of unprecedented activism among African Americans in St. Louis. Newcomers and old established residents worked on all manner of initiatives, but they did so without Henry's participation.[89] Toward the end of 1878, when the *Globe-Democrat* ran an article on prominent men of color in the city and the roles they played in promoting everything from education to religious and charitable endeavors, Henry's name was absent.[90] With the passage of the Fifteenth Amendment, he could vote, and he may have availed himself of that right, but he did not become involved in politics, as so many other black St. Louisans did. On at least one occasion he was summoned for jury duty, something that would have been unthinkable before the war.[91] There is no evidence that he relished this as a belated recognition of his status as a citizen. He may have thought it a time waster: he could have been working in his barbershop or keeping an eye on his lawsuits.

The census taker who called on the other Clamorgans in 1880 got some of his facts straight. Julia, the child of an Irish father and a Missouri-born mother, was the head of household. With her lived her sons: bachelor Léon, a bookkeeper, and the widowed Julius, a barber. Three people boarded with the family: a young woman, Emily Grice, and a middle-aged couple, the Postlewaites. Eliza Postlewaite, supposedly Julia's cousin, was from Ohio, while her husband, Joseph, a musician, was a Missouri native. On the question of race, the census taker was clear: everyone was white.[92] This was not the only subtlety he missed. Eliza was not Julia's cousin; Joseph was. He was the son of her long-dead aunt Phyllis Benito, alias Felicité Crevier. And to describe him simply as a musician was to ignore both his accomplishments and his entrepreneurial spirit. Joseph was a prolific composer whose marches and polkas, waltzes and quicksteps, delighted white upper-class St. Louisans.[93]

Back before the war, Joseph Postlewaite's closest ties had been within the free community of color. Louis Clamorgan, his cousin by marriage, had helped him get his start, giving him an outlet from which to sell his sheet music and advertise the services of the small band he led. Joseph had met and married Eliza Lee while on a trip to Cincinnati, where her father, like Joseph himself for a brief period, and many of his friends, worked on the river. During the war, Joseph and Eliza decamped along with Julia and her sons, and like them, they returned to St. Louis when things quieted down. In the postwar city Joseph's career flourished. He was commissioned to write music for all manner of occasions. His small Quadrille Band became the Great Western Reed and String Band, and eventually Postlewaite's Orchestra. As his fame grew, Joseph slipped imperceptibly across the racial divide. His patrons and fellow performers assumed he was white, and he never troubled to inform them otherwise.[94] While professional demands kept Joseph on the road for weeks at a time, Eliza and Julia were company for each other, and when he returned he regaled them with stories of the cities he had visited and the fashionable people who had graced his concerts. However, there were certain things he did not share with his wife or his cousin.

When Joseph died on New Year's Day 1889, after a lengthy illness during which he had been nursed around the clock by the faithful Eliza, the newspapers announced his passing. This was when the first of his secrets was exposed. On the morning of the funeral a young white woman turned up on Eliza's doorstep with two children in tow. She announced that she was Mrs. Postlewaite. She had seen the death notice and she had brought the children to pay their respects to their father. Eliza refused at first to believe the tale Annie Postlewaite—born Annie Papin and kin to the Chouteaus—told.[95] It soon emerged, though, that Joseph had maintained two households. He featured twice in the 1880 census, once with Eliza and Julia in the city, and again on a farm a couple of miles outside the city with Annie and their children.[96] The story of the two Mrs. Postlewaites was a gift to reporters, who clamored to get both women's stories. Eliza insisted she and Joseph had lived together ever since their marriage in 1851, except for his absences with his band and her occasional visits to her family back in Ohio. Annie countered that she could furnish proof that she and Joseph had been married in St. Louis in 1871.[97]

Soon the second of Joseph's secrets came out. When Eliza started giving interviews, the gentlemen of the press got a good look at her. She was "comely" and "intelligent-looking," but was it possible she was "colored"? Then they started asking searching questions about her late husband, and this was when the scandal truly erupted. Surely the members of the white establishment who had welcomed Joseph Postlewaite into their homes would have known if he had been a man of color. They could not have been mistaken. He had been given a send-off worthy of "the best-known band leader in the West." Hundreds of his professional associates had accompanied his body to its final resting place at Calvary, and many prominent white citizens had joined the throng of mourners (including a no doubt heavily veiled Eliza). He simply could not have breached the racial barrier. A few discreet inquiries soon established the truth. Many older people of color knew Joseph and knew his history, but they had kept silent. If he had "passed," what business was it of theirs to enlighten white folks?[98]

Although the story created a sensation, other news items soon chased it from the headlines. And frankly, upper-class white St. Louis preferred it that way. It was not a pleasant thought to realize that a man they believed they knew so well had fooled them so completely—and married (albeit bigamously) a white woman, and a Chouteau into the bargain. If Joseph Postlewaite had "passed," who else was doing so? As for those Joseph left behind, Eliza slipped back across the color line and lived the rest of her life as a white woman, while Annie and the children faded into obscurity.[99]

Julius and Julia Clamorgan were untouched by the secrets Joseph's death revealed. In the spring of 1881, Julius helped some 150 of his fellow barbers in their bid to unionize. These men did not own their own shops: they were subcontractors at the mercy of the shop owners. Julius understood the hardships they faced because he shared them. He had toiled away in the employ of others, never amassing sufficient capital to go into business for himself. The Journeymen Barbers' Union was a rare interracial undertaking, with about one third of its members being African American. Julius was elected to be the union's vice-president. What he might have achieved as a labor leader we will never know. Before the year was out, he was dead from tuberculosis.[100]

Julia did not long survive him. After a lifetime of loss—her husband and all but one of her children—the poor woman succumbed to stomach cancer on January 12, 1883, at the age of sixty-one. She was buried beside Julius at Calvary.[101] Léon stayed on in the family home and took whatever work he could find. He had struggled financially for years as the family's cases made their way through the courts, promising riches but ultimately failing to deliver. He sometimes labored as a porter. At other times he worked as a bath attendant. Occasionally he was hired by his uncle or one of his uncle's friends. For him there was not the wealth and security his father had enjoyed when he presided over Clamorgans. Had Louis lived, Léon would have become a junior partner, but the business was under Uncle Henry's control, and Henry had other plans.[102]

Across town Henry realized he would not long outlive his sister-in-law. He was suffering from heart disease, and by his sixtieth birthday his deteriorating health had forced him into retirement. There was no need to make a will, since all the real estate was in Amanda's name. Henry did, however, address the matter of Clamorgans. Joseph Roeser agreed to take over the unexpired portion of the lease for fifty dollars a month and the payment to Henry and his heirs of one-half of the profits. It was an arrangement that suited them both: Roeser could continue trading under the Clamorgan name, and Henry and his family would have a steady income.[103]

Henry had attended to matters none too soon. He and Roeser shook hands on the transfer of the lease on January 20, 1883. On March 9, Henry died. His funeral, attended by "A large number of prominent colored citizens . . . and several old Creole residents," took place two days later at the Church of St. Thomas of Aquin, after which he was interred in the family plot in Calvary. Although the official death register listed Henry as white, the press knew differently. He was a "well-known colored barber." As for his lifelong obsession, in a telling obituary the *Globe-Democrat* observed, "Those who knew Clamorgan can hardly remember the time he was not talking about some case . . . in which he was interested. He passed the greater part of his life in expectation of judgments and decisions." In the end, although he did not die a pauper, years of struggle saw him leave his wife and children in what the newspaper described as "moderate circumstances."[104]

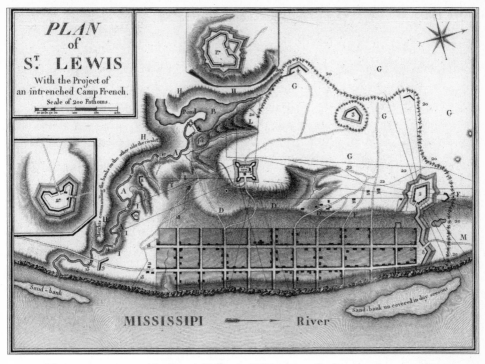

ABOVE: This map, composed by Victor Collet in 1796, shows St. Louis as Jacques Clamorgan would have known it when he was one of its wealthiest inhabitants and when the faithful Ester was superintending his household.

BELOW: Jacques Clamorgan's home, which doubled as his place of business, would have looked very much like one of the residences depicted here, as would the house he constructed for his children.

Jacques Clamorgan had many dealings with the half-brothers Auguste (1749–1829, shown here) and Pierre Chouteau (1758–1849), representatives of St. Louis's immensely rich and powerful "first family."

Jacques Clamorgan's business relationship with Manuel Lisa (1772–1820) was an uneasy one. Their partnership to take trade goods to Santa Fé ended acrimoniously and resulted in a lengthy court battle.

TOP: Images like this one of boatmen working their way downriver would have been very familiar to Jacques Clamorgan and his children. Note the presence of an African American crew member.

BOTTOM: John Caspar Wild's beautiful lithograph depicts the bustling waterfront of St. Louis that Jacques Clamorgan's grandsons would have known in their youth.

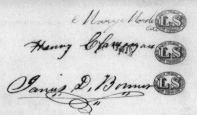

The Clamorgans were fortunate that their homes and their place of business were beyond the reach of the fire that broke out on one of the riverboats, spread rapidly, and devastated much of downtown St. Louis in 1849.

As a free person of color born outside Missouri, Mary Mordecai was required by state law to get a license in order to reside there. Her brother-in-law, Henry Clamorgan, was one of her sureties. On the same day Mary got her license, her sister, Harriet Clamorgan, applied for and got hers.

L. & H. CLAMORGAN,

IMPORTERS OF

Choice French and English

PERFUMERY,

COMBS, BRUSHES, RAZORS,

TOILET ARTICLES, &C., &C.,

No. 88, Chesnut Street,

OPPOSITE THE POST OFFICE,

SAINT LOUIS, MO.

The attention of the Ladies and Gentlemen of St. Louis is respectfully called to their extensive and elegant assortment of

Pure French and English Perfumery,

embracing the choicest and most fashionable products from the eminent houses of Lubin, Guerlain, Prevost, Piver, Monpelas, Mailly, Violet, Mangenet, Condray, and Chardin of Paris. Bayly & Co., Smith & Co., Ede & Co., and Pabey & Co., of London, and Farina's Cologne genuine.

As we will be continually receiving all the new and fashionable production, from the above houses, our stock will always be full and complete. Ladies and Gentlemen are respectfully requested to call and examine for themselves.

This full-page advertisement that Louis and Henry Clamorgan took out in *St. Louis Merchants, Mechanics and Manufacturers Business Directory* in 1850 illustrates the wide range of items they were offering for sale. Once Cyprian joined the partnership and the brothers moved into new premises at Fourth and Pine, they were able to stock an even wider variety of goods.

T R A N S A T L A N T I C   S K E T C H E S.

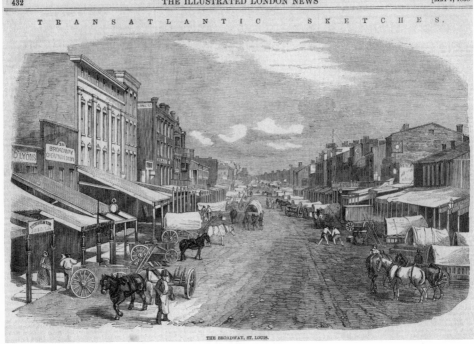

THE BROADWAY, ST. LOUIS.

ABOVE: This picture, titled *The Broadway, St. Louis*, appeared in *The Illustrated London News* in 1858, the same year Cyprian Clamorgan published his *Colored Aristocracy of St. Louis*.

BELOW: This lithograph by E. Sachse shows St. Louis as Henry Clamorgan knew it at the end of the Civil War, when he prepared to consolidate his business interests and embark on another series of legal battles to claim his grandfather's lands.

TOP LEFT: Henry Clamorgan, Jr., the son of Henry Clamorgan and Amanda Woodside, reinvented himself as Dr. Fordé Morgan, "passed" as white, and had a successful career as a pharmaceutical expert with the Charles H. Phillips Chemical Company and its successor, Sterling Products. (*Appleton (Wis.) Post-Crescent*, November 4, 1925, Courtesy of Heritage Microfilm, Inc.)

TOP RIGHT: Blanche, the eldest daughter of Louis P. Clamorgan and Louise McDougal, had several suitors. When she rejected one of them, he took his revenge by publicizing the Clamorgans' complex racial history and subjecting Blanche and the rest of her family to all manner of harassment. Photograph supplied by and used with the kind permission of her descendants)

RIGHT: In 1911 the Clamorgans found themselves at the center of a legal battle when Cora Clamorgan's white husband, Jack Collins, learned of her ancestry and, pressured by his father, tried to have their marriage annulled. (*St. Louis Post-Dispatch*, July 3, 1911, image courtesy of Clark Hickman)

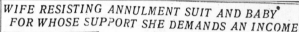

WIFE RESISTING ANNULMENT SUIT AND BABY FOR WHOSE SUPPORT SHE DEMANDS AN INCOME

Annulment Would Not Affect Status of Child

ANNULMENT of the marriage of J. B. Collins and Cor Clamorgan would not affect the legal standing of their 3-months-old daughter, Louise, John C. Higdon, the wife's lawyer, cites section 2918 of the Missouri statutes, which reads as follows:

"The issue of all marriages declared null in law, or dissolved by divorce, shall be legitimate."

MRS. CORA CLAMORGAN COLLINS.

MRS. CORA COLLINS AND HER BABY, LOUISE.

WHITE MAN PLANS TO MARRY SECOND CLAMORGAN GIRL

Engagement of Collins' Sister-in-Law to Charles Wass Announced by Her Mother.

Miss Blanche Clamorgan, elder sister of Mrs. Cora Clamorgan Collins, who is being sued by John B. Collins for annulment of their marriage on the charge that she has taint of negro blood, is engaged to marry Charles Wass of 200 Delmar avenue, the white foreman of an Olive street automobile repair shop.

Mrs. Louis P. Clamorgan of Ellendale, the young woman's mother, announced the engagement to a Post-Dispatch reporter Monday, and said that the wedding would take place in the fall.

Wass was a regular caller at the Clamorgan home at the time when the annulment suit gave publicity to the question of the family's racial standing. He has continued his visits since and has expressed contempt for the action taken by Collins.

Will Wed Despite Blood.

He is tall, broad-shouldered and handsome. He declared recently that he had

NAVY LIEUTENANT KILLS HIMSELF

Native of Murphysboro, Ill., Dies by Bullet on Board the Tacoma.

WASHINGTON, July 3.—Lieutenant Thomas L. Ozburn of the United States Navy killed himself on the gunboat Tacoma at the New York navy yard by shooting.

Details of the affair have not been received.

Lieutenant Ozburn was born in Murphysboro, Ill., and was senior engineering officer of the Tacoma.

LADY CONSTANCE FAILS TO APPEAR FOR HER WEDDING

Society Folk and Her Minister Fiance Wait in Vain at Church.

ABOVE LEFT AND RIGHT: These two photos of Louise and Louis P. Clamorgan appeared side by side in a family album. It is not clear which of the daughters is in the background here with her father. Note the strong family resemblance between Louis and his half-brother Henry Jr., alias Dr. Fordé Morgan, pictured earlier. (Photograph supplied by and used with kind permission of their descendants)

RIGHT: Shown in this carefully posed family portrait are Cyprian Clamorgan's daughter, Mary Belle (seated), her Canadian-born husband, François Bélanger, and their children Hebe and Minor. (Courtesy of the Clamorgan descendant Ronda Barnes)

9

The Mathematics of Race

WHEN ALL WAS SAID AND DONE, it came down to appearances. Henry Clamorgan had understood that. In legal terms it did not count that his grandfather had been French and his father Irish. His grandmother had been black, and in the eyes of the law in Missouri and much of the nation that had made him black, too. But appearances could be deceptive. People judged a man or woman by the hallmarks they associated with blackness or whiteness. The sheer complexity of Henry's ancestry had placed him in the racial borderlands. He had been black or white according to who was making that determination. It had been no concern of his to go into detail when dealing with the census taker or some other functionary. Let them categorize him as they chose. Occasionally he had "passed." He had not done so his entire life, but when the need arose and the opportunity presented itself, he had recrafted his identity.

Once Henry was dead, his wife and children took the process several steps further. A name change, a judicious pruning of the family tree, and appearances took care of the rest. There *were* times when it became necessary to reestablish descent from the notorious Jacques Clamorgan, but they hoped that could be done in such a way as to avoid bringing

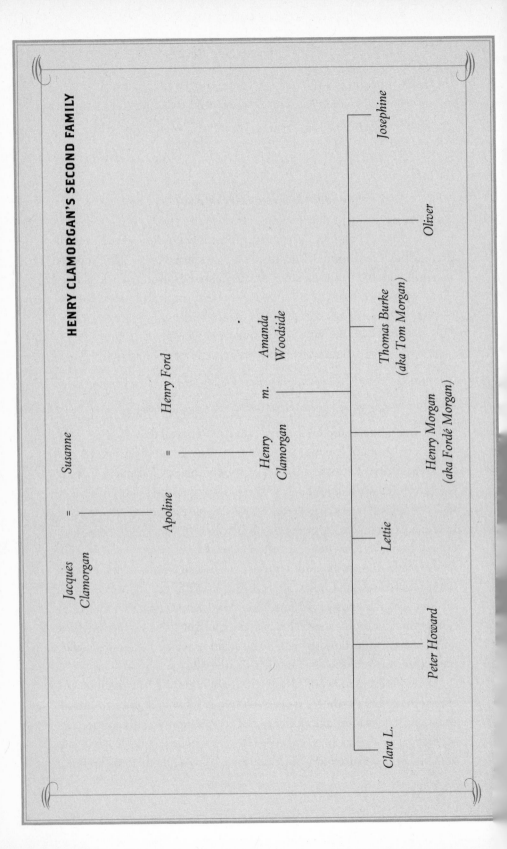

HENRY CLAMORGAN'S SECOND FAMILY

Jacques
Clamorgan = Susanne

Apoline = Henry Ford

Henry
Clamorgan m. Amanda
Woodside

Clara L. Peter Howard Lettie Henry Morgan
(aka Fordé Morgan) Thomas Burke
(aka Tom Morgan) Oliver Josephine

his black concubine Susanne into the picture. It was all about appearances, all about perceptions and images. And that toying with images began almost as soon as the "well-known colored barber," as the *St. Louis Globe-Democrat* described Henry, was in his grave.[1] His widow knew all about crafting the right image to suit the occasion.

Amanda's first reworking of her public persona in the days after Henry's death centered not on her race but on her supposedly weak and dependent state. She presented herself to the judges of the Probate Court as a helpless, near-destitute widow burdened with six children, all of them minors and two "of . . . tender years." Unprepared and quite unable to administer her late husband's estate, she explained that she had prevailed on her stepson to perform that onerous duty for her. He was doing his best. He had some cash on hand, but without the court's permission he could not disburse any funds until every last cent had been accounted for and the estate officially wound up. However, she needed money right away for living expenses. Could the court come to her aid and the aid of her fatherless children and authorize her stepson Louis P. Clamorgan to pay her at least a few dollars?[2]

Amanda handled her role of forlorn widow with real dramatic flair, but it *was* only a role. Her petition was nothing more than a carefully thought out tactic to circumvent a lengthy legal process. Far from an unschooled woman bereft of the guidance of her husband and scarcely able to keep her home together, she was a sophisticated businesswoman who knew enough to get a good lawyer and work with her stepson to speed up the tedious business of probate.

She bent the truth about her family situation. Two of her children, Oliver and Josephine, were indeed "of . . . tender years," but Lettie, Henry Jr., and Thomas were teenagers, and at twenty-three, Clara was not a minor. Neither Amanda nor Louis brought to the attention of the court the two-thousand-dollar life insurance policy Henry had taken out, with Amanda and the children as beneficiaries. And of course all the real estate Amanda and Henry had purchased was in her name. She intended to manage the property to keep herself and her family solvent. In the short term, though, she used it to overcome a legal hurdle.

To get the money from Henry's insurance policy Amanda needed to have the St. Louis Probate Court name her as the guardian of her minor children, and that entailed finding two individuals, neither of them related to her, to act as sureties. Both had to be able to state under oath that they possessed real estate worth a minimum of two thousand dollars. Here, as in so much else, Amanda proved how adept she could be at getting around the law. She sold one of her properties to Clara, who styled herself Clara L. Morgan, and hence did not appear to be related to Amanda. The day before she was scheduled to appear in court, Amanda sold another piece of land to her widowed sister Jane Royal.[3] The court did not ask about relationships, or about how and when the requisite amount of real estate had been obtained, and Mrs. Royal, Miss Morgan, and Mrs. Clamorgan did not see any need to enlighten the judges. Within hours of the hearing, Jane sold "her" real estate back to Amanda, and so eventually did Clara.[4] What Amanda had arranged was a neat maneuver that fulfilled the letter of the law, if not the law's true intent.

Meanwhile, Louis P. Clamorgan was hard at work liquidating his father's business. Since Amanda had told the Probate Court she was happy to have him act for her, he had no difficulty getting the court to appoint him as administrator. Two members of the colored aristocracy, barber Albert White and restaurant owner Felix Dora, posted bond for him. With two witnesses on hand—Amanda's half-brother, Charles Vandine; and a white friend, Frederick A. Beckman—Louis began an inventory, and then he recruited Beckman and two other men as appraisers. The three were well chosen. Beckman and George Werner were themselves barbers, while Julius Lang owned the shooting gallery at 401 Pine—a fact that must occasionally have rattled nerves at Clamorgans, which was located just a couple of doors away![5]

The appraisers worked methodically through the premises, putting a cash value on everything: the marble bathtubs, the massage tables, the mahogany barber's chairs, the bronze chandeliers, the mirrors, the pictures, the hot-water cistern, the soap dishes, the counter and safe. The firm did its own laundry. There were washtubs, flatirons, and so forth, as well as a large stove and an ironing table. Everything was split fifty-fifty with Samuel Mordecai, Henry's partner of many years.[6]

Henry's estate also had a one-quarter interest in various external fixtures, including an elegant glass sign and a barber's pole. Joseph Roeser,

who ran the barbershop, owned one-half, and Clamorgan and Mordecai a quarter each. Louis testified that his father's estate was a modest
one: he put its value at a thousand dollars. The Clamorgan-Mordecai
concern was also encumbered by a six-thousand-dollar mortgage, two-
thirds of which was unpaid. Roeser had offered to buy Henry's interest
and take up the mortgage, and Louis thought it seemed a proposition
well worth accepting.[7]

With Henry dead and Samuel Mordecai unwilling to run the business, either alone or with anyone else, it made sense for Roeser to take
it over. Henry's sons by his second marriage were still in school, and
Louis P. Clamorgan had made a career for himself in a very different
field from barbering. In the short term, Roeser joined forces with African American barber Norton E. Reynolds, but the arrangement did
not last long. Roeser's health failed, and Reynolds could not carry on
alone for more than a few years.[8] In 1895, Clamorgans closed its doors
for good. As far away as Portland, Oregon, this news was greeted with
dismay. The editor of the *Morning Oregonian* reminisced about the
famed establishment and its "octoroon" proprietors, who had bathed
and shaved the likes of Ulysses S. Grant and the Prince of Wales. The
marble bathtubs were auctioned off and the barber's chairs sold to the
highest bidder. The shutters came down, and an era ended.[9]

The business changed hands and eventually closed, but the history of
the Clamorgan family continued. By the end of 1883, when everything
was wrapped up and the barbershop and its contents were traded to
Roeser, Amanda and the children received less than six hundred dollars.
Of course, they actually had much more. The real estate Amanda controlled was worth thousands, and there was Henry's insurance policy.
Although he was Henry's eldest son, Louis P. Clamorgan inherited nothing. He had expended much time and energy for no reward other than
the knowledge that he had carried out his father's wishes. While Amanda
and Louis do not seem to have been at odds over the estate—she acknowledged he had performed his duties as administrator promptly and
honestly—once the necessary paperwork had been filed, Amanda and
her children had little contact with him. There were reasons for this. At

this point in his life Louis was a man of color, while the members of Henry Clamorgan's second family were rapidly making their move into the white community. To speed that move, the children, and sometimes their mother, jettisoned "Clamorgan" in favor of "Morgan."[10]

The Clamorgan ranks were thinning. Cyprian drifted in and out of St. Louis, turning up on Amanda's doorstep when it suited him. His daughter lived clear across the country. Amanda and her children knew she existed, but they had never met her. Henry's elder half-brother had died long before Amanda came on the scene. Henry's second family knew Louis's widow, Julia, but she had passed away two months before Henry, and the younger of her two sons had predeceased her, dying childless and unmarried.

In 1884, Léon, the only surviving member of Louis and Julia's branch of the family, wed Emily Grice, a young woman of mixed racial ancestry from New Orleans. Her mother, Cora Barden, who died when Emily was a child, had belonged to that city's free community of color. Her father, Warren Grice, was English.[11] Léon and Emily had known each other for years, and Léon was well aware of the troubled life Emily had led. She had come to St. Louis in her early teens, friendless and vulnerable. In 1869, when she was just fourteen, she had given birth to an illegitimate son. She had been saved from a life on the streets by Julia Clamorgan's aunt, Thérèse Crevier, the same Thérèse who had once been Jacques Clamorgan's slave and had testified on behalf of the Clamorgan family in the Baden case. Thérèse kept house for a wealthy widow, Anne Lucas Hunt, and Mrs. Hunt had raised no objections to the presence in her household of Emily and her baby. After Thérèse's death, and the death of her young son, Emily moved in with Julia. Julia became deeply attached to her, describing her as her adopted daughter.[12]

When Julia and Julius died within months of each other, Léon and Emily were drawn together by grief, and it is hardly surprising that they should have married. However, their life together was soon over. Léon contracted tuberculosis, the same disease that had claimed his brother, and he died early in 1888. The following year Emily wed a German immigrant, Charles Mottmueller.[13] Although she quietly assumed her new husband's racial identity, she remained close to Léon's extended family. She and Charles had three children, two of whom died in infancy.

The Clamorgans and the Mordecais allowed the Mottmuellers to bury their children in the family plot at Calvary. The babies were not Léon's, for his and Emily's marriage had been childless, but in a sense they were "family."[14] In various ways over the years, Léon's relatives, including Amanda and her children, came to the aid of Emily and her husband. She had inherited next to nothing from Léon, and Charles never graduated beyond the ranks of the laboring poor.[15] When the couple's daughter married an Irishman, it added still further to the racial complexity of the Clamorgan clan. Technically, Emily and her daughter were women of color, and hence their marriages to white men were illegal under Missouri law, but who was there to denounce them to the authorities? Certainly none of the Clamorgans.[16]

Amanda kept alive her ties to at least a few of Henry's relatives and a couple of members of her own extended family. She was closest to her elder sister, Jane. Around the time Amanda became Henry Clamorgan's second wife, Jane wed African American barber and riverboat steward Joseph Henry Royal. The couple had one child, Laura, who married Robert Hickman, the son of Barriteer Hickman, one of Henry's former partners. Jane was widowed relatively young, and their shared loss may have drawn the sisters even closer. Tragically, in the spring of 1884, Jane succumbed to cancer.[17] The links with Jane's daughter and her family endured, though. Jane had been "mulatto" at some points in her life and "white" at others, and the Hickmans made similar passages back and forth across the lines of racial demarcation.[18]

Amanda's other sister, Adeline; her husband, George Sass; and their children had relocated to Kansas City by 1870. In St. Louis, George had worked as a pastry cook, and in Kansas City he and Adeline capitalized on his skill by opening a restaurant. Although white himself, George had lived with Adeline's family for several years before the couple married, and he knew they were people of color. The Sass children, however, were apparently unaware of that fact. They had no contact with their kinfolk back in St. Louis. Amanda may never even have seen Adeline again after her move to Kansas City.[19]

Amanda's half-sister, Sophia Vandine, lived in St. Louis with her husband and their growing family. On December 8, 1875, Sophia had wed John W. Booth, a white man from Ohio. Whether she was classified as white before her marriage, she was white thereafter. Successive census takers differed over where she had been born and where her parents were from, but none questioned her designation of herself as white.[20]

Charles Vandine had come to Amanda's aid after Henry's death and had played a part in settling the estate. She was rather closer to him than to Sophia, although for a brief time in the 1890s Sophia and her family did in fact board with Amanda.[21] Charles lived with their mother and for several years managed Clamorgans for Norton E. Reynolds. He waited a long time before establishing a household of his own. He was forty-eight in 1897 when he married Jennie Davidson, a much younger white woman. By 1900, the "Van Dykes" (as the census taker called them) had one child, Mary Grace, and were firmly entrenched in the white community.[22]

Where did that leave the one member of Amanda's family who never permanently crossed the racial divide? Lucinda Vandine did not move in with any of her children, even when she became old and frail. As late as 1910, when she was almost ninety, she lived alone in lodgings. When Lucinda died in the St. Louis Infirmary on February 2, 1912, the superintendent registered her death and supplied the information that she was black. Amanda did not come forward to claim her mother's body, and Lucinda was buried not in the Clamorgan family plot at Calvary but in St. Peter's Cemetery.[23]

Amanda was a savvy money manager and she made excellent use of the real estate she and Henry had bought. Some of it she pledged as security for loans to make improvements to her home and her various rental properties. She apparently never had problems paying off those loans. She hung on to each of her houses as long as she could, and when she did sell she usually managed to negotiate a good price.[24] She was a shrewd landlord, constantly on the lookout for reliable tenants. She was even willing to rent out all or part of the family home if she thought she could make money on the arrangement.[25] Her property holdings were compact—two two-story brick houses on Iowa Avenue, several more around the corner on Chippewa Street, and of course the substantial home she and her children usually occupied. Having all her properties concentrated in such a small area meant she could keep a watchful eye on them and either she or one of her older children could collect the rents. Her tenants were mostly Irish or German tradesmen and their families. There was no black presence in the neighborhood for most of the time the "Morgans" were there . . . at least no acknowledged black presence.[26]

By the early 1890s the Morgans had passed without question into the white community. Daughter Clara wrote gossipy letters describing parties she had been invited to and calls she and the family had made and received.[27] The siblings attended masquerade balls with their friends. They went to the opera. (Clara noted that her ticket for one operatic evening cost $3.50. She said she would rather have had the cash, but that did not stop her asking her brother Thomas for a hat and gloves so she could go again.)[28] The family was Republican, and "Garfield picnics" were a regular feature of their summer fun.[29] It was Tom, though, who received the ultimate accolade. In 1894 he was *"honered* [sic] with an invitation to the V[eiled] P[rophet's] Ball." This was an exclusively white event, and remained so well into the last quarter of the twentieth century. Had his ancestry been known, Tom Morgan, alias Thomas Clamorgan, would never have been so *"honered."*[30]

In 1900 the census taker found only two members of the Clamorgan family, Amanda and Josephine, in residence at 2736 Chippewa Street. They shared the home with Johanna Gutzmann, a widow of about Amanda's age, and her daughter, Minnie.[31] Where were the rest of Amanda's children? Clara and Lettie were living elsewhere in St. Louis, with Lettie keeping house and Clara earning money as a piano teacher. One of Amanda's sons was a man of professional standing who had made his home far away from St. Louis. Another was across town, trying somewhat belatedly to claw his way to middle-class respectability. Sadly, a third had not survived childhood. In November 1884, eight-year-old Oliver, known to his family as Ollie, had died of scarlet fever.[32]

Henry Clamorgan, Jr., had gone out to work within months of his father's death, taking a position as a clerk at a downtown business. He aspired to something far better, though. In 1886, Amanda terminated her guardianship of Henry and handed over to him his share of his father's insurance money. It wasn't a princely sum, but it was enough to get him started.[33] After learning that tuition was free at the University of California, Henry headed west. Whatever schooling he had received in St. Louis—and he probably took advantage of the parochial schools, as did other members of the city's light-skinned Catholic elite—it had prepared him well enough to be able to pursue a degree in pharmacy. In 1889 he came back across the country to enroll in New York University's Bellevue Medical College, and in 1892 he emerged as a full-fledged M.D. It need hardly be said that along the way he had ceased to be black. After graduation he taught at the New York School of Clinical Medicine, where his specialty was diseases of the skin, before setting up in private practice.[34]

California and New York offered opportunities Henry would never have had in St. Louis, where the link with the "colored" Clamorgans could be made at any time by anyone who cared to pry into his history. For good measure he took a new name. He had dropped Clamorgan in favor of Morgan after his father's death. Now he altered his name again, becoming Fordé Morgan. Ford was the maiden name of the woman he eventually married, but it was also the name of his mysterious Irish grandfather, although why he gave it a French twist is anyone's guess. Perhaps he was associating himself, however cautiously, with the old French families of colonial St. Louis. And that, of course, was no fiction. He was Jacques Clamorgan's great-grandson.[35]

Secure in his new persona as Dr. Fordé Morgan, Henry, once a man of color but now white, traveled where he wished. In 1895, for instance, he was a guest at the fashionable Montrose Hotel in Biloxi, Mississippi, a venue he would not have been received at except as "help" had there been any doubts about his race. His photograph and physical description when he applied for a passport make it easy to see why no one questioned the racial identity of the tall, gray-eyed Midwesterner.[36] While his complexion was dark, he was confident no one would ever take him for other than a white man of Mediterranean descent, and apparently no one ever did. Henry never cut his ties to his kinfolk back in St. Louis. His mother and sisters stayed with him in New York for months at a time, but then they had also made the transition to white. His secret was safe, as was theirs.[37]

By the time the 1900 census was taken, Dr. Morgan, now a married man, was comfortably ensconced in Manhattan.[38] His wife, Harriet Ford, was a white New Englander. When the couple met, Harriet, who was three years older than Henry, had graduated from the American Academy of Dramatic Arts and was enjoying some success as an actress. Soon after their marriage, which took place around 1897, she gave up acting, but she did not abandon the theater. As Harriet Ford (professionally she never used Henry's name) she established herself as a playwright, crafting plays on her own and in collaboration with other dramatists, and adapting novels for the stage. Her first hit came in 1900 with *The Greatest Thing in the World*, which she wrote with Beatrice DeMille, the mother of famed director Cecil B. DeMille. For decades, plays Harriet had written, wholly or in part, were produced in theaters on both sides of the Atlantic, and as the film industry evolved she worked on screenplays.[39] When Henry's relatives came to New York, they enjoyed glimpses of backstage life at the theater, courtesy of Harriet, and had seats for the opening night of one or other of her plays.

Thomas Burke Clamorgan, alias Tom Morgan, probably got heartily sick of hearing that he should emulate his brother Henry. Tom's letters reveal how different he was from the studious Henry. Of course, he never meant his letters to be seen by anyone other than himself. He tucked them away in a box, which he put in a storage space in the family home. Other items were removed and consigned to the trash over the years, but the box of letters remained undisturbed. It finally surfaced in 2003, when 2736 Chippewa Street came into the possession of an owner with a keen eye and a real sense of the past. From time to time Tom Morgan's correspondents, especially the female ones, wrote "burn this" or "please destroy this" after revealing an intimate detail or two. Perhaps Tom *meant* to comply. Happily he did not, and the secrets of his reckless youth make for fascinating reading.

When he left school, Tom worked for a year or two as a machinist, but he was restless, itching to travel, and eager to escape the watchful eyes of his mother and eldest sister. Tom was a sociable sort—too sociable for his own good, according to Amanda and Clara—but his talent for conversing easily and turning strangers into friends made him an ideal salesman. By 1889 he had quit the machine shop to work for two millinery wholesalers, S. Strauss and Co. and A. H. Fuchs.[40] S. Strauss and Co. was a partnership of Simon and Benjamin Strauss and Adolph Samish. Simon was a native of Bavaria, Benjamin was his son, and Adolph Samish was his son-in-law.[41] Adam H. Fuchs and Thomas B. Morgan were close in age, and may have known each other from parochial school or from church, since both were Catholics. When Fuchs went into business he hired Tom Morgan.[42] It was Tom's job to go out on the road for weeks at a time and peddle everything from children's sun bonnets to trimmings, artificial flowers, feathers, lace for ladies' hats, and the hats themselves. At least in the early 1890s, his route included much of Missouri, Kansas, and Texas, with an occasional trip into "Indian Territory" in Oklahoma.[43]

Tom fared well with S. Strauss and Co. and worked for them for years, but Fuchs had a love-hate relationship with him. While Tom was a good salesman in that he moved considerable quantities of merchandise, he could be frustrating to deal with. He was quite capable of going off with another salesman's route list and conveniently forgetting to send his employer regular reports, although his requests for money came in often enough. Henry, the office manager, had the measure of him. On one occasion, when Tom was on the road, Henry sent him fifty dollars "for Gambling Expenses, [I] should say traveling."[44] Fuchs himself became increasingly irritated, and at one point almost fired Tom, declaring that he gave the firm more trouble than all the other salesmen combined. The home office never knew where he was or what he was doing. "These foxing games must be stopped and will be stopped at once." But then Fuchs relented—probably when Tom sent in more orders—and dispatched his traveling money, albeit with an admonition that none of it was to be spent on cigars and drinks.[45]

Judging from his correspondence, at this stage in his life Tom ran with a rather disreputable crowd. He and his friends were perennially short of money and fond of drinking, gambling, and womanizing.[46]

Tom's irresponsible ways and his tendency to help out his worthless cronies before his own flesh and blood precipitated a bitter quarrel with Clara in the fall of 1893. Yes, she and Mama knew he paid his board, but he had to stop pawning everything he owned and buying up other people's pawn tickets. The money he squandered was needed at home. On his last visit he had told Mama he had nothing to give her, and yet that very night he had taken his no-account friends out to supper. He had hocked his ring to pay for the spree, and had arrived home at 3:00 a.m. Clara gave him dire warnings about the need to save for the future. He had called her a "crazy old crank," and she wasn't above quoting his words back to him.[47] In fairness to Tom, he did send money home while he was on the road, and from time to time he authorized Clara to request an advance from his employers against his wages.[48]

Clara and Amanda were in agreement that the best way to make Tom mend his ways was to match him with a good woman, and they believed they had found just the one for him. Corinne McMillan was around Tom's age. Tom had probably met her and her sister, Mae, through his job, since both of the McMillans were employed by Starr Brothers, wholesalers of notions, on Fourth and Washington. S. Strauss and Co. was on Eighth and Washington. Corinne was a bookkeeper and Mae a clerk.[49] Corinne was set on marrying Tom and saving him from the idle and dissolute life she believed he was leading. Her letters dwelled on his unkind behavior, her willingness to forgive him, and the hope that he would come to appreciate the affection of a worthy young woman such as she.[50]

Tom's family did everything in their power to promote what they believed would be an eminently suitable alliance, and Corinne capitalized on this.[51] In the fall of 1892 she took the initiative and proposed to Tom. She told him that she would leave with him on his next trip. "I will accompany you to your first stopping place, become your wedded wife and keep same a secret . . . until such time as we can embark in a bussiness [sic]." His mother, brother, and sister thoroughly approved of her plan. They might even have shared with her the family's most closely guarded secret, for Corinne wrote, "I know your circumstance *history* and etc. and know I will prove true to the end."[52]

Unbeknownst to Corinne, she had a rival for Tom's affections. Fannie Cleary, her brother, Alfred, and her sister, Mary Josephine (Minnie), had trekked down from Canada in search of work. They were soon followed by their parents.[53] Fannie was several years younger than Tom and Corinne, and while Corinne had a certain status as a bookkeeper, Fannie was hard put to find and keep a job, especially at a time when the economy was far from robust. She worked as a sales clerk at different downtown stores, but she also endured lengthy periods of unemployment. Tom enjoyed being pursued by her, and he encouraged her with gifts of hats and other finery (courtesy of his employers) that she could not afford to buy for herself.[54]

Fannie was every bit as determined as Corinne to marry Tom. Corinne offered to elope with him, but only if marriage were indeed his intention. Fannie was less cautious, perhaps reasoning that if she became pregnant by him, or if the two became the subject of gossip, Tom would *have* to marry her. In January 1894, with Tom on the road again, Fannie slipped away to spend a couple of days with him. When her parents found out and demanded to know who had accompanied her, she lied and said Tom's sister had gone with her.[55] Mrs. Cleary talked with Clara, who quickly disabused her of the notion that she had played chaperone. All hell let loose. "[T]hey came to the conclusion that we were married and if not ought to be . . . And they say if . . . we are not married . . . it will be the only way to make all well." Rather ungraciously Tom replied that it was her own fault. Fannie was mortified and more than a little angry. "I don't see why *I* should . . . bear all the blame even if I did forget myself so far but it was all for you."[56]

Things got worse rather than better, although admittedly Fannie had a tendency to dramatize. "Min opened my letter . . . and told them all that was in it so you can imagine how it is here." Under the circumstances, Tom might not want to call at her home, but she would meet him anywhere he cared to name.[57] What Fannie did not know was that Minnie also had designs on Tom. He loaned her money, gave her presents, and carried on a correspondence with her. When Minnie finally gave up on him and began seeing someone she considered a better marriage prospect, Tom saved her from making a dreadful mistake. Through his network of friends—the same friends everyone was always nagging him about—he found out that the new man in Minnie's life already had a wife![58]

For all that they pursued him, neither Fannie nor Corinne got Tom to the altar. The young woman who pulled off that feat was an Illinois native, Nevada Belle Garrissine.[59] She and Tom wed around the same time that Henry married Harriet Ford. Nevada Belle might not have been the wife Amanda and Clara had picked out for the wayward Tom, but by all accounts their marriage was a happy one and, to the relief of his family, Tom finally settled down.

Whatever names they went by, and however they identified themselves as regards race, Amanda and her children were Clamorgans to the core. They proved this by suing every individual and every entity they could think of to get what they insisted was *their* land—or its value in hard cash. Henry had fought almost to his dying breath. Julia and her sons had fought. Cyprian would do battle with anyone and everyone until his health gave out, and his daughter would carry on the struggle. Henry's son from his first marriage would keep fighting, and there was every reason to believe *his* children would do so. Through deaths of claimants, changes of name and race, and setbacks in the courts and in Congress, Jacques Clamorgan's descendants were determined to have every square foot of land he had bequeathed them.

A defeat was never a defeat: it was simply a truce. This was the Clamorgans' attitude toward all their claims, and the Baden one was no exception. Although Henry Sr. had lost in the Missouri Supreme Court back in 1880, he had refused to accept the verdict as final. Perhaps it was just as well he did not live to hear the outcome of his appeal: several weeks after his death the Appeals Court ruled against him. The family fought on, and in 1884 the case went to the Missouri Supreme Court on a writ of error. Yet again the judgment was upheld, and yet again the Clamorgans tried to get it overturned on a technicality. This went nowhere, but still they refused to give up, and in 1892 they put matters to the test by threatening to haul into court the most prominent of the Baden landholders, Archbishop Peter Richard Kenrick. The Clamorgans might be Catholics, but when money and land were at stake they set aside religious loyalties.[60] And for good measure they sued their lawyers, Messrs. Johnson and Hall, for (so they said) bungling the Baden case over the preceding two decades.[61]

The Clamorgans acted as boldly as they did because they had found a new and aggressive young lawyer who promised them speedy results. Amanda had initially hired George C. Worth to represent her in a dispute with two local contractors—a routine affair involving allegations of property damage arising from renovations done to her home and countercharges of nonpayment for work carried out.[62] Apparently Worth saw the chance to make more money when he learned about the Baden claim in casual conversation with his client.

On Worth's advice, the family began their pursuit of the archbishop in the St. Louis Circuit Court, only to have Worth sell them out at a critical juncture. Was he, as some accounts had it, an honest lawyer who concluded, once he delved into the matter, that Kenrick had right on his side? Was he overawed by Kenrick's legal team? Or was he playing a double game, extorting money from the archdiocese to drop the whole matter, and then telling his clients he had thought it best to compromise?[63]

Through the summer and early autumn of 1892, before they learned of Worth's duplicity, the Clamorgans agonized over the case. They had decided to expand the scope of the action to include not only the archbishop but most of the other Baden landholders.[64] If they could win just one victory it would net them a fortune, since it would force all the rest of the defendants to settle. But the family had been down this path so many times before. Would the outcome be different this time? Clara, ever the voice of doom, feared it would not. On September 5 she wrote Tom, then on his travels: "I suppose it will be our luck to lose."[65] Amanda was more optimistic. On September 14 she reported to Tom that "prospects are better than they were last week." A week later her optimism had faded: "I have had a good deal of trouble with Mr. Worth . . . [I]t is such a long story I could not tell you on paper but will tell you all about it when you come home."[66] Worth had settled with the archbishop for just a hundred dollars.

This was the point at which Henry Jr., the newly minted physician, decided to return to St. Louis to take charge. For the duration of the court battle he resumed his birth name and risked the associations people might make. Yes, his own and his family's racial status was on the line, but so was a great deal of money—enough to justify the risk.

Henry immediately moved to have the settlement with Kenrick overturned, contending that Worth had made it without his knowledge or consent and then perjured himself by saying Henry had agreed to it. It was outrageous. The Clamorgans had demanded fifty thousand dollars in damages and additional sums in rent as long as the unlawful occupation of their land continued. Why had Worth settled for a paltry hundred dollars?[67] Henry fired Worth and hired another attorney, William S. Field. Although Field did his best for his clients—Amanda had also rejected the settlement and was a party to the suit—he was fighting an uphill battle. Yet again the Baden case went down to defeat.[68]

Given that Worth had sold them out, the Clamorgans balked at paying his fee. He retaliated by suing Amanda and Henry. Clara informed Tom that Worth was demanding three hundred dollars "for doing work that no one . . . ever authorized him to do." By the end of October, Worth's suit against Henry had been dismissed and he had requested a continuance in his case against Amanda. Clara did some investigating and learned that Worth was delinquent on his rent. She suspected he planned to skip town, and it turned out she was right. His failure to appear led to the dismissal of the suit.[69]

It was all very disheartening. The Clamorgans had defeated Worth, but this was a hollow victory. They were no closer to getting their land. Would they ever get it? Tom enlisted supernatural aid to try to find out. He consulted a medium. Nellie Whitlock assured him that her spirit control, "Miss Lotta," had sent word that "there is a large estate coming to you," but Tom needed to watch out for the interference of a "light complexted woman & a dark complexted man." Mrs. Whitlock could not tell him any more at that time, "as your little heart is *young* & *tender*," but if he wrote her by return (and sent more money), she would divulge more. A disappointed Tom Morgan scrawled across the letter "Rats."[70]

———

It had been a grave mistake to hire George C. Worth. Clara knew it. She placed her faith in Mr. Gray. He could easily "do [Worth] up."[71] If anyone could get the Clamorgans what they deserved it was Mr. Gray. Alexander Gray, the champion who would take on all comers and earn the trust of the perennially suspicious Clara and the rest of her family, is one of the most remarkable characters in the entire Clamorgan saga.

Neither a lawyer nor a native of St. Louis, Alexander Gray had been born in the fishing port of Fraserburgh, on the northeast coast of Scotland, and he and his wife, Elizabeth, had immigrated to the United States in 1875, when he was thirty-one and she was twenty. Gray was not a rich man, but he had been trained back in Scotland as a bookkeeper, and he managed to find employment in St. Louis, eventually becoming an accountant for a railroad company, the Missouri, Kansas and Texas, the famed KATY.[72]

What was the link between Gray and the Clamorgans? As he explained it, shortly after the death of Henry Clamorgan, Amanda and her children, along with Louis P. Clamorgan and Cyprian, had empowered him to act for them.[73] Gray never said who had approached whom. Maybe he heard about the Clamorgans' battles or read about them in the newspapers and thought there might be an opportunity for a savvy accountant with a talent for investigation. Or maybe he had run into one of the members of the family and been recruited. Clearly there was money to be made, and with a growing family to support, Gray could use more than he was getting from his regular employment. Although he did not explicitly say so, he must have expected to be compensated for his efforts with a share of anything he could recover. Aside from the profit motive, however, Gray does seem to have seen himself as a crusader for justice and the defender of a much-wronged group of people. He threw himself into the battle, marshalling every scrap of evidence that might substantiate this or that title. The Clamorgans furnished him with masses of documents, but he still needed to do a lot of sleuthing on his own. And with or without some prodding from the Clamorgans, he understood the need to tread carefully when it came to matters of race.

Well before George C. Worth came on the scene, seducing Amanda and her children with promises of a swift and profitable victory in the Baden case, Alexander Gray had already proven himself. In 1885, with the ink scarcely dry on his power of attorney from the Clamorgans, he had gone after the rich and socially prominent Theophile Papin, demanding to know how he and his brother, Sylvester, had managed to cheat Henry Sr. and Cyprian over the Cedar Island tract back in the 1850s. The Papins had no deed proving that they had, as they claimed, acquired the certificate of relocation from the Clamorgan heirs. Theophile and Sylvester were experienced real estate dealers who knew enough to have insisted on a deed if a legitimate conveyance had taken place. Why had the Clamorgans ended up with no land and little money, while the Papin brothers had gotten the land title? Despite his best efforts, Gray could not get from Theophile Papin what he knew his clients deserved, but he pressed on.[74]

He did his best as regards the Washington Avenue claim that Henry, Louis, and Cyprian had fought such a spirited battle over in the 1840s. In the late 1880s the National Boatmen's Savings Bank relocated from its old premises to a handsome new building on Washington Avenue. Gray insisted the bank was moving onto Clamorgan land to which it had no legal title, and he offered, on behalf of the family, to settle matters for a sizable cash payment. The bank's senior attorney was ready to talk terms, but a colleague intervened, asserting that the bank had acquired the land legally. At this late date the Clamorgans could not afford to reopen the mass of litigation from almost half a century earlier. They had come close to getting hundreds of thousands of dollars from an entity that simply wanted quiet possession of the land on which its new corporate headquarters stood, but close was not good enough.[75]

Around the time he tackled the Boatmen's Savings Bank, Gray approached no less an individual than President Grover Cleveland, begging him, as a matter of simple justice, to help get the Baden claim confirmed. The White House passed the matter on to Attorney General Augustus H. Garland, who referred it to Thomas P. Bashaw, the district attorney for the eastern district of Missouri. When Gray heard nothing further he contacted Bashaw, who told him Garland's actions had caused much alarm among those who held the land. He professed not to know why the matter had been dropped, and promised to investigate. Gray subsequently discovered that Bashaw was himself aligned with the adverse claimants and was not about to do anything for the Clamorgans.[76] It was after Gray's failure that George C. Worth stepped in, complicating the situation even further. Following that debacle, the Clamorgans handed the whole business of the claims back to Gray. He might not be a lawyer, but Gray was tenacious, and that was a quality the Clamorgans valued, because it was one they shared.

Year after year the issue of the Clamorgan claims dragged on, with Gray trying first one tactic and then another. On his clients' behalf he eventually enlisted the aid of Congressman Richard Bartholdt, who represented the district that included St. Louis. In June 1906, Bartholdt presented a petition from Gray to the House of Representatives. Gray and the Clamorgans must have spent months assembling the petition itself and all the supporting documentation. In the petition, Gray summarized the history of the various concessions to Jacques Clamorgan. The lands had been granted him by the Spanish Crown in lieu of money for services rendered. The federal government had done very badly by his heirs, in some instances confirming titles to whoever requested confirmation, and then refusing to backtrack when it emerged that those people were not the rightful heirs. In answer to an inquiry from Gray, the Government Land Office had reported that it had about twenty Clamorgan claims on file, but it could not spare a clerk to go through them all. His clients were poor people who could not pay for it to be done on their behalf. Could Congress take action to see that justice delayed was not justice denied?[77]

Gray's petition was referred to the Committee on Private Land Claims, and the Clamorgans waited with baited breath. Would they finally get their inheritance? When the matter came up early in 1907, the subcommittee on the Clamorgan claims submitted two reports. Martin Luther Smyser of Ohio voiced the opinion of the majority that the state and federal statutes of limitations precluded any further action. The heirs had "slept upon their rights." Moreover, most of the claims had been taken to court, and in only two instances had the plaintiffs been victorious.[78] However, in an all too rare bipartisan move, Republican Marion E. Rhodes of Missouri and his Democratic colleague Robert M. Wallace of Arkansas produced a minority report that heartened Gray and the heirs.[79]

Rhodes explained that he lived in a part of southwestern Missouri where some of the disputed lands were located. He had investigated and was satisfied that the Clamorgan claims were valid. Nothing in the Treaty of Paris transferring the vast Louisiana Territory from France to the United States had given the government the right to deprive individuals of their lands, and yet Jacques Clamorgan's property had effectively been stolen from him and his heirs. Various individuals had appropriated great swaths of Clamorgan real estate. They had perfected their titles under the federal homestead laws and under Missouri state law, while the heirs were barred from getting *their* titles confirmed. A rider in the 1824 bill authorizing other claimants of Spanish and French lands to go to court had prevented *them* from getting a hearing on the vast St. Charles grant, and this represented a major part of their inheritance, but there were other titles still unresolved. Rhodes and Wallace offered a bill that validated the Clamorgans' title to the Meramec claim, since it had never been ruled against in any court of law and had actually been confirmed by the U.S. Land Office. The family should get that even if they got nothing else.

This did not sit well with the other members of the subcommittee. They regarded it as a gross injustice to people who had acquired the land legitimately and would now have to go to court to validate their titles. Rhodes explained that he and his colleague hoped it would not come to a court fight. What they really wanted was to pressure the Government Land Office to look into the Clamorgan claims and compensate the heirs for all those that could be proven. The people who held the land could remain in quiet possession of it, while the Clamorgans received a substantial payout from the government. Rhodes got nowhere with this. The prevailing opinion was that too much time had elapsed and the matter should simply be left alone.[80]

The heirs—Amanda and her children in St. Louis; her stepson, Louis P. and his children; Dr. Morgan in faraway New York City; and Cyprian's daughter—were understandably disappointed. However, accustomed to fighting, they would not back down now. They were heartened that Gray had recruited Congressman Bartholdt to their cause. They needed a friend in Washington.

On June 2, 1910, another round of committee hearings got under way. Bartholdt opened the proceedings, describing what he regarded as the nation's breach of faith in regards to Jacques Clamorgan. As a result, "his heirs are not now in possession of one foot of [his] land." Bartholdt talked about the rider in the 1824 act regarding the St. Charles grant. Alexander Gray had discovered that "a number of interested parties" had gone to Washington to see that such a rider was introduced. He himself had searched the records and found that it had been "railroaded through in the wee hours of the morning." It reeked of double-dealing.[81]

Ex-congressman Rhodes was on hand to make a statement. He explained that he was appearing at the request of Mr. Gray, who had taken up the Clamorgans' case because of his faith in the justice of it. Did Rhodes know the heirs? Yes, he knew a good many of them. As for their claims, some had been confirmed to other people, but not all of them had been, and he reeled off a list. He conceded that there had been a trial in the Missouri Supreme Court regarding one of the claims, but the fundamental rights to the claims in toto had never been tried since 1824. He hoped the heirs would not have to go to court and that the federal government would compensate them, since it was the government that had given away the bulk of their land.[82]

Not surprisingly, the matter went no further, and once more the Clamorgans' hopes were dashed. With the help of Alexander Gray, now in his eighties and almost as obsessed with the claims as the Clamorgans themselves, Bartholdt did his best to keep the matter alive.[83] In 1915 he introduced another bill, only to see it referred to the Committee on Claims, which buried it. He might have tried again, but he had his own problems. He had been born in Germany, and the virulent anti-German sentiment that prevailed in the United States even before the nation entered the conflict in Europe prompted him not to seek reelection.[84] In 1916 another congressman from Missouri, Jacob E. Meeker, introduced a private bill. Nothing came of it, and with the nation on the brink of war, it was hardly a propitious time to call for yet another round of hearings on what many legislators regarded as ancient history. Meeker did not give up, however, and as peace returned he was preparing for another attempt to get the claims aired when he was felled in the influenza pandemic, and the Clamorgans lost yet another ally. Before his death, however, Meeker had managed to start things moving, and as late as 1919, bills for the relief of the Clamorgan heirs were still floating around in congressional committee rooms.[85] Nothing could move matters forward, though. Jacques Clamorgan had been dead for a century, and his claims were "old business." His descendants finally had to face facts: they must live on what they had, not what they had so fervently hoped to have.

Of all the heirs, Henry Clamorgan, Jr., alias Dr. Fordé Morgan, was the least in need financially, although he would hardly have turned up his nose at millions of dollars in restitution if the federal government had finally decided to do right by his family. In 1910, Henry and Harriet were living in Manhattan and doing very well. According to the census taker, Henry was a physician with his own office.[86] Actually, although he did spend some time in private practice, he had a long-standing relationship with the Charles H. Phillips pharmaceutical company, and at some point he began working for the company full time, interviewing doctors and dentists, visiting hospitals and pharmacies, and demonstrating the company's products. He was especially zealous in promoting Milk of Magnesia. At one point in the 1920s the Phillips Company featured him as its resident expert in an advertising campaign for its new and improved Milk of Magnesia toothpaste. When Phillips was bought by Sterling Products, Henry stayed on as the medical director. Today, in fact, company literature describes the important role Dr. Fordé Morgan played in Sterling's early growth.[87]

Before her marriage Harriet had traveled extensively as she established her stage career. Now that she had opted to craft plays instead of appear in them, she continued to travel in the United States and overseas, and Henry sometimes accompanied her.[88] In the summer of 1914, for instance, they crossed the Atlantic to see one of Harriet's plays produced on the London stage. The outbreak of hostilities almost trapped them in Europe, and they hurried back to New York via Canada on one of the first available ships. The fate of the *Lusitania*—sunk by a German U-boat with heavy loss of life—was enough to make any American think long and hard about an ocean voyage during the war years. After the armistice, though, venturing to sea on a luxury liner became once more a comfortable and elegant way to see the world. The Morgans traveled together for vacations, and in his professional capacity, Henry sailed to various ports in the Caribbean and Central America.[89] He and Harriet lived well.

Back in St. Louis Henry's mother juggled her real estate and continued pledging it to secure loans. Rental income from her properties kept Amanda afloat financially, and although she did sell a piece here and a piece there, she kept her own home and what she considered the most valuable of her rental properties, 3821 Iowa Avenue. The neighborhood was changing in some respects. Amanda can hardly have been pleased when one of the properties she had sold on Chippewa, the one right next to her own home, became a pool hall and saloon. Still, she made the best of the situation. She never sold up and moved. She had friends in the area. She had her tenants to oversee and her rents to collect. This was where she belonged.[90]

Amanda shared her home with Tom and his family. Tom Morgan continued working as a salesman.[91] For the first two decades of their married life he and Belle were childless, but on September 21, 1918, when Tom was fifty and Belle forty, their son, Thomas Burke Morgan, Jr., was born.[92] Growing up, the boy was surrounded by older relatives. After Belle and Tom wed, various members of her family had moved to St. Louis. Young Thomas never knew his maternal grandmother, Rebecca Travis Garrissine, for she died almost a decade before he was born, but his grandfather John Garrissine spent his last days in the Morgan household. Belle's younger brother, John Jr., lived with her and Tom until he married and moved out.[93] Two of Belle's sisters, Lucy and Adelaide, both of whom were widowed young, took refuge with Belle and Tom at different times. And of course Tom Jr. would have known his grandmother Amanda and one of his Morgan aunts, Lettie.[94]

Josephine was the only one of Amanda's daughters who married. John Court Kendal was born in Lancashire, but when he was in his early twenties he forsook England for the United States. For some years he bounced around from state to state. When he registered for the draft, for instance, he was working as a hired hand on a farm in Texas.[95] How and where the English drifter met Josephine is a mystery, but meet they did. They married in 1919, when she was forty-one and he was twenty-nine. Their only child, Sarah Amanda, was born in Missouri, most likely in St. Louis, on January 16, 1920. Soon after her birth the Kendals relocated to Los Angeles.[96]

Clara had tried in many ways over the years to assert her independence. Whether on Chippewa Street with her mother or elsewhere in the city in lodgings, she had earned her living by giving piano lessons. By 1920 she had given in to the same desire to travel that had afflicted both of her brothers, leaving St. Louis and moving to the community of Peoria, Arizona, where she lived alone, supporting herself as she had done for many years by teaching music.[97] When her health began to fail—she was battling chronic kidney disease—she turned not to her mother and brother back in St. Louis but to her sister in California. Clara died in Methodist Hospital in Los Angeles on July 7, 1923, and Josephine took care of the formalities. When she registered the death she named Clara's parents as Henry Morgan and Amanda Woodside, and gave her sister's occupation simply as "at home." She answered the question of race with "white." Josephine confused Clara's birth year with Lettie's: she stated that Clara had been born in 1865, and hence was fifty-eight, when she was in fact sixty-three. Josephine did not arrange for Clara to be taken back home for burial at Calvary. Instead she had her interred in Woodlawn Cemetery in Santa Monica.[98]

Difficulties arose over Clara's estate. She had not written a will, she had died in California, and such property interests as she had were in St. Louis. Attorney Albert E. Hausman applied to the St. Louis Probate Court to be appointed administrator. He listed as Clara's survivors her mother, two sisters, two brothers, her niece (although not her nephew), and one Tillie Louise Lang of Los Angeles, whom he identified as sole devisee. Clara's only asset was a piece of unimproved land on the outskirts of St. Louis, and Hausman requested permission to sell it for the benefit of her creditors, Leonhard and Johanna Herdt. Judging by the various legal and financial maneuverings, the Herdts had sold the real estate to Clara at some point and she had never paid them for it. They wanted it back and hired Hausman to get it for them.[99] Much about the matter of Clara's estate is unclear. Who was Tillie Lang? Had she befriended Clara or loaned her money?[100] Did Josephine get nothing when she had taken care of Clara in her last days and presumably paid for her funeral? Did Clara's family in St. Louis not contest Hausman's appointment as administrator? And what had Clara intended to do with the land she had acquired from the Herdts? In the end, the answers to those questions mattered very little to her family, at least in material terms. They got nothing from her estate because she had left nothing for them to inherit.

A little more than two months after the settlement of Clara's estate, Amanda began putting her own affairs in order. On August 17, 1925, she made (or perhaps revised) her will. Her one remaining piece of rental property was to pass jointly to Josephine, Lettie, and Henry. Thomas was to have the Chippewa Street property. Amanda had already arranged this by having a deed of transfer drawn up, with Belle's father acting as intermediary.[101]

Amanda was eighty-seven when she died in the early hours of January 31, 1927, in the home she and Henry had built. Thomas framed the brief death notice for the *Post-Dispatch*. It listed Amanda's four surviving children, Thomas himself, Josephine, Henry, and Lettie, and referred to the "late" Clara. Nothing was said of Peter, who had died before Thomas was born, or Oliver, who was probably only a hazy memory. On the death certificate Thomas was creative when it came to Amanda's name and background. Amanda "Cla Morgan" was, of course, white. He gave her place of birth as Belleville, Illinois. Her father was one Mr. Woodside, whose origins were unknown. In the space on the form for the name of the mother of the deceased, Thomas wrote "unknown," although he surely must have met Lucinda Vandine, since he was in his forties when his grandmother died.[102]

Amanda had outlived both of her sisters, but her half-brother and half-sister may well have attended her funeral, since they were both living in St. Louis and were presumably in contact with Amanda and her children. After her husband's death, Sophia Vandine Booth had moved in with one of her daughters. Although she might not have been especially close to Amanda toward the end of her life, she had shared a home with her at one point, and for a few years at least the Booths and the Clamorgans had lived in the same neighborhood.[103] Charles may have seen more of Amanda and her children. He had married much later than Sophia, and while her family had moved about the city, he and his wife and daughter had lived just a block or two away from Amanda for several decades. In financial terms Charles had not done as well as Sophia or, for that matter, Amanda. Nevertheless, he had made enough to support himself and his family. Like Sophia, Charles had been widowed, and like her he had moved in with his daughter.[104] Charles and Sophia died within months of each other in 1929. Their children were much younger than Amanda's, but even so they had had the opportunity to meet their grandmother, who lived until 1912. Charles's daughter, Mary Grace, insisted "Lucinda Woodworth" had been Dutch, while Sophia's daughter denied all knowledge of her grandparents.[105]

Amanda had named Henry to be her executor, but he was happy to let Thomas act in his stead. There were various payments to be made, the most significant being for a private nurse and the cost of the funeral. Since the Chippewa Street property had already been made over to Thomas, it did not appear on the inventory. The Iowa Avenue rooming house was appraised at $3,200. Independently wealthy, Henry did not need to push for it to be sold, but the money from its eventual sale no doubt came in handy for Lettie and Josephine.[106]

Lettie, the most elusive of all of Amanda's children, got her inheritance and remained in the only home she had ever really known. For whatever reason, poor Lettie never seems to have impressed herself as having much of a personality, even within her own family circle. She faded into the background to such an extent that when she died in 1934 her brother confused her birthdate with Clara's. Perhaps she had seemed older than the more energetic and at times more outspoken and more forceful Clara.[107]

In the early 1920s, Dr. Fordé Morgan and his wife left Manhattan for an even more luxurious home (complete with live-in housekeeper) in the Bronx.[108] Harriet continued writing, and Henry kept working for Phillips, and then its successor, Sterling Products, as the company's chief pharmacist. Although raised a Catholic, he left the fold and became an Episcopalian. He was also attracted to Freemasonry, rising to the rank of Master of Prince of Orange Lodge, No. 16. When he died on October 8, 1938, at age seventy-one, he left the bulk of his estate to Harriet, but his will contained generous bequests to his niece and nephew. Harriet outlived Henry by eleven years. As befitted someone who had made her mark on the stage and whose plays were still being performed, she rated a longer obituary in the *New York Times* than he had.[109]

Thomas Burke Morgan died at age seventy-two on June 23, 1940.[110] He left no will. Presumably he had seen no need to write one, since everything would automatically pass to his widow and son. Soon after Thomas's death, Belle sold the last piece of Clamorgan real estate in St. Louis and she and Thomas Jr., together with her sister Adelaide Weisbrod, relocated to California. Belle died in 1959; Adelaide outlived her by five years.[111] Thomas Jr. had a lifelong love affair with cars. Back in St. Louis he had been a driver and had worked at a service station. The legacies from his parents and his uncle gave him the capital to open a tire dealership. He married, had at least one child, and died in Riverside County on March 14, 1993, at the age of seventy-four.[112]

After their move to Southern California, Belle and Thomas Jr. may have seen something of the Kendals.[113] John Kendal worked a variety of jobs in the family's early years in Los Angeles, but eventually he found a position as a foreman for the water and power department in Los Angeles. After his death in 1948, Josephine remained in Los Angeles, dying there at the age of eighty on January 10, 1959. Like the rest of the family, she had long since become white. And there was no question about the racial identity of her daughter.[114]

Henry Clamorgan's second family had fought the good fight as far as the family's material inheritance was concerned. They had waged war, as he had done, but ultimately they had been defeated. They never saw a penny of Jacques Clamorgan's multimillion-dollar estate. But there was a battle they did win, and it, too, centered on their inheritance. If Jacques had left them his land claims, Susanne had left them her racial status. While they embraced the one legacy, the other they rejected, knowing all too well the consequences of being black in a society that privileged whiteness in innumerable ways. Henry's second family shunned that part of their inheritance until the knowledge of it was lost. His grandchildren probably never knew the complexity of the Clamorgans' racial legacy. For Henry's first family, though, it was a subtly different story.

10

"Well Known in Negro Circles"

LTHOUGH HE WILLINGLY ASSUMED the burden of settling his father's estate and was on civil (if not exactly friendly) terms with his stepmother and her children, Louis P. Clamorgan, Henry's only surviving child from his first marriage, was more a Mordecai than a Clamorgan. This was hardly surprising. At just three years old, he had gone to live with Mary Mordecai, his mother's sister, and her husband, Samuel. His father did not marry again until Louis was seven, by which time he had become fully integrated into the Mordecai household. He probably knew little of his siblings, two of whom died before he was even born. Elder brother Henry Jacques might have made an impression—Louis was two when Henry died—but his loss and the loss of a baby sister were likely eclipsed for Louis by the far more traumatic loss of his mother.[1]

Mary and Samuel Mordecai were in no hurry to hand Louis back to his father in 1859 when Henry married again, and Amanda Woodside, only nineteen when she wed Henry, might not have been eager to take on a stepson. Louis stayed where he was. He was in close enough contact with Henry and Amanda in the years that followed to know he had a brood of half-brothers and -sisters, but he considered the Mor-

LOUIS P. CLAMORGAN'S FAMILY

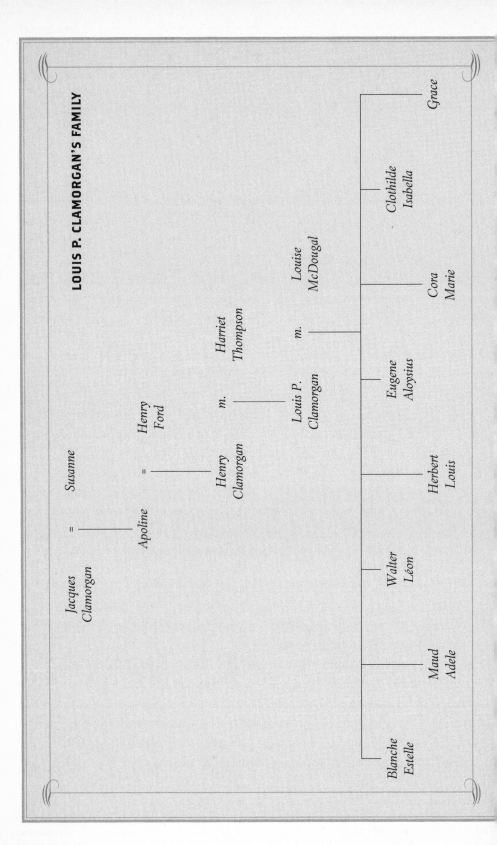

LOUISE McDOUGAL CLAMORGAN AND HER FAMILY

Andrew Tate m. Adele Livingston   Thomas McDougal = Hannah

Margaret m.   Harrison   Rachel m. Henry Blair

Adele m. William T. Fizer   Louise m. Louis P. Clamorgan

Harrison   Eugene   Minnie   Colota

decai daughters his "real" siblings and their parents his parents. As for Mary and Samuel, the informal adoption of their nephew helped them deal with their own grief. In four years they had buried a daughter and all three of their sons.[2]

When Louis went to live with the Mordecais in 1855, he immediately acquired an older sister and a younger one. Julia Augustina, the Mordecais' firstborn, was eleven.[3] Emilie would have come next, followed by Harry, William, and Samuel Jr. As it was, Louis's presence went some way toward filling the aching void left by their deaths. Virginia, Samuel and Mary's only other surviving child, was a year younger than Louis. He was firmly entrenched as a member of the family when the other Mordecai children—Harriet, Mary Blanche (who died in infancy), Mabel, and Edith—came along.[4]

Louis grew up in a household in which education mattered. Samuel Mordecai had money—the result of his labors as a riverboat steward and, if one is to believe Louis's uncle Cyprian, his luck and skill as a gambler. Samuel and Mary used some of that money to have Julia schooled in England. The risks involved in sending her so far away at such a tender age were more than compensated for by the knowledge that in England she would not be denied an education on account of her race.[5]

Julia was not the only one of the Mordecai daughters to receive a decidedly superior education. As an adult, Edith was a talented musician, having made good use of the early training her parents arranged for her to receive. She also spoke German "with the fluency of a Berliner."[6] If they did not marry young, the Mordecai daughters became teachers. Louis Clamorgan benefited from the emphasis his adoptive family placed on sound schooling and self-improvement. He attended parochial school (probably the school attached to St. Vincent de Paul, where the Mordecais worshipped for many years) and was then enrolled at the Christian Brothers College. The church authorities knew he was of African descent, but his light skin and his own and his family's Catholic faith carried the day. No objections were made to his presence, and he completed his education without incident, as in fact did other youngsters from the city's old established free community of color.[7]

When the Civil War began, Louis was nine, far too young for military service, but old enough to be aware of the conflict and of the deep divisions within St. Louis itself. There were profound changes in the city as thousands of soldiers poured in and took possession of Jefferson Barracks. With river traffic severely disrupted, Samuel Mordecai stayed closer to home. But if the steamboats were not calling at St. Louis as regularly as they had before the war, there were plenty of new arrivals, civilian and military, in need of the services of a good barber. And doubtless Mordecai, the inveterate gambler, had ample opportunity to turn a profit from his skill as a poker player.

The wartime influx into St. Louis included significant numbers of men and women of color, some fleeing slavery and others from the ranks of the freeborn in search of fresh opportunities. Two of the newcomers were the McLeod brothers, Donald and Murdoch. If their names are any indication, they were of Scottish as well as African descent. The McLeods were enterprising young men, willing to turn their hand to everything from barbering to operating a lottery office.[8] Not long after his arrival, Donald McLeod began courting Julia Mordecai. Her parents approved of the match, even giving the couple a valuable piece of real estate to help them get established. Julia and Donald were married in 1863 or early 1864. Their eldest child, a boy, died young, but their second child, Mary, survived. In the summer of 1869, Julia and Donald probably assumed they were about to become parents again, but in reality Julia was suffering from ascites, a dangerous accumulation of fluid in the abdomen. The medical attention she received did little to help. She was just twenty-five when she died.[9] Her grief-stricken parents took in their baby granddaughter, just as they had done their nephew when *his* mother died. Although the family remained on good terms with Donald McLeod, even after he married again, Mary did not go back to live with him until she was an adult. Like her aunts, she became a teacher—and yet another member of Louis P. Clamorgan's network of kinfolk. Louis also maintained a friendship with her father. To all intents and purposes, the two were brothers-in-law and not merely cousins by marriage, for Julia had been as close to Louis as a sister.[10]

Louis did not follow his father and uncle into the "tonsorial profession."
In the 1870 census he was listed as a cashier, not a barber. He had
moved out of the Mordecai home and into a boardinghouse in the Sixth
Ward with some two dozen other single men as he began his working
life. By 1873 he had returned to live with his aunt and uncle and had
been hired as a bookkeeper by the ill-fated Freedman's Savings and
Trust Company, the bank established by act of Congress in 1865 to
encourage thrift among the nation's four million ex-slaves. One of the
highly placed men of color who served on the board of the St. Louis
branch was none other than James P. Thomas, someone Louis had known
from infancy.[11]

When the 1880 census was taken, Louis was still living with the
Mordecais. The household was actually enumerated twice. The details
were the same except for one glaring difference: the first official categorized the Mordecais and their kinfolk, Louis among them, as mulattoes, and the second judged the same set of individuals to be white.
Louis's aunt and one of his cousins kept house, while Virginia and Mabel worked as teachers, and Edith and young Mary McLeod attended
school. Mattie Yeizer, a niece of Samuel's from Kentucky, boarded with
the family and earned her keep as a seamstress. As for Louis, he was a
clerk. The Freedman's Bank had collapsed amid scandal in 1874, but
by then he had been hired to work in the Collector's Department at
the St. Louis Courthouse.[12]

With a reasonably secure job and a stable home, Louis began to contemplate marriage. On October 2, 1882, now thirty years old, he wed
eighteen-year-old Louise McDougal. It was a wedding that attracted
the attention of the *St. Louis Globe-Democrat* for a couple of reasons.
First, it took place in a private home. The couple was to have been married at the Church of St. Thomas of Aquin, but it was still under construction, and the archbishop of the diocese issued a special dispensation
to the priest to conduct the ceremony in the Mordecai home. Second,
the wedding gave the newspaper's white readers a glimpse into "colored
society." The guest list included such prominent members of the African American community as the well-to-do riverman Alfred White,

Henry Clamorgan's onetime business partner Barriteer Hickman, and Louis's friend and patron James P. Thomas, and the array of gifts was suitably expensive, in keeping with the company. Samuel and Mary Mordecai hosted the event. However, there was no mention of the groom's father and stepmother even being present.[13]

After the wedding, Louis moved his young bride into the Mordecai home, and there the couple remained until shortly before the birth of their first child. Henry Clamorgan, Sr., never lived to see his grandchild. He died on March 9, 1883, and Blanche Estelle was born almost exactly six months later.[14] The only "grandparents" she and her younger siblings knew as they grew up were Mary and Samuel Mordecai.

In an interview she gave when she and Louis had been married almost thirty years, Louise McDougal Clamorgan claimed she had no knowledge of her husband's African ancestry. She had always believed him to be of Spanish descent. She lied out of necessity. She could hardly have avoided knowing about Louis's background, for it closely resembled her own. The casual white observer might have judged Louise to be of unmixed European descent. Indeed, she was described by a reporter for the *St. Louis Republic* as being "so nearly white that no one would suspect there is negro blood in her veins." But the same reporter noted that "She is a member of the McDougal family, well known in negro circles."[15] Louise's family, like her husband's, was rooted in the free community of color of the Upper South.

Louis P. Clamorgan never knew his grandparents. Apoline had died when his father was a child, and Henry Ford, the mysterious Irishman who had been one of Apoline's lovers and had fathered Henry Clamorgan, had long since disappeared. Louise McDougal, on the other hand, could trace her lineage back several generations. She had been born in 1864 in Nashville, Tennessee, the bustling river town where her mother's parents had lived for decades. It was in Nashville, on October 21, 1833, that Andrew Tate, a free black riverman, twenty-four years old and a native of Tennessee, had wed nineteen-year-old Adele Livingston.[16] Their eldest child, Margaret, was Louise's mother.

The backgrounds of Andrew Tate and Adele Livingston are obscure, but there are a few clues as to their origins. Adele was born in Georgia in 1814.[17] Whether slave-born or freeborn, she was legally free by the time her first child was born. In Tennessee, as elsewhere, children followed the condition of their mother, and no question was ever raised about the status of Margaret Tate and her siblings. As for Andrew, it is possible he was of Scottish as well as African descent. "Tate" is a common Scottish name, and Andrew is Scotland's patron saint. The names that Andrew Tate chose for a couple of his children reflect Scottish roots. Margaret was a Scottish queen, and a saint into the bargain. The name Caledonia, which the Tates bestowed on another of their daughters, speaks for itself. Regardless of whether or not Andrew had Scottish roots, all that mattered to most of Nashville's white residents, and indeed most whites outside Nashville, was that he and his family were people of color.

By 1850, Adele and Andrew had six children, ranging in age from fifteen-year-old Margaret to seven-month-old Priscilla. Andrew worked at various jobs, but his principal employment was as a steward on the various steamboats that called at Nashville. Admittedly this meant he was often away for weeks at a time, but kickbacks from the suppliers he patronized as he shopped for luxuries to please the palates of his wealthy passengers, and the tips those passengers gave him, meant he earned a good income. He did well enough that by 1850 he had acquired a home of his own valued at a thousand dollars. A decade later he had increased his property holdings to four thousand dollars.[18]

The Tates needed a decent income, for by 1860 there were more mouths to feed, but the burden of three additional children had been offset by the fact that Franklin, the couple's eldest son, had joined his father on the river, and Margaret had brought her new husband, another African American riverman, to live with the family and contribute his earnings to the maintenance of the household.[19]

The Tates' son-in-law was Harrison McDougal. He and Margaret had been married in Nashville on November 21, 1859. She was twenty-one at the time of their wedding, and he was several years older.[20] Harrison's mother, Hannah, was a slave. His father may well have been the same Thomas McDougal, a white planter from Montgomery County, Tennessee, who had left Harrison and his sister, Rachel, their freedom when he died in 1850. Not only had Thomas McDougal freed the pair, but he had bequeathed them five hundred dollars apiece.[21] Six years before Harrison's marriage, Rachel had made a most advantageous match. Like Harrison and Rachel McDougal, Henry Blair had been born into slavery and emancipated upon his master's death. Soon after their wedding, Henry and Rachel made their way to Pin Oak, a settlement of freed slaves near Edwardsville, Illinois, across the river from St. Louis. There, by a combination of hard work and good fortune, they became substantial landowners. In time the Blairs would play an important role in the lives of Harrison and Margaret McDougal's children, including Louise, Louis P. Clamorgan's wife.[22]

The Civil War brought dramatic changes to Nashville, as it did to so many communities. Tennessee seceded, but Nashville itself was soon taken by Union forces and martial law was imposed as the work of reconstruction commenced. Among the city's African American residents the Union victory ignited the hope that their lives would be changed for the better. Leading the charge for sweeping social and political reforms was Andrew Tate. In January 1865, with the collapse of the Confederacy all but assured, he mobilized more than fifty other African American men to petition the state's Union Convention. They wanted passage of the Thirteenth Amendment to "cut up by the roots the system of slavery." They wanted the right to vote, a right that, as they reminded the delegates, Tennessee's free men of color had enjoyed until 1835. They also wanted their testimony ruled admissible in court. Black soldiers had fought and died for the Union cause, some of them in repelling the Confederate assault on Nashville just a few months earlier. Black civilians had put their lives on the line to help white Union soldiers fleeing from Confederate prisons. "Will you declare in your revised constitution that a pardoned traitor may appear in court and his testimony be heard, but that no colored loyalist shall be believed even upon oath?" Andrew Tate and his fellow petitioners asked.[23] Whether Tate involved his son-in-law in his protests we do not know, but he made his own stand and insisted on his right to be heard.

As the war dragged painfully to a close, Margaret and Harrison moved out of her parents' household. Where exactly they went is not clear, but it is likely they relocated several times. Their eldest, Adele, was born in Tennessee in 1861, probably in the Tate home. Harrison Jr. was born in Illinois the following year, either while the McDougals were staying with the Blairs in Pin Oak or when they were on the farm Harrison owned in Marine, the neighboring township.[24] Louise was born in Tennessee on March 11, 1864. According to the 1870 census, two more of the McDougal children were born in Tennessee—Eugene in 1866 and Minnie in 1870—but other evidence suggests both were in fact born in St. Louis.[25]

Although he kept the land he had purchased in Illinois, by 1866, Harrison McDougal was working as a barber in St. Louis with the firm of Robert J. Wilkinson. In December of that same year he paid the not inconsiderable sum of $2,300 to the Blairs to buy a home for himself and his family. Just as the McDougals had maintained their landholdings in Illinois even though they made their home in St. Louis, the Blairs of Pin Oak had been extending their real estate investments across the Mississippi into Missouri.[26] By 1870, the McDougal family was in comfortable circumstances. Margaret had no need to work outside the home, and the couple's three eldest children were attending school. When it came to defining the McDougals with regard to race, the census taker that year had to decide in which category they belonged. They were not black, but neither were they white (although the city directories often omitted "col'd" after Harrison's name). The designation he decided fit the family was "mulatto." As his superiors in Washington had set it down in their instructions, "The word is . . . generic, and includes . . . all persons having any perceptible trace of African blood." Whatever that "trace" was, the census taker detected it in the McDougals.[27]

In the spring of 1873 tragedy struck. Margaret died of pneumonia while recovering from yet another confinement.[28] The members of Harrison and Margaret's extended family rallied around. Rachel Blair and her husband took charge of the infant Colota and Harrison Jr. Eugene and Minnie went to live with their maternal grandparents.[29] As for Adele and Louise, they stayed with their father in St. Louis.

Harrison rented out the McDougal home and moved in with friends on the same block with Adele and Louise in tow. He knew the Davises from Nashville. William B. Davis and his brother-in-law Thomas Richmond were steamboat stewards like Harrison and Andrew Tate, the elite of the old free community of color.[30] Just as she would later insist she did not know her husband was a man of color, so Louise McDougal would deny any knowledge of the background of the Davises, but back in the 1870s the need for such a denial lay far in the future.

Harrison McDougal stayed on in St. Louis for some years, boarding with the Davises and working as a barber. By 1877 he was running the barbershop at the Union Depot Hotel, on Seventh and Spruce. He was still there in 1879, but he disappeared from the city directories after that, and his establishment at the Union Depot was taken over by the Mordecais' son-in-law Donald McLeod and McLeod's partner, William H. Mosby.[31]

Two significant events, one happy and the other sad, took place in the McDougal-Blair family circle within the space of a few months. Adele McDougal began keeping company with a young man Harrison thoroughly approved of. Although he could pass as white anytime he chose, William T. Fizer was firmly rooted in the African American community. Born in Mississippi, he was a newcomer to St. Louis, but he had excellent job prospects. He had a clerkship in the Pension Office, and he was clearly ambitious. Harrison gave his blessing to the match, and on September 8, 1879, before a justice of the peace in Edwardsville, Adele and William were married.[32] The white official may not have appreciated just how much personal history William was revealing as he filled out the application for a marriage license. William had been born a slave, the son of one Maria Brown and her much older white master, John B. Fizer. In 1861, a little more than two years after William's birth, his father signed Mississippi's ordinance of secession and helped take his state out of the Union.[33] When William came of age, he went to work for the very government John B. had turned his back on, processing the pension applications of men who had fought in the war to bring Mississippi and the rest of the Confederate states back into the Union.

After their wedding, Adele and William made their home in St. Louis and they took in Adele's sister Louise. Living with them in the city, she met and eventually married Louis P. Clamorgan. Had she stayed with her father, she would probably have become the wife of one of Pin Oak's African American farmers. Soon after Adele and William married, Harrison McDougal abandoned barbering, and St. Louis, for good. On January 11, 1880, his brother-in-law died. Harrison had always been close to his sister and to the Pin Oak community. His elderly mother lived there. Colota and Harrison Jr. were there. Harrison helped Rachel and her children settle Henry Blair's estate, and then he moved in with them.[34] He sold his land in Marine and purchased a farm in Pin Oak, which he leased to a tenant, Caesar Brown. When Harrison Jr. was old enough to begin working, his father boarded him with Brown in the expectation that he, too, would become a farmer.

The census taker never caught up with Harrison Sr. in 1880, but it is intriguing to note how differently his children were classified. In St. Louis, Adele and Louise were "white," as was William Fizer, although when they married the year before, both Adele and William were identified on the marriage license as people of color. Across the river in Pin Oak, where dozens of African American families had farmed their own land for decades, and where the enumerator was well aware that affluence was not the exclusive preserve of white people, Harrison Jr. and Colota were "mulatto." And in Nashville, where Andrew Tate had spoken up so forcefully for the rights of his community and had proudly asserted his identity as a man of color, all the members of his family, including Eugene and Minnie, were set down as "black."[35] Of course, the McDougal siblings may also have differed in complexion. But equally, degrees of blackness and whiteness may have existed not so much in the individuals being classified as in the minds of those doing the classifying.

When he gave up his barbershop and made the move to Pin Oak, Harrison McDougal may have known his health was failing. He died on May 30, 1882, after what, to judge from the doctor's bills, was a protracted illness. Before he died, he did his best to put his affairs in order. He had enough property to leave each of his children a decent legacy. In addition to his farm in Pin Oak, he still owned the family home in St. Louis, and a town lot in Edwardsville. Adele did not need his land. William had secured a promotion and the couple had moved to Washington, D.C. Harrison left Adele a thousand dollars in cash. His real estate he bequeathed to his other five children, along with his personal property and his life insurance policy. The Pin Oak farm was not to be sold until the youngest, Colota, was of age, and he expressed the hope that until then his executors, Louise and Harrison Jr., would allow Caesar Brown to continue working the farm as a tenant. On the matter of guardianship, Harrison McDougal wanted Colota to remain with her aunt Rachel in Pin Oak and Minnie with the Tates in Nashville. Eugene was to be boarded with a family friend, and Harrison Jr. would stay with Caesar Brown. As for Louise, Harrison McDougal died secure in the knowledge that she would soon be married, for she was already engaged to Louis P. Clamorgan.[36]

After Louise and Louis wed, three of the McDougal siblings made their way back to St. Louis. Adele remained in Washington with her husband, and Colota stayed in Pin Oak, the only home she had ever really known. Eugene was in St. Louis by 1884. Thanks to his sister and her husband, he was soon receiving invitations to various social events organized by the city's colored aristocracy. He also found employment, and because he could "pass" with ease, his opportunities were greater than those of many young men of color. He worked as a "wrapper" in a downtown store before graduating to sales clerk for a tailoring firm. After a stint as a salesman at another business, he returned to the tailor's shop.[37] Soon after Eugene's arrival, his sister Minnie left Nashville and moved to St. Louis.[38] Harrison Jr. often came over to St. Louis from the farm in Pin Oak. Eventually he quit farming, settled in St. Louis, and was hired by the post office as a letter carrier. He boarded with Louise and Louis P. Clamorgan before finding a home of his own.[39]

The increasingly congested city of St. Louis was not the healthiest of environments. By 1893 Louise had lost her sister Minnie. Colota was now of age, though, and the surviving siblings were able to sell the family home in St. Louis.[40] Eugene's share soon came back to his brother and sisters: they were his only heirs when he died less than a year later of tuberculosis. The same individual who had been classed as black in the 1880 census was white when the authorities at St. John's Hospital reported his death. The notice in the *St. Louis Republic* said that he was mourned by many in "the fraternity of salesmen." He had been respected and well liked, and it went without saying that his acquaintances had never questioned his race. They assumed that he had been white like them.[41]

Meanwhile, Louis P. and Louise Clamorgan were busy moving from one home to another in the city and raising a family. Blanche Estelle was born in their first home on August 8, 1883, and her sister, Maud Adele, fourteen months later. By the time Walter Léon came along on April 30, 1887, the family had moved again.[42] Eventually the Clamorgans moved back into a house where the Mordecais had once lived. This was where three more of their children were born—Herbert Louis on April 10, 1889, Eugene Aloysius on April 22, 1891, and Cora Marie on September 9, 1892. When Clothilde Isabella was born in 1894, the family had moved to another house, at 3459 Missouri Avenue. It was there where their youngest child, Grace, was born on March 11, 1898.[43]

It is worth noting that Louis did not ask his stepmother or any of his half-siblings to serve as godparents to his children, although all were practicing Catholics. Back in 1868, his father and stepmother had invited him to be the godfather to their new son, Thomas. When he became a father, Louis did not return the favor. If there was no overt animosity, there was certainly no strong sense of kinship between him and his father's second family.[44]

Louis's ties were, first and foremost, with the Mordecais. He and Louise asked each of the Mordecai sisters to sponsor a child. Julia, of course, was dead by the time Louis's children were born, but he and Louise invited her husband and daughter to be godparents. Louise also turned to a member of her own family. Her brother Harrison was their son Walter's godfather.[45]

When it came to the choice of other sponsors for their children, Louis and Louise moved beyond their immediate families, but not far beyond. They approached men and women Louis (and in some cases Louise) had known for years. The ties that bound the Clamorgans to other members of the city's African American upper class were complex. They were ties forged by intermarriage, by shared faith, by business dealings, and by friendships that extended back over generations. They were labyrinthine and multilayered. Virtually everyone was a cousin of some sort. Admittedly there might have been some people they could not ask to become godparents because they were not Catholics, but the Clamorgans evidently had as their closest friends people like them: people of color who were Catholics by birth or conversion. And every one of the people they asked to sponsor a child was African American. Some were so light skinned that the census taker often classed them as white, but the Clamorgans knew their friends' histories, just as those friends knew theirs. White acquaintances they might have had, but something as personal as selecting godparents led them to look within their own circle.

Blanche's godfather, Felix Dora, was an old friend of Louis P. Clamorgan's, and had in fact been a guest at his wedding. He kept a restaurant just a few doors away from the Mordecais and was married to Theodosia Haslett, whom Louis's uncle Cyprian had celebrated as the "colored belle of St. Louis." Louis knew Felix's older brother George, who was a barber, and their mother, Nancy Lyons. The family's complex heritage—African American, white, and Native American—baffled officials, who were constantly shifting them from one racial category to another.[46]

Clothilde's godfather was Charles P. Badeau. Badeau was a barber, like so many of the Clamorgans' friends and relatives. The link between Badeau and Louis P. Clamorgan involved more than barbering, though. Charles was courting Edith Mordecai, and in a matter of months after Clothilde's baptism he joined Louis's extended family.[47]

Brothers Joseph and William Wilkinson were godfathers to Herbert and Grace. Yet again there were strong ties, not only of faith but of family and friendship, between the Clamorgans, the McDougals, and the Wilkinsons. Joseph and William's father was Robert J. Wilkinson. Harrison McDougal had worked for him when he first came to St. Louis, but this was only one link. Wilkinson's first wife was Julie Speers, Ester's great-granddaughter. When Julie died, Robert married Caroline Thompson, who was Louis's aunt, the widow of his mother's brother. In a roundabout way, Robert and Caroline's sons were Louis's cousins.[48] As for Caroline's own background, she had been born Caroline Vashon. The Vashons, a prominent African American family from Pennsylvania, with links to the free people of color of the Caribbean and the black Brahmins of Boston, added a few more complexities to the Clamorgans' dizzying array of kinship ties.[49]

Several of the women in the Clamorgans' circle were teachers. All three of the unmarried Mordecai sisters, Virginia, Harriet, and Mabel, taught school. Minnie A. Crosswhite, who boarded with the Mordecais for some years and eventually became principal of the all-black Aldridge Elementary School, was Cora Clamorgan's godmother.[50]

The Clamorgans asked yet another teacher, Carrie Helms, to act as Grace's godmother. Born Caroline Hamilton, Carrie Helms had married Louis G. Helms, a steward on the river, in 1883, when she was nearly eighteen and he was almost twice her age. Before her twenty-first birthday Carrie was widowed. She had taught before her marriage and she returned to teaching after her husband's death.[51] Carrie was also a member of the Clamorgans' network of kinfolk. Her husband's father was Gabriel Helms, and his mother was Matilda Selina Speers, another of Ester's great-granddaughters.[52]

Cora Clamorgan's godfather was James P. Thomas, heir, through his wife, Antoinette, to the Rutgers fortune. Louis knew Thomas through his partnership with Henry Clamorgan and Samuel Mordecai and his role as a director of the Freedman's Savings Bank. Louise also knew him, since her mother's family was from Thomas's hometown, and her father, uncle, and grandfather had been boat stewards, as had Thomas at one point in his remarkably varied career. And in years to come there would be yet another link when one of Louise's Pin Oak cousins, Ulysses Jefferson Blair, married Thomas's daughter, Pelagie.[53]

Louis and Louise Clamorgan were not the richest members of their community, but they were "comfortable." Over the years Louis held positions in various city departments, thanks to an influential patron. James P. Thomas had helped him get his first job. A rising white politician would get him his second. Henry Ziegenhein had had a humble enough start. The child of German immigrants, he had begun his working life as a carpenter. After a stint in the Union army, he had begun his climb through the ranks of the Republican Party, his success bolstered by his own ambition and the power of the German vote in St. Louis.

Louis P. Clamorgan had long been active in black Republican circles in the city, and at some point that involvement brought him to Ziegenhein's attention. In a modest way Louis became one of his protégés.[54] When Ziegenhein was elected city collector he found a position for Louis. As his patron moved up the ranks of city government, Louis moved up with him. Among other responsibilities, he handled the accounts of the police courts and the workhouse. In 1897, Ziegenhein became the mayor of St. Louis and he named Louis P. Clamorgan his chief page. By 1901, when Ziegenhein's term ended, Louis was a water meter inspector. After that he went to the Janitorial Department at City Hall, where he worked as a clerk. He was always carried on the city's so-called "colored list." There were positions he could never aspire to, positions reserved for white men, but thanks to the boost Ziegenhein had given him, he always had steady employment, and he was not condemned to the menial labor that was the lot of most black workingmen in St. Louis.[55]

As their family grew and their means improved, the Clamorgans moved from one home to another. The house that they occupied for the longest period of time, at 3459 Missouri Avenue, actually belonged to Louise, who had purchased it with the money she had inherited from her father (although Louis would later claim that his great-grandfather had owned the land on which it was built).[56] It was in that home that they would bring up their children, and sadly it was there that they would suffer the loss of two of their three sons. Nine-year-old Herbert died in 1898 of enteritis, and in 1902, just two days after his eleventh birthday, Eugene succumbed to heart and kidney problems.[57]

Through the 1880s and the 1890s the Clamorgans lived in the heart of St. Louis's affluent community of color. They worshipped with people like them and they socialized with people like them. Louis was an officer of a black fraternal organization and a member of a "council of the representative colored men of the City of St. Louis." He traveled to Cincinnati one year and to Philadelphia another year with his old friend Donald L. McLeod to attend the Convention of Colored Catholics.[58] The Mordecais' home was the scene of elegant, although suitably decorous, social events at which members of the African American elite from St. Louis and beyond were entertained. The Clamorgans were invited to these gatherings and to others around the city.[59] A white acquaintance who became "very neighborly" with Louise Clamorgan during those years on Missouri Avenue later recalled, "It was generally understood that the family had negro blood, for negro relatives visited them, but the white people esteemed them, and the color line was not drawn."[60]

Slowly, though, Louis and Louise began to distance themselves and their children from at least some of their old associations. In a city that had become far more rigidly segregated by race than it had been before the Civil War, the Clamorgans, like some of their most intimate friends, were only too well aware that a better life awaited them and their offspring if they could reinvent themselves as white. To become white did not mean cutting all the ties to everyone and everything they had ever known at one fell swoop. The passage of time was severing some of those ties for them. Louis's adoptive parents died within months of each other: Mary Mordecai in December 1900, and Samuel the following summer. Cousin Harriet passed away in 1906.[61] The other Mordecai kin were scattered across the city: Charles and Edith Badeau and Edith's unmarried sisters in one household, Mary McLeod and her father in another.[62] Louis's family saw very little of his stepmother and her children, and anyway most of the members of Henry Clamorgan's second family had long since changed their name to "Morgan" and passed into the white community. As for Louise's family, only her unmarried brother, Harrison, remained in St. Louis. He lived in his own home a few blocks away from the Clamorgans.[63] Colota was a member of the Blair household in Pin Oak. Adele was in Washington, D.C. The other two McDougal siblings were dead.

As late as 1900 the Clamorgans were still "colored." This was how they had answered the question about race when they registered the births of their children. This was how they were classified in the census. Louis and Louise were truthful about their origins and the origins of their respective parents. The family exuded respectability. They were homeowners, Louis reported that he was a city functionary, and five of the seven Clamorgan children (Eugene was still alive in 1900) attended school.[64]

The census taker saw an African American family, but others did not. By 1900 the move into the white community had already begun. One by one, the Clamorgan children were enrolled in parochial schools, according to their father, "with the full understanding of the authorities as to their race." From the parochial schools they moved into the white public schools, where he said they "were admitted without question." It subsequently emerged, though, that there had been bumps along the way. Blanche had been sent to Central High, a white school, but somehow her African ancestry had been discovered and she had been forced to transfer to the all-black Sumner High School.[65]

Bruised by her experiences, Blanche did what her father's stepmother and her children across town did. She jettisoned the name "Clamorgan" and opted for "Morgan." Her parents and siblings did not bother to change their name. They gambled on their appearance and on people's hazy memories. They simply let it be assumed they were white. In the summer of 1907 the Clamorgans sold their home on Missouri Avenue and purchased one in Maplewood, a neighborhood on the outskirts of St. Louis "which has long prided itself on its exclusive white residents."[66] Of course, there were those who knew Louis to be the son of the barber Henry Clamorgan, a man of color, and the descendant of Jacques Clamorgan by one of his "Negro wives." But the men Louis worked with at City Hall, the other men on the "colored list," either did not venture into his all-white section of town or else did not know or care what he claimed to be. Each day when he traveled across the city, Louis crossed an imperceptible line—the line that separated black from white. Downtown he was black, but in Maplewood his neighbors simply took it for granted that he was white. Clamorgan explained to a reporter how he viewed his racial identity: "I am of mixed Spanish and negro descent, and never represented myself as a white person. I did not think it my business to proclaim my race from the housetops, but I never made a false statement to anyone about it. I associated with negroes, and if a white man wished my acquaintance, he was welcome to it."[67]

In fact, Louis was rather disingenuous. A few of their new neighbors had asked the Clamorgans about their antecedents, and one or two had taken note of their "unusually dark complexion." Louis and his wife had an explanation. They told everyone they were descended from an aristocratic Spanish family, and they mentioned that through one of their illustrious ancestors they had a claim to a vast estate granted to that individual by the king of Spain in recognition of his valiant services.[68] "Susanne, Négresse," as Louis's great-grandmother had been described by the parish priest of St. Louis more than a century before, was conveniently forgotten, while his great-grandfather, Jacques Clamorgan, notorious in his day for both his sharp business practices and his bevy of black concubines, was transformed into a Spanish nobleman.

By the time the enumerator caught up with the family in 1910, the "colored" Clamorgans had become white, at least in the neighborhood where they lived. Their modest home in Maplewood stood on its own lot, and the garden boasted fruit trees, a lawn, and a grape arbor.[69] Of the Clamorgans' six surviving children, Maud was married and Clothilde and Grace were still in school—both at all-white institutions. The other three had entered the workforce. Walter was employed at an auto dealership, while Blanche and Cora were stenographers, an occupation reserved exclusively for white women. Unlike their father, Walter and his sisters were white downtown as well as in Maplewood.[70]

Walter was a leading member of the local athletic club, and his baseball-playing friends would gather at his home on a Sunday. As for his sisters, they were talented musicians who often organized entertainments for the other young people in the neighborhood.[71] They were also very handsome and had no shortage of suitors, all of them white. Blanche had departed from her family's Catholic faith and joined Maplewood's new (and exclusively white) Christian Science Church. She was a reader at the church, and many of the members visited her at her parents' home. All of them accepted the story of Spanish ancestry. Joseph De Witt, the son of one of the church's most prominent members, was much taken with Blanche, but he had a rival for her affections. One of Walter's friends, Charles Wass, was plucking up the courage to propose to Blanche. And then there was a third man pursuing Blanche, whom she angered by rejecting outright.[72]

Meanwhile, Cora had caught the eye of Jack B. Collins, the son of Owen L. Collins, one of the richest men in Maplewood. Jack was an acquaintance of Walter's from the athletic club. He started visiting the Clamorgan home to see his friend, and when he met his friend's sister his visits became more frequent. At first the couple studied together. Jack was trying to learn Spanish and Cora helped him with his lessons.[73]

Louis and Louise Clamorgan had seen nothing to worry them at first, but then they realized Cora and Jack were becoming more than friends. What exactly her parents told Cora depended on which newspaper account one read. According to the *Post-Dispatch*, Louis said he and his wife talked to Cora, who knew the truth about her ancestry. "We told her that a marriage between her and a white man would not be suitable or happy, and she promised us that she would not think of doing such a thing." The *Star* said Cora was not aware of her racial heritage. Louise lectured her for three hours straight and told her there were "reasons that would prevent her marrying Collins," although she never divulged what those reasons were. The next time Jack came to call he was told he could not see Cora again. And that, so Louis and Louise believed, was the end of the matter.[74]

As for Maud Clamorgan, she had already married one of her family's neighbors. Maud lived not far from her parents in a home she and her husband and their infant daughter shared with her in-laws. By an odd coincidence her husband's family rented their home from Jack Collins's father. The Clamorgans would later tell reporters that their daughter's in-laws, the Davises, had *seemed* respectable enough. There had, however, been gossip when the family arrived in Maplewood. One neighbor had observed that "they looked like negroes," and allegations that they were "passing" started flying about. The newcomers promptly squelched those rumors, threatening legal action and presenting "proof" of their Native American descent. And "Indian" descent, in the context of white St. Louis society in the early years of the twentieth century, was acceptable. As the city celebrated the centenary of the Lewis and Clark expedition, Native American descent even had a tinge of romance. "Black" or "Negro" descent most definitely did not. If they were "Indians," the Davises were welcome in Maplewood. When Louis Davis had begun courting Maud, Louis and Louise Clamorgan insisted they saw no reason to object.[75]

Maud and Louis Davis's first child, a daughter, was born in Febru-

ary 1910. One glance was enough to make her grandparents fear for
her future and for their own. Little Laura Jane was a healthy baby, but
her "distinctive" appearance, as the newspapers delicately phrased it,
threatened her family's tenuous grasp on whiteness. The Clamorgans
had gambled on the appearance of whiteness when it came to the choice
of schools for their children, employment, and the purchase of a home
in a "good" neighborhood. They had also gambled when it came to marriage. The union of the light-skinned Louis P. Clamorgan and the equally
light-skinned Louise McDougal had produced children who could
easily "pass." What they had not factored in when they gave their consent to Maud's marriage was the unpredictability of genetics. Louis
Clamorgan might not have realized the Davises were "passing," but
Louise undoubtedly did, for this was the very same Davis family with
whom she and her father and sister had boarded so many years before.
The birth of little Laura Jane Clamorgan Davis would not only jeopar-
dize the future of the Clamorgans and the Davises but would force an
entire community to question how, where, and even if lines of race
could be drawn. If these two families had crossed the racial divide, how
many other "white" families were keeping secret certain crucial facts
about their own racial identity?[76]

11

Defining Whiteness

"NEGRO BLOOD, Shown by Birth, Shatters Two County Homes," screamed the front-page headline in the *St. Louis Republic* on the morning of June 9, 1911. Within hours the story had reached Kansas City. Throughout the day telegraph wires buzzed with the tale of forbidden love and long-buried secrets. On June 10, in far-off New Jersey, the *Trenton Evening Times* picked up the report from Missouri. It garbled some of the details, but the outline was there, and the Clamorgan name featured prominently. In neighboring Pennsylvania the *Wilkes-Barre Leader-Times* had the story the same day. By June 15 it had made its way to the *Washington Post*. By July 4, it was in the *Los Angeles Times*. As the summer wore on, newspapers across the nation carried the tale of the "colored" family that had grasped at whiteness, only to have the truth revealed by the birth of a black baby.[1]

Contrary to what might have been expected, the scandal that rocked St. Louis in 1911 was only indirectly about Laura Jane Clamorgan Davis and her parents. Maud and Louis Davis and their daughter were actors in the drama, but they were relegated to the supporting cast. The leading players were another couple, their baby, and the young man's father. Despite the best efforts of her parents to separate her from Jack

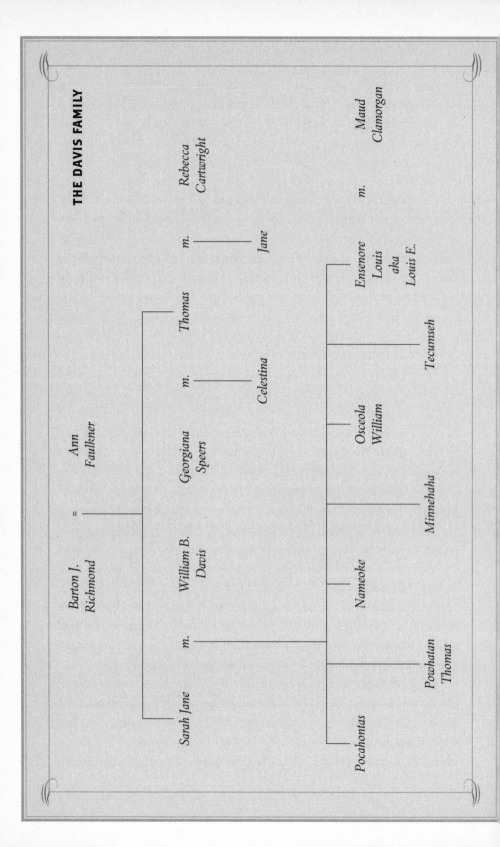

THE DAVIS FAMILY

Barton J. Richmond = Ann Faulkner

Sarah Jane   m.   William B. Davis   Georgiana Speers   m.   Thomas   m.   Rebecca Cartwright

Celestina   Jane

Pocahontas   Nameoke   Minnehaha   Osceola William   Ensenore Louis aka Louis E.   m.   Maud Clamorgan

Powhatan Thomas   Tecumseh

Collins, Cora Clamorgan had eloped with him. Their union had been blessed with a daughter who bore no resemblance to her dark-skinned cousin. Depending on one's point of view, Jack's father, Owen L. Collins, was either a heartless fiend intent on destroying the happiness of his son and daughter-in-law or a tragic figure whose only wish was to shield his family from "contamination." As for the roles the Clamorgans and the Davises played, their level of complicity in the unfolding drama was a matter of opinion. They were either luckless pawns caught up in events beyond their control or abettors whose crime of "passing" deserved to be exposed for all to see. Guilt or innocence, sympathy or shame, depended on one's perspective. Somewhere in the welter of claims and counterclaims lay the truth. Teasing it out is no easy matter. Still, one has to start the winnowing process with one of the principal players, and Owen L. Collins, either the villain of the piece or a heartbroken father, is as good a choice as any.

Originally from Louisiana (a state where race was defined rather more rigidly than in Missouri), Collins had come to St. Louis in the mid-1880s. He had worked hard to establish himself as an engineer, and his efforts had paid off. By 1889 he was the superintendent of the Pond Engineering Company. After a brief sojourn in Seattle, Owen and his wife, St. Louis native Mary Burrell, and their young family returned to St. Louis and moved into a comfortable home in the exclusive neighborhood of Maplewood.[2]

By the early 1900s, Collins had money and connections. Following a stint as the city's chief engineer, he had started his own engineering company. As each of his five sons left school, he used his extensive network of business contacts to place them in good jobs. In 1910, Owen and Mary's fourth son, John Berwick Collins, who generally went by the name of Jack, was working as construction superintendent of the Ball Engine Company.[3] Most of his free time was spent at the Clamorgan home until Cora's parents told him his visits must cease.

The Collinses expected their sons to establish themselves professionally before settling down with the daughters of other successful businessmen. In December 1910, though, Owen and Mary learned that nineteen-year-old Jack had his own ideas about matrimony. He had run off to the town of Hermann, in neighboring Gasconade County, with eighteen-year-old Cora Clamorgan, a young woman they hardly knew. The pair had been married by a justice of the peace, and Owen and Mary could expect to become grandparents in the spring. The news was broken not by Jack himself but by his mother-in-law. Louise Clamorgan called on Mary Collins and told her just how matters stood.[4]

At this point the Collinses had no suspicions about Cora's ancestry, although they did have some misgivings about the youth of the bride and groom and the relatively humble status of Cora's parents. Ironically, Owen Collins and Louis P. Clamorgan had worked just floors away from each other at City Hall in the 1890s. Had Owen ever left his office and visited the Collector's Department, he would have met Louis. He might even have uncovered the Clamorgan family's secret, for Louis was carried on the city payroll as a man of color.[5] When the Collinses and the Clamorgans did eventually meet, though, it was not downtown but in Maplewood, where the Clamorgans were "white." Louis and Louise assured Owen and Mary Collins that they had done all they could to prevent a marriage between Cora and Jack, only to have the young people take matters into their own hands. In an interview some months later, Louis P. Clamorgan observed, "That was all we thought [it] worth while to say."[6]

Jack and Cora moved in with her parents, and it was in their home that Virginia Blanche Clamorgan Collins was born on April 18, 1911.[7] Jack's parents still considered the couple too young for the responsibilities of marriage and parenthood, but they were gradually reconciling themselves to the situation. Then, on the evening of June 7, Owen received an unsigned letter. The Clamorgans believed they knew who had sent it—their daughter Blanche's rejected suitor, who had done a little delving into her past and had decided to repay her coldness by (as he saw it) ruining her life. The letter he wrote to Owen Collins informed him "that two negro families had invaded" Maplewood, "and that [his] own son had married into one . . . while one of [his] houses sheltered the other." Collins did some hasty investigating and learned, to his horror, that the allegations were true. He immediately started proceedings to extricate Jack from his marital entanglement and turn his tenants, the Davises, out of their home.[8]

Owen Collins hired the influential law firm of Johnson and Young to handle the matter of annulling Jack's marriage. As it happened, senior partner Charles P. Johnson had been a regular customer at Henry Clamorgan's barbershop. He remembered the barber as "a mulatto, about half white." He foresaw no difficulty in proving that Henry's granddaughter was a woman of color and hence prohibited under Missouri law from marrying a white man.[9]

Not surprisingly, Collins claimed his son had been "grossly deceived." Jack had moved back into his parents' home and would be staying there. As for his infant granddaughter, he confessed he dreaded for her future. This "innocent child . . . in whom the negro blood is not now discernible, may . . . give birth to a child, and the negro characteristics may predominate. Or several generations may elapse before the negro blood comes to the surface." He was unrelenting in his rage against the Clamorgans. "How these people could thrust themselves on a white community . . . and permit their children to intermarry with white people . . . is beyond my comprehension." He conveniently ignored the fact that Cora and Jack had never sought the consent of either set of parents. He was amazed and appalled that his family had been the last to hear the rumors swirling about Maplewood, but he did reveal that a sister of his had met the Clamorgans and had admitted, once the story got out, that she had realized they were "colored." Not knowing what to say, she had said nothing.[10]

A reporter from the *St. Louis Republic* cornered Jack Collins and got *him* to talk. His version of events echoed his father's. Jack told the man the Clamorgans had lived in Maplewood for four years, during which time "No one . . . suspected that there was a taint of negro blood in the . . . family." Cora was beautiful and refined. He had never thought twice about her delicate olive complexion. He had always understood her family to be of Spanish origin.

Jack recounted how, on the fateful evening of June 7, his parents had told him the rumors about Cora's family. He had confronted her with the disclosure in the anonymous letter and sent her to talk to her parents. When she came back she was sobbing. She would not share with him what they had told her, but she had said they must separate. He was trying, so he claimed, to spare her feelings as much as possible. "I believe she has been imposed on almost as badly as I have been." In another interview the following day he declared that, much as he loved Cora, their marriage must be ended.[11]

Once the annulment suit became public knowledge, the Clamorgans set about reevaluating their situation. They put their house on the market. They also kept their school-age daughters home in an effort to shield them from the scandal, but things seemed to be spiraling out of control. Ben Blewett, the superintendent of schools, announced he would have Clothilde and Grace reassigned to black schools forthwith.[12] Of course, he could do nothing about their siblings, who, with the exception of Blanche, had already graduated from white schools. Presumably, though, they could expect dismissal from their jobs—white-collar jobs that were the preserve of whites in St. Louis.

Reporters clamored to talk with Cora and her parents to get their side of the story. Newsmen tracked down Louis at his desk in the basement of City Hall. The reporter from the *Republic* wrote of his surprise at finding himself face-to-face with someone who "could easily pass for a white man." Louis vehemently denied being of African ancestry, insisting his father had been a Spaniard. When pressed as to whether or not his father had been the same Henry Clamorgan who had kept a barbershop at Fourth and Pine, he cut the interview short. The man from the *St. Louis Star* did a little better. He did not get an admission that the Clamorgans were people of color, but he did wring from Louis a confession that, had Jack Collins told him of his intention to marry Cora, he would have withheld his consent and disclosed "everything" to the young man, although he would not elaborate on precisely what he meant by this.[13]

The reporter from the *Post-Dispatch* outdid his rivals. He got from Louis not only an admission that "there is negro blood in the family" but a brief (if inaccurate) genealogy. Louis explained he was descended from "a Spanish army lieutenant of noble lineage . . . who contracted a marriage with a Cuban woman of part negro blood." The couple had four children, one of whom, Apoline, married her cousin "St. Elmo." Louis's father was their son. His mother, he said, came from Pennsylvania, and was of French and Irish extraction. The *Post-Dispatch* did some digging of its own and corrected one part of Louis's family history. Ester, Jacques Clamorgan's mistress, whom the newspaper assumed was the mother of his children, was not from Cuba. She was "a free mulatto woman, supposed to have been the child of one of the French founders of St. Louis." Louis's real great-grandmother, Susanne, was forgotten entirely.[14]

After the interviews he gave on June 9, Louis stopped speaking.[15] While one group of reporters staked out his workplace, another group descended upon the Clamorgan home. The man from the *Republic* spotted Louise attending to the laundry in her neatly kept garden. As luck would have it, Maud Davis and Laura Jane were visiting. When the women caught sight of the caller, Maud scooped up several items of clothing from the laundry basket and tried to screen Laura Jane. But the reporter wrote that "a glimpse was sufficient to betray the negro characteristics in the child, many of which were missing in the mother." Louise insisted her husband was a Spaniard, but under the reporter's relentless questioning she broke down, declaring, "I have dreaded this for thirty years. Now that it has come, we will have to bear it." With that she went indoors and refused to comment further.[16]

Over the following days and weeks, Louise Clamorgan proved adamant on the subject of their ancestry. She was white and her husband was Spanish. "If he is recorded at city hall as a negro, I never knew about it." She alluded to his illustrious ancestor, Jacques Clamorgan, and to the claim pending in Washington regarding his lands. As for her son-in-law, she characterized him as a young man callous enough to use any pretext to rid himself of a wife who was a semi-invalid. Cora suffered from rheumatism, and it had flared up again during her pregnancy. Jack had been attentive for a time, a fact Cora herself confirmed, but then he had come to regard his wife as a burden.[17]

Louise's disclosures cast the Collinses, father and son, in an unflattering light. She told the *Star* that Jack had headed off to Texas to find a job on a ranch and scrape together enough money to make a home for himself and Cora.[18] Things hadn't worked out, and on Christmas Eve he was on the Clamorgans' doorstep. He had been to see his father, who had heartlessly turned him away. Owen was still furious about the marriage and told Jack if he was old enough to take a wife he could keep her himself. The Clamorgans decided that Jack and Cora could live with them.[19]

Reporters clamored to interview and photograph the young woman at the center of the scandal. Not surprisingly, Cora had her own version of events. She recounted how, on the very day the storm broke, Owen Collins had come to see his granddaughter for the first time. Owen had cooed over his grandchild and said he longed for the day when she would "pull my coat-tails and call me grand-daddy." When he left to go home for supper—and to open his mail—they discovered Virginia had a ten-dollar bill clutched in her tiny fist. Jack just missed his father, returning from work a few minutes after Owen left.

After supper Jack went to call on his father and thank him for his gift to Virginia. Cora recalled he was gone much longer than she expected. It was a fine evening, and she sat with her baby in the garden. When Jack finally came home he broke the news to her. Taking Virginia from her, he told her she must talk to her father at once. Cora found Louis tending to his chicken coop. According to her, he remained silent for several moments "and then told me that my great-great-grandfather had married a Cuban woman who had some negro blood, how much he didn't know."

She repeated to Jack what her father had told her. He was torn. His father, he said, would force them apart, and it was best that they separate for a while. He vowed, however, that he would return to her. Would she wait for him? In a little over a year he would be of age and free from his father's control. Cora promised to wait. Although Owen had ordered his son to quit the Clamorgan home immediately if the rumors about her ancestry proved to be true, Jack spent one last night with her. Now he was back with his parents, and what the future held for her and Virginia, Cora confessed she did not know.[20]

In danger of being lost in the Collins-Clamorgan contest was the other family whose members faced an uncertain future in the wake of the disclosures that had sent Owen Collins running to his lawyer. It was, after all, the birth of Laura Jane, and the revelation that her father as well as her mother was "passing," that had caused the uproar. The Davises had never claimed to their neighbors in Maplewood to be wholly white. They had simply not admitted to being of African descent.

On the day the Clamorgan scandal broke, a representative from the *St. Louis Republic* turned up on the Davises' doorstep. He spoke with Nameoke Coleman, Louis Davis's widowed sister. She was adamant that the family was not black. They were of Creek and Choctaw descent. Her claims were backed up by her sister Pocahontas and their mother, Sarah Jane. They were Native Americans. They had never been anything else. As for the Clamorgans, Nameoke said she had always taken them at their word that they were Spanish. However, on closer questioning, Sarah Jane admitted that she had long suspected her son "had married a woman with negro blood in her veins."[21]

The Davises soon found themselves targets of an investigation. Reporters worked overtime, talking with people, checking records, and ferreting out every scrap of information they could about the family. It was established that Louis Davis had been appointed "as a negro" in the post office. Brother Osceola was employed at the Turkish baths in the Planters' House hotel, and his fellow workers claimed that "for twenty years he has been known to them as a negro." Their sister Pocahontas might have had a Native American name, but she taught at the all-black Dumas School. The superintendent of schools, the same Ben Blewitt who had pledged to reassign Grace and Clothilde Clamorgan to all-black schools, confirmed that Pocahontas "was carried on the records . . . as a negress." Pocahontas tried to explain this away. Yes, she taught in a black school, but only "because her skin was so dark she could not get a place in a white school . . . When she took the position . . . she told the . . . authorities she was . . . an Indian."[22] As the Clamorgans' white middle-class world began to collapse, so did the Davises'—and they had been working on refashioning their identity for decades with even more industry and imagination than the Clamorgans. As for their insistence that they did not know the family into which Louis Davis had married, this was revealed to be a patent lie, albeit a lie told out of dire necessity.

Sarah Jane Davis, born Sarah Jane Richmond, had crossed the lines of race many times over the years. Back in Nashville in 1850, she and her family had been "white." They had lived comfortably, they had money, and they looked white to the census taker. His silence about the absent Mr. Richmond may have been the result of discretion or genuine ignorance. Sarah Jane knew who her father was. He was a Rhode Islander by the name of Barton J. Richmond. He had come to Nashville and prospered, and like so many affluent white men, he had maintained two families, one white and one "colored."[23]

On March 10, 1849, Sarah Jane married William B. Davis, a free man of color. Davis was a riverman. By the early 1850s the couple had moved to Cincinnati, and it was there, on February 29, 1852, that their eldest child was born. In a nod to William's supposed Native American ancestry, the Davises named her Pocahontas. The Davises were not in Ohio for very long. They relocated to New Orleans, and it was actually in the Crescent City that they registered Pocahontas's birth. They stayed put in the city for several years, and two more children were born while they were there, Powhatan Thomas in 1854 and another daughter, Nameoke, in 1856.[24]

By 1860 they had moved again, this time to St. Louis, and Sarah's brother Thomas soon joined them.[25] William Davis continued working as a riverboat steward, but Thomas alternated between the river and Robert J. Wilkinson's barbershop. It was at the barbershop that he befriended another recent arrival from Nashville, Harrison McDougal, whose daughter Louise would become Louis P. Clamorgan's wife. He also met the young woman who would become his own wife. Georgiana Speers was Julie Wilkinson's sister. In a roundabout way, Georgiana and Julie were Clamorgans, for their great-grandmother was none other than Ester, Jacques's longtime mistress.[26]

Georgiana and Thomas wed on Christmas Day, 1861. Their marriage was short-lived. In the summer of 1864, nearing her second confinement, Georgiana became seriously ill. Nothing could be done to save her or her unborn child. Thomas was left alone to raise their eighteen-month-old daughter, Celestina. Georgiana's mother, Theresa Speers, was overburdened with family responsibilities. Julie Wilkinson had died a year after Georgiana and Thomas wed.[27] Her other siblings either were dead or had their hands full with their own children. Desperate, Thomas sought help from his sister. With the birth of Minnehaha, Sarah Jane had four children of her own to care for, but she assumed the task of raising her niece. Sadly, Celestina died in 1867 at age four.[28]

The Richmonds and the Davises lived quietly and attracted little attention beyond their own circle. The Davises had three more children, Osceola William, Tecumseh (who died young), and Ensenore Louis.[29] As for Thomas Richmond, in 1873 he married again, and he and his new bride, Rebecca Cartwright, moved into a home of their own. They had three children together, only one of whom survived infancy. By 1880, Thomas's widowed mother, Ann Faulkner, had come to live with him. The Richmond household was captured twice in the census. On the vexed question of race, the first enumerator classed them all as black; the second, as mulatto.[30]

The census taker had no qualms about identifying the Davises as mulattoes, and they were routinely listed as "colored" in the city directory, but William and Sarah Jane had been struggling for years to define themselves and their children as Native American. William may have been of Indian as well as African and European descent. In 1911 his children produced an affidavit he had supposedly secured half a century earlier. A man who claimed to have known William's parents testified that his mother was one "Indian Sally" and his father was Jackson Davis, a dark-skinned white man.[31]

The names that William and Sarah Jane chose for their children owed more to literature than affinity with any specific Indian nation. Minnehaha was, of course, the wife of Hiawatha in Longfellow's epic, while Nameoke was an Indian enchantress in a turgid mid-nineteenth-century romance.[32] Osceola had been a celebrated warrior during the Second Seminole War. Tecumseh, the great Shawnee leader, had forged an intertribal alliance that struck terror in the hearts of whites before the defeat of that alliance at Tippecanoe. Ensenore was an Algonquin leader the English had encountered at Roanoke, while Pocahontas and Powhatan are too well known to need to be identified here.

Indian their names might have been, but long before Louis Davis's marriage to Maud Clamorgan, the Davis children had made certain choices that compromised the family's slow drift away from their African ancestry. They sometimes dropped their Indian names. As an adult, Ensenore Louis invariably called himself Louis E., and at various times Powhatan and Osceola went by their middle names, becoming Thomas P. and William O. Davis. Louis and Osceola attended the Christian Brothers College, but they were unable to climb the social and economic ladder as nimbly as Louis P. Clamorgan, an earlier alumnus.[33] When he left school, Powhatan took a job as a porter, a job likely to fall to the lot of any unskilled man, regardless of race, but after *his* stint as a porter Osceola became a bath attendant and masseur, work monopolized in St. Louis by men of color. By 1879, Pocahontas was a teacher, and that was the job she held for almost her entire working life. However, in the early 1880s she was briefly employed as a cashier at James P. Thomas's barbershop. In light of the racial and gender conventions of the time, it was unthinkable that a white woman would work for a man of color in such a male environment as a barbershop. Her employment marked Pocahontas out as African American. And when Pocahontas returned to the classroom, Minnehaha took her place at the cashier's desk of the firm that had now become Dora and Thomas.[34] Most important, the association of the Davis daughters with James P. Thomas and Felix Dora, both friends of Louis P. Clamorgan and godfathers to his children, further undercut the claim that the Davises and the Clamorgans existed in complete ignorance of one another.

Of even greater significance than the choice of employment on the part of the younger Davises was their selection of marriage partners. In 1882, Powhatan wed one Mary Baker. The wedding took place at a black church with a black minister officiating, and Mary herself was almost certainly a woman of color.[35] Nameoke Davis's husband was Alexander Coleman, a post office clerk, who was originally from Louisiana. Like Nameoke, he was light-skinned, but also like her, he was of African descent. The couple married in 1883. They had one child, Alexander Andrew Aloysius, born on February 2, 1889. By 1892, Nameoke was a widow.[36]

On November 23, 1887, at the Church of St. Francis Xavier, the youngest Davis daughter, Minnehaha, wed Robert Benton Fillmore, a native of Virginia. For some years he had worked as a household servant for a white banker. By 1887, though, he had graduated to a white-collar job, clerking for a company that published law books. Over the next few years he moved back and forth, from porter to clerk to janitor at the all-black Delaney School.[37] Despite her choice of husband, Minnehaha continued the process of racial redefinition begun by her parents. Her firstborn was Robert Jr., but his brothers were baptized Powhatan and Osceola, and his sisters Juanita and Pocahontas. It is interesting to see how Robert and Minnehaha responded to the question of race when registering their children's births. They listed the boys as "white" and the girls as "Indian."[38]

By 1900 the members of the Davis-Richmond-Fillmore clan were making a determined effort to be other than black. Some were successful, while others were not. The census recorded an extended family whose members were scattered across the city and across the various categories of race. William B. Davis died in the summer of 1882. He was "colored" in the death register.[39] Sarah Jane's mother and brother died within weeks of each other in 1899. Ann Faulkner had actually been living with Sarah Jane at the time of her death. She was listed as "colored." Thomas was "white." Although they had been "black" or "mulatto" in the past, Thomas's wife and daughter crossed the racial divide. In 1900 the census taker classed both women as white, and white they remained.[40]

The official who called on the Fillmores in 1900 was unimpressed by their Indian names. He classed them as black. In a different part of the city, Sarah Jane presided over a household that comprised five of her adult children and her grandson, Nameoke's child, Alexander. Their enumerator *was* impressed by Native American names. He listed everyone in the home as "Indian."[41]

Soon after the Davises arrived in Maplewood, Louis began courting Maud Clamorgan. He was twelve years older than she, but he had a steady job with the post office and impressed Louis and Louise as a suitable husband for their daughter. At some point the two families met. Although nearly four decades had passed since Harrison McDougal had boarded with the Davises, Louise McDougal, now Louise Clamorgan, almost certainly recognized in Sarah Jane Davis her father's old friend, while Sarah Jane saw in the woman now representing herself in Maplewood as white the African American girl she had helped care for so many years before.

The marriage went ahead in 1909, and in the spring of the following year Maud and Louis Davis had their first child. George Watson, the census taker who visited the Davises when Laura Jane was three months old, probably never saw her. He recorded her name, age, and place of birth, and concluded she must be white because, to his way of thinking, so was everyone else in the household, but rumors of the "colored" baby in lily-white Maplewood soon began to spread.[42] By the summer of 1911 it seemed that everyone in the neighborhood knew about Laura Jane—everyone except the Collinses, until Owen Collins received an anonymous letter.

As the Clamorgan-Collins annulment battle proceeded, the press had a field day. Racial definition was obviously the main issue, but it was not the only one. Sexual impropriety was also there. When the press got hold of the papers Owen Collins's lawyer had filed, it emerged that Jack and Cora had wed in December 1910, not August, as Cora had always insisted. She stuck to her story, steadfastly denying that the marriage had occurred in December. Perhaps to spare her any additional distress, Jack went along with her assertion that they had wed in August. There was no getting around the fact of the marriage license, though. The couple had married on December 5, when Cora was four months pregnant. The recorder of deeds for Gasconade County remembered Cora and Jack. He had thought them a very handsome young couple.[43]

Premarital sex was one part of the story, but the fallout from "race mixing" was a much larger part. According to one paper, the Clamorgans were so angry over the bid to annul the marriage that they proposed renaming Jack and Cora's baby. She had been called Virginia after Jack's grandmother, but if the Collinses pushed ahead with the annulment, her name would be changed to Louise Blanche.[44] Then a bizarre rumor started circulating to the effect that Cora had been adopted by the Clamorgans. The Collinses were accused of having begun the rumor to put an end to the annulment suit. If Cora were not the Clamorgans' biological child, but the child of some nameless white woman who had abandoned her at birth, she was white, and therefore she and Jack could remain married. This was soon disproved by friends of the family and by an appeal to common sense. Cora was a Clamorgan by birth, not by adoption, and this made her . . . whatever the Clamorgans were.[45]

The Sunday editions of the city newspapers soon weighed in at much greater length than the dailies. On June 18 the *St. Louis Republic* devoted two entire pages to revelation and speculation. Attention was focused on Cora. She was "a little doll-like woman," but "[h]er eyes are dark, faintly tinged with the tell-tale shades that the Southerner knows from afar off." She was fiercely protective of her baby, vowing to take her "where she will never hear of this accursed thing." That mother and child were doomed the paper had no doubt. "What Will Become of Little Virginia Collins?" one headline asked. A Catholic priest lamented: "Doubtless the shadow will always be over her. Memories are long." A retired judge condemned prejudice, saying that, as a Jew, he had had more than a taste of it himself. If he were Jack Collins he would stick with his wife and child, no matter what. Even so, he and the other civic and religious leaders who held forth on the matter made dire predictions about the fate that awaited little Virginia.[46] No one had anything to say about Cora's sister and her child, though. They were "colored folks" and that was the end of the matter.

The following Sunday a lengthy article in the *Post-Dispatch* explored the dilemma confronting the man who looked white but knew himself to be of African descent. Could one blame him for wanting "release from . . . endless proscription"? Sometimes the gamble paid off, and within a generation or two "the fatal secret is buried beyond resurrection." In other cases, exposure damned the individual to a life far worse than the one he had lived before he "passed." Relegated once more to the black community, he was tormented by the loss of all he had enjoyed when he had been white.

The paper did its own genealogical investigation. Cora's great-great-grandfather was identified as a Spaniard, an associate of Auguste Chouteau and Antoine Soulard. Jacques Clamorgan had "brought with him the Latin indifference to the intermixture of blood," and he had taken as his common-law wife a woman of color, Ester. The fate of the couple's descendants was bound up with changing perceptions of race, with most of them becoming "pallid ghosts, flitting from side to side of the color line." The newspaper speculated that little Virginia might be no more than one-sixty-fourth black, but if the court did indeed annul her parents' marriage on the grounds of miscegenation, she would be tainted lifelong. And even if the court decided no impediment existed, as long as her story was known she would be blighted.[47]

As more and more details emerged, deep-seated fears bubbled to the surface about the racial purity of the white community.[48] Others besides the Clamorgans and the Davises came under scrutiny. A member of the Wilkinson clan was set to graduate from the Christian Brothers College. Although no attempt had ever been made to conceal his ancestry, "some of the teachers did not know he was colored." However, half a dozen classmates found out and told the school's president they would boycott the commencement exercises if young Wilkinson received his diploma. The president took a firm stand, replying that they could do as they pleased, but Wilkinson would get his diploma. It was noted that the young man had not encountered any problems until the Clamorgan case came up.[49]

The news that there were "colored" families in their midst left many of Maplewood's white residents stunned, but not everyone was hostile. The day after the annulment suit was filed, a reporter who had come to the Clamorgan home seeking more comments from the family ran into half a dozen young white men and women who had called to commiserate with Cora.[50] A neighbor launched a petition drive on the family's behalf. Another neighbor observed, "This thing about the Clamorgans' negro blood was well known in a general way." They were decent people. "They did not thrust themselves on their neighbors. When any attention was shown them they were appreciative."[51] Louise informed a reporter that the family home had been taken off the market, observing, "We never knew how many friends we had . . . Our neighbors have stood by us nobly, and we are going to stay here."[52] As for Cora, the *Post-Dispatch* noted she had already had a proposal from a well-to-do white man. Moved by her beauty, the fortune that might come her way if the Clamorgan land claims were confirmed, or beauty and riches combined, he declared he was eager to marry her the minute she was legally free from Jack Collins.[53]

The marital and social prospects of Cora's elder sister also brightened. One of Blanche's suitors, Joseph De Witt, left town, and his mother would have nothing to do with the young woman who could easily have become her daughter-in-law. But when De Witt abandoned Blanche, his rival did not. Charles Wass continued visiting the Clamorgan home. One paper quoted him as saying that having "so small a trace of negro blood" that the family was accused of was unimportant to him. He loved Blanche and planned to marry her. According to another paper, though, he was not ready to commit himself, saying, in response to Louise Clamorgan's assertion of an impending marriage, "When you see the license you may know I am going to get married, but not until then."[54] There was also encouraging news for Blanche from another quarter. The board of the Maplewood Christian Science Church voted not to expel her. One of the readers declared that "The divine love of Christ is over all." Blanche was "a beautiful, refined and faithful church worker" who was welcome to remain in fellowship.[55]

In one of the earliest articles on the annulment suit a reporter from the *Globe-Democrat* warned the Collinses they could expect a fierce battle if the Clamorgans decided to challenge them in court. "The Clamorgans are fighters. The entire . . . family has been conducting an organized legal battle against the United States Government for more than half a century."[56] On the day after the annulment suit was filed, Louise informed a reporter that the family had consulted a lawyer, John C. Higdon, whom they had known for many years. They would agree to a divorce, but not an annulment, which "would be an injustice to Mrs. Collins and leave her child fatherless."[57]

When the suit was first filed, the Collinses' legal team insisted that getting an annulment on the grounds of race would be simple, but they began to find that it was actually a tougher proposition than they had thought. The 1909 *Revised Statutes of Missouri* defined as illegal any marriage between a white person and another person "having one-eighth part or more of negro blood." However, the determination of the degree of "negro blood" was left up to a jury based on appearance. There was a distinct possibility that jurors would conclude that Cora was white, or at the very least not black enough to be barred from marrying Jack.[58]

Attorney Higdon recommended that Cora seek a divorce. She should sue Jack for abandoning her, and Owen Collins for alienation of his son's affections.[59] Louise said she and her husband approved of his recommendation. They would never consent to the Collinses' suit, for "she and the family did not wish it made a matter of court record that they are negroes by having the marriage annulled on that ground." An action for divorce on the grounds of desertion was another matter. Louise spoke of suing Collins Sr. for fifty thousand dollars, adding she didn't expect to get it because she had learned that he had put his real estate in his wife's name, but it would at least give her own family a degree of satisfaction.[60]

All talk of annulments and divorces came to an end in the waning days of the summer. Attorney Higdon and his clients had made it clearly understood that the Collinses would pay a hefty price if they pressed ahead. There would be legal fees, plus maintenance and medical costs for Cora and Virginia.[61] Probing the history of the Clamorgan clan, Owen Collins had proved to his own satisfaction that Cora was a woman of color. Proving it to a court of law was another matter. And a young wife abandoned by her husband as a result of the machinations of her father-in-law was likely to cut a very sympathetic figure when it came to awarding alimony and damages. On the evening of August 27, his twentieth birthday, Jack Collins called on Louis Clamorgan. He had been sent by his father to say he would abandon the suit if the Clamorgans promised not to bring a countersuit. Louis agreed.[62]

Was it understood that the price of giving up the suit was exile for the Clamorgans and Jack Collins? They were gone from St. Louis by year's end. Louis, Louise, all but one of their children, their son-in-law, and their infant granddaughter headed as far west as they could to seek a new home in California. Owen and Mary Collins were left to contemplate the aftermath. They had effectively lost their son and granddaughter. To make that loss even more poignant, they soon received word that Cora was pregnant again with a child they might never get to see. The accidental death of Jack's elder brother, Irwin, the following year intensified their sense of loss.[63]

As for upholding the racial purity of Maplewood, the Collinses had suffered a humiliating defeat in that quarter. They had evicted the Davises from their home, but the Davises had found another landlord less squeamish about race and more appreciative of tenants who paid their rent on time. The Davises were no longer the Collinses' tenants; they were now their neighbors. Owen and Mary could expect to run into members of the family, including Laura Jane, first cousin to their own granddaughter, on a regular basis. And for good measure the Davises invited some of their relatives to move in with them. The Fillmores— Minnehaha, Robert, and their children, all of them black according to the 1900 census—took up residence.[64] The Davises and the Fillmores had never set out to integrate Maplewood. They had placed a premium on whiteness. But their secret had been dragged into the open, and they had essentially become racial pioneers on the urban frontier.

Left out of the whole brouhaha was another St. Louis family. No one made the connection between Louis and Louise Clamorgan and their children in lily-white Maplewood and the "Morgans" on equally white Chippewa Street. Although born to different mothers, Louis P. Clamorgan and Tom, Clara, Lettie, and Josephine Morgan all had the same father, and all were descended from Jacques and Susanne. All were engaged in proving that they were indeed Jacques Clamorgan's heirs in order to get his land claims confirmed, but somehow the inquisitive gentlemen from the press never picked up on precisely what this implied. The Morgans were white and they stayed white, even as the "colored" Clamorgans packed up and moved west.

Louis and Louise Clamorgan and their children moved into a home in Los Angeles and began the process of reclaiming their identity as white people. They went by the name "Morgan," like their kinfolk back in St. Louis, but in time some of them changed that to "Demorgan." This was a sensible precaution, for the *Los Angeles Times* had published stories about the annulment case, and the Clamorgan name was unusual enough that readers might hear it and remember what they had read.[65]

Louis had no occupation in 1912. Whether he ever found employment after he became more settled in California is not clear. By 1920, he and Louise had relocated to South Pasadena with Cora, Jack, and their children. In the census, Louis took a few liberties with the truth. He gave his name as Louis Morgan, and said he had been born in Pennsylvania, which was actually his mother's home state. He claimed his father was from Spain. His race, not surprisingly, he reported as white. Shortly after the census was taken, Louis and Louise headed to Sierra

Madre, and it was there that Louis died on December 29, 1922, at age seventy. His name appeared in the death record as "De Morgan," and that was the name his widow continued to use.[66] After her husband's death Louise returned to Los Angeles. In 1930, as Louise Demorgan, a white widow from Tennessee, she was living in a boardinghouse in the city. She spent her remaining years in Los Angeles, dying there at the age of eighty-two in 1946.[67]

Blanche Clamorgan may have become engaged to Charles Wass, the more liberal-minded of her two suitors, but she did not marry him. Instead she joined her parents in California. As she had in St. Louis, she found work as a stenographer. In August 1912 she married a recent immigrant from England, Albert Vincent Leat. Blanche continued working as a stenographer until the birth of the couple's only child, Hazel, in March 1914. Albert was a stage carpenter who worked as a crew foreman in one of the area's new film studios. As a skilled craftsman he earned good wages, and the little family prospered, graduating swiftly to the rank of homeowners. Albert died in 1957, and Blanche outlived him by almost twelve years, dying in Los Angeles County on October 10, 1969, at the age of eighty-six, her race unquestioned.[68]

Louis and Louise Clamorgan's only surviving son, Walter, was living on his own by 1913 and working as a mailman. That was the job he held for some years before he was able to get back to his first love, automobiles. By 1920, Walter had found work in a garage, and before too long he was plying the trade he had had back in St. Louis: selling cars.[69] Walter and his wife, Agnes, were married in 1915 and likely had no children. After Agnes's death Walter turned to Blanche for emotional support. It was probably Blanche's husband who got him a job as a maintenance man at the 20th Century Fox Studios. The movie industry took care of Walter in his last days. He died in the Motion Picture Hospital in Woodland Hills on January 28, 1965, at age seventy-five. For the greater part of his life he had been without question white, and Blanche made sure that was how he was identified on his death certificate.[70]

Clothilde was just sixteen in the summer of 1911 when her world was turned upside down. Once in Los Angeles, however, she adjusted quickly to her new environment. She jettisoned her first name in favor of her middle name, Isabel, and used "Morgan" as her last name. In 1916 she wed William Alexander Dommes, a Californian of German extraction who worked as a bookkeeper. The couple had one son, Richard, born in 1919. Like almost all of her siblings, Isabel spent the rest of her life in California, dying in Los Angeles County on May 26, 1978, at age eighty-three, her identity as a white woman unchallenged.[71]

The youngest of the Clamorgans, Grace, moved with her parents to California, where she completed her schooling. It was in California that she met a young electrician, Raymond Roney. The couple married in 1917, when Grace was nineteen. Soon after their marriage they headed to Newark, New Jersey, where Raymond worked as a salesman for an electrical business. Their only child, Jeannette, was born in New York in 1919. That same year, Grace lied outright to the census taker. Her father, she said, had been born in Spain. The Roneys' sojourn in the East was relatively brief. By 1930, they were in Pasadena. Grace Demorgan Roney died in Los Angeles on July 24, 1990, at age ninety-two.[72]

Cora's story is not as straightforward as those of her siblings. Her life took many twists and turns. In their early years in California she and Jack maintained their own home, apart from her parents. On September 18, 1912, Cora gave birth to the couple's second child, Herbert Jack Collins. Jack had none of his father's connections to help him in Los Angeles, but he did manage to get a job with the post office. The young family did not have much money, and they were seldom at the same address longer than a year. Finally, in 1920, they moved in with Cora's parents.[73]

At some point over the next decade Cora and Jack separated, and she took refuge with her sister Clothilde and her family. Well aware that she could not rely on Jack to support her and their children, Cora made use of the office skills she had acquired back in St. Louis and went out to work as a bookkeeper.[74] Did Jack's parents play a role in the breakup? There is no way of knowing for sure, but it seems likely. Owen had done his best to get his son's marriage annulled and he had failed. Rather than cut Jack out of their lives entirely and irrevocably, the Collinses eventually sold up and followed him to California. With Irwin dead, Owen and Mary simply could not endure the loss of another son. By 1920 they were in Burbank, in Los Angeles County, and they were laying claim to their son, but not to his wife or his children. In the census, they listed Jack as a member of their household, although he was still with Cora and her parents at the time.[75] The Collinses were not reconciled to a marriage they had so bitterly opposed, and Jack, burdened with a family and looking at a life filled with dead-end jobs and continuing financial hardship when he had been raised with much brighter prospects, seems to have caved in under pressure. His father's death intensified the demands upon him. His mother was alone, and he turned his back on Cora to be with her.[76]

The marital woes of Jack and Cora could not help but have an impact on their children. Herbert struck out on his own as soon as he could, and Virginia, about whose future there had been so many dire predictions, married young. She was seventeen in 1929 when she wed Orville N. Maloy. The couple made their home in Pasadena, and on July 22, 1931, Virginia gave birth to a daughter, Jeanne Margaret.[77] The "accursed thing" that Cora had vowed to shield Virginia from, namely the truth about her ancestry, remained a secret. Virginia married a white man, and the child she bore was white.

Cora stayed close to Virginia, Orville, and her granddaughter. She shared a home with them at various times, and when she and Jack briefly reconciled in the late 1930s, so did he.[78] Within a year or two, though, Jack had faded out of their lives again. Cora never divorced him, but she made a determined effort to become independent of him. She decided on a new career. She qualified as a nurse and worked until she was in her sixties. Throughout the upheavals in Virginia's life—when Orville died after a long and happy marriage, Virginia wed a second time, divorced, and then made a far more successful third match—mother and daughter remained close.[79] Cora Clamorgan Collins passed away at age ninety-six in Van Nuys, Los Angeles County, on January 6, 1989, with Virginia by her side. Like her siblings, whatever she may have been, she was white when she died.[80]

Despite or perhaps because of all they had endured, Louis Davis and Maud Clamorgan remained together. They stayed in St. Louis. In 1913 or 1914, Maud gave birth to another daughter. She was named Sarah, after Louis's mother. Their third child was born in October 1916 and lived just five days. (The baby's death certificate listed her as "colored.") In 1919 the Davises had another daughter, Louise. Louis Davis's elder brother, Osceola, had succumbed to tuberculosis in 1916, leaving Louis as the only male representative of the Davis clan. (Like his infant niece, Osceola was "colored" on his death certificate.) Matriarch Sarah Jane Davis, recorded at the time of her death as white, died in 1919 at age eighty-seven.[81]

The Davises stayed in their home in Maplewood long after the Collinses had decamped to California. In 1920, Louis, Maud, and their daughters shared the house with Nameoke and Pocahontas. The census taker assumed he was seeing two separate households. He classed Louis as Indian, the same designation Louis had claimed for himself in 1918 when he registered for the draft, and Nameoke Coleman and Pocahontas Davis as white, not knowing the three were siblings. Louis he judged to be Indian, but Maud and the children, including Laura Jane, he classified as white.[82]

The following year the Davises headed across the river to Illinois. Two sons, Louis and Leon, and a daughter, Ramona, were born after the move. In 1930 the family was living in an integrated neighborhood in the town of Lebanon. Louis was still working for the post office. The five surviving Davis children—Sarah had apparently died in her early teens—were living at home. On this occasion the census listed all the members of the household as "Negroes."[83]

Maud never lost touch with her siblings, and in the early 1930s she and her family moved to California to join them. In this new setting the Davises quietly "passed." Louis predeceased his wife, dying in 1935. All of the Davis children, even Laura Jane, managed to integrate themselves into the white community, and all of them remained close to their mother. Maud Clamorgan Davis died in Los Angeles on December 31, 1950, at age sixty-six. Her daughter Louise Davis Lillard supplied the information that appeared on the death certificate: Maud's maiden name was "De Morgan" and she was white.[84]

As for the other members of the Davis clan, soon after the 1920 census was taken, Pocahontas and Nameoke moved from Maplewood to the suburb of Webster Groves. It was there in 1924 that Pocahontas died. After her sister's death, Nameoke relocated to East St. Louis to share a home with her son, who worked for the Illinois Highway Department.[85]

Alexander Coleman had long since moved into the white community. As the nation mobilized for World War I, he registered for the draft. In response to the question about his race he wrote "Caucasian." He was inducted into the army on April 30, 1918, and he shipped out for Europe in a matter of weeks. Promoted to corporal, he served for the duration, returned unscathed, and was honorably discharged in 1919. He had enlisted as a white man, and the U.S. Army had seen no reason to alter that.[86]

Back in civilian life, Alexander divided his time between the Davis home and his lodgings across the river in East St. Louis. By 1920, as Andrew Coleman (Andrew being one of his middle names), he was boarding with a family in East St. Louis. Like everyone else in the home, he was white. He moved back to St. Louis for a time to live with his mother and aunt, but after Pocahontas's death he returned to East St. Louis, taking his elderly mother with him. Alexander never married. He spent the rest of his long life in East St. Louis, dying there at the age of eighty-one in 1970.[87]

Minnehaha Davis Fillmore and her family, all of whom had been black in 1900, became Indian in the 1910 census. Following the crisis that beset the Davis clan in 1911, the Fillmores moved into the home that Minnehaha's mother and siblings had rented after Owen Collins evicted them from the house they leased from him. The Fillmores remained with the Davises until 1914, when they headed off to Chicago.[88]

It was in Chicago that the three Fillmore sons registered for the draft. All reported on the same day and all gave the same information when it came to race. They were Indians. All requested exemptions. Robert was a post office stenographer and hence in a reserved occupation. Powhatan referred to a physical disability. Osceola, who worked as a chauffeur for the American Express Company, cited his need to support his parents.[89]

Robert Fillmore, Sr., died in 1919. In the census that was taken the following year, "Minnie A." Fillmore headed a household that included Powhatan; his wife, Jennie; and his siblings, Osceola, Juanita, and Pocahontas. Everyone was Native American, except for Jennie, who was white. Minnehaha's eldest child, Robert, lived across town. He was identified as white. Interestingly, although he listed himself as having been born in Missouri, he told the enumerator that both his parents were from Oklahoma, perhaps to suggest that anything about him that might indicate he was other than white could be attributed to Native American ancestry.[90]

Juanita Fillmore died in 1924. (Her death certificate listed her as white.) By the time of the 1930 census, Osceola, his wife, Olive, and their children lived with her parents. Everyone in the household was white. Across town the enumerator who called on Powhatan was perplexed. His wife and son were white, but how should *he* be listed? The man wrote "Red" and corrected that to "IN" for "Indian."[91]

The other siblings lived just blocks apart in the suburb of Jefferson. Although both were white in the census, they gave different versions of their ancestry. Robert said he and his parents had been born in Missouri. (A decade earlier he reported that his parents were from Oklahoma.) Pocahontas, who was married to a prosperous car dealer, told a different story. Everyone in her home, including her mother and her son from her first marriage, was white, although her father had been born on an Indian reservation.[92]

As for some of the other players in the Clamorgan saga, Louise Clamorgan's brother Harrison McDougal moved to the Los Angeles area in 1917. Around 1922, indigent and ailing, he became an inmate at the Los Angeles County Farm. He died at the farm on December 21, 1930, his racial designation given as "white."[93]

Adele McDougal's married life with William T. Fizer seemed happy enough. The couple had two children, Charles and Camille, and William got various promotions at the Pension Office. But William was an ambitious man eager to better himself and fulfill his intellectual potential. Once he and his family were settled in Washington, D.C., he enrolled in Howard University's medical school, somehow managing to juggle his studies with his demanding work schedule. In 1883, he graduated as a full-fledged M.D. But if William thought he could graduate from the position of clerk to that of surgeon or medical examiner now that he was Dr. Fizer, he was bitterly disappointed. He had been appointed as a clerk, and for a man of color, that was the highest rank he could aspire to.[94]

William T. Fizer cut quite a figure in the African American community in Washington, but in the summer of 1888 his and his family's respectable middle-class existence was shattered.[95] Adele Fizer discovered that her husband had been leading a double life. Presenting himself as Portuguese, he had become friendly with a white family who owned a successful restaurant. The family literally took the charming and well-educated man at face value, and when he began courting their daughter, they encouraged the relationship. It was only when he proposed marriage that the young woman's parents thought it prudent to learn a little more about their prospective son-in-law. Their inquiries not only revealed that he already had a wife and two children, but ripped to shreds the story about his Portuguese origins. William immediately resigned his position at the Pension Office and fled the city. Newspapers across the country got hold of the story and it was almost as widely reported as the misfortunes of Adele's sister's family would be two decades later.[96]

Adele, described in the press as "a good-looking mulatto," was understandably distraught when William abandoned her and their two children, but once she recovered from the shock she turned for help to the network of friends she had made in Washington. Someone got her a job as a clerk working on the upcoming census. When that job came to an end, she spent some time with her mother's family in Nashville. In that city's directory for 1890–91 she was "colored," but she and her children managed to shed that label once they returned to the nation's capital. Adele got another civil service appointment and regained a measure of financial stability.[97] Not only did she remake her own and her children's racial identity but she also bent the truth about her marital status, calling herself a widow. By 1930, still working for the federal government, she was living in Washington with her grandson and his wife.[98] Her errant husband had tried to "pass," with disastrous consequences. Although she had not at first set out to become white, Adele was ultimately far more successful at maneuvering across the racial borderlands.

Colota was the only one of the McDougal siblings who spent her entire life as African American, and for her it was apparently a matter of choice. She received her early education in Pin Oak, but there was enough money from her father's estate to make it possible for her to move out of the area to continue her schooling and train as a nurse.[99] She kept her ties with the Blairs, though, for they were the only "family" she had ever really known. By 1900, Colota had relocated to the Chicago area with her widowed aunt Rachel and her cousin Henry. All three were classed as black. A decade later, Colota and Rachel were in Indianapolis with another of Rachel's children, Margaret, and her husband, John B. Bates. Bates was a chiropodist and Colota earned her keep as a nurse.[100]

The Bates-Blair marriage broke up amid scandal when John abandoned Margaret and their young daughter and ran off to St. Louis with Colota. They arrived just after Louise and her family had departed for California. Margaret never divorced John, although he obviously did not consider himself bound to her any longer. In 1920 he described himself as a widower. When the census taker called on *her* that year, Margaret insisted she was a married woman. A decade later, when she was living with her married daughter and did not care to admit that she had been deserted by her husband, she said she was a widow.[101]

In St. Louis, firmly entrenched in the black community, Colota continued to work as a nurse and John as a chiropodist. They never married. Either Margaret steadfastly refused to give John a divorce, or he and Colota saw no need to legalize their union. They were still together when Colota died on March 30, 1937, at age sixty-four.[102] So separate had their lives become that in faraway Los Angeles, Louise probably never learned of her sister's death.

It took decades, but ultimately Louis and Louise Clamorgan, their children, their in-laws, and virtually every member of their extended family made the transition from "colored" to "white" or, in a few cases, "Indian." This transition did not come without a price. Maintaining whiteness meant reinventing themselves, but one by one that is exactly what they did. And although there were painful missteps along the way, each one of them—Fizers, McDougals, Fillmores, Davises, and of course Clamorgans—accomplished what they had set out to do: they left their past behind them.

12

On the Fringes

THE SCANDAL in 1911 surrounding Cora Clamorgan's marriage revived interest in that most elusive member of the Clamorgan clan, Cyprian. Reporters digging for every titillating detail they could find about the family unearthed his long-forgotten exposé of St. Louis's colored aristocracy. Readers of the *St. Louis Star*, the *Globe-Democrat*, and the *Post-Dispatch* were also reminded that it was Cyprian who had led the Clamorgans into battle against no less an entity than the U.S. government, and that battle was still ongoing.[1] Another generation of Clamorgans were the major players now, but Cyprian still merited a paragraph or two in the press for the book he had had the temerity to write and the barrage of lawsuits he had begun.

Author and perennial litigant—Cyprian was both of those things, but he was much more besides. He never wrote his autobiography, and had he done so he would surely have played fast and loose with the truth. As regards the core question of his identity, since a fortune was at stake, he had always been eager to prove his descent from Jacques Clamorgan. His readiness to claim Susanne as his grandmother varied, though, according to time and place. Sometimes he embraced the to-

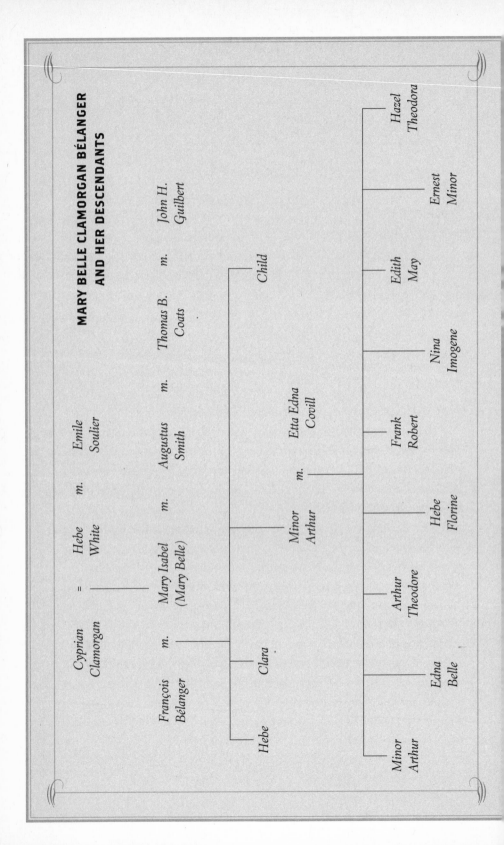

MARY BELLE CLAMORGAN BÉLANGER
AND HER DESCENDANTS

Cyprian Clamorgan = Hebe White

Hebe White m. Emile Soulier

Mary Isabel (Mary Belle) m. Augustus Smith

Thomas B. Coats m. John H. Guilbert

François Bélanger m. Clara

Hebe

Minor Arthur m. Etta Edna Covill

Child

Minor Arthur

Edna Belle

Arthur Theodore

Hebe Florine

Frank Robert

Nina Imogene

Edith May

Ernest Minor

Hazel Theodora

tality of his family's history, while at other times he shied away from any hint of African ancestry.

Racially and geographically, Cyprian Clamorgan was a moving target. He changed his name whenever the need arose. Sometimes he used his birth name; at other times he was C. C. Morgan and occasionally C. Clay Morgan. Tracking a man who often had no wish to be found or who chose to reveal only a few sketchy details about his life is a challenging proposition. And yet Cyprian fascinates even as he frustrates. What is true of him is equally true of his daughter and grandson. Time and again, their capacity for refashioning themselves proved beyond any shadow of a doubt that they were indeed Cyprian's heirs. It is with Cyprian, though, that the story must begin.

On the evening of September 1, 1868, Pinckney Benton Stewart Pinchback was taking a stroll along Canal Street in New Orleans. The son of a Mississippi planter and a former slave, he had been born in Macon, Georgia, but New Orleans had been his home for some years. Now that the war was over and black men in Louisiana were not only free but enfranchised, Pinchback was emerging as a leading light in Radical Republican circles. His affiliation with the Radicals, the wing of the Republican Party that advocated the most sweeping changes at the national and local levels, including the granting of full civil rights to African Americans and the ouster from public life of any individual suspected of ever having been loyal to the Confederacy, earned him a legion of enemies. He was accustomed to going armed at all times. He was keenly aware of the volatile nature of life in the Crescent City and the deep hatred many whites bore him. He was a very obvious example of a black man who did not "know his place." In the April elections he had run for a seat in the Louisiana Senate against a white Democrat, Edwin L. Jewell. Jewell had won, but the Republicans asserted that his victory had been tainted by voting irregularities, and in a face-off between the two parties Jewell had been ousted and Pinchback confirmed in his stead. He had been sworn in on August 31, and tensions were running high.[2] Democrats, many of them unreconstructed and unrepentant Confederates, were literally baying for Pinchback's blood.

Pinchback was just crossing the street when he heard behind him the click of a pistol being cocked. Reaching into his pocket to draw his own weapon, he spun around expecting to see a white man taking aim at him. The casual white observer might have taken the would-be assassin for a white man, but Pinchback knew better. Not only did he recognize his adversary as a man of color like him, but he could put a name to him. The man called himself C. C. Morgan. Rumor had it that he was a barber from St. Louis, although he had been many things over the years.[3] More to the point, he was an old enemy who had every reason to want Pinchback dead. Morgan loosed off a couple of shots, and Pinchback returned fire. Bystanders ducked for cover. The gun-toting C. C. Morgan—none other, of course, than Cyprian Clamorgan—was determined to avenge the wrong Pinchback had done him. But Pinchback could counter that Morgan had wronged *him*. What happened that September evening on Canal Street had been years in the making, but, then, Cyprian's decade-long residence in New Orleans had been replete with drama. This was merely the latest episode.

How Cyprian made a living in New Orleans before the war is anyone's guess, although he almost certainly relied on his wits and his ability to pass as white. The outbreak of hostilities brought new opportunities. In the early months of 1862, when the city was still under Confederate control, he was the prime mover in C. C. Morgan and Co., a soap-manufacturing concern. As the junior partner in Clamorgans back in St. Louis, he had sold soap and he had a fairly good notion of how to make it. The citizens of the hot and humid metropolis appreciated a good cleansing bath, but with the Union navy mounting a tight blockade of New Orleans, soap was not easy to obtain. Cyprian was happy to make money by supplying it.[4]

Once Union forces took the city, he scented more alluring possibilities. New Orleans was suffering from a dearth of lawyers. Many of the younger members of the legal fraternity had dashed off to join the Confederate army. Others had fled as the Yankees approached, and of those who remained, scores were deemed too disloyal to be allowed to practice before the Provost Court. Cyprian was loyal: he had demonstrated as much by being among the first to greet General Benjamin F.

Butler when he made his entrance into the captured city.[5] Cyprian assessed his opportunities now that New Orleans was in Union hands. He was eloquent, as his speeches to the newly formed Union Association and other pro-Union organizations in the city had demonstrated.[6] He was well versed in the law. His and his half-brothers' court battles had proven an excellent primer in the laws of inheritance and land tenure—and then there was the little matter of his forgery trial. Just as important as his background in the law was the fact that he was white if he chose to be. As a man of color he would have been ineligible to become an officer of the court, but the military authorities were none too sure about racial definitions in a city with such a mix of peoples. Quite simply, to the Union officers, most of them Northern-born, C. C. Morgan Esq., self-proclaimed attorney-at-law, looked white enough.[7]

It was in his professional capacity that Cyprian first encountered P.B.S. Pinchback. On May 16, 1862, Pinchback got into a fight with his brother-in-law John Keppard. Keppard pulled a knife on Pinchback, and Pinchback defended himself—or retaliated, according to which version of the ugly little episode one believed. Both were arrested, but Keppard's wounds were so serious that the Provost Court ordered Pinchback to post bond in case Keppard died. Although Keppard recovered, he was not in a forgiving mood. On the advice of his attorney, and expecting nothing more than a slap on the wrist, Pinchback pled guilty to assault with intent to kill. To his horror he was sentenced to two years' confinement. Before he was led away he was approached by C. C. Morgan, who told him the matter could be resolved if he handed over five hundred dollars. Pinchback refused. He ended up serving two months rather than two years, but not surprisingly the whole episode rankled.[8]

Shortly after the attempt to squeeze money out of Pinchback, Cyprian was brought before General George F. Shepley, the acting mayor, on a complaint from the wife of the former mayor, John T. Monroe. Monroe was Confederate in his sympathies, and General Butler had wasted no time putting him under lock and key. Mrs. Monroe hired Cyprian to get her husband released. He said his fee was two thousand dollars, half of which he wanted up front as a retainer. She alleged he had tried to extort the money from her. Shepley reviewed her complaint and rendered his decision: Attorney Morgan was entitled to demand whatever fee he chose for his services. Moreover, "as an honest man and a loyal citizen, he should be protected" in his right to make a living.[9]

Uneasy perhaps about the complaint filed against him, Cyprian promptly announced to the public that he wished to pursue some occupation more congenial to him than the law. "Believing a refreshment stand, for the sale of coffee, sandwiches, lemonade and other light articles of food and drink . . . would be equally requisite as beneficial [to] the many soldiers and citizens" who flocked to the Custom House each day on business, he planned to become a caterer.[10] Never let it be said that Cyprian Clamorgan, whatever he called himself, was not a man of ingenuity!

Cyprian got the necessary license to operate his new business, but the legal profession still beckoned and he continued accepting clients. In the spring of 1863 he was summoned to appear before the Provost Court on a charge of taking money from one of those clients, doing nothing to earn it, and lying about being a lawyer. Cyprian snapped back that he did have a law license, and accused the prosecutor of not being a member of the Bar![11] Cyprian realized, though, that his enemies' list was growing. It was time for another career change. He began dealing in shinplasters, currency notes of dubious value. In a chaotic situation where legitimate notes were in short supply and specie was almost nonexistent, an unscrupulous individual could make a killing. He could also court trouble.

In January 1864, Cyprian became embroiled in a lengthy dispute with the authorities that the editor of the *Times-Picayune* gleefully predicted would see the erstwhile soapmaker, legal expert, caterer, and banker cast himself in an entirely new role, that of martyred innocent.[12] As Cyprian told the story, he was walking home one evening when he encountered a white policeman, William Nutley. After a few words of cordial conversation, Cyprian was about to continue on his way when Nutley demanded he hand over all the money he had on him. Fearing violence from the club-wielding Nutley, Cyprian complied. Nutley pocketed three ten-dollar bills, handed back the rest, and sent Cyprian about his business. "[A]fter a short reflection," Cyprian went to the police station to report what had happened. Nutley denied everything.

However, a search revealed Cyprian's three bills concealed in Nutley's clothing, and he was arrested for robbery.

Cyprian turned up for the hearing the next morning, but the recorder continued the case and released Nutley on bail. Cyprian's angry protest was ignored. As he was exiting the building, an army officer approached him and told him that the mayor, Captain James F. Miller, Shepley's replacement, wanted to see him. Cyprian was ushered into Miller's office. Miller asked if he was Mr. Morgan. When Cyprian replied in the affirmative, Miller left the room "like a man with a guilt stained heart," and Cyprian was arrested for bribing an officer of the law, a charge he vehemently denied.

When Cyprian was brought to trial he faced Nutley and "a tribe of his villainous associates," all of whom (according to Cyprian) committed perjury. The prosecutor was Rufus Long, a man who, in Cyprian's words, was known "from one end of this city to the other as . . . an unmitigated . . . scoundrel." Not surprisingly, the prosecution's version of events differed markedly from Cyprian's. Nutley said that on the evening in question he had encountered the defendant in company with a black man. Cyprian was in a passion and declared "that if he and other citizens had their way the Mayor and Ruf[us] Long would be hung higher than a kite." Nutley told him to be quiet, but Cyprian compounded his initial offense by speaking of the "highest officers . . . in authority here" as "Yankee thieves." What in peacetime was freedom of expression constituted criminal behavior under martial law. Nutley promptly arrested Cyprian, who drew thirty dollars out of his pocket, remarking, "'I have a bushel of money; it is better for you to take this than to take me in.'" Nutley took the bribe, but then Cyprian tried to get his cash back with a pack of lies about threats of violence. The Provost Court weighed Nutley's story against Cyprian's and found Cyprian guilty as charged. He was fined one hundred dollars, sent to prison for a month, and bound over for six months after that. When he argued, he got another month of jail time for contempt.[13]

Seething with fury, Cyprian sat in his cell and penned a statement to the public. His adversaries would rue the day they had targeted him. He might not have learned to write until he was in his late teens, but the lessons in penmanship he had forced his guardian to arrange for paid dividends now. His handwriting was elegant. More to the point, his account of the affair was coherent and compelling. If he could put over a case in court as well as he could express himself on paper, Cyprian Clamorgan, alias C. C. Morgan, alias C. Clay Morgan, must have been formidable as an attorney. On this occasion, however, his biting wit and flair for the dramatic proved his undoing. When he tried to circulate his statement, he was given more jail time for this additional display of contempt.[14]

In his predicament Cyprian was not without friends. A white Union soldier, Private Reuben F. Briggs, thought Cyprian was getting a raw deal and wrote a confidential letter to no less a person than the commander in chief. Briggs told President Lincoln that "the Press here were afraid of the authorities" and refused to publish Cyprian's statement, but Lincoln should read it for himself. Mr. Morgan "is . . . an honest unassuming loyal citizen." The people of New Orleans were aware of what had befallen him, "and . . . the honest and loyal portion . . . exclaim on ev[e]ry corner we are not safe . . . now." It was well known that Prosecutor Long and Mayor Miller were enriching themselves by preying on the populace. Morgan was just their latest victim. No one in a position of authority would come to his aid. General Shepley, now Louisiana's military governor, refused to intervene. Major General Nathaniel P. Banks acknowledged that "a great outr[a]ge had been perpetrated," but that was as far as he would go. Surely President Lincoln would not stand back and let an innocent man suffer in this way.[15]

One would like to be able to report that Briggs's letter (written at considerable risk to himself) prompted Lincoln to step in. It did not. In fact, even more trouble was in store for Cyprian. Nutley had lost his job on the police force back in January for accepting a bribe. In November, after various continuances, he finally stood trial in the Provost Court on the charge of armed robbery. Cyprian, who had by then completed his sentence, was allowed to appear against him, and he mounted a spirited attack. However, Nutley produced witnesses to paint his accuser as "the most arrant liar."[16] Nutley was convicted on the robbery charge and sentenced to a year at hard labor. However, Cyprian himself did not fare much better. In a stunning turn of events, he found himself under arrest again, this time for having sent an anonymous letter to army headquarters "full of bitter and scurrilous falsehoods." His home had been searched, drafts of the letter found, and the handwriting identified as his. According to a reporter in the courtroom, Cyprian took the matter very coolly. When one man asserted that he "was crazy on the subject of revenging himself on persons whom he thought had injured him," he shrugged his shoulders and smiled sarcastically. Cyprian was soon released. Perhaps he greased a few palms, or perhaps certain high-placed individuals feared a lengthy period of incarceration might lead to a probe of their activities.[17]

Cyprian's race did not become a matter for open discussion at his trial, although the suspicion that he was "passing" might have emboldened Nutley to target him in the first place. The policeman had, after all, come upon him "in company with a negro man." Private Briggs never mentioned to President Lincoln that his friend was a man of color. He may have been supremely indifferent to issues of race, but he may not have known Cyprian's background.[18] The fact was, though, that Cyprian had begun (albeit cautiously) to reveal his identity. On November 5, 1863, a couple of months before he tangled with Nutley, he had attended a meeting of "free Colored Citizens" at the city's Economy Hall. (Addressing the meeting was none other than P.B.S. Pinchback, now a captain in the U.S. Colored Troops.)[19] Caution might have dictated that Cyprian not involve himself in the various civil rights campaigns the African American community was mounting in 1864. His legal woes were only likely to become worse if he openly proclaimed himself to be a man of color.[20] However, after his first taste of prison life, and perhaps because of it, he became bolder.

Within weeks of his release after his first run-in with the authorities on the bribery charge, Cyprian Clamorgan, alias C. C. Morgan, publicly acknowledged himself to be a man of color. His eloquence and the sheer force of his personality thrust him into the limelight, and he relished it. In the summer of 1864, when slavery was officially outlawed in Louisiana, he was one of those on the speaker's platform at a rally to celebrate the event. As yet his role was a fairly minor one—he got to introduce the preacher who gave the invocation—but he was attracting attention.[21] Of course, this attention increased in December, when he was jailed a second time.

By January 1865, with a Union victory all but assured, Louisiana's free men of color held a statewide convention to consider their future, and among the delegates, his name mangled as "C. C. Gellorgan," was Cyprian.[22] He had stepped from his jail cell into public life. Within weeks of the convention he addressed a huge meeting at the Economy Hall on the need for a complete change of national policy with regard to the rights of black people.[23] Throughout 1865, as one of the most radical of the Radical Republicans, he spoke at one rally after another in the city—castigating former Confederates; condemning Lincoln's successor, Andrew Johnson, for being too soft on former rebels; and above all, urging black men to vote as soon as they had the chance.[24]

Cyprian was very much alive to the need for African American men to have a voice in the political process. He held firm to his belief, proclaimed back in 1858 in *The Colored Aristocracy*, that while abolishing slavery was an essential first step along the way to creating a more just society, freedom without the fundamental rights of citizenship was at best half-freedom. These were volatile times, however. The defeat of the Confederacy found the vast majority of Southern whites (and not a few Northerners) determined to keep all black people, no matter how wealthy and well educated, in a state of dependency. Although Cyprian may not have witnessed firsthand the riot that rocked New Orleans on July 30, 1866, its impact could hardly have been lost on him. The attack on several hundred black people and their white sympathizers assembling peacefully to discuss how to put an end to policies of racial exclusion was well coordinated and involved not only white civilians but many of the city's police and firefighters. The official toll—37 dead and almost 150 injured—fell far short of the actual numbers. To openly advocate rights for African Americans was a course of action fraught with danger, but it was one that Cyprian Clamorgan and many others were emboldened to take.

Cyprian made plenty of friends in the African American community and he supported them as they supported him. For instance, when an auctioneer contemptuously rejected the bid of a black physician for much-needed medical supplies, only to accept a lower bid from a white man, Cyprian was on hand to speak up about the injustice.[25] On another occasion he discovered that a planter in an outlying parish was refusing to relinquish ownership of a young woman and continuing to hold her as his slave. Black people in the neighborhood were understandably outraged, but they needed someone who knew the ways of officialdom to get something done about the situation. They turned to Cyprian. Their faith was not misplaced. He made it his business to get word to the military authorities and ensure that the unfortunate woman was released.[26]

In that heady postwar period when it seemed change would truly come about, Cyprian was everywhere, urging black men to flock to the polls. He often ventured outside of New Orleans into the rural parishes. In the spring and summer of 1867 he made one stump speech after another. In St. Bernard Parish he begged the newly enfranchised black residents to grill candidates in the upcoming election about what they had done during the war. If they had risked their lives on the battlefield to defend the Union, or spoken out against slavery and in favor of civil rights when it was hazardous to do so, then they deserved to be supported. If they had been Confederate sympathizers, they should be scorned and treated with contempt.[27]

From St. Bernard Parish, Cyprian moved on to Iberville Parish. Audiences, the majority of them black, warmed to this "indefatigable champion of our cause," as one commentator described him.[28] After a brief return to New Orleans to address an enormous Radical Republican gathering, he was off again.[29] As he took the stage in St. John the Baptist Parish, those who came to hear him expected an inspiring speech, and they were not disappointed. Cyprian told them straight out, "[I]f you vote for old masters or any rebels, you ought to sink into the depths of slavery lower than you ever were before." He also used the occasion to take a swipe at Banks, Shepley, and the other men who had either conspired to send him to prison in 1864 or refused to intervene to get him out of prison.[30]

On July 4, Cyprian was in Pointe Coupée Parish to speak at an Independence Day celebration. Then he headed back to New Orleans for the elections to the Radical Republicans' Central Committee. His powers of oratory, combined with the energy he had displayed in the rural parishes, garnered him a place on the committee. Fresh from that triumph, he went back out to Pointe Coupée, where he spoke for an hour and a half to an audience of two thousand, who punctuated his speech with enthusiastic applause. He was implored to make a return visit as soon as he could fit it into his busy schedule.[31]

His growing involvement in political life inevitably exposed Cyprian to the realities of party intrigue. The Republicans depicted their Democratic opponents as the party of reaction, the party of disloyalty. And while there was a good deal of truth to that charge, the Republicans were not to a man honest brokers. There were a good many in Republican circles happy to exploit black voters for their own and their party's benefit. And some of those doing the exploiting were themselves men of color. Even during the war, long-simmering tensions born of differences of caste and class had occasionally boiled over. Some among the ranks of the freeborn had resented what they saw as the refusal of the ex-slaves to heed the advice of their betters. Newcomers clashed with those who could trace their lineage in the Crescent City back to the time before the Louisiana Purchase. Name-calling, cynical politicking, intimidation, and outright fraud seemed to be the order of the day. Was Cyprian shocked by such goings-on? Probably not. He was no standard-bearer for truth and honesty. The turmoil throughout the states of the erstwhile Confederacy in the early days of Reconstruction spelled opportunity for the quick-witted and politically astute, regardless of race. Cyprian might have been taking a stand for good government when he clashed with Pinchback on Canal Street that September evening in 1868, but more likely he wanted to eliminate a rival, for the truth was that Cyprian had not done as well as he had hoped. Yes, he had held audiences enthralled in the countryside, and he had often graced the speaker's platform in New Orleans. Somehow, though, he had failed to make his way into the innermost circles of political power. His influence was at its height in that hectic summer of 1867, but he had failed to get himself elected to the state's constitutional convention, or to have any role other than as a spectator in that pivotal event that shaped the future of Louisiana.[32] And always, it seemed, Pinchback was able to do better than he. Cyprian felt very aggrieved, and not without good reason. To avenge a whole series of affronts and injuries, he purchased a gun and ammunition. He would show that jumped-up, ignorant demagogue that Cyprian Clamorgan, whatever he chose to call himself, was not to be trifled with.

Tensions in New Orleans in the late summer of 1868 were running so high that any spark could ignite a full-blown race riot. The confrontation on Canal Street almost touched off just such an explosion. While Pinchback "bore unmistakable evidence of his negro origin," his opponent was someone who at first glance would be taken for white. Black onlookers began rooting for Pinchback, while whites cheered on his attacker. Finally, someone in the crowd recognized Cyprian as a light-skinned man of color, and the whites dispersed, figuring it was no affair of theirs, as long as no white people were hit by stray bullets.[33] Luckily, both Cyprian and Pinchback proved appallingly bad shots: they hit neither each other nor any of the dozens of passersby. When he ran out of bullets, Cyprian charged at Pinchback and began pummeling him with his fists, but Pinchback struck back. At that point the authorities intervened, and both men were taken into custody. While Pinchback was unscathed, Cyprian had sustained a scalp wound as a result of a blow from a policeman's club. Pinchback was turned loose, but once his head had been bandaged, Cyprian was lodged in jail.[34]

The press clamored to interview both parties, and Cyprian was happy to oblige. He had not won what he wanted by his skill with a pistol; maybe he could win it with his ability to tell a good tale. The previous January, so he explained, he had turned up at Republican headquarters to protest the party's shameless exploitation of rank-and-file black voters. Leaving the building after what he conceded had been a heated exchange with a couple of the party faithful, he had been set upon by an unknown assailant, who beat him unmercifully and left him for dead. When he recovered, he learned that his attacker had been none other than P.B.S. Pinchback, who had been "instigated . . . to assassinate him" by Henry C. Warmoth (at the time of the shooting, the new Republican governor), because, "dissatisfied with the nominations of the Republican party," Cyprian had been canvassing for Warmoth's Democratic opponent. Since the attack, he admitted he had cherished the thought of vengeance. He had bought a gun, but he really did not know how to use it. Pinchback, who had lived a rough-and-tumble existence as a riverboat gambler before the war, was far more proficient with firearms than he was. Cyprian contended that when he encountered Pinchback on Canal Street, the two had drawn on each other simultaneously. As the injured party in the January affray, he felt he had been justified in his actions.[35]

Pinchback's supporters gave a different version of events. C. C. Morgan had turned up at Republican headquarters in January and "ranted rather disgustingly." Pinchback had told him to moderate his language, whereupon Morgan assaulted him. Yes, Pinchback had hit him, but only in self-defense. Before the April elections, Morgan had stirred up all sorts of trouble, and he had finally agreed to be the trigger man in a Democratic plot to kill Pinchback.[36] In an impassioned speech in the Louisiana Senate the day after the shooting, this was exactly how Pinchback characterized the affair.[37]

Pinchback's fiery rhetoric ensured the story would not die. One newspaper dredged up a witness who was ready to swear that Pinchback had fired the first shot, while another paper made a hero out of his opponent, whom it described as "one of the most intelligent and enterprising of the colored men of this city." This high-minded citizen had become disgusted with the Republicans. What he had first believed to be the party of freedom and morality was, he realized, "the party of oppression, plunder and usurpation." The scalawags and carpetbaggers who dominated the political process cared less about the well-being of black people than did the majority of white Southerners. "Hurrah for Morgan!" the editorial concluded.[38]

Although assailed by Pinchback's friends as "a Judas, a Cain, a Benedict Arnold, *a traitor to his race*," Cyprian soon proved he was no hireling of the Democrats.[39] His flirtation with the Democratic Party lasted just a few months, after which he quickly bolstered his Radical Republican credentials. In January 1869, U.S. senator Charles D. Drake, a Radical Republican from Missouri, testified that Cyprian was and always had been a steadfast Republican.[40] (Drake knew more about Cyprian's background than most people. He had practiced law in St. Louis and had had dealings with the Clamorgan clan.) Then there was the com-

plaint of Dr. Clarence Ward, a self-confessed member of the white su-
premacist Knights of the White Camelia. Questioned by a congressional
subcommittee about election irregularities in Louisiana in 1869, he declared that the Democrats could have taken his own parish of Iberville
if not for the likes of that rabble-rouser "Clay Morgan," who told black
voters if they backed the Republicans they would get forty acres and a
mule and "run the white people out of the parish."[41]

By the spring of 1872, however, Cyprian was yet again assessing
where his loyalties lay. At the national level a deep fissure had opened
up within GOP ranks, and incumbent Ulysses S. Grant's Radical Republicans found themselves facing a challenge from the so-called Liberal Republicans, a coalition of disaffected moderate Republicans and
Democrats. The Liberal Republicans' platform was built around the
eradication of governmental corruption, and, somewhat surprisingly,
the belief that Reconstruction had gone far enough. The leaders of the
new party lambasted "carpetbag" governments. Black people now had
all the rights they needed. It was time to end the military presence in
the South, restore civilian rule, give amnesty to former Confederates,
and let things settle down.

Cyprian Clamorgan decided to become a Liberal Republican.[42] On
May 8, just days after the party held its convention in Cincinnati and
nominated Horace Greeley, editor of the *New York Tribune*, as its presidential candidate, Cyprian spoke at a large, boisterous gathering in
New Orleans's famed Congo Square. He touted his credentials, maintaining that he "had addressed twenty-five thousand people in Louisiana
since the days of Gen. Butler." He read from the Liberal Republicans'
manifesto and then insisted on sharing with the crowd a letter he had
written to the *Times-Picayune* explaining his decision to switch parties.
It was a well-argued piece that proved once again that "Mr. C. C. Morgan"
must have been a force to be reckoned with in the courtroom. According to Cyprian, as far back as 1867 he had urged Louisiana's white citizens to make common cause with their black brethren or risk having "a
set of unprincipled adventurers" descend upon the state and ride into
power by manipulating the black vote. No one had listened to him, and
the result was that Louisiana had been given over to "the vampire
Warmoth" and his friends. It was time for a change.[43] Eloquent though

Cyprian was, this was not a situation in which oratory carried the day. His call for blacks and whites to unite against "carpet-bagger rule" was a highly unpopular one. Amid a chorus of catcalls, he struggled on, until the crescendo of booing and insults forced him to return to his seat.[44] It was a sad comedown for one who had been listened to by thousands just a few years earlier. When *they* had interrupted him it had been with bursts of applause, not hisses and jeers.

The rough handling he received at the Congo Square rally was disheartening, but it was the outcome of the election that finally killed Cyprian's dreams of achieving real power and influence in a "redeemed" Louisiana where the Liberal Republicans held sway. When the Democratic National Convention met in Baltimore in July, delegates adopted wholesale the Liberal Republican ticket in hopes of destroying the GOP. At *their* convention the Radical Republicans backed amnesty for former Confederates, but they held fast to the need for rigorous enforcement of the Fourteenth and Fifteenth amendments, and they demanded the passage of civil rights laws in the individual states. With a strong economy and a bona fide war hero in the White House, they romped home.

In Louisiana the paying off of old scores in 1872 produced a volatile situation. The Republicans were deeply divided. On one side were the Radical Republicans—the so-called Custom House Faction. They were led by William Pitt Kellogg, who was running for governor. The incumbent, Henry C. Warmoth, was himself a Republican, but he loathed the Custom House Faction and came out in support of the Democratic gubernatorial candidate, John McEnery. McEnery also secured the backing of the Liberal Republicans. (In his statement to the public, Cyprian Clamorgan had been just as scathing about the Custom House Faction as he had been about Warmoth and his cronies.) In a flagrant abuse of power, Warmoth created the State Returning Board to scrutinize and rule on election returns. The Board could and did decide that the votes from certain precincts were invalid. Since Warmoth and his cronies controlled the Returning Board, they were able to manipulate the results and have McEnery declared the victor. So enraged were the Radicals that they commenced impeachment proceedings against Warmoth. With Warmoth's ouster, the lieutenant governor stepped in to serve the remaining month of Warmoth's term. When he heard about the handover of power, Cyprian must have had quite a few sleepless nights, for the acting governor was none other than P.B.S. Pinchback! Had Cyprian proven a better shot back in 1868, he might have changed history, for the man he had tried to kill achieved the distinction of becoming the nation's first black governor. Now Cyprian had to worry about what Pinchback might dream up by way of revenge. Fortunately for Cyprian, Pinchback had other matters to attend to during his brief tenure. Although Warmoth had engineered a victory for McEnery, another returning board declared Kellogg the winner. When President Grant intervened on Kellogg's behalf, McEnery's supporters refused to back down. Violence ensued, and federal troops had to be called in to restore some semblance of order.

Amid all the chaos, the resourceful Mr. C. C. Morgan somehow managed to worm his way into the office of collector of taxes for St. Charles Parish.[45] Before long, though, Cyprian decided to quit Louisiana for good and turn his attention to something other than politics. As he headed north he once more jettisoned his identity as a man of color. What had all too briefly been an advantage became a liability. Let white people see him and judge for themselves who and what he was, and if they concluded that he was white, he saw no need to tell them otherwise. By the spring of 1876, when he began fighting the U.S. government over his grandfather's lands, Cyprian had settled in Hardin, Illinois, across the river from St. Charles County, Missouri.[46] After a relatively brief sojourn there, he moved again, this time to St. Louis, so he could more effectively wage war in the courts. In July 1876 the *Globe-Democrat* noted that "the institutor of the great Clamorgan land suits" had arrived in town, vowing to stay as long as he had to in order to see the rights of his family vindicated. And it seemed Cyprian would be true to his word. In 1879 he was in the city directory as a "traveler," the usual description for a traveling salesman.[47] It was a distinct comedown for a man who had dreamed of a thriving law practice, a seat in the Louisiana legislature, even a stint in Congress, but it was only a temporary setback. If Cyprian could not have an important political office, or the respectability that came with being a professional man, he would have money. Any day now the courts would make him very rich indeed. Any day now . . .

Meanwhile, Cyprian's daughter had grown up regarding another man as her father. Under the circumstances, her mother probably preferred it that way. After she and Cyprian separated, Hebe White settled down with Emile Soulier in New Iberia. Emile looked upon Mary Belle as his child and was apparently a good father to her. In time he and Hebe had two sons together, Auguste Maurice, born in 1860, and Edouard Emile in 1863.[48] Although a wife and mother, Hebe continued working as a teacher, as she had on and off for years. She enjoyed some success, teaching first on her own and then joining forces with several other women to operate a private school for girls. The school survived the chaos of the war, but it could not weather the yellow fever epidemic that brought so much misery to New Iberia in 1867. While the Souliers emerged unscathed from that crisis, their good fortune did not last. In 1869, Hebe's health failed, and at age forty-three she died.[49]

The family struggled on without her. When the census taker called at the Soulier home in 1870, he did not inquire too closely into relationships. The head of household was Emile, a retired merchant. The official had no way of knowing that the teenager whose name he wrote down as Belle Soulier was in fact Mary Isabel, or Mary Belle, Clamorgan, the out-of-wedlock child of Emile's deceased wife. There was another puzzle that the man never tried to unravel: One Emma Silcot, a native of Belgium, kept house for Emile, and her daughter, Flora, attended school with Mary Belle. Emma was of course Hebe's older sister. William Silcot had died in St. Louis in 1864, leaving Emma to raise their three daughters.[50] Hebe took in Emma and her children, and when Hebe died, Emma stayed on to manage the home. Although Mary Belle might have grown up in ignorance of her birth father's family, she learned a lot about her mother's people from Hebe and then from Emma.

In the spring of 1872, when sixteen-year-old Mary Belle married,

she was led to the altar not by Cyprian Clamorgan but by the man who
had raised her. Mary Belle had eventually been told that Emile was not
her biological father. She was listed in the marriage register at St. Peter's Church as "Mary Bella Clay Morgan," and on the civil license as
the legitimate daughter of one "Claymorgan" and Hebe White. Cyprian
and Hebe never had been man and wife, but there was no need to be
overly scrupulous about such things. As regards the solemnizing of the
marriage, Father Chassé, the priest at St. Peter's, had agreed to it on
one condition: Mary Belle had been baptized an Episcopalian, but she
must promise to convert if she wanted him to perform the ceremony.
She gave him that promise. The wedding took place on April 20, and a
couple of weeks later Mary Belle returned to church to be received
into the Catholic faith.[51] Then she and her husband settled down in
New Iberia to begin their lives together.

The man Mary Belle married, François Bélanger, was a Canadian,
and at twenty-eight he was almost twice her age. François was from
Montmagny, a farming community on the St. Lawrence River. He was
one of a dozen children born to Paul Bélanger and Henriette Méthot.
As a younger son, François realized early in life that his inheritance
would be a meager one.[52] He must reconcile himself to being a land-
less laborer or strike out on his own. He chose the latter course, coming to the United States and raising enough capital to go into trade. It
was trade that brought him to New Iberia, and probably trade that led
to his meeting with merchant Emile Soulier's adopted daughter.

Why did Mary Belle accept a proposal of marriage from a man who
was so much older than she, and after what was probably a brief court-
ship, since François was a relative newcomer to New Iberia? She may
genuinely have been in love with him, but there could have been another
factor in her decision. Her stepfather planned to marry again, and staying on in the Soulier home to watch Marianne Labyche take the place
of her beloved mother might have been more than Mary Belle could
stomach. François Bélanger offered her a respectable means of escape.
Some months after Mary Belle's marriage to François, Emile wed Marianne and the two proceeded to raise a family. Child followed child in
rapid succession, and there was no place in the new ménage for the

members of Emile's first family. Edouard and Auguste left home as soon as they were able. Aunt Emma and Cousin Flora were given their marching orders. Emma Silcot returned to St. Louis, where she sank into poverty and died in The Home of the Friendless, while Flora trekked out to Washington Territory to live with a stepbrother.[53] Thanks to François, Mary Belle fared better. The couple stayed in New Iberia for a while, and it was there on January 27, 1873, that their daughter was born. Hebe Bélanger's birth a full nine months after her parents wed silenced any rumors floating around New Iberia that the couple had married in haste to cover up a premarital pregnancy.[54] Later that year or early the next, the Bélangers headed to New Orleans. Just possibly they met up with the father from whom Mary Belle had been so long separated, but a reunion was not what had brought them to town. New Orleans was their port of departure for Central America.

The Mosquito Coast was a narrow strip of land on the Atlantic Coast of Central America named by Europeans for the region's indigenous people, the Miskito. Control of the area had been hotly contested over the centuries. The United States had tried to exert its authority, and would do so again. Nicaragua insisted the Mosquito Coast was part of *its* sovereign territory. However, the British had reached an understanding with the most powerful of the Miskito chiefs: they recognized him as ruler and paid him an annual tribute, in return for which he acquiesced to British authority. As a result, the Mosquito Coast had a strongly British flavor by the time the Bélangers arrived.

The bustling town of Bluefields, where the Bélangers made their home, had a romantic past. It was named for a seventeenth-century Dutch pirate, Abraham Blauvelt or Blauveldt, who had anchored his ship in Bluefields Bay between raids. Captain Blauvelt was not the only buccaneer to use the bay as a hideout: for more than two centuries the area was known as a pirates' lair. By the 1870s, however, those lawless times were long gone. Bluefields was a rapidly growing commercial hub from which tropical fruits and hardwoods were exported to the United States and Europe. The town was thriving, and it would do even better if the interoceanic canal the British, the French, and the Americans were talking about building was to be located anywhere in the vicinity. Rumor had it that a route across the isthmus that would cut through the Mosquito Coast was a very real possibility.

In Bluefields the Bélangers found themselves in a setting where various cultures coexisted, albeit not on equal terms. Mary Belle and François belonged to the Euro-American minority whose members dominated the area's business interests. However, they had to reckon with the presence of the Miskito majority, as well as other local peoples, such as the Sumu, Rama, and Garinagu, or Garifunu, who were descended from escaped African slaves and the native peoples with whom they had intermarried. While some newspapers back in the United States used terms such as "hostile" and "savage" when they talked about the Miskito rulers, this was simply not the case, at least as far as white residents such as the Bélangers were concerned. The kings of the Mosquito nation in the 1870s and '80s, William Henry Clarence, and his successor, George William Albert Hendy, cheerfully accepted their salaries from the British Crown and cooperated with white traders in the business of making money.[55]

The mingling of peoples was only one aspect of life in and around Bluefields to which the Bélangers had to accustom themselves. Topography and climate also affected their day-to-day existence. Only 750 miles north of the equator, and just 20 feet above sea level, Bluefields was swampy and humid. Malaria was an ever-present threat, as was dengue fever. Mary Belle was probably less bothered by her new environment than her Canadian-born husband, for she had spent her entire life alongside the Bayou Teche. Mosquitoes, torrential downpours, and constant heat, even during the supposedly cool months, were not as injurious to her health as they were to his. She may actually have preferred Bluefields, with its refreshing ocean breezes, to the stifling summer heat of landlocked New Iberia. What Mary Belle had learned to respect in her native Louisiana, though, was what a tropical weather system could unleash. François had probably never lived through a hurricane, but she had. The Mosquito Coast had its share of hurricanes, including a late-season monster in 1876 that destroyed three hundred homes in Bluefields and killed several dozen residents. Although the Bélangers must have been affected to some degree, they survived, salvaged what they could, rebuilt, and soldiered on.[56]

Details of the Bélangers' business activities are sparse. They apparently had a store in Bluefields and a wharf on the Escondido River, where it opened up into Bluefields Bay. Like a number of the other white residents, they may also have owned or part-owned a banana plantation. As for the source of capital for their initial investment, there is no telling what that may have been. François was not a rich man when he left Canada, but he could have linked up with shipping and banking interests in New Orleans. The Morgan Steamship Company, for instance, was eager to develop its interests on the Mosquito Coast. François and Mary Belle did not become really wealthy in Bluefields, but they did well enough to be able to support themselves and their growing family.

In Bluefields, little Hebe Bélanger flourished. Mary Belle gave birth to another daughter, Clara, in 1876, and a son, Minor Arthur, in 1878. Hebe had been baptized in New Iberia, but if François and Mary Belle had promised Father Chassé to see to it that all their children were baptized as Catholics, they could not fulfill that promise in Bluefields. De facto British control meant that the religious establishment was Protestant. The Bélangers could not find a Catholic priest, so they asked one of the Protestant missionaries to christen Minor. Clara and the couple's fourth child, who died in infancy, were almost certainly baptized at one or other of the Protestant missions.[57]

Although Mary Belle and François made return visits to the United States fairly often, they seldom traveled together. Mary Belle routinely handled business matters back in the United States while François literally minded the store in Bluefields. Ocean travel was not without its hazards: vessels could and did founder, sometimes with the loss of the entire ship's company. Mary Belle was undaunted, and generally took one or more of the children along with her.[58]

In December 1883, François took Minor with him to New Orleans.[59] This was a rare instance in which the entire family left Bluefields around the same time, for François had arranged for Mary Belle and Hebe to rendezvous with him and Minor in Canada for a homecoming of sorts. François took his wife and their two surviving children—Clara's name never surfaced again after an 1880 trip to New York—to meet his relatives. His parents were dead, but he had siblings in and around Montmagny. The family spent time there and then traveled to Cap-St-Ignace, where François's mother had been born. While they were in Cap-St-Ignace, François asked the parish priest to baptize Minor.[60]

The reunion with François's extended family brought about a significant change in the Bélangers' business arrangements. Jules Amadée Bélanger was the son of François's elder brother, Jules Adolphe, and a close bond developed between uncle and nephew. Jules Amadée accompanied François and his family back to the Mosquito Coast and became a junior partner in Bélanger and Co. In 1887, François and Jules returned to Canada so Jules could marry Josephine Fournier, whom he had been courting before he left home. His father was unable to attend the ceremony, but standing in for him was François, described in the church register as "a retired merchant."[61]

François had not actually retired when he sailed to Canada with Jules, although it seems that he was planning to do so. He and the newlyweds returned to Bluefields, and early in 1888, François made what was almost certainly his last business trip to the United States, arriving once more in New Orleans.[62] At some point over the next year he and Mary Belle and the children left the Mosquito Coast and headed to Fall River, Massachusetts. Why they chose Fall River is a mystery. It had a growing French Canadian population, and François may have had family there. On the other hand, the Bélangers might just have been making a brief stopover before going on to Canada. They were certainly not in town long enough to put down roots. Their names do not appear in the Fall River directory. And when François died of pneumonia on August 6, 1889, by a tragic coincidence his son's eleventh birthday, the local French language newspaper, *L'Indépendant*, made no mention of his passing. François's body was taken back to Cap-St-Ignace for burial. The Bélanger clan took charge, quite possibly giving poor Mary Belle no chance to object. She and the children might not even have been at the funeral.[63]

Stranded in Fall River with little to live on, Mary Belle contemplated her future and that of her children. She did not have many options. She and François had done moderately well in Bluefields, but despite their early dreams of becoming really rich, those dreams had never been fulfilled. François had not written a will. There was no real estate for Mary Belle and the children to inherit, and apparently nothing much by way of cash. With François gone, where were they to live? She could not take Minor and Hebe to New Iberia. Emile Soulier was dead, Edouard and Auguste had their own families to care for, and Emile's widow was hardly likely to help her. Her mother's kinfolk were in no position to come to her aid. What about her birth father? By now Mary Belle knew Cyprian Clamorgan as more than just a name. If she had not met him in New Orleans when she and François were getting ready to leave for the Mosquito Coast, she had had the opportunity to spend several weeks in his company later on. Out of the blue one day in 1881, Cyprian had turned up on her doorstep. Whatever was said between father and daughter it was not sufficient to prompt Mary Belle to reach out to Cyprian in her hour of need. Given the timing of Cyprian's trip to Bluefields—the year after the Supreme Court rejected the Clamorgan land claims—he undoubtedly hoped Mary Belle would help him out financially. He had not gotten what he wanted and had soon sailed back to the United States.[64] No, there was no home waiting for Mary Belle and her children in St. Louis with Cyprian.

She could, of course, seek out François's relatives. Perhaps she did and was rebuffed. Perhaps they intimated that she and the children would have to work on the family farm if they wanted a home in Montmagny. A return to the Mosquito Coast was a possibility, but Jules had installed Josephine as mistress of the household in Bluefields. And with François out of the picture, he had found other business partners.[65] Mary Belle realized she must fend for herself and her children.

The wedding that took place in New Bedford, Massachusetts, on November 18, 1889, provided ample fodder for the neighborhood gossips. It was hardly unusual for a widow to marry again, but Mary Belle Bélanger was not yet out of mourning. On the other hand, she did have her children to think of. Although she had tried to support them by working as a seamstress in the months since François's death, it had been a struggle. When Augustus Smith made her an offer of marriage she gladly accepted it. What set tongues wagging was not just Mary Belle's hasty second marriage but the age difference between bride and groom: she was thirty-three and he was sixty-seven. And while it was Mary Belle's second trip to the altar, it was Augustus's fourth.[66]

Augustus Smith was a printer by trade. Born in Rhode Island, he had apprenticed in newspaper offices in Boston, and it was in Boston that he had married for the first time. From Boston he had moved to Illinois, from there to St. Louis, and then to Memphis, before returning to Boston, and finally settling in New Bedford.[67] Mary Belle may have envisaged a relatively brief union with Augustus that would guarantee her children's financial security until they were old enough to fend for themselves. At sixty-seven, how long was he likely to live? In the short term, though, she and Minor and Hebe tried to adjust to the realities of their new life. For at least a couple of years they shared a home with Augustus's son from his first marriage, who was older than his father's new bride.[68]

Contrary to expectations, Augustus Sr. lived a very long life. He did not retire from his job as a compositor at the *New Bedford Standard* until 1906, when he turned eighty-four. Mary Belle worked from home as a dressmaker, assisted by Hebe. They were renters rather than homeowners, and over the years they moved from one address to another in New Bedford. Once Augustus retired, the household got by on his savings and whatever Mary Belle and her children could bring in. Minor finished his schooling in New Bedford. Either Augustus made no attempt to secure an apprenticeship for him, or he did arrange one and the boy proved uncooperative. Minor entered the workforce as an operative in a textile mill.[69]

As for Mary Belle's father, after his foray to Central America, Cyprian had had to survive as best he could in St. Louis. He turned to candy making, one of the many trades he had picked up in the course of his travels. It was as a candy maker by the name of Cyprian P. Morgan that he appeared in the 1893 city directory. The following year, as John Clamorgan, he was working at the same trade and living in a boardinghouse.[70]

Toward the end of 1894, Cyprian pulled off a spectacular coup. He induced two speculators, George Bradley and Henry Kieferle, to pay him ten thousand dollars for his title to the parcel of land he had fought Fanny Deaver over back in the 1870s. It was a significant sum of money, equivalent today to almost a quarter of a million dollars, but six acres of prime real estate was a valuable commodity. Presumably Bradley and Kieferle had acquired the land from Deaver's heirs when she died in 1891 and then discovered that there was an encumbrance, which they needed to remove. Did Cyprian have the exclusive title? This was a moot point. Louis Clamorgan was dead, and neither of his sons had left heirs, but Henry had no fewer than six children living. Nothing in the deed implied that Cyprian would split the proceeds with them, though.[71]

Assuming he got his hands on the cash before Kieferle drank himself to death some months after the sale, Cyprian should have been able to live in style for the rest of his days. He did not. Within a few years he was destitute. He may have squandered the money, or he may have been cheated out of it, for his mental health was deteriorating. Alone, impoverished, and increasingly confused, he found a temporary refuge in one of St. Louis's many Catholic charitable institutions. In the spring of 1900 he entered the Alexian Brothers' Hospital, suffering from what was simply termed "senility." The Brothers assumed Cyprian was white, and even in his impaired state he appreciated that it would not do to tell them otherwise. His stay lasted until the autumn, when Peter J. Doerr, the senior cashier of St. Louis's Lafayette Bank, took him out of the hospital and promised to provide for him.[72]

Perhaps Doerr was a kindly individual who took pity on an old acquaintance, but he may have been an opportunist eager to exploit an elderly man who could no longer protect his own interests. With the Clamorgan claims still unresolved, Cyprian (or Doerr acting on his behalf) milked them for a few hundred dollars. People were willing to part with cash to cleanse their titles. A couple of deals in 1901 netted a grand total of three hundred dollars.[73] It was a pittance compared to the riches Cyprian had hoped to win from the courts or from Congress, but his days of fighting were over. For a few months at least, the money kept a roof over his head, food in his belly, and clothes on his back.

The ultimate tragedy of Cyprian's life was that a man who had fought so long and so hard to win a fortune died in poverty. Doerr tired of caring for him, or maybe the burden of nursing someone suffering from senile dementia became too great. On June 16, 1902, Cyprian went into the St. Louis Poor House. His daughter could not or would not help him. As for his St. Louis kin, Henry's widow was the natural choice for a caretaker, but in the early 1900s she was spending months at a time with her eldest son in New York City. Neither her children nor Henry's son from his first marriage seemed willing to do more than check in on the old man occasionally. No one stepped forward when Cyprian died on November 13, 1902. He was buried not in the Clamorgan plot in Calvary but in an unmarked grave in St. Matthew's U.C.C. Cemetery as a charity case. In death as in life he was estranged from his family. The authorities also inflicted upon him what he would surely have considered one final indignity. Since his departure from Louisiana, Cyprian had struggled to shed his identity as a man of color. The overseers of the Poor House knew his history, however, and labeled him "colored."[74]

Meanwhile, Mary Belle was managing as best she could in New Bedford. On New Year's Day 1908 she suffered an appalling tragedy. Hebe had been rushed to St. Luke's Hospital a day earlier suffering from a massive infection. It turned out to be a pelvic abscess, virtually untreatable in an era before antibiotics, and she died in excruciating pain. Mother and daughter had been through so much together. Hebe had never married and had made her home with her mother and stepfather. Mary Belle buried her child in New Bedford's French Cemetery and tried to pick up the pieces of her life.[75]

Fourteen months after Hebe's death, Mary Belle lost her husband. The death was reported not by Mary Belle but by Amy Bloomfield, Augustus's widowed sister.[76] Augustus had little to leave—certainly not enough to warrant making a will. Mary Belle had long since relinquished any hope of a comfortable inheritance from him, and after Hebe's death she may well have given the elderly man over to the care of his sister. A Clamorgan to the core, Mary Belle was pinning her hopes on her family's land claims. Although she and her father had gone their separate ways, in the brief time the two of them had spent in each other's company in Bluefields, Mary Belle had learned enough from Cyprian to understand what it meant to be a Clamorgan. Was she not, when all was said and done, Jacques Clamorgan's great-granddaughter, and entitled to her share of his legacy? For some time Mary Belle had been squirreling away a portion of her earnings to carry on the fight. Hebe had helped and encouraged her. Now Mary Belle pressed on alone. She convinced a local attorney in Massachusetts of the viability of her claims, and a few months before Augustus's death she had gone to consult with her cousins in St. Louis. It was a bold move, but then a woman who had made and remade her life since her teenage years was unlikely to be deterred by a lengthy journey to a city she had never visited before and a meeting with people who might be kin but who were basically strangers. She returned to New Bedford in time to bury her husband, but she did not stay put for long.[77]

In 1910 the widowed Mary Belle appeared in the census as a nurse-companion to an elderly spinster, Sarah Tilden.[78] Toward the end of 1910, or early the following year, she left New Bedford for good. The 1911 city directory reported that she had gone to California.[79] She was in her mid-fifties. She had outlived two husbands and three of her four children. Her travels had taken her from Louisiana to Central America, from there to Canada, and then to New England. A move across the United States was hardly a bigger upheaval than those she had already faced. It was time to begin life anew. And she just might inherit a fortune.

Like his mother, Minor Arthur Bélanger was a restless soul, and he lost no time breaking free. There may have been tensions with his stepfather. Augustus Smith was so much older than Minor, more like a grandfather than a replacement for the father he had lost. But maybe what Minor found so tough to accept was not so much his elderly stepfather as the tedium of life in the mills of New Bedford.

No sooner had Minor turned twenty-one than he headed down to

Bluefields. By this time Jules Amadée Bélanger was a man of considerable wealth and consequence: he headed the firm of Bélanger and Co. and he was also the British consul in the region.[80] He and Josephine had no children, and Minor may have hoped they would take him in and make him a partner in the firm, since he was the son of the company's founder. These were also stirring times. In 1894, Nicaraguan forces led by José Santos Zelaya had forcibly annexed the Mosquito Coast. However, early in 1899, Nicaragua's control of the region was challenged by Juan Pablo Reyes, and Reyes's insurgency was aided by the arrival of some of Teddy Roosevelt's Rough Riders fresh from their victories in Cuba. As the senior representative for British interests on the Mosquito Coast, Cousin Jules was in the thick of things.[81] Surely he could help his adventurous young kinsman, assuming Minor did not mean to throw in his lot with Reyes and his American allies. Whether he had come looking for profit or glory, Minor had his hopes dashed. Reyes's rebellion was defeated, and Jules made it clear he did not intend to take Minor into business with him. In the spring of 1900 the dejected young man arrived in New Orleans and began the trek back to New Bedford.[82]

He did not stay long. The United States was at war and the army beckoned. With or without his mother's knowledge, Minor made his way to Fall River and enlisted. The recruiter described him as being of medium height, with brown eyes, black hair, and a complexion that the official categorized as dark. Yes, he was foreign-born, but then, as now, there was no barrier against resident aliens serving in the military. Minor was assigned to a Pennsylvania regiment, the Fifth Infantry, nicknamed the Bobcats.[83] The fighting in Cuba was long since over, but another theater had opened. Soon Minor was on a troop ship heading to Manila. The Fifth Infantry was in the Philippines for many months trying to pacify those areas still outside American control after the capture of the Filipino nationalist leader Emilio Aguinaldo. Private Bélanger's conduct in the army was described in the official record as "Very Good." He received an honorable discharge in November 1902 and headed back to New Bedford.[84]

On February 27, 1904, at New Bedford's First Primitive Methodist

Church, Minor, then almost twenty-six, married seventeen-year-old Etta Edna Covill, a packer in one of the mills. Etta had been born in Rhode Island, the daughter of David Covill, from Massachusetts, and Imogene Elmes, a native of Hallowell, Maine. On the application for a marriage license, Minor gave his occupation as "spindle-maker" and identified his parents as Frank Bélanger and Mary B. Clamorgan.[85]

Soon after the wedding the couple moved to Philadelphia. What seems like an odd decision was actually one that had solid good sense behind it. Minor had served in a Pennsylvania regiment. He had friends in and around Philadelphia from his army days, and those friends could help him and Etta get settled. It was in Philadelphia that the couple's first child, Minor Arthur, Jr., was born, on January 7, 1906. Sadly, he died when he was little more than a month old.[86] The Bélangers' second child, Edna Belle, was born on February 27, 1907. Shortly after her birth, Minor made another foray into Central America in the hope of finding the brighter economic prospects that had so far eluded him. In a repetition of his parents' move to the Mosquito Coast more than thirty years earlier, he and Etta set off with their baby daughter and whatever cash they had managed to save to seek their fortunes. Disappointment awaited them, and after a stay of less than a year they moved back to the United States. They arrived in New York in early 1908 and decided not to head to Philadelphia but to return to New Bedford.[87] With his sister's death, Minor may have felt a great deal of emotional pressure to be closer to his mother.

The Bélangers were back in time for Minor's name to appear in the 1908 New Bedford directory, and it was in New Bedford that their third child, Arthur Theodore, was born, on September 4 of that year.[88] Another daughter, Hebe Florine, was born a year and a half later. The "Balingers"—somewhat surprisingly, in a city with more than a few French Canadian residents, the census taker had a problem with their name—were listed in the 1910 census. Minor had returned to labor in the mills as a shuttle maker. He acknowledged that he was an alien and claimed that both his parents were French-speaking Canadians. The enumerator had no way of knowing that Minor's mother, who lived a few streets away, had declared herself to be a native of Louisiana.[89]

After Mary Belle left for California, Minor and Etta stayed on in New Bedford. In 1912, Etta gave birth to Frank Robert. Two years later Nina Imogene was born. Now that he was settled permanently in the United States, Minor took a long overdue step: on June 6, 1916, he became a U.S. citizen.[90]

Around the time of his naturalization Minor received some unexpected news from the West Coast. His mother had married again. Her new husband was Thomas Benton Coats, and he was far closer to her in age than either François Bélanger or Augustus Smith. Thomas was originally from Polk County, Missouri. That was where he had spent at least the first three decades of his life, and it was where he had married for the first time, and where he and his wife, Matilda, had begun raising a family.[91] In the mid-1880s the Coatses moved to Kansas, and from there they went to California. When Matilda died on July 3, 1914, most of the Coats children had already moved away to begin their own lives. Thomas sold his farm in Hemet and relocated to Los Angeles, where he met Mary Belle. On December 1 the two married.[92]

Not surprisingly, the Coats children regarded their father's new wife as a gold digger, and apparently Mary Belle let it be known that she believed she had done well for herself in ensnaring Thomas. She proceeded to go through his money, persuading him to invest in a tailoring business. It did not prosper, despite her skill as a seamstress, and Thomas was obliged to turn to one of his sons for a loan until he and Mary Belle could find some other way of supporting themselves— or until Mary Belle got her share of the Clamorgan inheritance.[93] In 1918 the couple left Los Angeles for the small community of Lakeport. Thomas purchased a fruit farm, and although Mary Belle sometimes did dressmaking, she was to all intents and purposes a farmer's wife. In 1920 she lied a little about her age, but the rest of her answers to the census taker were truthful: she had been born in Louisiana, her father in Missouri, and her mother in Belgium.[94]

Mary Belle and Thomas remained in Lakeport until 1924, when they moved to Santa Barbara. In the spring of 1925, Mary Belle was widowed for the third time.[95] Each of Thomas's eight children had a claim on his estate, but he had made some provision for Mary Belle.

While Thomas's relatives may have expected Mary Belle to live out her remaining years quietly in Santa Barbara, she had other ideas.[96] She embarked on a fourth marriage, this one with a man many years her junior. Back east, Minor can hardly have been pleased to receive a letter from his mother informing him that he now had a stepfather younger than he was! Mary Belle's new husband was John H. Guilbert, a Dutch immigrant and a carpenter by trade. He had arrived in the United States in 1901, when he was twenty-one. In 1930 the census taker found the Guilberts living fairly comfortably, probably on Mary Belle's inheritance from Thomas. They had a home in Compton Township, in Los Angeles County, and a live-in housekeeper. The money did not last long, however, and they soon became renters, living at various addresses in and around Los Angeles. It was in Los Angeles that Mary Belle died on December 1, 1936, at the age of eighty-one. John Guilbert supplied what information he could: most of it was correct, except that he gave his wife's father's name as *Cytrian* Clamorgan.[97]

By the summer of 1917, when their daughter Edith May was born, the Bélangers were back in Pennsylvania. At first they settled just outside Philadelphia, and Minor commuted into the city each day to his job as a machinist. The family eventually moved into Philadelphia proper, and that was where the census taker found them in 1920. The year after the census was taken, Minor and Etta lost two of their children. Newborn Ernest Minor died in April 1921 and his thirteen-year-old brother, Arthur Theodore, five months later. Both were buried in the plot in Hillside Cemetery in rural Montgomery County that Minor and Etta had bought when their firstborn died.[98]

The Bélangers remained in Philadelphia through the 1920s. They never amassed the money to buy a home, and they were obliged to move every year or two in search of a lower rent or a little more space. The arrival of one of Etta's brothers helped them by adding another income to the household, although it meant even closer quarters. By the time the 1930 census was taken, "Mina Bellinger" (the census taker's rendering of Minor's name) reported that he worked as a machinist for an automobile company. His son Frank was also working, as was one of his daughters, Hebe.[99] No directories were published for Philadelphia during the depths of the Depression, but when they resumed in 1935, the Bélangers were long gone. Like so many others looking for brighter prospects, they had headed west. Minor, Etta, Frank, Hebe, Edith, Nina, and the baby of the family, Hazel Theodora, settled in Riverside, California. Accompanying them to the Golden State was their eldest child, Edna, her husband, and their two sons.[100]

Minor was not in good health. Within months of settling in Riverside he entered the Veterans' Hospital in Sawtelle, suffering from multiple ailments. The treatment he received proved effective, and he was discharged in a far more robust state than when he entered, although he seems to have retired on his army pension after leaving the hospital.[101] Contrary to what he and the family probably expected, he outlived Etta. She died of pneumonia in the spring of 1942, and Minor had her body brought back to Hillside Cemetery for burial.[102] For several years after Etta's death, Minor lived with Frank in Santa Monica, but in 1950, Minor married again and moved to Los Angeles. His second marriage was of fairly short duration, not because of any disharmony between him and his new wife, Marie, but because of Minor's deteriorating health. He spent the last few weeks of his life—possibly the last few months—in the Los Angeles National Military Home.[103] He died on December 26, 1954, at the age of seventy-six, and was buried with full military honors in the Los Angeles Veterans' Cemetery.

While the information Minor's family supplied to the authorities was less than accurate in one respect, they passed on what they knew. They gave his mother's maiden name as Soulier, and this was what appeared on his death certificate.[104] In a final ironic twist, Cyprian Clamorgan's role in his daughter's life was forgotten. Presumably the man Minor had heard his mother talk about as the father figure she remembered from her youth was Emile Soulier, and it was his name that Minor handed down to his own children. He had met his grandfather just once, but when Cyprian arrived at the Bélanger home in Bluefields, Minor was only four years old. As a grown man and a father himself, he had no recollection of the mystery visitor. Yes, when he and Etta wed in 1904 he had put his mother's name down on the marriage license application as Mary B. Clamorgan. Over the years, though, he had simply forgotten. Emile Soulier? Cyprian Clamorgan? Neither had been a presence in his life. What did it matter what he told his children about someone he had never known? Their grandmother could have set the record straight, but by the time Minor's children were of an age to know or care about their ancestry, Mary Belle was no longer around. And with the fading from family memory of Cyprian Clamorgan, the Clamorgan inheritance was lost—an inheritance that was about untold riches, epic court battles, and so very much more besides.

Epilogue: Clamorgan Alley

THERE ARE ALWAYS PROBLEMS with the counterfactual, but it is tempting to indulge for a moment or two in the "what-ifs" of the Clamorgan saga. Had things fallen out differently, what might we have seen? Perhaps Clamorgan Street or Clamorgan Boulevard, rather than the two-block alley in downtown St. Louis that bears Jacques Clamorgan's name today. Farther afield, if Jacques or his descendants had secured recognition of their land claims, might there have been a Clamorganville somewhere in Missouri or Arkansas, or far upriver in the Dakotas, at the site of the great Cedar Island claim? Had Jacques and Susanne's grandson, that consummate trickster figure Cyprian Clamorgan, alias Mr. C. C. Morgan, seen his dreams of political power come to fruition, he might have won a seat in Congress or secured for himself a term in Louisiana's Governor's Mansion. If he had been a better shot, he might have gone down in history as a notorious assassin. Had he developed his literary talents further, he could have emerged as a leading African American writer, challenging the nation in the post–Civil War years to examine anew its understanding of race. Or perhaps he would have slipped quietly into the white community and found success as an author with no one any the wiser about his complex genealogy.

And if Cyprian, Henry, Julia, Léon, Julius, Louis, and the rest of the Clamorgan clan had achieved a victory in just one of their cases—the contest over the great St. Charles grant, perhaps, or the Baden claim, or the Washington Avenue–Little Prairie title—it would not have been the physical landscape alone that would have had to change. An immensely wealthy multiracial family would have challenged by their very presence the "borderland" between black and white in nineteenth-century America. All it would have taken was just one verdict in their favor, one ruling, one congressional subcommittee report that declared them not only Jacques Clamorgan's lineal descendants but also the inheritors of his vast fortune.

The what-ifs tantalize. We can speculate about what might have been, but that is all we can do. Look for the Clamorgan name today and you will not find it borne by any family in the United States. Two centuries after Jacques Clamorgan's death, his name has disappeared, although his and Susanne's heirs have not. Without the help of several of the women and men who can trace their descent back to the notorious Frenchman and his enslaved "housekeeper," I could not have maneuvered my way through the twists and turns of the Clamorgan story. My heartfelt thanks go out to them.

And finally, what of the prize that at least six generations of Clamorgans agonized over? What of Jacques Clamorgan's claims to a million acres or more of prime real estate in the American heartland? At least a few of those claims remain unresolved. They are waiting to be fought over anew if any of his heirs care to step forward, dust off a yellowing case file or two, and begin working their way through the crabbed and faded handwriting. Today it is not a matter of millions of dollars at stake. With the passage of time, the inheritance must be measured in terms of billions. But perhaps any legal case that the Clamorgan heirs could mount would end like Charles Dickens's *Jarndyce v. Jarndyce*, with the costs of the fight swallowing up every last cent and the prize forever eluding them.

Notes

Abbreviations

BMHS	*Bulletin of the Missouri Historical Society*
BPL	Boston Public Library
COLARCH	Colonial Archives of St. Louis
COVR	California Office of Vital Records
CSLRD	City of St. Louis, Recorder of Deeds
FHL	Family History Library, Salt Lake City
IGI	International Genealogical Index, Church of Jesus Christ of Latter-Day Saints
ISA	Illinois State Archives, Springfield
JSH	*Journal of Southern History*
KSA	Kentucky State Archives, Frankfort
LH	*Louisiana History*
LHQ	*Louisiana Historical Quarterly*
LSA	Louisiana State Archives, Baton Rouge
MHS	Missouri Historical Society, St. Louis
MHR	*Missouri Historical Review*
MOSA	Missouri State Archives, Jefferson City
MOSL	Missouri State Archives, St. Louis
MSA	Massachusetts State Archives, Boston
MVHR	*Mississippi Valley Historical Review*
NEHGS	New England Historic Genealogical Society, Boston

NMHR   *New Mexico Historical Review*
PCA   Philadelphia City Archives
SLCOL   St. Louis County Library
SLGS   St. Louis Genealogical Society
SSDI   Social Security Death Index
TSA   Tennessee State Archives, Nashville

1. Sieur Jacques

1. "Index to the Spanish Judicial Records of Louisiana, August–September 1781," *LHQ* 17 (Jan. 1934): 220–21; Abraham P. Nasatir, "Jacques Clamorgan," in Leroy R. Hafen, ed., *French Fur Traders and Voyageurs in the American West* (Lincoln: University of Nebraska Press, 1997), 124.

2. Frederick A. Hodes, *Beyond the Frontier: A History of St. Louis to 1821* (Tucson, Ariz.: Patrice Press, 2004), 216. On Marmillon, see the reconstructed 1776 St. Louis Census at www.stlgs.org/DBgovernmentCensus1776.htm.

3. Hodes, *Beyond the Frontier*, 126–32.

4. Ibid., 155.

5. David J. Weber, *The Spanish Frontier in North America* (New Haven, Conn.: Yale University Press, 1992), 198–99; François Furstenberg, "The Significance of the Trans-Appalachian Frontier in Atlantic History," *AHR* 113 (June 2008): 656.

6. On the origins of the Chouteau clan, see Shirley Christian, *Before Lewis and Clark: The Story of the Chouteaus, The French Dynasty That Ruled America's Frontier* (New York: Farrar, Straus and Giroux, 2004), esp. chaps. 1–3; and William E. Foley and C. David Rice, *The First Chouteaus: River Barons of Early St. Louis* (Urbana and Chicago: University of Illinois Press, 1983), 22–23.

7. Nasatir, "Jacques Clamorgan," in Hafen, ed., *French Fur Traders*, 124–25.

8. Thomas James, *Three Years Among the Indians and Mexicans* (Waterloo, Ill. Printed at the Office of the "War Eagle," 1846; repr. St. Louis, Mo.: MHS, 1916), 96; Richard Edward Oglesby, *Manuel Lisa and the Opening of the Missouri Fur Trade* (Norman: University of Oklahoma Press, 1963), 17; *Missouri Republican*, Mar. 20, 1863; *Claim of Heirs of Jacques Clamorgan* (Washington, D.C.: Government Printing Office, 1910), 7; A. P. Nasatir, "Jacques Clamorgan: Colonial Promoter of the Northern Border of New Spain," *NMHR* 17 (Apr. 1942): 104; David Williams, "John Evans' Strange Journey: Part II. Following the Trail," *AHR* 54 (Apr. 1949): 511; Gwyn A. Williams, "Welsh Indians: The Madoc Legend and the First Welsh Radicalism," *History Workshop* 1 (Spring 1976): 143, 147.

9. Juliette Augusta Magill Kinzie, *Wau-Bun: The Early Day in the Northwest* (Philadelphia: J. B. Lippincott, 1873), 150–51. On the inconsistencies in Kinzie's book (the first edition of which appeared in 1856), see Milo M. Quaife, *Checagou: From Indian Wigwam to Modern City, 1673–1835* (Chicago: University of Illinois Press, 1933), 43–44. The myth about a link between the two men persists. See Richard C. Lindberg, "Jean Baptiste Point Du Sable," in John A. Garraty and

Mark C. Carnes, eds., *American National Biography* (New York: Oxford University Press, 1999), vol. 7, pp. 166–68.

10. See, for example, Joseph J. Hill, ed., "An Unknown Expedition to Santa Fé in 1807," *MVHR* 6 (Mar. 1920): 561–62.

11. *Dictionnaire des familles françaises anciennes ou notables à la fin du XIXe siècle* (Evreux: Charles Hérissey, 1912), vol. 11, p. 19.

12. E. C. Abendanon, "An Important Atlas in the British Museum," *The Geographical Journal* 57 (Apr. 1921): 284–89.

13. Jean Canu, *Les mille ans d'une famille normande: les Clamorgan, 1066–1980* (St. Lô: Société d'archéologie de la Manche, 1980).

14. The editor of "Journal of Jean Baptiste Truteau on the Upper Missouri," *AHR* 19 (Jan. 1914), says he was from Guadeloupe and cites (302n) the journal of naturalist André Michaux. However, Michaux never met Clamorgan, whom he referred to as "Charles Morgan" and described simply as "a creole from the Islands." *André Michaux's Travels into Kentucky, 1793–96* (vol. 3, p. 80), in Reuben Gold Thwaites, ed., *Early Western Travels, 1748–1846* (Cleveland, Oh.: A. H. Clark, 1904–1907).

15. When Jacques died in 1814, the priest who officiated at his funeral gave his age as "about eighty," indicating he had been born about 1734. However, in the 1787 census, Jacques reported he was forty-two, so his birth year would have been 1744 or 1745. Old Cathedral, Burials (1781–1832), 92 (SLCOL); "Census of St. Louis and Districts, 1787," Census Collection, MHS.

16. John Francis McDermott, *Private Libraries in Creole Saint Louis* (Baltimore, Md.: Johns Hopkins University Press, 1938), 56, 79–83.

17. "Index to the Spanish Judicial Records of Louisiana, Aug.–Sept. 1781," 220–21.

18. *New Jersey Gazette*, Mar. 22, 1780; *Pennsylvania Gazette*, Mar. 20, 1780.

19. "Index to the Spanish Judicial Records of Louisiana, October 1783," *LHQ* 22 (Jan. 1939): 298–301; "Index to the Spanish Judicial Records of Louisiana, March 1784," *LHQ* 23 (Jan. 1940): 297–304.

20. COLARCH, vol. 3, no. 2223-4. On Clamorgan's dealings with Mercier, see Poepping Family Papers, box 1, f. 1, MHS.

21. St. Louis Deeds, Book A, p. 203; COLARCH, vol. 2, nos. 384, 396, and 441; Minutes of the Board of Land Commissioners, Book 1, p. 423, MOSA; "Land Claims in the Missouri Territory, Communicated to the House of Representatives, December 1, 1812," in *American State Papers: Public Lands* (Washington, D.C.: Gales and Seaton, 1861; repr. Greenville, S.C.: Southern Historical Press, 1994), vol. 2, p. 655.

22. 1787 Census of St. Louis; COLARCH, vol. 3, no. 2239. On deals between Clamorgan and Tardif, see COLARCH, vol. 2, no. 768.

23. Clarence Walworth Alvord, ed., *Cahokia Records, 1778–1790* (Springfield: Illinois State Historical Library, 1907), 370–73.

24. Ibid., 409–11. In 1780–81 the British had evacuated the old colonial trading post and relocated to Mackinac Island.

25. Alvord, ed., *Cahokia Records*, 239–41, 305, 331, 355–57, 363–67, 409–11, 421, 435.

26. John Dodge to William Croghan, Jan. 13, 1788; Croghan to Hugh Howard, Feb. 23, 1788; Howard to Croghan, Jan. 31, 1788, Draper MSS, Ser. N, Croghan Papers, 1, nos. 6 and 8, and Ser. M, William Clark Papers, 2, no. 43 (microfilm, BPL).

27. Hodes, *Beyond the Frontier*, 217; Lorenzo J. Greene, Gary R. Kremer, and Antonio F. Holland, *Missouri's Black Heritage* (Columbia: University of Missouri Press, 1993), 8–17.

28. Hodes, *Beyond the Frontier*, 77.

29. For records of some of the slaves Clamorgan owned, see COLARCH, vol. 2: nos. 376, 418, 533, 556, 566, 571, 596, 599, 604, 797B, 848, 929, 987; ibid., vol. 4, nos. 1676, 1700; and Teresa Blattner, comp., *People of Color: Black Genealogical Records and Abstracts from Missouri Sources* (Bowie, Md.: Heritage Books, 1998), 135, 138, 139.

30. "Afro-Louisiana History and Genealogy, 1718–1820," www.ibiblio.org/laslave; "Ste. Geneviève Co., Missouri, Slave Bills of Sale, 1766–1827," in Sherida K. Eddleman, comp., *Missouri Genealogical Records and Abstracts*, vol. 1 (Bowie, Md.: Heritage Books, 1990), 48, 49, 50, 51; Kaskaskia Manuscripts, 1714–1816, ISA.

31. Blattner, comp., *People of Color*, 135–41; COLARCH, vol. 2, nos. 556, 572, 595, 931.

32. *Proceso entre Dn. Carlos Sanguinet y Dn. Santiago Clamorgan* (Feb. 27–Mar. 28, 1787), in Poepping Coll., MHS, cited in Stuart Banner, "Written Law and Unwritten Norms in Colonial St. Louis," *Law and History Review* 14 (Spring 1996): 61–62.

33. Alvord, ed., *Cahokia Records*, 384–87.

34. Helen C. Marsh and Timothy R. Marsh, comps., *Davidson County, Tennessee, Wills and Inventories, vol. 1 (1783–1816)* (Greenville, S.C.: Southern Historical Press, 1990), 23, 27; St. Louis Deeds, Book C, p. 437.

35. Hodes, *Beyond the Frontier*, 224.

36. Old Cathedral, Baptisms (1769–1804), 43, 49, 54, 56, 60, 67 (SLCOL); COLARCH, vol. 2, nos. 596, 599.

37. On Clamorgan's investments in the saltworks, see COLARCH, vol. 2, nos. 555, 566, and ibid., vol. 4, no. 1676.

38. Frederic Louis Billon, *Annals of St. Louis in Its Early Days Under the French and Spanish Dominations* (St. Louis: self-published, 1886), 248–50; Louis Houck, *A History of Missouri, From Its Earliest Explorations and Settlements Until the Admission of the State into the Union* (St. Louis: R. R. Donnelly and Sons, 1908), 73, 74. Minutes of the Board of Land Commissioners, Book 1, p. 422, MOSA.

39. Jacques Clamorgan to Trudeau, Apr. 1, 1793, and Carondelet to Jacques Clamorgan, July 22, 1794, in Abraham P. Nasatir, ed., *Before Lewis and Clark: Documents Illustrating the History of the Missouri, 1785–1804* (St. Louis, Mo.: St.

Louis Historical Documents Foundation, 1952; repr. Norman: University of Oklahoma Press, 1990), 169–71, 236–37.

40. "Land Claims in the Missouri Territory," in *American State Papers: Public Lands*, vol. 2, pp. 567, 662; Houck, *History of Missouri*, 75; Minutes of the Board of Land Commissioners, Book 1, pp. 410, 422, and Book 4, pp. 493–94.

41. "People of Illinois to Carondelet, 1792," and "Inhabitants of Spanish Illinois to the King, July 7, 1793," in Lawrence Kinnaird, ed., *Spain in the Mississippi Valley, 1765–1794. Annual Report of the American Historical Association for the Year 1943* (Washington, D.C.: Government Printing Office, 1946), vol. 4, pp. 44–46, 181–90.

42. Foley and Rice, *First Chouteaus*, 37–38; Abraham P. Nasatir, "The Formation of the Missouri Company," *MHR* 25 (Oct. 1930): 10–11.

43. Hodes, *Beyond the Frontier*, 256; Nasatir, "Anglo-Spanish Rivalry on the Upper Missouri, Part 2," *MVHR* 16 (Mar. 1930): 526; Williams, "John Evans," 510–11.

44. Jacques Clamorgan to Carondelet, Oct. 4, 1793, in Kinnaird, ed., *Spain in the Mississippi Valley*, vol. 4, pp. 208–15.

45. Nasatir, "Formation," 12–13.

46. Nasatir, "Anglo-Spanish Rivalry on the Upper Missouri, Part 1," *MVHR* 16 (Dec. 1929): 369–70; "Regulations for the Illinois Trade," in Nasatir, ed., *Before Lewis*, 186–94.

47. "Allotment of the Missouri Trading Posts," in Kinnaird, ed., *Spain in the Mississippi Valley*, vol. 4, pp. 277–79.

48. "Articles of Incorporation of the Missouri Company," in Nasatir, ed., *Before Lewis*, 217–26.

49. Jacques Clamorgan to Carondelet, May 12, 1794, in Nasatir, ed., *Before Lewis*, 226–27; Nasatir, "Formation," 15–16.

50. Trudeau to Carondelet, May 31, 1794, in Nasatir, ed., *Before Lewis*, 228–29.

51. Carondelet to Trudeau, July 12, 1794, in Nasatir, ed., *Before Lewis*, 236.

52. On his role in equipping one early foray, see COLARCH, vol. 4, no. 1699.

53. Billon, *Early Days*, 295–96; "Instructions to Truteau," in Nasatir, ed., *Before Lewis*, 243–53.

54. "Truteau's Journal," in Nasatir, ed., *Before Lewis*, 302.

55. "Report of Santiago Clamorgan and Antoine Reihle, July 8, 1794," in Nasatir, ed., *Before Lewis*, 335–40; Noel M. Loomis and Abraham P. Nasatir, *Pedro Vial and the Roads to Santa Fé* (Norman: University of Oklahoma Press, 1967), 90. Santiago Clamorgan and Jacques Clamorgan were one and the same. Which version of his name, the French or the Spanish, appeared in any document depended on the whim and the linguistic background of the individual writing that document.

56. Trudeau to Carondelet, July 20, 1795, and Aug. 30, 1795, in Nasatir, ed., *Before Lewis*, 343–45.

57. Nasatir, "Anglo-Spanish Rivalry, Part 2," 508; Mackay to Jacques Clamorgan, Oct. 24–27, 1795, in Nasatir, ed., *Before Lewis*, 351–52.

58. Jacques Clamorgan to Carondelet, Dec. 15, 1795; and Trudeau to Carondelet, Dec. 19, 1795, in Nasatir, ed., *Before Lewis*, 364n, 374.

59. Carondelet to Manuel Godoy, Jan. 8, 1796, and Trudeau to Gayoso de Lemos, May 6, 1798, in Nasatir, ed., *Before Lewis*, 400–404, 557–58.

60. Nasatir, "Jacques Clamorgan," in Hafen, ed., *French Fur Traders*, 131.

61. Jacques Clamorgan to Carondelet, Apr. 15 and 30, 1796, in Nasatir, ed., *Before Lewis*, 421–24, 424–25.

62. Jacques Clamorgan to Carondelet, Apr. 10, 1796, in Nasatir, ed., *Before Lewis*, 417–21.

63. Carondelet to Jacques Clamorgan, May 11, 1796, in Nasatir, ed., *Before Lewis*, 420–21n.

64. Jacques Clamorgan to Carondelet, n.d., and May 26, 1796, in Nasatir, ed., *Before Lewis*, 429, 431–32.

65. *Title Papers of the Clamorgan Grant of 536,904 Arpens of Alluvial Lands in Missouri and Arkansas* (New York: T. Snowden, 1837), 3–5, 6–7.

66. Jacques Clamorgan to Carondelet, Sept. 15, 1796, in Nasatir, ed., *Before Lewis*, 444–50.

67. Trudeau to Carondelet, July 3 and Aug. 4, 1796, in Nasatir, ed., *Before Lewis*, 441–42.

68. Carondelet to Jacques Clamorgan, Sept. 13, 1796, and Carondelet to Jacques Clamorgan, Nov. 8, 1796, in *Petition of Clamorgan's Representatives* (1818), 6–7.

69. "Agreement between Todd and Clamorgan," in Nasatir, ed., *Before Lewis*, 464–67.

70. The financial fallout from Todd's death is described in detail in Juan Ventura Morales to Don Diego de Gardoquil, Dec. 1, 1796, in Nasatir, ed., *Before Lewis*, 481–82.

71. Carondelet to Manuel Godoy, Mar. 20, 1797, in Nasatir, ed., *Before Lewis*, 507–12. On Clark, see www.enlou.com/people/clarkd.htm.

72. Trudeau to Gayoso de Lemos, May 6, 1797, in Nasatir, ed., *Before Lewis*, 557–58.

73. Jacques Clamorgan to Trudeau, Mar. 1, 1797; Trudeau to Jacques Clamorgan, Mar. 3 and July 3, 1797, in *Petition of Clamorgan's Representatives . . . 1818*, 1–4.

74. Trudeau to Gayoso de Lemos, Nov. 15, 1798, in Nasatir, ed., *Before Lewis*, 561n.

75. Robidoux to Gayoso de Lemos, Mar. 7, 1798, in Nasatir, ed., *Before Lewis*, 548–53.

76. Trudeau to Gayoso de Lemos, May 6, 1798, in Nasatir, ed., *Before Lewis*, 558.

77. Jacques Clamorgan to Trudeau, June 18, 1798, in Nasatir, ed., *Before Lewis*, 563–66.

78. Trudeau to Gayoso de Lemos, June 20, 1798, in Nasatir, ed., *Before Lewis*, 567.

79. COLARCH, vol. 4, nos. 760–58 and 1915. For one heated exchange between Clamorgan and an individual who considered himself ill-used as a result of Clamorgan's financial wheeling and dealing, see Poepping Family Papers, box 1, f. 22.

80. Jacques Clamorgan to Daniel Clark, Jr., June 18, 1798, in COLARCH, vol. 5, pt. 3; Jacques Clamorgan to Daniel Clark, Jr., July 13, 1798, in Nasatir, ed., *Before Lewis*, 569–70.

81. Jay Gitlin, *The Bourgeois Frontier: French Towns, French Traders and American Expansion* (New Haven, Conn.: Yale University Press, 2010), 58–59; Database of Illinois Marriages (ISA); W. C. Walton, *A Brief History of St. Clair County, Illinois* (1928), in www.rootsweb.ancestry.com/~ilstclai/chap4.htm; John Hay to Regis Loisel, Oct. 4, 1798, in COLARCH, vol. 5, pt. 3.

82. Memorial of Jacques Clamorgan to Trudeau, Sept. 27, 1798, in Nasatir, ed., *Before Lewis*, 571–81; COLARCH, vol. 5, pt. 3.

83. COLARCH, vol. 5, pt. 3.

84. Ibid.

85. Nasatir, ed., *Before Lewis*, 570n; Nasatir, "Jacques Clamorgan," in *French Fur Traders*, 133; Rice and Foley, *First Chouteaus*, 78.

86. Isaac Todd to John Askin, July 15, 1799, in Milo M. Quaife, ed., *The John Askin Papers* (Detroit, Mich.: Detroit Library Commission, 1928–31), vol. 2, p. 569n.

87. Petition of Jacques Clamorgan, Jan. 15, 1800, in Nasatir, ed., *Before Lewis*, 608–11.

88. Jacques Clamorgan to Salcedo, Apr. 18, 1801, in Nasatir, ed., *Before Lewis*, 632–35.

89. Jacques Clamorgan to Delassus, Nov. 24, 1800, in Nasatir, ed., *Before Lewis*, 618–22.

90. Oglesby, *Manuel Lisa*, 18, 19.

91. Robidoux and Others to Governor of Louisiana, Dec. 8, 1800, in Nasatir, ed., *Before Lewis*, 624–27. On the alliance with Manuel Lisa, see Nasatir, ed., *Before Lewis*, 553n.

92. Foley and Rice, *First Chouteaus*, 83; Robidoux to Jacques Clamorgan, Nov. 26, 1803, in Nasatir, ed., *Before Lewis*, 718.

93. Foley and Rice, *First Chouteaus*, 88.

94. Weber, *Spanish Frontier*, 290–91; Furstenberg, "Significance," 668–69.

95. Foley and Rice, *First Chouteaus*, 87–89.

96. Landon Y. Jones, ed., *The Essential Lewis and Clark* (New York: HarperCollins, 2000), 2.

97. Lemont K. Richardson, "Private Land Claims in Missouri, Part 1," *MHR* 50 (Jan. 1956): 138.

98. *Representation and Petition of the Representatives Elected by the Freemen of the Territory of Louisiana* (Washington, D.C.: William Duane and Son, 1805).

99. Lloyd A. Hunter, "Slavery in St. Louis, 1804–1860," *BMHS* 30 (July 1974): 237; Hodes, *Beyond the Frontier*, 310–12.

100. Richardson, "Private Land Claims, Part 2," *MHR* 50 (Apr. 1956): 271.

101. "Petition to Congress by Inhabitants of the Territory, February 1, 1806," in Clarence Edwin Carter, ed., *The Territorial Papers of the United States* (Washington, D.C.: Government Printing Office, 1948), vol. 13, pp. 425–30.

102. St. Louis Deeds, Book A, pp. 29, 38, 51, 100, 179, 214, 228, 230, 251, 277, 393, 415, 474, and 480; ibid., Book C, p. 222 (CSLRD). St. Charles Co. Deeds, Book A, pp. 106 and 107; ibid., Book C, pp. 160 and 453, MOSA.

103. John James Ingalls, "Regis Loisel," *Kansas Magazine*, Feb. 1873, in *Atchison Globe*, July 6, 1891; "Land Claims in the Missouri Territory," 567; St. Louis probate file no. 0005, MOSA.

104. "Minutes of a Meeting at St. Louis," in Carter, ed., *The Territorial Papers*, vol. 13, pp. 43–46; Richardson, "Private Land Claims, Pt. 1," 139.

105. Hodes, *Beyond the Frontier*, 308–10; Richardson, "Private Land Claims, Pt. 1," 143.

106. Richardson, "Private Land Claims, Pt. 2," 272–75.

107. Hodes, *Beyond the Frontier*, 310; Richardson, "Private Land Claims, Pt. 2," 280–81.

108. Richardson, "Private Land Claims, Pt. 2," 282.

109. Nasatir, "Jacques Clamorgan," 110; Frederic L. Billon, *Annals of St. Louis in Its Territorial Days from 1804 to 1821* (St. Louis: self-published, 1888), 9, 10.

110. Kate L. Gregg, "Building the First American Fort West of the Mississippi," *MHR* 30 (July 1936): 349.

111. Carter, ed., *The Territorial Papers*, vol. 13, pp. 329–51, 385–88, 455–56.

112. "Missouri Judicial Records" (MOSA online database).

113. Delassus-LeDuc Collection, MHS, cited by Nasatir in introduction to Walter B. Douglas, *Manuel Lisa* (New York: Argosy-Antiquarian, 1964), 31–32; Hodes, *Beyond the Frontier*, 296.

114. Oglesby, *Manuel Lisa*, 35–40; "List of Licenses Granted to Trade with Indians in the Superintendency of Louisiana, April 7–September 30, 1807," in Thomas Maitland Marshall, ed., *The Life and Papers of Frederick Bates* (St. Louis: Missouri Historical Society, 1926), vol. 1, 202.

115. Hill, ed., "An Unknown Expedition," 560–62.

116. Even Marie-Philippe Leduc, who drew up Clamorgan's will and knew he had "natural" children, testified after Clamorgan's death that he was a man without a family. "Opinions and Arguments Respecting Land Claims in Missouri, Communicated to the House of Representatives, June 3, 1836," *American State Papers: Public Lands*, vol. 8, p. 800.

2. "Ester, a Free Woman of Color"

1. See, for instance, *St. Louis Globe-Democrat*, Aug. 14, 1876; *St. Louis Post-Dispatch*, June 9, 1911; ibid., June 25, 1911; *St. Louis Republic*, June 11, 1911; *St. Louis Star*, June 11, 1911.

2. Kaskaskia MSS, Aug. 21, 1784, ISA; Otto Lohrenz, "The Rev. Ichabod Camp, First American Preacher on the Ohio and Mississippi Rivers," *Filson Club History Quarterly* 65 (July 1991): 358–67.

3. Lohrenz, "Ichabod Camp," 369–77.

4. Kaskaskia MSS, June 17, 1785. Clamorgan actually went into debt to buy Siley. See Litigation Collection Translations, box 1, f. 18, MHS.

5. Lohrenz, "Ichabod Camp," 380.

6. Ibid., 381; Frederic Louis Billon, *Annals of St. Louis in Its Early Days Under the*

French and Spanish Dominations (St. Louis: self-published, 1886), 232; Louisa Wherry and Catherine Dodge, in *Ester, Free Mulatto Woman, v. Jacques Clamorgan*, Missouri Superior Court, 1809, MOSA.

7. The entry for "Don Santiago Clermorgan" in the 1791 Spanish census gives a sense of the complex household and farming operation Ester oversaw for Jacques. See 1791 Census of St. Louis and Its Districts (MHS).

8. Pascal L. Cerré, in *Ester v. William C. Carr*, St. Charles Circuit Court (1831), recapitulated in *George Speers, Adm. of Ester, A Free Mulatto Woman, v. William C. Carr*, Missouri Supreme Court, 1842 (MOSA); David Delany, Catherine Dodge and Joseph Brazeau, in *Ester v. Clamorgan*.

9. *Ester v. Carr*.

10. COLARCH, vol. 2, no. 597 (MHS).

11. Daniel Gahan, "'Journey After My Own Heart': Lord Edward Fitzgerald in America, 1788–90," *New Hibernia Review* 8 (Summer 2004): 86–87, 88, 99; Jon Kukla, *A Wilderness So Immense: The Louisiana Purchase and the Destiny of America* (New York: Random House, 2003), 115–16. For an account of Fitzgerald's life, see Stella Tillyard, *Citizen Lord* (New York: Farrar, Straus and Giroux, 1997).

12. Old Cathedral, Baptisms (1769–1804), 45 (SLCOL). The child's mother is named as "Catherine," but the timing of the birth, and Brazeau's sponsorship, make it clear that this was Siley's child.

13. COLARCH, vol. 2, no. 594.

14. Ibid., vol. 1, no. 587; St. Louis Deeds, Book A, p. 219: and ibid., Book F, p. 8 (CSLRD).

15. Livre Terrien, Book 4, p. 34, MHS; St. Louis Deeds, Book B, p. 313. On Spain's land policies, see Judith A. Gilbert, "Esther and Her Sisters: Free Women of Color as Property Owners in Colonial St. Louis, 1765–1804," *Gateway Heritage* 17 (Summer 1996): 17.

16. Livre Terrien, Book 5, pp. 2, 10–11; St. Louis Deeds, Book A, p. 205; ibid., Book B, p. 318.

17. COLARCH, vol. 1, no. 602; ibid., vol. 2, no. 592; St. Louis Deeds, Book E, p. 80.

18. Joseph Brazeau, Pascal Cerré, and John Hay, in *Ester v. Clamorgan*. On Sophie and Hélène, see COLARCH, vol. 4, no. 1935, and ibid., vol. 5, no. 742.

19. Elizabeth Hortez, in Minutes of the Board of Land Commissioners, vol. 6, pp. 160–61 (MOSA).

20. COLARCH, vol. 1, no. 754.

21. Frederick A. Hodes, *Beyond the Frontier: A History of St. Louis to 1821* (Tucson, Ariz.: Patrice Press, 2004), 221. The racial identity of the Labadies perplexed the recordkeepers in St. Louis. However, the Labadie children all married into the free community of color. Old Cathedral, Marriages (1781–1828), 95 (SLCOL); St. Louis probate file no. 611 (MOSA), and St. Louis Deeds, Book V3, p. 451.

22. John Cooms and Rosanna Berry, in *Ester v. Clamorgan*. For a plat showing who Ester's neighbors were, see *Gabriel Helms v. George Speers and wife*, St. Louis Circuit Court, Mar. 1840 term (MOSL).

23. *Ester v. Carr.* On the Camp-Reihle-McNair family, see Lohrenz, "Ichabod Camp," 388n.

24. Old Cathedral, Baptisms (1769–1804), 102, 128, 131 (SLCOL).

25. Ibid. (1804–14), 20.

26. Joseph Brazeau and John Cooms, in *Ester v. Clamorgan.*

27. Catherine Dodge, in ibid.

28. Account Book of Bernard Gaines Farrar (MHS); Old Cathedral, Burials (1781–1832), 138 (SLCOL).

29. Jacques Clamorgan to "Madame Ester," Feb. 4, 1809, in *George Speers v. William Myers et al.,* St. Charles Circuit Court, June 1837 term, no. 2845 (MOSA).

30. An old friend was murdered on a similar expedition. See Lansing B. Bloom, "The Death of Jacques D'Eglise," *NMHR* 2 (Oct. 1927): 369–79.

31. Board of Land Commissioners, vol. 1, pp. 427, 485.

32. St. Louis Deeds, Book A, p. 210; Joseph Brazeau, in *Ester v. Clamorgan.*

33. St. Louis Deeds, Book F, p. 267.

34. Old Cathedral, Baptisms (1769–1804), 89 (Aurore), 121 (Adelle), 141 (Agatha), (SLCOL). St. Louis Deeds, Book F, p. 267 (Joseph).

35. Old Cathedral, Baptisms (1769–1804), 89, 141 (SLCOL).

36. St. Louis Deeds, Book A, pp. 205–8; ibid., Book K, p. 216.

37. Joseph Brazeau, in *Ester v. Clamorgan.*

38. Marie-Philippe Leduc, in ibid.

39. Affidavit of Ester, in *Ester v. Carr.*

40. Ibid.

41. Ibid.

42. Jacques Clamorgan to "Madame Ester," in *Speers v. William Myers et al.*

43. *Ester v. Carr.*

44. James Mackay, Antoine Soulard, Thérèse Demoulin, Patrick Lee, and David Wade in *Ester v. Clamorgan.*

45. Jacques Clamorgan, in ibid.

46. Louisa Wherry, Catherine Dodge, John Hay, and Joseph Brazeau, in ibid.

47. Affidavit of Ester, in ibid.

48. St. Louis Deeds, Book B, p. 314; ibid., Book C, pp. 267, 552–54.

49. Board of Land Commissioners, vol. 5, p. 406. On Carr's involvement in Clamorgan's affairs, see Frederick Bates to Rufus Easton, Dec. 10, 1814, in Thomas Maitland Marshall, ed., *The Life and Papers of Frederick Bates* (St. Louis: Missouri Historical Society, 1926), vol. 2, pp. 291–93.

50. For payments from Clamorgan's executors to Ester for the maintenance of his children, see St. Louis probate file no. 168A.

51. St. Louis Deeds, Book F, p. 8; ibid., Book Z4, pp. 317, 323. Jacques Clamorgan had indeed secured title to Edward's land, either with Brazeau's consent or through trickery on his own part. St. Louis Deeds, Book A, p. 219.

52. *Missouri Gazette,* Apr. 1, 1815.

53. St. Louis Deeds, Book F, p. 267; Old Cathedral, Baptisms (1804–14), 69; ibid. (1814–23), 20, 54 (SLCOL).

54. St. Louis Deeds, Book K, p. 379.

55. Ibid., Book I, p. 233; ibid., Book L, p. 407; ibid., Book I2, p. 120; St. Louis Tax Records, 1826, 1828, 1829, 1831, CSLRD.

56. Old Cathedral, Burials (1781–1832), 145 (SLCOL); St. Louis city directory, 1821.

57. St. Louis probate file no. 1065; St. Louis Deeds, Book Y, p. 105.

58. St. Louis Deeds, Book O, p. 483.

59. Ibid., Book E2, p. 356.

60. *Ester v. Carr*.

61. St. Louis Deeds, Book Y, pp. 77, 105.

62. *Ester v. Carr*. For the property transfers Ester supposedly consented to, see St. Louis Deeds, Book B, pp. 312–19.

63. *Ester v. Carr*.

64. Ibid.

65. John Cooms, William Cooms, and Rosanna Berry, in ibid.

66. Alexander Bellassus, David Delany, and others, in ibid. Riddick eventually married Carr's sister.

67. Marie-Philippe Leduc, in *Ester v. Carr*.

68. Pierre Chouteau, Sr., in ibid. On the claims Chouteau derived from Clamorgan, and ultimately from Ester, see "Opinion of Gamble & Spaulding, October 1, 1836," Albert Todd Papers, f. 1, MHS.

69. For Ester's death date, see affidavit of George Speers in *Speers et al. v. Carr*.

70. Board of Land Commissioners, vol. 6, pp. 111, 160–61, 310; *American State Papers: Public Lands* (Washington, D.C.: Gales and Seaton, 1861); repr. Greenville, S.C.: Southern Historical Press, 1994), vol. 6, p. 820.

71. The funeral of "Francis a black man, aged 23 years," took place on August 20, 1833 (Old Cathedral, Burials [1832–47], 24, SLCOL).

72. St. Louis probate file no. 1065.

73. Ibid., file no. 524; *George Speers, Adm. of Edward Fitzgerald, v. Jean P. Cabanné*, St. Louis Circuit Court, Mar. 1831 term, no. 64; St. Louis Circuit Court, Minutes (1830–33), 6: 268, 278, 284, 328, 366. Cabanné's widow eventually freed Charlotte. See St. Louis Circuit Court Records, vol. 14, p. 227, www.nps.gov/jeff/historyculture/upload/EMANCIPATIONS.pdf.

74. St. Louis Deeds, Book Y, p. 105.

75. Ibid., Book Y, p. 274.

76. See, for instance, William E. Ewing to Hamilton R. Gamble, Mar. 25, 1837, box 6, f. 4, Hamilton R. Gamble Papers, MHS; *Daily Missouri Republican*, Aug. 18, 1851; "Opinion of Gamble & Spaulding"; *John Magwire v. Mary Tyler et al.*, St. Louis Land Court, Oct. 1855 term (MHS).

77. St. Louis directory, 1838–39; St. Louis County Court Records, vol. 1, p. 455 (SLCOL).

78. Old Cathedral, Marriages (1828–40), 38 (SLCOL); St. Louis Marriages, vol. 1, p. 182 (CSLRD); St. Louis County Court Records, vol. 1, p. 458.

79. *Gabriel Helms v. George Speers and wife*, St. Louis Circuit Court, Mar. 1840 term, no. 679; St. Louis Deeds, Book I2, p. 410; ibid., Book K2, pp. 140, 283; ibid., Book K4, p. 179; and ibid., Book Z3, p. 89.

80. In 1852, for instance, they were forced to pledge the property on Fifth and Myrtle as security for a loan. St. Louis Deeds, Book H6, p. 120.

81. Ibid., Book T2, p. 74.

82. Ibid., Book R2, p. 339; St. Louis probate file no. 1715. There is little information on the Butchers beyond what is in the city directories. In 1835, Agatha, a twenty-nine-year-old "light mulatto . . . stout made," was licensed to reside in St. Louis (St. Louis County Court Records, vol. 1, p. 461). Thomas never bothered to file the paperwork to get a license, so there is no description of him and no indication of his origins in the records of the St. Louis County Court. The 1840 census (roll 231, p. 120) lists both Agatha and Thomas as people of color between the ages of twenty-four and thirty-six.

83. St. Louis Deeds, Book T2, p. 305.

84. Affidavit of George Speers, and "Brief on behalf of Administrator," in *Speers et al. v. Carr*.

85. St. Louis Deeds, Book Z4, pp. 317, 323.

86. The 1840 census lists one Joseph "Cavenor" in East Baton Rouge. U.S. Census (1840), roll 129, p. 81.

87. Old Cathedral, Baptisms (1814–23), 170, and (1823–35), 94, 213, 343; Old Cathedral, Marriages (1840–49), 20; Old Cathedral, Burials (1781–1832), 156, 163; ibid. (1832–47), 225; ibid. (1847–52), 28, 409; ibid. (1852–70), 30, 213 (SLCOL); St. Louis Death Registers, vol. A, p. 115; ibid., vol. B, p. 223; and ibid., vol. D, p. 155.

88. St. Louis Marriages, vol. 2, p. 428; St. Louis Death Registers, vol. J, pp. 380, 383; ibid., vol. K, p. 55; Old Cathedral, Burials (1852–70), 529, 530, 555 (SLCOL).

89. St. Louis Death Registers, vol. K, p. 358; ibid., vol. 1, p. 632. When Georgiana was baptized in August 1838, the priest mistakenly recorded her name as Josephine (Old Cathedral, Baptisms [1835–44], 91, SLCOL).

90. St. Louis Death Registers, vol. K, pp. 219, 223; ibid., vol. 1, p. 212; Interments at Calvary, www.search.stlcathcem.org.

91. St. Louis Deeds, Book 334, p. 241.

92. St. Louis Marriages, vol. 13, p. 417. Shavière made his first appearance in the city directory in 1868.

93. U.S. Census (1870), St. Louis, Ward 2, roll 811, p. 395; ibid. (1880), St. Louis, roll 717, e.d. 4, p. 69; and ibid., roll 732, e.d. 253, p. 78.

94. St. Vincent de Paul, Marriages (1867–91), 6 (SLCOL); St. Louis Death Registers, vol. 4, p. 216. On Geneva's identity, see St. Louis probate files no. 13428 (Gabriel Helms) and no. 15465 (Joseph Helms), and U.S. Census (1870), St. Louis, Ward 2, roll 811, p. 527.

95. St. Louis probate file no. 14226. Gabriel Helms and Robert J. Wilkinson both died in 1879. St. Louis Death Registers, vol. 9, pp. 638, 713.

96. Interments at Calvary; St. Louis Death Registers, vol. 11, p. 258; *St. Louis Post-Dispatch*, July 26, 1881. For the eventual division of Theresa's real estate among her heirs, see St. Louis Deeds, Book 692, p. 247.

97. When Theresa Sawyer's husband died in 1896, his only heir was his second wife. St. Louis probate files, no. 14159 (Theresa Sawyer), no. 25074 (Francis Sawyer).

98. St. Louis Death Registers, vol. 17, pp. 70, 92; ibid., vol. 18, p. 438. Geneva moved to Arkansas. (St. Louis probate file no. 15465 [Joseph Helms]). Virginia Cox married James T. Cole, and Mary wed Allen Wallace Wilkinson (St. Louis Marriages, vol. 21, p. 514 [no. 5468]; and ibid., vol. 22, p. 581 [no. 3612]). Cole and Wilkinson (no relation to Mary's Wilkinson cousins) were African American barbers, although Cole was better known as an arranger of social events for the city's white elite (*St. Louis Post-Dispatch*, Apr. 14, 1918; *St. Louis Argus*, Apr. 19, 1918).

3. Natural Children

1. St. Louis probate file no. 168A (MOSA).

2. For the Chouteau genealogy, see Mary B. Cunningham and Jeanne C. Blythe, comps., *The Founding Family of St. Louis* (St. Louis: Piraeus, 1977).

3. Jacques Clamorgan to Mme. Manuel Lisa and Hiacinthe Egliz, July 21, 1807; Marie Lisa and Hiacinthe Egliz to Jacques Clamorgan, July 22, 1807, Manuel Lisa Papers, MHS. For one reason for Lisa's defection, see Richard Edward Oglesby, *Manuel Lisa and the Opening of the Missouri Fur Trade* (Norman: University of Oklahoma Press, 1963), 36–40.

4. Joseph J. Hill, ed., "An Unknown Expedition to Santa Fé in 1807," *MVHR* 6 (Mar. 1920): 560–62; Walter B. Douglas, *Manuel Lisa* (New York: Argosy-Antiquarian, 1964), 159.

5. *National Intelligencer and Washington Advertiser*, Aug. 28, 1809.

6. St. Charles Court of Common Pleas (MOSA, microfilm); Lemont K. Richardson, "Private Land Claims in Missouri, Part 3," *MHR* 50 (July 1956): 391; St. Louis Deeds, Book B, p. 160; ibid., Book C, pp. 63, 65 (CSLRD).

7. St. Louis Deeds, Book C, p. 255.

8. Douglas, *Manuel Lisa*, 69n, 126, 159; 35; Oglesby, *Manuel Lisa*, 35.

9. St. Louis Court of Common Pleas, Nov. 1811 term. For the problems the debt caused later on, see *Clamorgan & Lisa's Executors, Appellants, v. Geisse, Snyder, Morrison & Summers, Appellees*, 1 Mo 141 (Oct. 1821 term), and *Philipson, to use of Menard, v. Bates' Executor*, 2 Mo 116 (April 1829 term).

10. St. Louis Deeds, Book B, p. 160.

11. Ibid., Book C, p. 353.

12. Pierre Chouteau, Jr., in *Landes et al. v. Perkins*, 12 Mo 238 (Oct. 1848 term).

13. On Chouteau and Lisa's new venture, see William E. Foley and C. David Rice,

The First Chouteaus: River Barons of Early St. Louis (Urbana: University of Illinois Press, 1983), 144–45.

14. St. Charles County Deeds, Book A, pp. 522, 525 (MOSA); St. Louis Deeds, Book B, pp. 265, 267, 300; ibid., Book C, p. 179.

15. St. Louis Deeds, Book C, p. 109.

16. St. Charles County Deeds, Book C, p. 480; St. Louis Deeds, Book C, pp. 179, 243.

17. St. Louis Deeds, Book C, p. 257.

18. Ibid., Book C, pp. 555, 558.

19. Jacques Clamorgan to Frederick Bates, Nov. 3, 1812, 1st Board of Land Commissioners, Papers of Original Claimants, RG 951, MOSA.

20. Gates, "Private Land Claims," 184–85.

21. On the claims he still had in and around the town, see St. Louis Deeds, Book B, pp. 278, 299; ibid., Book C, pp. 33, 125, 137, 138, 404; *Missouri Gazette*, June 5, 1813.

22. *Missouri Gazette*, Aug. 1, 1812; ibid., Aug. 14, 1813.

23. St. Louis Court of Common Pleas, Nov. 1809 term; ibid., Mar. 7, 1810; ibid., July 4–5, 1810; Nov. 10, 1810; ibid., Nov. 12, 1810; ibid., Mar. 1811 term, pp. 116, 122–23; ibid., July 1811 term, p. 138; ibid., July 1813 term, pp. 258, 262; St. Louis probate records, file no. 0004; *Jacques Clamorgan v. Thomas Williams*, St. Louis Circuit Court, July 1810 term, no. 38.

24. See, for instance, St. Louis probate file no. 00073, and *Missouri Gazette*, July 26, 1810.

25. *Missouri Gazette*, Nov. 30, 1809; ibid., Dec. 21, 1809; ibid., Jan. 25, 1810.

26. Ibid., Oct. 19, 1809.

27. "Recommendation of Citizens of the Territory," in Clarence E. Carter, ed., *The Territorial Papers of the United States* (Washington, D.C.: Government Printing Office, 1949), vol. 14, p. 340.

28. William Russell to Silas Bent, Jan. 25, 1812, in Carter, ed., *The Territorial Papers*, vol. 14, p. 511.

29. Frederick A. Hodes, *Beyond the Frontier: A History of St. Louis to 1821* (Tucson, Ariz.: Patrice Press, 2004), 347–49, 451.

30. For the deal Jacques and Catherine negotiated, see St. Louis Deeds, Book T, p. 132.

31. Old Cathedral, Baptisms (1769–1804), 102, 128, 131; ibid. (1804–14), 20 (SLCOL).

32. St. Louis Deeds, Book B, pp. 367–68, 370.

33. Charles E. Peterson, *Colonial St. Louis: Building a Creole Capital* (St. Louis: Missouri Historical Society, 1949), 34; COLARCH, vol. 2, no. 769, no. 827; and ibid., vol. 4, no. 1441.

34. COLARCH, vol. 1, no. 930.

35. When the clerk recorded the emancipations in the St. Louis Deed Books, he did not note the endorsements, but when the documents themselves were entered into evidence in *Landes et al. v. Perkins*, those endorsements were noted.

36. There are references in various St. Louis records to one Jean-Baptiste Pelletier, but he was evidently white and not connected in any way to Julie.
37. St. Charles County Deeds, Book C, pp. 380, 382.
38. St. Louis Deeds, Book E, p. 457.
39. Old Cathedral, Burials (1781–1832), 92 (SLCOL); *Missouri Gazette*, Nov. 19, 1814.
40. St. Louis probate file no. 168A (Jacques Clamorgan), MOSA.
41. Ibid.
42. Ibid.
43. Ibid. For the announcement of the sale, see *Missouri Gazette*, Nov. 12, 1814.
44. *Missouri Gazette*, Mar. 2, 1816; ibid., Apr. 29, 1816; St. Louis Court of Common Pleas (Apr.–July 1815), 357–58, 392–93; ibid. (Oct.–Nov. 1815), 412–13; St. Louis Circuit Court, vol. 2, p. 138.
45. St. Louis Court of Common Pleas, 2: 514–15; St. Louis Circuit Court (1816–19), 419.
46. Supreme Court of Missouri, vol. 1 (1821–27), 90–92, 220.
47. St. Charles County Deeds, Book D, pp. 94, 425.
48. Ibid., Book C, p. 475.
49. Tholozan had even paid the taxes due on the land to be sure St. Charles County officials did not seize it for nonpayment (*Petition of Clamorgan's Representatives*, n.p., 1818, p. 3).
50. H.R. 15th Cong., 1st sess., 144; *Petition of Clamorgan's Representatives*.
51. H.R. 18th Cong., 1st sess., 312–13; Gates, "Private Land Claims," 204.
52. *Missouri Republican*, July 6, 1826.
53. For an overview of this period, see Glen E. Holt, "St. Louis's Transition Decade, 1819–1830," *MHR* 76 (July 1982): 365–81.
54. John F. Darby, *Personal Recollections of Many Prominent People Whom I Have Known, and Events—Especially of Those Relating to the History of St. Louis—During the First Half of the Present Century* (St. Louis: G. I. Jones and Co., 1880), 5.
55. Testimony of James Mackay in *Ester, Free Mulatto Woman, v. Jacques Clamorgan*, Missouri Superior Court, 1809, MOSA.
56. Jacques Clamorgan to "Madame Ester," Feb. 4, 1809, in *George Speers v. William Myers et al.*, St. Charles County, Circuit Court, June 1837 term, no. 2845 (MOSA).
57. J. M. Krum and C. H. Krum, *Henry Clamorgan, Cyprian Clamorgan, Leon A. Clamorgan and Julius Clamorgan, Appellants, v. The Baden and St. Louis Railway Company, Respondent. Statement and Brief for Respondent* (St. Louis: Chancy R. Barns, 1880), 17; Jacques Clamorgan probate; St. Louis directory, 1821.
58. Old Cathedral, Marriages (1781–1828), 92; Baptisms (1814–23), 184 (SLCOL).
59. Krum and Krum, *Brief . . . 1880*, 15.
60. St. Louis Circuit Court, vol. 3 (1821–24), 127, 181, 273.
61. Krum and Krum, *Brief . . . 1880*, 14; St. Louis Circuit Court, vol. 3 (1821–24), 333; testimony of Charles Collins in *Louis Clamorgan v. John Seigle*, Circuit Court, St. Charles County, Oct. 1844 term, no. 1699 (MOSA).

62. St. Louis probate file no. 637 (St. Eutrope Clamorgan).

63. Ibid.

64. Jacques Clamorgan probate; Old Cathedral, Burials (1781–1832), 140 (SLCOL).

65. 18th Cong., 1st sess., Ch. 173, 52–56.

66. St. Louis probate file no. 511 (James Irwin); *Thomas H. Benton v. Robinson Kelly and Margaret A. Irwin*, St. Louis Circuit Court (March 1827 term), Chancery, Civil Case file, box 10, f. 15, MOSL.

67. On Benton's pivotal role in the matter of the 1824 Act, see Jay Gitlin, *The Bourgeois Frontier: French Towns, French Traders and American Expansion* (New Haven, Conn.: Yale University Press, 2010), 69–70. On Cyprian Martial's presence in Washington, and his ability to read and write, see *Daily National Intelligencer*, Apr. 3, 1823.

68. Krum and Krum, *Brief . . . 1880*, 16.

69. St. Louis Deeds, Book M, p. 469.

70. St. Louis probate file no. 769 (Cyprian M. Clamorgan).

71. Louis Houck, *A History of Missouri, From the Earliest Explorations and Settlements Until the Admission of the State into the Union* (Chicago: R. R. Donnelley and Sons, 1908), 1: 22–23n; *Missouri Republican*, July 20, 1826; *Baltimore Patriot*, Oct. 17, 1826.

72. *William R. Grimsley v. Charles Collins and Apoline Clamorgan, administrators*, July 1828 term, box 118, f. 41, case no. 74, St. Louis Circuit Court; Circuit Court Minutes, vol. 5 (1827–30), 188–89, 201. The court record says that Cyprian Martial's purchase of the bureau, the cause of the whole complicated dispute, took place on January 18, 1827, but the circumstances clearly indicate it occurred in 1826.

73. Cyprian M. Clamorgan probate file.

74. Ibid.

75. St. Louis Circuit Court, vol. 4 (1824–27), 88, 91, 106, 311, 366, 372–73; ibid., vol. 5 (1827–30), 191–92, 201–2; ibid., vol. 6 (1830–33), 56, 99, 255, 320–21, 330.

76. Cyprian M. Clamorgan probate file.

77. St. Louis Deeds, Book N, p. 456. St. Louis Tax Lists, 1824, 1825, 1827 (CSLRD).

78. Cyprian M. Clamorgan probate file.

79. Ibid.

80. Old Cathedral, Burials (1781–1832), 147 (SLCOL).

4. "In Them Days Everything Was Free and Easy"

1. Testimony of Gabriel Helms in J. M. Krum and C. H. Krum, *Henry Clamorgan, Cyprian Clamorgan, Leon A. Clamorgan and Julius Clamorgan, Appellants, v. The Baden and St. Louis Railway Company, Respondent: Statement and Brief for Respondent* (St. Louis: Chancy R. Barns, 1880), 18.

2. Old Cathedral, Baptisms (1769–1804), 149 (SLCOL); St. Louis probate file no. 302 (Marie Louise Papin), MOSA.

3. Old Cathedral, Baptisms (1814–23), 97 (SLCOL).

4. Ibid., Burials (1781–1832), 108 (SLCOL).

5. Ibid., Baptisms (1814–23), 160 (SLCOL).

6. Ibid., Marriages (1781–1828), 94 (SLCOL).

7. See, for instance, *Arkansas Gazette*, Sept. 2, 1834; *Essex* (Mass.) *Register*, July 17, 1813; *Chillicothe* (Ohio) *Telegraph*, July 31, 1813; *Missouri Gazette*, June 19, 1813.

8. On Langham's business activities, see "Town of Osage," *MHR* 2 (Oct. 1907): 78–80; Breckinridge Jones, "One Hundred Years of Banking in Missouri," *MHR* 15 (Jan. 1921): 368–69, 390; Perry S. Rader, "The Location of the Permanent Seat of Government," *MHR* 21 (Oct. 1927): 13, 15, 17.

9. Krum and Krum, *Brief for Respondent . . . 1880*, 19.

10. Old Cathedral, Baptisms (1814–23), 230 (SLCOL). Langham was back in St. Louis within months of Henry's birth. In the summer of 1823 he was the second in a duel in St. Louis. *Louisville Public Advertiser*, July 23, 1823.

11. Old Cathedral, Baptisms (1823–35), 45 (SLCOL).

12. On Langham's role in the expedition, see Richard E. Jensen and James S. Hutchins, eds., *Wheel Boats on the Missouri: The Journals and Documents of the Atkinson-O'Fallon Expedition, 1824–26* (Helena: Montana Historical Society, 2001). For Louisa's approximate date of birth, see St. Louis Probate Court, 1816–1901: Guardianship Records, box 2, f. 70, MOSA.

13. Old Cathedral, Baptisms (1823–35), 172 (SLCOL).

14. St. Louis probate file no. 870 (Apoline Clamorgan), MOSA.

15. *Apoline Clamorgan v. Armstead Lawless*, St. Louis Circuit Court, Nov. 1826 term, no. 4096; St. Louis Circuit Court, vol. 4 (1824–27), 409, MOSL.

16. St. Louis probate file no. 769 (Cyprian M. Clamorgan).

17. St. Louis Deeds, Book N, p. 538 (CSLRD); *Missouri Republican*, Dec. 13, 1827.

18. On issues arising from the estate, see Cyprian M. Clamorgan probate file, and St. Louis Circuit Court Minutes, vol. 5 (1827–30), 133.

19. *Missouri Republican*, Mar. 18, 1828.

20. Cyprian M. Clamorgan probate file.

21. St. Louis Deeds, Book O, p. 94; *Dougal v. Fryer*, 3 Mo 39.

22. *Collins v. Administrator of Pauline Clamorgan*, 5 Mo 272 and 6 Mo 169.

23. St. Louis Deeds, Book O, p. 284.

24. Ibid., Book O, p. 514.

25. St. Louis Probate Court, 1816–1901: Guardianship Records, box 2, f. 70.

26. Ibid., box 2, f. 69, and box 4, f. 1.

27. Apoline Clamorgan probate file.

28. For the text of Apoline's will, see St. Louis Deeds, Book N2, p. 186.

29. For the mortgage Apoline gave Fryer, see ibid., Book P, p. 223.

30. Ibid., Book N2, p. 186.

31. Old Cathedral, Baptisms (1823–35), 398 (SLCOL); Apoline Clamorgan probate file.
32. Old Cathedral, Burials (1781–1832), 166 (SLCOL); Apoline Clamorgan probate file; Krum and Krum, *Brief for Respondent . . . 1880*, 18.
33. *Arkansas Gazette*, Sept. 2, 1834; St. Louis probate file no. 1178 (Angus L. Langham).
34. Apoline Clamorgan probate file.
35. Ibid.
36. Ibid.
37. Cyprian M. Clamorgan probate file; St. Louis Probate Court: Guardianship Records, box 2, f. 64.
38. Apoline Clamorgan probate file.
39. *Missouri Republican*, Feb. 28, 1832; St. Louis Deeds, Book S, p. 358; ibid., Book T, p. 45.
40. *Dougal v. Fryer*.
41. St. Louis Deeds, Book S, p. 361.
42. *Collins v. Administrator of Pauline Clamorgan*.
43. Apoline Clamorgan probate file.
44. Cyprian Clamorgan Guardianship, box 3, f. 70, case no. 200; U.S. Census (1840), St. Louis, roll 231, p. 137; Old Cathedral, Baptisms (1823–35), 398 (SLCOL).
45. Isabel Jeanette was probably related to seamstress Susanne Jeanette (ca. 1777–1845). There is nothing in the record to help identify Eliza. Apoline Clamorgan probate file; Old Cathedral, Burials (1832–47), 34 (SLCOL); Guardianship Records, box 2, f. 70.
46. Cyprian M. Clamorgan probate file.
47. *Clamorgan et al. v. Lane*, 9 Mo 446.
48. *Prospectus for Raising a Loan of £54,000 upon Shares in the Clamorgan Land Association, U.S., at Six Per Cent Interest, With a Valuable Bonus to the Lenders* (n.p., ca. 1837, at www.jstor.org/stable/60206421); Clamorgan Land Association, *Papers Relating to the Clamorgan Grant* (n.p., ca. 1838, at www.jstor.org/stable/60207085); *Title Papers of the Clamorgan Grant, of 536,904 Arpens of Alluvial Lands in Missouri and Arkansas* (New York: T. Snowden, 1837).
49. *Argument on Behalf of the Claimants in the Claim of the Representatives of Jacques Clamorgan, to a Tract on the Rivers Cuivre and Dardenne, in the State of Missouri* (n.p., ca. 1837); Joseph M. White and Victor Monroe, *Clamorgan's Case* (St. Louis, ca. 1836), in Collections of the St. Louis Mercantile Library, University of Missouri–St. Louis; Minutes of the Board of Land Commissioners, vol. 6, p. 221; ibid., vol. 7, p. 37, MOSA.
50. White and Monroe, *Clamorgan's Case*. See also the opinion of Luke E. Lawless, with supporting documentation, in *Argument on Behalf of the Claimants . . . to a Tract on the Rivers Cuivre and Dardenne*.
51. St. Louis probate file no. 168A (Jacques Clamorgan).

5. The Aristocracy of Color

1. Old Cathedral, Marriages (1840–49), 31 (SLCOL).
2. U.S. Census (1840), St. Louis, roll 231, p. 134; ibid. (1880), St. Louis, roll 728, p. 122 (www.ancestry.com); Old Cathedral, Baptisms (1835–44), 283 (SLCOL); St. Louis County Court Records, vol. 1, p. 460 (SLCOL). *Crevier v. Bertrand et al.* (1858) Mo. Supreme Court case files, box 401, f. 6 (MOSA) reveals a great deal about the history of Julia's family.
3. Old Cathedral, Baptisms (1835–44), 283, 414 (SLCOL); *Missouri Republican,* Oct. 1, 1846; Old Cathedral, Burials (1832–47), 208 (SLCOL).
4. Old Cathedral, Marriages (1840–49), 135 (SLCOL); St. Louis Marriages, vol. 2, p. 401 (www.ancestry.com).
5. *St. Louis Star,* June 9, 1911; U.S. Census (1830), Harrisburg, Dauphin Co., Penn., roll 151, p. 66; ibid. (1840), Harrisburg, North Ward, roll 456, p. 199.
6. On William Eagleson, see Old Cathedral, Marriages (1828–40), 119 (SLCOL), and St. Louis County Court Records, vol. 2, p. 333.
7. St. Louis City Census (1840), MHS; St. Louis directories, 1843, 1845, 1847, 1851.
8. Old Cathedral, Baptisms (1835–44), 414; ibid. (1844–51), 260; Burials (1847–52), 471 (SLCOL).
9. *Missouri Republican,* Oct. 1, 1846, and *Weekly Reveille,* Mar. 27, 1848, in Lois Stanley, George F. Wilson, and Maryellen Wilson, comps., *More Deaths from Missouri Newspapers, 1810–1857* (Greenville, S.C.: Southern Historical Press, 1990), 20; Old Cathedral, Burials (1832–47), 208; ibid. (1847–52), 28, 56; Baptisms (1844–51), 244, 340 (SLCOL).
10. St. Louis County Court Records, vol. 2, p. 134; ibid., vol. 4, p. 405.
11. Louis S. Gerteis, *Civil War St. Louis* (Lawrence: University Press of Kansas, 2001), 7–17.
12. St. Louis County Court Records, vol. 3, pp. 86, 159; Tiffany Papers, box 63, f. 6 and f. 11, MHS.
13. Lloyd A. Hunter, "Slavery in St. Louis, 1804–1860," *BMHS* 30 (July 1974): 236–37, 255, 260.
14. Ibid., 260.
15. *Lewis A. Clamorgan v. Geo. C. Fisher, Morgan V. Halls & James G. Shaw,* and *Lewis A. Clamorgan v. Peter W. Johnstone,* St. Louis Circuit Court, May 1841 term, no. 171 and no. 172, and *Lewis A. Clamorgan v. Peter W. Johnstone,* ibid., Nov. 1841 term, no. 323, MOSL.
16. *James Madden and wife v. Louis Clay Morgan,* St. Louis Circuit Court, Nov. 1844 term, no. 329.
17. St. Louis Deeds, Book O2, p. 28; ibid., Book E3, p. 317, CSLRD.
18. St. Louis Deeds, Book N2, p. 363; ibid., Book T2, p. 148.
19. St. Louis Deeds, Book N2, p. 222; ibid., Book W2, pp. 216, 280; ibid., Book C3, pp. 257–58, 277; ibid., Book E3, p. 112; ibid., Book F3, p. 177; ibid., Book G3,

p. 149; ibid., Book I3, p. 237; ibid., Book Y3, p. 1; ibid., Book R5, p. 101; Richard Edwards and Menra Hopewell, *Edwards's Great West and Her Commercial Metropolis, Embracing a General View of the West and a Complete History of St. Louis* (St. Louis, Mo.: Office of "Edwards's Monthly," 1860), 289.

20. On the various transactions between Louis Clamorgan and Murry McConnell, see St. Louis Deeds, Book T2, pp. 146, 149; ibid., Book W2, p. 214.

21. *Hardage Lane v. Henry Clamorgan et al.*, St. Louis Circuit Court, July 1842 term, no. 111; St. Louis Circuit Court Records, 13 (1841–42), 293; *Clamorgan et al. v. Lane*, 9 Mo 446.

22. St. Louis Deeds, Book C3, pp. 257, 277; ibid., Book F3, p. 81; ibid., Book G3, p. 149; ibid., Book K4, p. 44; ibid., Book R5, p. 101; ibid., Book Y3, p. 1; ibid., Book Y4, p. 246; ibid., Book 168, p. 188; *Lane v. Henry Clamorgan et al.*

23. St. Louis probate file no. 870 (Apoline Clamorgan), MOSA; St. Louis Deeds, Book O2, pp. 100, 124; ibid., Book S2, p. 270.

24. St. Louis Deeds, Book F3, p. 187; ibid., Book M3, pp. 363, 446; ibid., Book R4, p. 78; ibid., Book S4, pp. 540–41; ibid., Book V4, p. 66; ibid., Book Z4, p. 326.

25. Minutes of the Board of Land Commissioners, vol. 1, p. 422; ibid., vol. 4, p. 181; ibid., vol. 5, p. 164 (MOSA); St. Louis Deeds, Book I3, p. 293.

26. St. Louis Deeds, Book 166, p. 86.

27. Ibid., Book R3, p. 296; ibid., Book U3, p. 450; ibid., Book X3, pp. 16, 25.

28. "Year of Disaster" (www.nps.gov/archives/jeff/disaster_year.html).

29. *St. Louis Daily New Era*, Nov. 15, 1849.

30. Old Cathedral, Baptisms (1769–1804), 140; ibid., Marriages (1781–1828), 125 (SLCOL); St. Louis Deeds, Book M, p. 441; ibid., Book L3, p. 165; ibid., Book P2, p. 191.

31. St. Louis Deeds, Book T, pp. 307–8; Loren Schweninger, ed., *From Tennessee Slave to St. Louis Entrepreneur: The Autobiography of James Thomas* (Columbia: University of Missouri Press, 1984), 103–4; *Laws of the State of Missouri, Passed at the First Session of the Fourteenth General Assembly, Begun and Held at the City of Jefferson, on Monday, the Sixteenth Day of November, Eighteen Hundred and Forty-Six* (Jefferson City: James Lusk, 1847), 307–8; *Laws of the State of Missouri, Passed at the Sixteenth General Assembly, Begun and Held at the City of Jefferson, on Monday the Thirtieth Day of December, A.D. 1850* (Jefferson City: James Lusk, 1851), 616. Old Cathedral Burials (1832–47), 223 (SLCOL). On the various leases and sales Louis Clamorgan negotiated for the family, see St. Louis Deeds, Book C3, p. 19; ibid., Book N3, p. 279; ibid., Book O3, p. 187; ibid., Book U5, pp. 4, 580, 597; ibid., Book Z3, p. 252; ibid., Book H5, p. 384; ibid., Book B5, p. 419; ibid., Book T5, p. 56.

32. On one series of interconnected transactions, see St. Louis Deeds, Book I3, p. 238; ibid., Book O3, pp. 208–209.

33. St. Louis Deeds, Book F2, p. 236; ibid., Book E3, p. 317; ibid., Book Z3, p. 397; ibid., Book L4, p. 492; ibid., Book M4, pp. 424, 483; ibid., Book X4, p. 94. Be-

tween 1840 and 1850 Louis and Henry were parties in more than eighty deeds recorded in St. Louis and a dozen more in neighboring St. Charles County.

34. St. Charles County Deeds, Book O, p. 450 (MOSA).

35. St. Louis Probate Court, 1816–1901: Guardianship Records, box 2, f. 70 (MOSA); *Missouri Republican*, Apr. 18, 1849; ibid., Apr. 22, 1849.

36. St. Charles County Deeds, Book O, p. 452; ibid., Book P, pp. 32, 409.

37. Ibid., Book P, pp. 403, 406, 408, 409, 411; ibid., Book Q, pp. 182, 287; ibid., Book T, p. 63.

38. *Louis Clamorgan v. John Hausan et al.*, St. Charles Circuit Court, April 1842 term, box no. 1703; *Louis Clamorgan v. John Seigle*, St. Charles Circuit Court, Oct. term 1844, box no. 1699 (MOSA).

39. House Report No. 506, 30th Cong., 1st sess. On the progress of the bill see 30th Cong., 1st sess., Senate, 271, and House, 638, 729–30; *Daily National Intelligencer*, Apr. 18, 1848. Warrick Tunstall made another move on behalf of himself and the brothers in the following session. See *Report on Claim of Heirs of Jacques Clamorgan*, Senate Reports, No. 328, 30th Cong., 2nd sess., and *Daily National Intelligencer*, Mar. 30, 1849.

40. St. Louis Deeds, Book I3, p. 238; ibid., Book O3, pp. 208, 294.

41. Ibid., Book P3, pp. 267, 450.

42. St. Louis Deeds, Book P3, p. 449; ibid., Book U3, p. 45; ibid., Book X3, p. 147.

43. St. Louis Deeds, Book T4, p. 116; ibid., Book O5, p. 476.

44. *Clamorgan v. O'Fallon & Lindell*, 10 Mo 112.

45. *Landes et al. v. Perkins*, 12 Mo 238.

46. *Isaac Landes, Plaintiff in Error, v. Joshua B. Brant*, 51 U.S. 348; *Missouri Daily Republican*, Feb. 11, 1851.

47. *Landes et al. v. Perkins*.

48. St. Louis Deeds, Book N4, p. 454; ibid., Book G5, pp. 347, 455, 457, 494, 501; ibid., Book H5, p. 181; ibid., Book I5, pp. 61, 95; ibid., Book K5, p. 272; ibid., Book L5, p. 385; ibid., Book N5, p. 246; ibid., Book T5, p. 100; ibid., Book K6, p. 500.

49. *Isaac Landes, Fidelio C. Sharp, Henry Clamorgan and Louis Clamorgan v. Michael Young*, St. Louis Circuit Court, Sept. 1847 term, case no. 3. See also cases no. 4–6, 183, 186–92, 194–96, 203; St. Louis Circuit Court, Minutes, vol. 12, pp. 78–80.

50. St. Louis Deeds, Book H4, p. 174; ibid., Book N4, p. 454.

51. St. Louis Circuit Court, Minutes, vol. 12, pp. 78–80.

52. *Finney, Respondent, v. Brant, Appellant*, 19 Mo 42, and *Lindell, Respondent, v. Brant, Appellant*, 19 Mo 50.

53. St. Louis directory, 1840–41; St. Louis Deeds, Book T2, p. 398.

54. St. Louis Deeds, Book S2, p. 132; St. Louis directory, 1843.

55. St. Louis County Court, Minutes, vol. 2, p. 134; U.S. Census (1830), Chowan County, North Carolina, roll 119, p. 335; ibid. (1840), St. Louis, roll 231, p. 106 (where his name appears as "Isle"); St. Louis directories, 1840–41, 1842, 1845, 1847.

56. *Missouri Republican*, June 10, 1845.

57. *Alexander Foster and James S. Temple v. John S. Clark, Geoffrey Iredell and Lewis A. Clamorgan*, St. Louis Circuit Court, Sept. 1845 term, no. 113. "Geoffrey" was a mistake on the part of the clerk. Iredell invariably spelled his first name "Jeffrey."

58. *Joseph Lamalfa v. Geoffrey G. Iredell and Lewis A. Clamorgan*, St. Louis Circuit Court, Sept. 1845 term, no. 246.

59. *Reveille* (St. Louis) in *Georgia Telegraph*, July 7, 1846.

60. *Baltimore Sun*, Nov. 9, 1848.

61. *Missouri Republican*, Mar. 9, 1849.

62. St. Louis Deeds, Book O3, p. 264; Milwaukee Mortgages, Book E, pp. 125–26 (FHL microfilm); *Milwaukee Daily Sentinel*, Oct. 13, 1845; St. Louis directories, 1843, 1845, 1848, 1851.

63. John Hogan, *Thoughts About the City of St. Louis, Her Commerce and Manufactures, Railroads, &c.* (St. Louis, Mo.: Republican Steam Press, 1854), 74; J. N. Taylor and M. O. Crooks, *Sketch Book of St. Louis* (St. Louis, Mo.: George Knapp & Co., 1858), 25–26; Gerteis, *Civil War St. Louis*, 49.

64. See, for instance, Edwards and Hopewell, *Edwards's Great West*.

65. Jeffrey S. Adler, *Yankee Merchants and the Making of the Urban West: The Rise and Fall of Antebellum St. Louis* (New York: Cambridge University Press, 1991), 86–88.

66. *Missouri Republican*, Jan. 28, 1850; *Sunday Republican*, Sept. 8, 1850.

67. Cyprian Clamorgan Guardianship, St. Louis Probate Court Records, box 3, f. 70, case no. 200; *Missouri Republican*, July 16, 1851.

68. St. Louis Deeds, Book Z5, p. 496.

69. On bandoline and how it was made, see B. Fenner, *Fenner's Complete Formulary*, 6th ed. (Westfield, N.Y.: self-published, 1888), 2–3.

70. On odors and odor boxes, see G. W. Septimus Piesse, *The Art of Perfumery, and Method of Obtaining the Odors of Plants* (Philadelphia: Lindsay and Blakiston, 1857), 52, 59, 73, 78.

71. St. Louis probate file no. 3685 (Louis Clamorgan).

6. A Settling of Scores

1. Old Cathedral, Burials (1847–52), 457 (SLCOL); St. Louis Death Registers, vol. B, p. 18 (www.ancestry.com); St. Louis Probate Court, file no. 3685 (Louis Clamorgan), MOSA.

2. Old Cathedral, Burials (1847–52), 465 (SLCOL).

3. Louis Clamorgan probate file.

4. Ibid.

5. Ibid.

6. Ibid.; St. Louis Deeds, Book 157, p. 106; ibid., Book 230, p. 138; ibid., Book 238, p. 336; ibid., Book 239, p. 400 (CSLRD).

7. Lloyd A. Hunter, "Slavery in St. Louis, 1804–1860," *BMHS* 30 (July 1974): 236.

8. Ibid., 242–45; Maximilian Reichard, "Black and White on the Urban Frontier: The St. Louis Community in Transition, 1800–1830," *BMHS* 33 (Oct. 1976): 9, 12.

9. Julie Winch, ed., *Cyprian Clamorgan's "The Colored Aristocracy of St. Louis"* (Columbia: University of Missouri Press, 1999), 56–57, 87–91.

10. Ibid., 101–102.

11. See, for instance, *Missouri Republican*, Jan. 15, 1851.

12. St. Louis Deeds, Book G6, p. 283.

13. *Frederick Douglass' Paper*, Mar. 31, 1854; U.S. Census (1860), Philadelphia, Ward 2, roll 1152, p. 296 (www.ancestry.com).

14. Franklin County Deeds, Book P, p. 351 (KSA).

15. St. Louis Circuit Court Records, vol. 3, p. 243 (MOSL); Old Cathedral, Marriages (1840–49), 184 (SLCOL).

16. Louis Clamorgan probate file.

17. St. Louis Deeds, Book I6, p. 223.

18. Ibid., Book H6, p. 583.

19. St. Louis Criminal Court, Record Books, vol. 8, pp. 30, 51, 52, 55, 73, 86 (case no. 73), MOSA.

20. *Morning Oregonian*, Dec. 27, 1895.

21. *Missouri Republican*, Dec. 6, 1858.

22. Ibid., June 21, 1852.

23. *Morning Oregonian*, Dec. 27, 1895.

24. St. Louis Deeds, Book 161, p. 108.

25. Ibid., Book 186, p. 431.

26. Winch, ed., *Clamorgan's Colored Aristocracy*, 52, 78–79.

27. For an account of Thomas's life, see Loren Schweninger, ed., *From Tennessee Slave to St. Louis Entrepreneur: The Autobiography of James Thomas* (Columbia: University of Missouri Press, 1984). For the "compliment" Thomas was paid, see Winch, ed., *Clamorgan's Colored Aristocracy*, 59.

28. St. Louis Deeds, Book 167, p. 220; ibid., Book 169, pp. 211–12; ibid., Book 202, p. 229.

29. St. Louis Marriages, vol. 6, p. 318 (www.ancestry.com).

30. St. Louis Deeds, Book N6, p. 466; ibid., Book U6, p. 200.

31. Ibid., Book 155, pp. 211–12; ibid., Book 161, pp. 155, 168; ibid., Book 170, pp. 537–38; ibid., Book 172, p. 333; ibid., Book 202, p. 229; ibid., Book 222, pp. 112, 347; ibid., Book 225, p. 391; ibid., Book 236, p. 221; ibid., Book 246, p. 281; *Pelagie Rutgers v. Leon Clamorgan et al.*, St. Louis Circuit Court, Feb. 1853 term, no. 63.

32. St. Louis Deeds, Book 217, p. 248; ibid., Book 231, p. 318. Henry also came to the aid of the family of Antoine Morin, helping Pelagie Morin settle her husband's estate. See St. Louis probate file no. 5227.

33. St. Louis Deeds, Book 153, p. 462; ibid., Book 155, p. 213.

34. For a deal Henry Clamorgan brokered between White and Pelagie Rutgers, see ibid., Book 195, p. 533.

35. Ibid., Book 184, p. 522; St. Louis probate file no. 3652 (Charles Sebastian).

36. St. Louis Deeds, Book 159, p. 33.

37. Ibid., Book 156, p. 460; ibid., Book 159, p. 33; ibid., Book 166, pp. 77, 284, 370; ibid., Book 168, pp. 29, 79.

38. *John Glenn and Charles M. Thruston, Appellants, v. The United States*, 54 U.S. 250. On Glenn, Thruston, Webster, and the early history of the Clamorgan Land Association, see *Prospectus for Raising a Loan of £54,000 Upon Shares in the Clamorgan Land Association, U.S., at Six Per Cent Interest, with a Valuable Bonus to the Lenders* (n.p., ca. 1837, Hume Tracts, at www.jstor.org/stable/60206421).

39. *New York Times*, Apr. 19, 1852.

40. St. Louis Deeds, Book C6, p. 624.

41. For Mumford's version of events, see his statements in St. Louis probate files no. 769 (Cyprian M. Clamorgan) and no. 5571 (Maximin Clamorgan).

42. See *Report No. 22 to accompany Bill H. R. No. 214*, 35th Cong., 1st sess.

43. For the wording of the act, see *Daily National Intelligencer*, June 7, 1858.

44. St. Louis Deeds, Book 234, p. 546.

45. Ibid., Book 229, p. 74; ibid., Book 231, p. 53. Guardianship files no. 3884 and no. 3885, St. Louis Probate Court (MOSA).

46. *Henry Clamorgan and Cyprian Clamorgan v. Isaac T. Greene*, St. Louis Circuit Court, Feb. term 1859, no. 454.

47. Ibid. For good measure the Clamorgans also brought suit against Loughborough to try to make him award the certificate of relocation to them. *Henry Clamorgan et al. v. John Loughborough*, St. Louis Circuit Court, Sept. 1859 term, no. 836.

48. St. Louis Deeds, Book O5, p. 476.

49. *Clamorgan et al. v. Greene*, St. Louis Circuit Court (1859).

50. *Henry Clamorgan et al., Defendants in Error, v. Isaac T. Greene, Plaintiff in Error*, 32 Mo. 285.

51. *Missouri Republican*, Mar. 20, 1863; J. M. Krum and C. H. Krum, *Henry Clamorgan, Cyprian Clamorgan, Leon A. Clamorgan and Julius Clamorgan, Appellants, v. The Baden and St. Louis Railway Company, Respondent: Statement and Brief for Respondent* (St. Louis: Chancy R. Barns, 1880), 25–26.

52. Cyprian Martial Clamorgan and Maximin Clamorgan probate files.

53. Ibid. It emerged that Mumford had tried to get the surveyor-general to give the certificate to him. When he learned it had been sent to Henry Clamorgan and the Papins, he hit on the tactic of having himself appointed to administer the two Clamorgan estates.

54. Cyprian Martial Clamorgan and Maximin Clamorgan probate files.

55. Ibid.

56. *Claim of Heirs of Jacques Clamorgan*, House Bill 17888, 61st Congress (Washington, D.C.: Government Printing Office, 1910), 18. On the Loisel-Papin connection, see Mary B. Cunningham and Jeanne C. Blythe, comps., *The Founding Family of St. Louis* (St. Louis: Piraeus Publishers, 1977), 193, 194.

57. Old Cathedral, Burials (1847–52), 471 (SLCOL); St. Louis Death Registers, vol. B, p. 42.
58. Louis P. DeMorgan death cert. (1922), COVR.
59. St. Louis Death Registers, vol. D, pp. 52, 62; Old Cathedral, Burials (1852–70), 169, 174 (SLCOL). The priest got Maria's gender wrong and the city registrar her age and sex, but she is included on the monument in Calvary Cemetery that Henry erected. All four Clamorgan children are "white" in the city death register.
60. Old Cathedral, Burials (1852–70), 201 (SLCOL); St. Louis Death Registers, vol. D, p. 127; Interments at Calvary, at www.search.stlcathcem.org.
61. St. Louis directories, 1854, 1859.
62. Old Cathedral, Burials (1852–70), 412 (SLCOL).
63. St. Louis Marriage Records, vol. 9, p. 366; Mo. Death Cert. (1927) no. 3507 (MOSA).
64. Mo. Death Cert. (1912) no. 1159; U.S. Census (1850), Ward 4, St. Louis, roll 417, p. 19; Old Cathedral, Marriages (1849–55), 71 (SLCOL).
65. U.S. Census (1860), Ward 2, St. Louis, roll 648, p. 633.
66. Howald Bailey, "Baron Renfrew Captivates America," *History Teacher* 4 (Nov. 1970), 37–46; *Morning Oregonian*, Dec. 27, 1895.

7. An Independent Man

1. Cyprian Clamorgan Guardianship, St. Louis Probate Court Records, box 3, f. 70, case no. 200 (MOSA); U.S. Census (1840), St. Louis, roll 231, p. 137 (www.ancestry.com).
2. Cyprian Clamorgan Guardianship.
3. Ibid.
4. Ibid.
5. Old Cathedral, Baptisms (1844–51), 244 (SLCOL); St. Louis directory, 1848.
6. Cyprian Clamorgan Guardianship.
7. St. Louis Deeds, Book I6, p. 223 (CSLRD).
8. *Joseph L. Papin v. Cyprian Clamorgan*, St. Louis Circuit Court, Sept. 1852 term, no. 36 (MOSL).
9. St. Louis directory, 1852.
10. St. Louis Deeds, Book K6, p. 38.
11. St. Louis directory 1854–55, 1859–60. Nash married into the family of prosperous barber William Johnson.
12. *New York Herald*, Feb. 15, 1857.
13. St. Louis Marriages, vol. 7, p. 241 (www.ancestry.com).
14. Old Cathedral, Baptisms (1844–51), 341 (SLCOL).
15. On Kretschmar, see U.S. Census (1850), St. Louis, roll 414, p. 341.
16. Old Cathedral, Burials (1847–52), 555 (SLCOL); St. Louis Death Registers, vol. B, p. 166 (www.ancestry.com).

17. St. Louis Deeds, Book C6, p. 624.

18. Ibid., Book O6, p. 18.

19. U.K. Census (1841), Liverpool HO/107/360/13; ibid. (1851) Liverpool HO/107/ 2189/12; ibid. (1861) Liverpool RG9 2686/40/25 (www.ancestry.com); St. John's Church, Haymarket, Liverpool, Baptisms; St. Louis Marriages, vol. 5, p. 341; U.S. Census (1860), St. Louis, Ward 10, roll 654, p. 214. I am grateful to Nick Schaefer, of Mullumbimby, New South Wales, Australia, for generously sharing with me his research on the White family.

20. For a brief description of the growth and development of New Iberia, see the sketch by historian Glenn E. Conrad at www.cityofnewiberia./com/historyarticle.

21. Mary Bell [sic] Guilbert Death Cert. (COVR); Church of the Epiphany, New Iberia, Baptisms, 6.

22. *St. Louis Post-Dispatch*, June 10, 1911.

23. Julie Winch, ed., *Cyprian Clamorgan's "The Colored Aristocracy of St. Louis"* (Columbia: University of Missouri Press, 1999), 46.

24. Ibid.

25. Julie Winch, ed., *"The Elite of Our People": Joseph Willson's Sketches of Black Upper-Class Life in Antebellum Philadelphia* (University Park: Penn State University Press, 2000), 86–87.

26. Winch, ed., *Clamorgan's Colored Aristocracy*, 54, 56, 61.

27. Ibid., 55.

28. Ibid., 52.

29. Ibid.

30. Ibid., 51, 52, 58, 59, 61, 62–63.

31. Ibid., 48–49.

32. Ibid., 59–60, 99–100.

33. Ibid., 55.

34. *Missouri Republican*, Feb. 26, 1851.

35. Winch, ed., *Clamorgan's Colored Aristocracy*, 53.

36. Ibid., 56, 62.

37. Ibid., 57–58.

38. Ibid., 45, 47.

39. Ibid., 57.

40. Ibid., 47.

41. Ibid., 47, 58.

42. Ibid., 60–61, 63.

43. *Cyprian Clamorgan v. Samuel Mordecai*, St. Louis Circuit Court, Sept. 1859 term.

44. St. Louis Criminal Court, Record Book, vol. 10, pp. 528, 541, 564, and ibid., vol. 11, p. 48 (case no. 78), *The State of Missouri v. Cyprian Clamorgan* (MOSA).

45. Only on rare occasions did Cyprian refer to Hebe as his wife. See, for instance, St. Louis Deeds, Book 196, p. 319.

46. St. Martin Parish Courthouse, Louisiana, Marriage License no. 2051 (FHL microfilm).

47. U.S. Census (1860), Attakapas, St. Martin Parish, Louisiana, roll 425, p. 103.

48. On racial dynamics in the city in the 1850s, see Richard Tansey, "Out-of-State Free Blacks in Late Antebellum New Orleans," *Louisiana History* 22 (Fall 1981): esp. 370, 376–83.

49. New Orleans Register of Free Colored Persons, vol. 3 (1859–61), 158–59 (FHL microfilm). This was not the first time Cyprian Clamorgan came to the aid of a free man of color in need of a "white" witness to vouch for him. See ibid., 35–36.

8. Thickets of the Law

1. Loren Schweninger, ed., *From Tennessee Slave to St. Louis Entrepreneur: The Autobiography of James Thomas* (Columbia: University of Missouri Press, 1984), 155–59. On ethnic tensions in the city, see Louis S. Gerteis, *Civil War St. Louis* (Lawrence: University Press of Kansas, 2001), 73–74.

2. Schweninger, *From Tennessee Slave*, 157, 158; Gerteis, *Civil War St. Louis*, 312–13.

3. Gerteis, *Civil War St. Louis*, 97–115.

4. William Wells Brown, "The Colored People of Canada," in C. Peter Ripley et al., eds., *The Black Abolitionist Papers* (Chapel Hill: University of North Carolina Press, 1986), vol. 2, p. 476; Guardianship Files no. 3884 and no. 3885, St. Louis Probate Court, 1816–1901 (MOSA); *St. Louis Post-Dispatch*, Jan. 13, 1883.

5. Gerteis, *Civil War St. Louis*, 78, 87, 169–201.

6. St. Louis Deeds, Book 245, p. 490; ibid., Book 256, p. 193 (CSLRD).

7. Gerteis, *Civil War St. Louis*, 88, 177.

8. *Henry Clamorgan et al. v. Isaac T. Greene*, 32 Mo. 285; *Henry and Cyprian Clamorgan et al. v. Isaac T. Greene*, St. Louis Circuit Court, Sept. 1862 term, no. 93.

9. Missouri Legislature, 22nd General Assembly, 1st sess.: Senate Journal, 78, 127, and House Journal, 187.

10. *Missouri Republican*, Mar. 20, 1863.

11. Ibid.

12. *Laws of the State of Missouri, Passed at the Regular Session of the Twenty-Second General Assembly, Begun and Held at the City of Jefferson on Monday, December 29, 1862* (Jefferson City, Mo.: J. P. Ament, 1863), 209–10.

13. St. Louis Probate Court file no. 769 (Cyprian Martial Clamorgan) and no. 5571 (Maximin Clamorgan); J. M. Krum and C. H. Krum, *Henry Clamorgan, Cyprian Clamorgan, Leon A. Clamorgan and Julius Clamorgan, Appellants, v. The Baden and St. Louis Railway Company, Respondent: Statement and Brief for Respondent* (St. Louis: Chancy R. Barns, 1880), 22–23.

14. St. Louis Deeds, Book 256, p. 193; ibid., Book 267, p. 73; ibid., Book 263, p. 475; ibid., Book 430, p. 288.

15. St. Vincent de Paul, Baptisms (1852–67), 403 (SLCOL).

16. Gerteis, *Civil War St. Louis*, 210–12, 255–59, 273.

17. St. Louis Deeds, Book 294, p. 333.

18. Lorenzo J. Greene, Gary R. Kremer, and Antonio F. Holland, *Missouri's Black Heritage*, 2nd ed. (Columbia: University of Missouri Press, 1993), 79–81; Gerteis, *Civil War St. Louis*, 224.

19. Gerteis, *Civil War St. Louis*, 310; St. Louis Death Registers, vol. L, p. 37 (www .ancestry.com).

20. U.S. IRS Tax Assessment Lists, 1862–1918 (www.ancestry.com); St. Louis Deeds, Book 303, p. 220.

21. St. Vincent de Paul, Baptisms (1867–77), 63 (SLCOL); Mo. Death Certificates no. 37625 (1934) and no. 20495 (1940), MOSA. In later years, family members confused the sisters' birth dates, but Clara was the elder by almost five years.

22. St. Louis Deeds, Book 351, p. 19; ibid., Book 451, p. 355.

23. Ibid., Book 349, p. 334; ibid., Book 353, p. 46.

24. Ibid., Book 375, p. 170.

25. Ibid., Book 354, p. 396; ibid., Book 369, p. 207; ibid., Book 370, p. 227.

26. U.S. Census (1870), St. Louis, Ward 1, roll 810, p. 132; *New York Daily Tribune*, July 6, 1871.

27. St. Louis probate file no. 7904 (Pelagie Rutgers); St. Louis Death Registers, vol. 1, p. 524. On Julia Rutgers, who died in infancy, see St. Vincent de Paul, Burials (1845–66), entry for July 29, 1865 (SLCOL), and St. Louis Death Registers, vol. L, p. 123.

28. St. Louis Marriages, vol. 13, p. 243 (www.ancestry.com).

29. *St. Louis Daily Times*, Feb. 13, 1868; *St. Louis Globe-Democrat*, Feb. 13, 1868; St. Vincent de Paul, Marriages (1867–91), 7 (SLCOL).

30. St. Louis Deeds, Book 382, p. 9.

31. *Henry Clamorgan v. John W. Bame and Jacob Stoutenberge*, St. Louis Circuit Court, Dec. 1868 term, no. 11041; St. Louis directory, 1868. (The clerk managed to misspell the name of one of the defendants. It was actually Stoutenburg.)

32. St. Louis Deeds, Book 372, p. 134; *Henry Clamorgan v. John Kavanagh*, St. Louis Circuit Court, Feb. 1872 term, no. 21285.

33. *Henry Clamorgan v. Thomas J. and William A. Albright*, St. Louis Circuit Court, June 1870 term, no. 16364; St. Louis directory, 1870.

34. St. Louis Deeds, Book 426, p. 371.

35. Ibid., Book 399, p. 174.

36. Julie Winch, ed., *Cyprian Clamorgan's "The Colored Aristocracy of St. Louis"* (Columbia: University of Missouri Press, 1999), 53, 80–81. On the links between the Clamorgans and the Hickmans, see Old Cathedral, Baptisms (1856–74), 28 (SLCOL).

37. St. Louis directory, 1873.

38. Ibid., 1866, 1869, 1871, 1873.

39. St. Louis Deeds, Book 386, p. 541; ibid., Book 391, p. 208.

40. Ibid., Book 413, p. 187; ibid., Book 602, p. 165; *St. Louis Globe-Democrat*, Nov. 17, 1876.

41. St. Louis Deeds, Book 434, p. 451; ibid., Book 485, p. 81.

42. St. Louis Death Registers, vol. 5, pp. 314, 326; St. Vincent de Paul, Burials (1867–1905), 22; Baptisms (1867–77), 263 (SLCOL); *Daily Arkansas Gazette* (Little Rock), July 30, 1873; Jay Gitlin, *The Bourgeois Frontier: French Towns, French Traders and American Expansion* (New Haven, Conn.: Yale University Press, 2010), 175–76.

43. John James Ingalls, "Regis Loisel," *Kansas Magazine* (Feb. 1873), in *Atchison* (Kansas) *Globe*, July 6, 1891.

44. *St. Louis Globe-Democrat*, Feb. 13, 1868; *Weekly Patriot and Union* (Harrisburg, Penn.), Feb. 27, 1868; *Frank Leslie's Illustrated Newspaper*, Mar. 7, 1868; John Rodabough, *Frenchtown* (St. Louis: Sunrise Publishing, 1980), 48–49; Old Cathedral, Marriages (1855–81), 181 (SLCOL).

45. *Cyprian Clamorgan v. Fanny Deaver et al.*, St. Louis Circuit Court, Feb. 1878 term, no. 45298; *St. Louis Globe-Democrat*, Dec. 20, 1877. For Jacques's original claim, see Minutes of the Board of Land Commissioners, vol. 4, p. 501 (MOSA).

46. St. Louis Deeds, Book 490, p. 354; ibid., Book 594, p. 363.

47. Ibid., Book 531, p. 275; St. Louis probate files no. 8835 (John Donnellan) and no. 13044 (Joanna Gibbons).

48. Mary B. Cunningham and Jeanne C. Blythe, comps., *The Founding Family of St. Louis* (St. Louis: Piraeus, 1977), 196; *Cyprian Clamorgan v. Fanny Deaver*, St. Louis Circuit Court, Nov. 1874 term, no. 29647; *St. Louis Globe-Democrat*, Jan. 24, 1877.

49. *St. Louis Globe-Democrat*, Dec. 20, 1877; *Cyprian Clamorgan v. Fanny Deaver et al.*, St. Louis Circuit Court, Feb. 1878 term.

50. St. Louis Deeds, Book 492, p. 271; *American State Papers: Public Lands* (Washington, D.C.: Gales and Seaton, 1861; repr. Greenville, S.C.: Southern Historical Press, 1994), vol. 2, pp. 469–70.

51. *Claims of Heirs of Jacques Clamorgan. House Bill 17888, 61st Congress* (Washington, D.C.: Government Printing Office, 1910), 11; *Cong. Record*, 43rd Cong., 1st sess., 967; St. Louis Deeds, Book 625, p. 284.

52. *United States v. Clamorgan; Clamorgan v. United States*, 101 U.S. 822.

53. The suit received extensive press coverage. See *Daily Arkansas Gazette*, July 30, 1873; *Little Rock Daily Republican*, July 30, 1873; *Cleveland Morning Daily Herald*, July 30, 1873; *St. Louis Globe-Democrat*, June 24, 1876.

54. *St. Louis Globe-Democrat*, June 13, 1875; *United States v. Clamorgan; Clamorgan v. United States*; Minutes of the Board of Land Commissioners, vol. 5, p. 417; ibid., vol. 6, pp. 179–81.

55. *Report to Accompany Senate Bill No. 551*, 32nd Cong., sess. 1; Senate 33rd Cong. sess. 1, p. 254.

56. *St. Louis Globe-Democrat*, June 13, 1875; ibid., Aug. 17, 1875; ibid., Jan. 4, 1876. The Blows' claim was based on the marriage of one of Louis Labeaume's daughters to Peter E. Blow (Old Cathedral, Marriages [1828–40], 157, SLCOL).

57. *St. Louis Globe-Democrat*, June 22, 1876.

58. Ibid., June 23, 1876; ibid., June 24, 1876.

59. Ibid., June 24, 1876; *United States v. Clamorgan; Clamorgan v. United States.*

60. *St. Louis Globe-Democrat*, Apr. 7, 1876; ibid., July 11, 1876; ibid., July 27, 1876; ibid., Aug. 14, 1876; ibid., Sept. 18, 1876.

61. Ibid., Aug. 14, 1876.

62. *United States v. Clamorgan; Clamorgan v. United States; New York Times*, Jan. 6, 1880.

63. *St. Louis Globe-Democrat*, Jan. 6, 1880; *Daily Inter-Ocean* (Chicago), Jan. 6, 1880; *North American* (Philadelphia), Jan. 6, 1880; *Daily Evening Bulletin* (San Francisco), Jan. 6, 1880; *Washington Post*, Jan. 6, 1880; *St. Louis Post-Dispatch*, June 10, 1911.

64. *St. Louis Globe-Democrat*, Apr. 13, 1884.

65. J. M. Krum and C. H. Krum, *Henry Clamorgan, Cyprian Clamorgan, Leon A. Clamorgan, and Julius Clamorgan, Appellants, v. The Baden and St. Louis Railway Company: Statement and Brief for Respondent* (St. Louis, Chancy R. Barns, 1878), 1–5, 8–11; Krum and Krum, *Brief for Respondent . . . 1880*, 3.

66. E. P. Johnson and G. W. Hall, *Henry Clamorgan et al., Appellants, v. The Baden & St. Louis R. R. Co., Respondent: Statement and Brief of Appellants* (St. Louis: Chancy R. Barns, 1880), 1, 2; Minutes of the Board of Land Commissioners, vol. 1, p. 422, and ibid., vol. 3, p. 10, in Krum and Krum, *Brief for Respondent . . . 1880*, 3, 4.

67. *St. Louis Globe-Democrat*, Nov. 17, 1876.

68. St. Louis Deeds, Book 485, p. 545.

69. See, for example, *Henry Clamorgan et al. v. John F. Walter*, St. Louis Circuit Court, June 1874 term, no. 29645; *Clamorgan et al. v. August Fogel*, Aug. 1874 term.

70. *Clamorgan v. Fogel.*

71. On one wave of litigation, see St. Louis Circuit Court, Apr. 1875 term, no. 33068-90, 33095-33103, 33111. On the progress of the various cases, see *St. Louis Globe-Democrat*, Dec. 7, 1875; ibid., May 9, 1876; ibid., Oct. 18, 1876; ibid., Nov. 1, 1876; ibid., Nov. 17, 1876; ibid., Dec. 5, 1876.

72. *St. Louis Globe-Democrat*, Jan. 16, 1877; ibid., Jan. 25, 1877; ibid., Feb. 7, 1877; ibid., Feb. 28, 1877; ibid., Oct. 12, 1877; ibid., Oct. 17, 1877; ibid., Nov. 14, 1877.

73. *Henry Clamorgan et al. v. George S. Case*, St. Louis Circuit Court, Apr. 1874 term, no. 28690.

74. St. Louis Death Registers, vol. 6B, p. 301.

75. Krum and Krum, *Brief for Respondent . . . 1878*, 10–11; Krum and Krum, *Brief for Respondent . . . 1880*, 2, 18–19; Johnson and Hall, *Brief of Appellants*, 7, 26–27. The lawyers said the judgment in Chouteau's favor was handed down in 1809, but he actually secured it the previous year. See St. Louis Deeds, Book C, p. 109.

76. *St. Louis Globe-Democrat*, June 15, 1880; ibid., Oct. 20, 1880. Krum and Krum, *Brief for Respondent . . . 1880*, 47, 50–51, 52, 53; *Clamorgan, Appellant, v. The Baden & St. Louis Railway Company*, 72 Mo. 139.

77. *Brief for Appellant . . . 1880*, 4, 5, 8.

78. *Clamorgan Claims*, 20.

79. *St. Louis Globe-Democrat*, Nov. 2, 1880.

80. Ibid., Mar. 23, 1882.

81. *Henry Clamorgan et al., Plaintiffs in Error, v. D.C. Hornsby et al., Defendants in Error*, 13 Mo. App. 550.

82. *St. Louis Globe-Democrat*, Mar. 10, 1883.

83. St. Louis Deeds, Book 583, p. 558; St. Louis directories, 1877–78.

84. St. Louis directories, 1874–79.

85. St. Louis Deeds, Book 369, p. 207; U.S. Census (1870), St. Louis, Ward 1, roll 810, p. 132.

86. U.S. Census (1880), St. Louis, roll 719, e.d. 52, p. 256; St. Louis directories, 1877, 1880–83.

87. U.S. Census (1880), St. Louis, roll 724, e.d. 155, p. 52; ibid., roll 735, e.d. 406, p. 6B.

88. On some of those links, see St. Louis probate file no. 12825 (Charles Cotonmais); St. Louis Deeds, Book 552, pp. 262, 443; ibid., Book 557, p. 55; Records of Calvary Cemetery; St. Louis Death Registers, vol. 6, p. 82; ibid., vol. 6B, p. 301; Mo. Death Certificate no. 31366 (1913); St. Vincent de Paul, Baptisms (1867–77), 155, 249 (SLCOL).

89. For a sense of that activism, see Lawrence O. Christiansen, "Black St. Louis: A Study in Race Relations, 1865–1918," (Ph.D. diss., University of Missouri, 1972), chap. 8, and Greene et al., *Missouri's Black Heritage*, chap. 6.

90. *St. Louis Globe-Democrat*, Dec. 23, 1878.

91. Ibid., Feb. 10, 1878.

92. U.S. Census (1880), St. Louis, roll 728, e.d. p. 122.

93. St. Louis probate file no. 2526 (1848). See also *Crevier v. Bertrand et al.*, Mo. Supreme Court Case files (1858), box 401, f. 6. On Postlewaite's musical career, see Samuel A. Floyd, "J. W. Postlewaite of St. Louis: A Search for His Identity," *Black Perspective in Music* 6 (Autumn 1978): esp. 151–60, and "A Black Composer in Nineteenth-Century St. Louis," *19th-Century Music* 4 (Autumn 1980): 121–33.

94. St. Louis County Court Records, vol. 6, p. 120 (SLCOL); *Daily Missouri Republican*, Jan. 6, 1851; ibid., Jan. 27, 1851; St. Louis directories, 1850, 1855, 1857, 1864, 1866–68, 1870, 1875, 1879, 1881–89.

95. *St. Louis Post-Dispatch*, Jan. 4, 1889.

96. U.S. Census (1880), Central Township, St. Louis Co., roll 715, p. 132, e.d. 177.

97. *St. Louis Post-Dispatch*, Jan. 4, 1889.

98. *New York Times*, Jan. 5, 1889; St. Louis Death Registers, vol. 22, p. 512; *St. Louis Globe-Democrat*, Jan. 3, 1889; *St. Louis Post-Dispatch*, Jan. 3, 1889; ibid., Jan. 4, 1889.

99. See St. Louis Death Registers, vol. 28, p. 379 (where Eliza's name appears as "Virginia").

100. St. Louis directories, 1873, 1875–79; *St. Louis Globe-Democrat*, May 25, 1881;

ibid., May 30, 1881; St. Louis Death Registers, vol. 12, p. 438; St. Vincent de Paul, Burials (1867–1905), 58–59 (SLCOL).

101. St. Vincent de Paul, Burials (1867–1905), 62–63 (SLCOL); St. Louis Death Registers, vol. 13, p. 261; *St. Louis Post-Dispatch*, Jan. 13, 1883; Interments at Calvary, www.search.stlcathcem.org.
102. St. Louis directories, 1875–83.
103. St. Louis Deeds, Book 697, p. 156.
104. St. Louis Death Registers, vol. 14, p. 337; *St. Louis Globe-Democrat*, Mar. 10, 1883; ibid., Mar. 12, 1883.

9. The Mathematics of Race

1. *St. Louis Globe-Democrat*, Mar. 12, 1883.
2. St. Louis probate file no. 14670 (Henry Clamorgan), MOSA.
3. St. Louis Deeds, Book 706, p. 540, ibid., Book 716, p. 52 (CSLRD); *St. Louis Globe-Democrat*, Sept. 13, 1883.
4. St. Louis Probate Court, 1816–1901, Guardianship Records, files no. 10988-10991 (MOSA). St. Louis Deeds, Book 722, p. 438; ibid., Book 962, p. 193.
5. St. Louis directories, 1881–85.
6. Henry Clamorgan probate file.
7. Ibid. See also *St. Louis Globe-Democrat*, Apr. 13, 1883.
8. *St. Louis Post-Dispatch*, July 28, 1888.
9. *Morning Oregonian*, Dec. 27, 1895.
10. St. Louis directories, 1884, 1886, 1892–95.
11. St. Vincent de Paul, Marriages (1867–92), 177 (SLCOL); Mo. Death Cert. no. 35998 (1916), MOSA; New Orleans directory, 1859; *Times-Picayune*, Dec. 24, 1865.
12. U.S. Census (1870), St. Louis, Ward 5, roll no. 815, p. 135; ibid. (1880), e.d. 112, roll no. 728, p. 122 (www.ancestry.com); St. Louis directory, 1878.
13. St. Vincent de Paul, Burials (1867–1905), 88–89 (SLCOL); St. Louis Death Register, vol. 21, p. 107 (www.ancestry.com); St. Vincent de Paul, Marriages (1867–91), 271 (SLCOL).
14. Interments at Calvary, www.search.stlcathcem.org; St. Louis Death Register, vol. 25, p. 227; ibid., Book 27, p. 153; ibid., Book 40, p. 241.
15. See, for instance, St. Vincent de Paul, Baptisms (1881–92), 222, 269, 397, 472 (SLCOL).
16. St. Vincent de Paul, Marriages (1892–1935), 238 (SLCOL); U.S. Census (1920), Camden, N.J., e.d. 56, roll 1023, p. 26A; ibid. (1930), Brooklyn, N.Y., e.d. 134, roll 1515, p. 9A.
17. *St. Louis Post-Dispatch*, Apr. 10, 1884; St. Louis Death Register, vol. 15, p. 496.
18. U.S. Census (1860), St. Louis, Ward 2, roll 648, p. 629; ibid. (1870), Ward 4, roll 813, p. 662; ibid. (1900), Ward 4, roll 890, p. 10A; ibid. (1920), Ward 10,

roll 951, p. 9A; Old Cathedral, Marriages (1881–1932), 8 (SLCOL); Mo. Death Certs. no. 12559 (1911) and no. 24069 (1938), MOSA.

19. U.S. Census (1850), St. Louis, Ward 4, roll 471, p. 19; ibid. (1860), St. Louis, Ward 2, roll 648, p. 635; ibid. (1870), Kansas City, Ward 2, roll 782, p. 469; ibid. (1880) Kansas City, roll 692, p. 247; ibid. (1900) Kansas City, Ward 9, roll 863, p. 3A; Kansas City directories, 1889–91. Adeline died at the age of seventy-two (Mo. Death Cert. [1912] no. 26316).

20. St. Louis Marriages, vol. 17, p. 231 (www.ancestry.com); U.S. Census (1880), St. Louis, roll 727, p. 429; ibid. (1900), Ward 7, roll 891, p. 13B; ibid. (1910), Ward 24, roll 814, p. 6B; ibid. (1920), Ward 11, roll 954, p. 4A.

21. St. Louis directory, 1897.

22. St. Louis Marriages, vol. 51, p. 441 (no. 72978); U.S. Census (1900), St. Louis, Ward 11, roll 893, p. 8B; St. Louis directories, 1883–1900.

23. U.S. Census (1900), St. Louis, Ward 7, roll 891, p. 8A; St. Louis directories, 1905, 1910; Mo. Death Cert. no. 1159 (1912).

24. St. Louis Deeds, Book 934, p. 190; ibid., Book 966, p. 162; ibid., Book 1004, p. 466; ibid., Book 1272, p. 403; ibid., Book 1378, p. 184; ibid., Book 1420, p. 136; ibid., Book 1529, p. 404. *St. Louis Republic*, Nov. 28, 1891.

25. St. Louis directories, 1885, 1887, 1889–90, 1898, 1901, 1902.

26. From the census, city directories, and vital records it is possible to identify nearly a dozen families who rented from the Clamorgans.

27. Clara Morgan to Thomas Morgan, Nov. 16, 1892; Clamorgan Papers, MHS.

28. Fannie Cleary to Thomas Morgan, Feb. 9, 1894; Clara Morgan to Thomas Morgan, Apr. 12, 1893[?].

29. Clara Morgan to Thomas Morgan, May 25, 1894.

30. Clara Morgan to Thomas Morgan, Sept. 27, 1894.

31. U.S. Census (1900), St. Louis, Ward 10, roll 893, p. 8B.

32. St. Louis Death Registers, vol. 16, p. 760; Guardianship Records, file no. 10990; Interments at Calvary.

33. St. Louis directories, 1885–86; Guardianship Records, file no. 10988.

34. *Directory of Graduates of the University of California, 1864–1916* (Berkeley: University of California, 1916), x–xi, 144; *General Alumni Catalogue of New York University, 1833–1907: Medical Alumni* (New York: General Alumni Society, 1908), 472.

35. U.S. Census (1900) Manhattan, N.Y., e.d. 551, roll 1106, p. 12A.

36. *Biloxi Herald*, July 27, 1895; "Fordé Morgan," in Passport Applications, Jan. 2, 1906–Mar. 31, 1925 (www.ancestry.com).

37. See, for instance, Clara Morgan to Thomas Morgan, Mar. 1, 1893, and May 4, 1894.

38. U.S. Census (1900), Manhattan, N.Y., e.d. 551, roll 1106, p. 12A.

39. W. C. Sharpe, comp., *Vital Statistics of Seymour, Connecticut* (Seymour, Conn.: Record Printing, 1883), 17; U.S. Census (1880), Seymour, New Haven Co., Conn., roll 104, p. 64B; *New York Times*, Dec. 14, 1949. On Harriet Ford's assess-

ment of her role as a playwright, see *New York Times*, Sept. 11, 1910; ibid., June 14, 1914; ibid., Dec. 13, 1914.

40. St. Louis directories, 1887–1900.
41. Ibid., 1889; U.S. Census (1880), St. Louis, roll 733, p. 458; ibid. (1900), St. Louis, Ward 25, roll 900, p. 15B.
42. On Fuchs's background, see U.S. Census (1900), St. Louis, Ward 28, e.d. 416, roll 901, p. 19A; Interments at Calvary; Mo. Death Cert. no. 8592 (1929).
43. Fannie Cleary to Thomas Morgan, May 7, 1894.
44. "Henry" to Thomas Morgan, Feb. 13, 1893.
45. A. H. Fuchs to Thomas Morgan, Aug. 6 and Aug. 8, 1893.
46. "Phil" to Thomas Morgan, Jan. 4, 1893, and Jan. 16, 1893; "Joe" to Thomas Morgan, Nov. 2, 1892, Feb. 11, 1893, and Jan. 18, 1894; John Z. to Thomas Morgan, Sept. 3, 1893; Fannie Cleary to Thomas Morgan, July 9, 1893, and July 18, 1893.
47. Clara Morgan to Thomas Morgan, Oct. 14, 1893.
48. See, for example, Thomas Morgan to Clara Morgan, May 14, 1893; A. H. Fuchs to Thomas Morgan, May 24, 1893, and May 26, 1893.
49. St. Louis directories, 1889, 1890; U.S. Census (1910), Ward 25, St. Louis, roll 822, p. 97A.
50. For a typical example, see Corinne McMillan to Thomas Morgan, Mar. 3, 1893.
51. See, for instance, Clara Morgan to Thomas Morgan, Sept. 5, 1892.
52. Corinne McMillan to Thomas Morgan, Oct. 9, 1892.
53. Canadian Census (1881), St. John's Ward, Toronto, Subdistrict D, div. 1, p. 33 (www.ancestry.com).
54. Fannie Cleary to Thomas Morgan, Mar. 13 and Mar. 16, 1894.
55. Fannie Cleary to Thomas Morgan, Jan. 25, 1894.
56. Fannie Cleary to Thomas Morgan, [undated] and May 21, 1894.
57. Fannie Cleary to Thomas Morgan, July 17, 1894.
58. Minnie Cleary to Thomas Morgan, July 11, 1893, and Nov. 20, 1893; Fannie Cleary to Thomas Morgan, Feb. 1, 1894.
59. U.S. Census (1880) Nokomis, Montgomery Co., Ill., roll 237, p. 22B; ibid. (1900) St. Louis, Ward 23, roll 899, p. 6B; Calif. Death Cert. (COVR).
60. *St. Louis Globe-Democrat*, Oct. 11, 1892: *H. Clamorgan et al., Plaintiffs in Error, v. D. C. Hornsby et al.* (13 Mo. App. 550) and *Clamorgan et al., Plaintiffs in Error, v. Hornsby et al.* (94 Mo. 83).
61. *St. Louis Republic*, June 9, 1892.
62. *Lassauer & Ehrlich v. Amanda Morgan*, St. Louis Circuit Court, June 1892 term, no. 88637.
63. *St. Louis Globe-Democrat*, Oct. 2, 1892.
64. *St. Louis Republic*, Oct. 11, 1892.
65. Clara Morgan to Thomas Morgan, Sept. 5, 1892.
66. Amanda Clamorgan to Thomas Morgan, Sept. 14 and Sept. 22, 1892.
67. *St. Louis Republic*, June 26, 1892; ibid., Oct. 2, 1892.
68. Ibid., Oct. 2, 1892; *St. Louis Globe-Democrat*, Oct. 11, 1892.

69. Clara Morgan to Thomas Morgan, Oct. 13, 1892, Oct. 31, 1892, and Nov. 16, 1892.
70. Nellie Whitlock to Thomas Morgan, Aug. 10, 1893.
71. Clara Morgan to Thomas Morgan, Nov. 16, 1892.
72. Fraserburgh Parish Registers (www.scotlandspeople.org); St. Louis directories, 1882–83, 1885, 1887–89, 1894–95, 1897–98, 1905–1908; U.S. Census (1880), St. Louis, roll 725, p. 176, e.d. 159; ibid. (1900), roll 897, p. 11B, e.d. 309; ibid. (1910), roll 821, p. 5A, e.d. 342.
73. *Claim of Heirs of Jacques Clamorgan. House Bill 17888, 61st Congress* (Washington, D.C.: Government Printing Office, 1910), 19.
74. Ibid., 18–19.
75. Ibid., 21; *Bismarck* (N.D.) *Daily Tribune*, Dec. 25, 1888.
76. *Clamorgan Claims*, 21.
77. Ibid., 15, 16–17, 18; 59th Cong., 1st sess., H.R., 1216.
78. 59th Cong., 2nd sess., H.R. (report no. 8080).
79. *Clamorgan Claims*, 2, 10.
80. Ibid., 3–4, 12, 13. The Meramec claim was one that the Clamorgans and their attorney Alexander D. Anderson had tried to act on in the 1870s.
81. Ibid., 1–2.
82. Ibid., 5–6.
83. Mo. Death Cert. no. 16718 (1922).
84. 63rd Cong., 3rd sess., H.R., 311.
85. 64th Cong., 1st sess., H.R., 504 (H.R. 13749); 64th Cong., 2nd sess., H.R., 448 (H.R. 202760); 65th Cong., 1st sess., Senate, 352 (Senate Bill 2310); 66th Cong., 2nd sess., Senate, 454 (Senate Bill 3993).
86. U.S. Census (1910) Manhattan, Ward 12, New York, roll 1028, p. 24A.
87. *Appleton* (Wisc.) *Post Crescent*, Nov. 4, 1925; *Wisconsin Rapids Daily Tribune*, Nov. 5, 1925; *New York Times*, Oct. 10, 1938; "Forde Morgan," www.americas greatestbrands.com.
88. *New Haven Register*, Aug. 23, 1888; ibid., Nov. 12, 1891; ibid., Oct. 20, 1892; *Daily Inter-Ocean*, Mar. 11, 1888; *St. Paul* (Minn.) *Daily News*, Oct. 31, 1889; *Daily Picayune*, Sept. 22, 1892. On one trip to England, see *Galveston* (Tex.) *Daily News*, June 10, 1910.
89. "Border Crossings from Canada to the United States, 1895–1956," and "New York Passenger Lists" 1918 (no. 2573) and 1922 (no. 3092) (www.ancestry.com).
90. The city directories and the federal censuses provide glimpses into the lives of the people in Amanda's immediate neighborhood.
91. St. Louis directories, 1910–40.
92. Calif. Death Cert.
93. St. Louis Burials (SLGS CD), vol. 2; U.S. Census (1910), St. Louis, ward 11, e.d. 179, roll 816, p. 4A. John Garrissine died at age eighty-nine on February 25, 1928 (Mo. Death Cert. [1928] no. 2217).
94. U.S. Census (1920), e.d. 211, St. Louis, Ward 11, roll 954, p. 4A.

95. Calif. Death Cert.; U.K. Census (1891) RG12/3464, folio 66, p. 33 (www.ancestry .com); World War I draft registrations (www.ancestry.com).
96. SSDI, Sarah Amanda Bantum (www.ancestry.com); U.S. Census (1930), Los Angeles, roll 143, e.d. 267, p. 16A.
97. St. Louis directories, 1907, 1910, 1911; U.S. Census (1920), Peoria, Maricopa Co., Ariz., roll 49, p. 2B, e.d. 39. Clara shaved a good many years off her age when she responded to the census taker's questions.
98. Calif. Death Cert.
99. St. Louis probate file no. 59594 (Clara Clamorgan).
100. On the Lang household, see U.S. Census (1920), Los Angeles, Calif., roll 108, e.d. 227, p. 12A.
101. St. Louis probate file no. 65229 (Amanda Clamorgan). For the transfer of 2736 Chippewa to Thomas, see St. Louis Deeds, Book 164, p. 2.
102. Mo. Death Cert. no. 3507 (1927); *St. Louis Post-Dispatch*, Feb. 1, 1927.
103. *St. Louis Post-Dispatch*, Sept. 21, 1923; ibid., Feb. 4, 1929; Mo. Death Cert., no. 28728 (1923) and no. 7993 (1929).
104. U.S. Census (1910), Ward 11, St. Louis, roll 816, p. 237B; ibid. (1920), Ward 11, St. Louis, e.d. 211, roll 954, p. 4B; Mo. Death Cert. no. 25499 (1920).
105. *St. Louis Globe-Democrat*, Dec. 20, 1929; Mo. Death Certs. no. 7993 and no. 42583 (1929).
106. Amanda Clamorgan probate.
107. Mo. Death Cert. no. 37625 (1934); *St. Louis Post-Dispatch*, Oct. 15, 1934.
108. New York directories, 1920–25; U.S. Census (1930), Bronx, N.Y., roll 1468, p. 10A.
109. *New York Times*, Oct. 10, 1938; ibid., Dec. 3, 1938; ibid., Dec. 14, 1949.
110. Mo. Death Cert. no. 20495 (1940); *St. Louis Post-Dispatch*, June 24, 1940; Interments at Calvary.
111. Calif. Deaths (www.vitalsearch-ca.com).
112. St. Louis directories, 1936–40; Calif. Death Cert.
113. Calif. Death Cert.; U.S. Census (1930), Los Angeles, roll 143, e.d. 267, p. 267.
114. Los Angeles directories, 1925–29; Calif. Death Cert.; *Los Angeles Times*, May 18, 1948; ibid., Jan. 14, 1959. Sarah Amanda (Kendal) Bantum died in Los Angeles County on June 16, 2000 (SSDI).

10. *"Well Known in Negro Circles"*

1. St. Louis Death Registers, vol. B, p. 42; ibid., vol. D, pp. 52, 62, 127 (www.ancestry .com); Old Cathedral, Burials (1847–52), 471; ibid. (1852–70), 169, 174, 201 (SLCOL).
2. *Missouri Republican*, Jan. 24, 1850, in Lois Stanley, George F. Wilson, and Maryellen Wilson, comps., *More Death Records from Missouri Newspapers, 1810–1857* (Greenville, S.C.: Southern Historical Press, 1990), 74; Old Cathedral, Burials

(1832–47), 123 (Emilie "Morgan"); ibid. (1852–70), 24, 108 (SLCOL); St. Louis Death Registers, vol. B, p. 213; ibid., vol. C, p. 171.

3. Old Cathedral, Baptisms (1844–51), 48 (SLCOL).
4. On Mary Blanche's short life, see St. Vincent de Paul, Baptisms (1852–67), 218 (SLCOL), and St. Louis Death Registers, vol. G, p. 1.
5. Julie Winch, ed., *Cyprian Clamorgan's "The Colored Aristocracy of St. Louis"* (Columbia: University of Missouri Press, 1999), 50–51.
6. *Western Appeal*, Nov. 30, 1890, and ibid., June 20, 1891, in Willard B. Gatewood, Jr., *Aristocrats of Color: The Black Elite, 1880–1920* (Bloomington: University of Indiana Press, 1990), 16.
7. *St. Louis Post-Dispatch*, June 9, 1911.
8. St. Louis directories, 1865, 1867–71, 1873–74, 1876.
9. St. Louis Deeds, Book 369, p. 290 (CSLRD); St. Louis Death Registers, vol. 2, p. 181; ibid., vol. 3, p. 111; Interments at Calvary, www.search.stlcathcem.org.
10. St. Louis Marriages, vol. 17, p. 367 (www.ancestry.com); U.S. Census (1900), St. Louis, Ward 12, roll 894, e.d. 193, p. 4B.
11. St. Louis directories, 1870, 1873; U.S. Census (1870), St. Louis, Ward 6, roll 816, p. 259.
12. U.S. Census (1880), St. Louis, roll 721, e.d. 82, p. 29; ibid., roll 730, e.d. 207, p. 21.
13. *St. Louis Globe-Democrat*, Oct. 3, 1882; St. Thomas of Aquin, Marriages (1882–1939), 71 (SLCOL); St. Louis Marriages, vol. 23, p. 339.
14. St. Thomas of Aquin, Baptisms (1882–93), 8 (SLCOL); *St. Louis Globe-Democrat*, Mar. 10, 1883.
15. *St. Louis Republic*, June 9, 1911; ibid., June 18, 1911.
16. Tennessee State Marriages, 1780–2002 (www.ancestry.com).
17. U.S. Census (1900), Nashville, Ward 7, roll 1564, e.d. 86, p. 4A.
18. Ibid. (1850), Nashville, Davidson Co., Tenn., roll 875, p. 91; ibid. (1860), Nashville, Ward 6, roll 1246, p. 434. Nashville directories, 1855, 1857, 1859, 1860–61.
19. U.S. Census (1860), Nashville, Ward 6, roll 1246, p. 434.
20. Tennessee State Marriages.
21. The transcript of Thomas McDougal's will is included in the emancipation records filed for Rachel and Harrison in Illinois. Madison County Emancipation Records, vol. 3, p. 88 (ISA).
22. Tennessee State Marriages. On the Blair family, see U.S. Census (1860), Madison Co., Ill., roll 208, p. 38; ibid. (1870), Madison Co., Ill., roll 251, p. 146; ibid. (1880), Pin Oak, Madison Co., Ill., roll 233, e.d. 23, p. 341. On Pin Oak's African American community and Henry Blair's role in its development, see W. T. Norton, comp., *Centennial History of Madison County, Illinois, and Its People, 1812 to 1912* (Chicago and New York: Lewis Publishing Co., 1912), vol. 1, pp. 595–96.
23. Andrew Tate et al. to the Union Convention of Tennessee, Jan. 9, 1865, uniden-

tified newspaper clipping in Col. R. D. Mussey to Capt. C. P. Brown, Jan. 23, 1865; in Ira Berlin, Leslie S. Rowland, and Joseph Patrick Reidy, eds., *Freedom's Soldiers: The Black Military Experience in the Civil War* (Cambridge, U.K.: Cambridge University Press, 1998), 141–48.

24. *Gazetteer of Madison County* (Alton, Ill.: James T. Hair, 1866), 184.
25. U.S. Census (1870), St. Louis, Ward 5, roll 815, p. 50. The entry for Eugene in the St. Louis Death Registers (vol. 30, p. 474) says he was born in St. Louis.
26. St. Louis directory, 1866; St. Louis Deeds, Book 341, p. 106.
27. St. Louis directories, 1869–70; U.S. Census (1870), St. Louis, Ward 5, roll 815, p. 50.
28. St. Louis Death Registers, vol. 5, p. 281 (as Margaret "McDengle").
29. U.S. Census (1880), Pin Oak, Madison Co., Ill., roll 233, e.d. 23, pp. 341, 343; ibid., Ward 5, Nashville, Tenn., roll 1249, e.d. 42, p. 1288.
30. St. Louis directories, 1864–69, 1871–75.
31. Ibid., 1875–85.
32. Madison Co., Ill., Marriages, vol. 8, p. 51 (ISA).
33. U.S. Census (1860), Panola, Miss., roll 589, p. 102. The 1860 slave census for Panola shows John B. Fizer as the owner of a two-year-old boy classed as mulatto. William was born in 1858. Also on the Fizer plantation was an eighteen-year-old mulatto woman who was almost certainly William's mother, Maria Brown. On the older Fizer's role in the secession crisis, see www.csawardept.com/documents/secess.
34. Madison County probate cases, file 29/090 (ISA).
35. U.S. Census (1880), St. Louis, roll 723, e.d. 131, p. 20; ibid., Pin Oak, Madison Co., Ill., roll 233, pp. 341, 343; ibid., Ward 5, Nashville, Tenn., roll 1249, e.d. 42, p. 6.
36. Madison County probate cases, file 53/159.
37. *Cleveland Gazette*, Jan. 31, 1885; St. Louis directory, 1886–94.
38. St. Louis directory, 1885.
39. *Cleveland Gazette*, Jan. 31, 1885; St. Louis directories, 1890–91, 1893–94, 1894–95, 1895–1900.
40. St. Louis Deeds, Book 1155, p. 549.
41. St. Louis City Death Registers, vol. 30, p. 474; Interments at Calvary; *St. Louis Republic*, Apr. 22, 1894.
42. St. Louis Birth Registers (MOSA).
43. Ibid.; St. Louis directories, 1884–86, 1888–89. The Clamorgans registered their third son as Arthur, but had him baptized as Eugene Aloysius.
44. St. Vincent de Paul, Baptisms (1867–77), 63 (SLCOL).
45. St. Thomas of Aquin, Baptisms (1882–93), 8, 16, 39, 52, 75 (SLCOL). The priest wrote down the wrong birth date for Walter: April 13 instead of April 30.
46. Winch, ed., *Clamorgan's Colored Aristocracy*, 50, 54: Mo. Death Certs., no. 3125 (1912), no. 10956 (1922) and no. 8947 (1924), MOSA; St. Louis directories, 1851, 1854, 1859, 1875, 1877–78, 1883–86, 1890, 1893; U.S. Census (1880), St.

Louis, roll 735, e.d. 403, p. 160 (Felix); ibid., roll 719, e.d. 49, p. 205 (George); ibid., roll 720, e.d. 75, p. 133 (Nancy); ibid. (1900), St. Louis, Ward 10, roll 893, e.d. 150, p. 2B (Felix and Nancy); ibid. (1910), St. Louis, Ward 11, roll 816, e.d. 179, p. 7B (Felix and Nancy); ibid. (1920), Ward 11, roll 954, e.d. 211, p. 8A (Felix and Nancy); Interments at Calvary. According to her obituary (*St. Louis Post-Dispatch*, Mar. 22, 1922), Nancy's maiden name was Washinga. Her mother was French and her father "of Indian descent."

47. St. Louis Marriages, vol. 53, p. 81 (no. 78702).

48. Ibid., vol. 2, p. 428; ibid., vol. 6, p. 318; ibid., vol. 11, p. 257; St. Louis Death Registers, vol. J, p. 380; ibid., vol. G, p. 97; ibid., vol. K, p. 55; ibid., vol. 9, p. 713; Old Cathedral, Burials (1852–70), 412 (SLCOL); U.S. Census (1870), St. Louis, Ward 3, roll 812, p. 250; ibid. (1880), St. Louis, roll 735, e.d. 401, p. 137C.

49. The Vashons were a prolific and far-flung family, and the literature on them is extensive. For a brief overview of the life of the most prominent member of the clan, George Boyer Vashon, see C. Peter Ripley et al., eds., *The Black Abolitionist Papers* (Chapel Hill: University of North Carolina Press, 1991), vol. 3, pp. 321–22.

50. St. Louis directories, 1887–91, 1893–1900; U.S. Census (1880), St. Louis, roll 735, e.d. 401, p. 137C.

51. IGI; St. Louis directories, 1884–86, 1889–95; St. Louis Death Registers, vol. 18, p. 438; *St. Louis Post-Dispatch*, Apr. 9, 1886. U.S. Census (1900), St. Louis, Ward 10, roll 893, e.d. 152, p. 2A; ibid. (1910), Ward 23, e.d. 364, roll 821, e.d. 364, p. 9A.

52. Old Cathedral, Marriages (1828–40), 38 (SLCOL); St. Louis Death Registers, vol. B, p. 223; Winch, ed., *Clamorgan's Colored Aristocracy*, 58–59.

53. Loren Schweninger, ed., *From Tennessee Slave to St. Louis Entrepreneur: The Autobiography of James Thomas* (Columbia: University of Missouri Press, 1984). For the Blair-Thomas marriage, see Illinois Statewide Marriage Index, 1763–1900 (ISA).

54. *Little Rock Daily Republican*, June 17, 1872; *St. Louis Globe-Democrat*, Mar. 11, 1880; ibid., Sept. 15, 1880; ibid., Nov. 13, 1880.

55. St. Louis directories, 1882–1911; *St. Louis Republic*, Mar. 31, 1889; ibid., July 6, 1894; ibid., Apr. 14, 1897; *St. Louis Post-Dispatch*, June 9, 1911.

56. St. Louis Deeds, Book 1087, p. 348; St. Louis directories, 1893–1907. *St. Louis Star*, June 9, 1911. Louise had money at her disposal. On the same day she bought the house, she and her siblings sold their father's farm in Pin Oak for $7,800 and split the proceeds. *Edwardsville Intelligencer*, June 8, 1892.

57. St. Louis Death Registers, Book 37, p. 90; ibid., Book 43, p. 149; Interments at Calvary. Both boys were listed as "colored" in the death registers.

58. *St. Louis Globe-Democrat*, May 17, 1881; ibid., Dec. 30, 1887; *Indianapolis Freeman*, July 12, 1890; *Cleveland Gazette*, July 19, 1890; *Irish World and American Industrial Liberator* (New York), Jan. 9, 1892.

59. See, for example, *Cleveland Gazette*, Jan. 31, 1885; *Western Appeal*, June 30, 1888; ibid., Dec. 29, 1888.

60. *St. Louis Post-Dispatch*, June 16, 1911.

61. St. Louis Death Registers, Book 41, p. 447; ibid., Book 42, p. 97; ibid., Book 4, p. 238; *St. Louis Globe-Democrat*, Dec. 31, 1900, and ibid., July 18, 1901.

62. In the 1910 census the Clamorgans were white, the Badeaus and Mordecais mulatto, and the McLeods black. U.S. Census (1910), St. Louis, Ward 10, roll 816, e.d. 157, p. 4A (Badeau and Mordecai); ibid., Ward 14, roll 818, e.d. 818, p. 1B (McLeod). Mabel and Virginia Mordecai taught at all-black schools (St. Louis directories, 1909–11). Mabel eventually married and moved to Chicago. Virginia taught at the Delaney School for the rest of her working life. *St. Louis Post-Dispatch*, Nov. 6, 1925.

63. U.S. Census (1900), St. Louis, Ward 8, roll 892, e.d. 123, p. 1B.

64. Ibid., Ward 9, roll 892, e.d. 144, p. 12B.

65. *St. Louis Post-Dispatch*, June 9, 1911; ibid., June 10, 1911; *St. Louis Globe-Democrat*, June 10, 1911.

66. St. Louis Deeds, Book 2035, p. 184; ibid., Book 2062, p. 20; *St. Louis Republic*, June 10, 1911; *St. Louis Post-Dispatch*, June 9, 1911.

67. *St. Louis Post-Dispatch*, June 9, 1911. The Clamorgans continued to attend "colored" social events, and their presence was noted in the African American press—which of course no one in all-white Maplewood read. See, for instance, *St. Louis Palladium*, Oct. 29, 1904.

68. *St. Louis Republic*, June 9, 1911.

69. Ibid., June 9, 1911; ibid., June 10, 1911, U.S. Census (1910), St. Louis, Ward 24, roll 814, e.d. 459, p. 2A.

70. St. Louis directories, 1905, 1907–10; *St. Louis Globe-Democrat*, June 10, 1911; *St. Louis Star*, June 11, 1911.

71. *St. Louis Star*, June 9, 1911; *St. Louis Post-Dispatch*, June 9, 1911.

72. *St. Louis Republic*, June 9, 1911; *St. Louis Post-Dispatch*, June 10, 1911.

73. *St. Louis Post-Dispatch*, June 9, 1911.

74. Ibid., June 9, 1911; *St. Louis Star*, June 9, 1911.

75. *St. Louis Republic*, June 9, 1911; ibid., June 18, 1911.

76. Ironically, just before the scandal broke, one of the hits of the theatrical season in St. Louis was a drama in which a supposedly white Southern aristocrat learned the truth about his African ancestry. *St. Louis Post-Dispatch*, June 9, 1911.

ii. Defining Whiteness

1. *St. Louis Republic*, June 9, 1911; *Kansas City Star*, June 9, 1911; *Trenton* (N.J.) *Evening Times*, June 10, 1911; *Wilkes-Barre* (Penn.) *Times-Leader*, June 10, 1911; *Kansas City Journal*, June 10, 1911; *Syracuse* (N.Y.) *Daily Journal*, June 13, 1911; *Columbus* (Ga.) *Daily Enquirer*, June 14, 1911; ibid., June 16, 1911; *Pawtucket* (R.I.) *Times*, June 14, 1911; *Washington Post*, June 15, 1911; *Los Angeles Times*, July 4, 1911; ibid., Aug. 30, 1911; *Tulsa World*, Sept. 10, 1911.

2. U.S. Census (1870), Ward 4, St. Mary Parish, La., roll 531, p. 592; IGI; St. Louis directory, 1890; Washington State Census, 1892 (www.ancestry.com).

3. U.S. Census (1910), Ward 24, roll 814, e.d. 459, p. 2B; St. Louis directory, 1911.

4. *St. Louis Post-Dispatch*, June 9, 1911.

5. St. Louis directories, 1898–99.

6. *St. Louis Post-Dispatch*, June 9, 1911.

7. Virginia B. Ferguson death cert. (COVR).

8. *St. Louis Republic*, June 9, 1911; *St. Louis Post-Dispatch*, June 9, 1911.

9. *St. Louis Republic*, June 9, 1911; *St. Louis Star*, June 10, 1911.

10. *St. Louis Republic*, June 9, 1911; *St. Louis Post-Dispatch*, June 9, 1911.

11. *St. Louis Republic*, June 9, 1911; ibid., June 10, 1911.

12. Ibid.; *St. Louis Globe-Democrat*, June 10, 1911; *St. Louis Star*, June 11, 1911.

13. *St. Louis Republic*, June 9, 1911; *St. Louis Star*, June 9, 1911.

14. *St. Louis Post-Dispatch*, June 9, 1911.

15. *St. Louis Star*, June 10, 1911.

16. *St. Louis Republic*, June 9, 1911.

17. *St. Louis Post-Dispatch*, June 9, 1911.

18. *St. Louis Star*, June 9, 1911.

19. Ibid., June 13, 1911.

20. *St. Louis Star*, June 13, 1911.

21. *St. Louis Republic*, June 9, 1911.

22. Ibid.; *St. Louis Star*, June 9, 1911.

23. U.S. Census (1820), Nashville, Tenn., roll 122, p. 76; ibid. (1830), Nashville, roll 174, p. 295; ibid. (1840), Nashville, roll 520, p. 269; ibid. (1850), Nashville, roll 875, p. 153; Mo. Death Cert. no. 23521 (1919), MOSA; Little Compton Historical Society, *Little Compton Families, from Records Compiled by Benjamin Franklin Wilbour* (Little Compton, R.I., 1967), 522; *Providence* (R.I.) *Gazette*, Nov. 22, 1817.

24. Tennessee State Marriages (www.ancestry.com); Mo. Death Cert. no. 12414 (1924), MOSA; New Orleans Birth Records, vol. 14, pp. 463, 464; ibid., vol. 19, p. 539 (LSA).

25. U.S. Census (1860), St. Louis, Ward 4, roll 649, p. 347.

26. St. Louis directories, 1865–67, 1869; U.S. Census (1850), St. Louis, Ward 4, roll 417, p. 53; ibid. (1860), Ward 4, roll 469, p. 47.

27. St. Louis Marriages, vol. 10, p. 440; St. Louis Death Registers, vol. K, pp. 58, 358. Her baptismal name was Julie, but Georgiana's elder sister generally went by the less French-sounding "Julia" as an adult. Although she was mulatto in the census, Georgiana was white in the death register.

28. St. Louis directories, 1864–67; St. Louis Death Registers, vol. 1, p. 632.

29. St. Louis Death Registers, vol. 6, p. 78.

30. St. Louis Marriages, vol. 16, p. 354; U.S. Census (1880), St. Louis roll 718, e.d. 23, p. 421 (1st enum.); roll 727, e.d. 61, p. 481 (2nd enum.).

31. U.S. Census (1880), St. Louis, roll 727, e.d. 33, p. 251; *St. Louis Star*, June 13, 1911.

32. Nameoke appears in Rufus Dawes's *Nix's Mate* (New York: Samuel Colman, 1839).

33. *St. Louis Star,* June 9, 1911.
34. St. Louis directories, 1875, 1881–82, 1884, 1886, 1888–1900.
35. St. Louis Marriages, vol. 22, p. 321 (no. 2819).
36. St. Louis directory, 1884; St. Louis Birth Records (MOSA). Alexander Andrew's parents gave his race as "white" when they registered his birth.
37. St. Francis Xavier, Marriages (1863–80), 278 (SLCOL); U.S. Census (1880), St. Louis, roll 723, e.d. 137, p. 135; St. Louis directories, 1886–89.
38. St. Louis Birth Records.
39. St. Louis Death Registers, vol. 13, p. 24. Tecumseh Davis had also been listed as "colored."
40. Ibid., vol. 38, pp. 455, 507; Interments at Calvary, www.search.stlcathcem.org; U.S. Census (1900), St. Louis, roll 893, e.d. 152, p. 4A; ibid. (1920), St. Louis, Ward 20, roll 957, e.d. 396, p. 1A; ibid. (1930), St. Louis, roll 1233, e.d. 565, p. 4B.
41. U.S. Census (1900), St. Louis, Ward 10, roll 893, e.d. 150, p. 6A; ibid., Ward 12, roll 894, e.d. 193, p. 21A.
42. Ibid. (1910), St. Louis, Ward 24, roll 814, e.d. 459, p. 1B.
43. *St. Louis Globe-Democrat,* June 10, 1911; *St. Louis Post-Dispatch,* June 10, 1911; World War I draft registration (www.ancestry.com); Gasconade County Marriages, vol. 6, p. 51 (MOSA).
44. *St. Louis Post-Dispatch,* July 3, 1911.
45. *St. Louis Star,* June 15, 1911; ibid., June 16, 1911; *St. Louis Post-Dispatch,* June 16, 1911.
46. *St. Louis Republic,* June 18, 1911.
47. *St. Louis Post-Dispatch,* June 25, 1911.
48. *St. Louis Republic,* June 10, 1911.
49. *St. Louis Post-Dispatch,* June 11, 1911; *St. Louis Globe-Democrat,* June 12, 1911; *St. Louis Star,* June 12, 1911; *St. Louis Star-Times,* June 15, 1911; *The Crisis,* Aug. 1911, 144.
50. *St. Louis Star,* June 11, 1911.
51. *St. Louis Post-Dispatch,* June 11, 1911.
52. Ibid., June 16, 1911; *St. Louis Globe-Democrat,* June 10, 1911.
53. *St. Louis Post-Dispatch,* July 3, 1911.
54. *St. Louis Republic,* June 9, 1911; *New York Times,* July 4, 1911; *Los Angeles Times,* July 4, 1911; *St. Louis Post-Dispatch,* July 3, 1911; *St. Louis Globe-Democrat,* July 4, 1911.
55. *St. Louis Republic,* June 10, 1911.
56. *St. Louis Globe-Democrat,* June 10, 1911.
57. *St. Louis Post-Dispatch,* June 10, 1911; *St. Louis Star,* June 10, 1911. Higdon knew Louis and he had known Louis's father. See St. Louis Deeds, Book 650, p. 499 (CSLRD).
58. *Revised Statutes of Missouri* (1909), sec. 4727.

59. *St. Louis Post-Dispatch*, June 11, 1911.
60. *St. Louis Star*, June 10, 1911; *St. Louis Post-Dispatch*, July 3, 1911.
61. *St. Louis Star*, July 3, 1911; *St. Louis Post-Dispatch*, July 3, 1911; *St. Louis Globe-Democrat*, July 4, 1911.
62. *St. Louis Republic*, Aug. 30, 1911; *Tulsa World*, Sept. 10, 1911.
63. Mo. Death Cert. no. 30683 (1912).
64. St. Louis directories, 1912–13.
65. Los Angeles directory, 1912; *Los Angeles Times*, July 4, 1911; ibid., Aug. 30, 1911.
66. Los Angeles directory, 1912, 1916; U.S. Census (1920), South Pasadena, Los Angeles Co., Calif., roll 119, e.d. 611, p. 4B; Louis P. De Morgan death cert. (1923), COVR. Louise gave her husband's birthplace as Pennsylvania and identified his parents as Henry De Morgan, a native of Spain, and Harriet Thomas (the name should actually have been Thompson), from Pennsylvania.
67. U.S. Census (1930), Los Angeles, roll 139, e.d. 158, p. 15B; Louise De Morgan death cert. (1946), COVR.
68. Los Angeles directory, 1912, 1913–17, 1920–21, 1924–25; U.S. Census (1920), Los Angeles, dist. 64, roll 108, e.d. 227, p. 18B; ibid. (1930), Los Angeles, roll 135, e.d. 85, p. 19B; Petition for Naturalization no. 43683, Los Angeles (www.ancestry.com); Calif. Births, 1905–96, and Calif. Deaths (www.vitalsearch-ca.com).
69. Los Angeles directories, 1913–17, 1920–21, 1926–29.
70. U.S. Census (1920), Los Angeles, dist. 75, roll 115, e.d. 458, p. 12B; ibid. (1930), Los Angeles, roll 143, e.d. 267, p. 13B; Walter L. Morgan death cert. (1965), COVR.
71. Los Angeles directory, 1913–17, 1923–30. U.S. Census (1930), Los Angeles, roll 135, e.d. 94, p. 15A; California Births, 1905–96; Calif. Deaths.
72. Los Angeles directory, 1917; U.S. Census (1920), Ward 1, Newark, N.J., roll 1031, e.d. 94, p. 17A; ibid. (1930), South Pasadena, Los Angeles Co., Calif., roll 175, e.d. 1516, p. 1A; Calif. Deaths.
73. Los Angeles directories, 1913–17; South Pasadena directory, 1920; Calif. Births, 1905–96; U.S. Census (1920), South Pasadena, Los Angeles Co., Calif., roll 119, e.d. 611, p. 4B.
74. Los Angeles directory, 1924; U.S. Census (1930), Los Angeles, roll 135, e.d. 94, p. 15A.
75. U.S. Census (1920), Burbank, Los Angeles Co., Calif., roll 102, e.d. 16, p. 14A.
76. Ibid. (1930), Inglewood, Los Angeles Co., Calif., roll 128, e.d. 1008, p. 1B; Calif. Deaths. Mary Collins died in 1935.
77. U.S. Census (1930), Pasadena, Los Angeles Co., Calif., roll 170, p. 12A, e.d. 1275; Calif. Births.
78. California Voter Registrations, 1934, 1940, 1942, 1944 (www.ancestry.com).
79. Information on Virginia's later life was kindly supplied by a Clamorgan descendant (e-mail communication with the author, Feb. 7, 2010).

80. Soc. Sec. Admin., form OAC-790 (Cora M. Collins); Cora Marie Collins death cert. (1989), COVR. Virginia gave her mother's maiden name as "Morgan."
81. Mo. Death Certs. no. 36390 and no. 42923 (1916), and no. 23521 (1919); Interments at Calvary.
82. U.S. Census (1920), St. Louis, Ward 24, roll 960, e.d. 464, p. 9B; World War I draft registration (www.ancestry.com).
83. St. Louis directories, 1921, 1925; Database of Illinois Death Certificates, 1916–50 (ISA); U.S. Census (1930), Lebanon, St. Clair Co., Ill., roll 555, e.d. 78, p. 13A.
84. Los Angeles directories, 1933–34; California Voter Registrations, 1934, 1936, 1938, 1940, 1944, 1946, 1948, 1952; Maud Adele Davis death cert. (1950), COVR. On Louise Davis Lillard's remarkable life, see *Los Angeles Times*, July 23, 2005.
85. Mo. Death Cert. no. 12414 (1924). (Pocahontas was classed as white on the death certificate.) U.S. Census (1930), East St. Louis, St. Clair Co., Ill., roll 556, e.d. 52, p. 4B; Database of Illinois Death Certificates, 1916–50; *St. Louis Post-Dispatch*, Mar. 26, 1944.
86. World War I draft registration; MOSA Soldiers' Database, World War I.
87. U.S. Census (1920), Ward 7, East St. Louis, St. Clair Co., Ill., roll 404, e.d. 175, p. 6A; Interments at Calvary.
88. U.S. Census (1910), St. Louis, Ward 10, roll 816, e.d. 157, p. 10B; Chicago directories, 1914.
89. World War I draft registrations.
90. U.S. Census (1920), Chicago, Ward 27, roll 338, e.d. 1611, p. 5A; ibid., Ward 26, roll 338, e.d. 1586, p. 3B.
91. Database of Illinois Death Certificates, 1916–50; U.S. Census (1930), Chicago, Ward 41, roll 480, e.d. 1488, p. 26A; ibid., Ward 39, roll 475, e.d. 1386, p. 15A.
92. U.S. Census (1930), Jefferson Township, Cook Co., Ill., roll 480, e.d. 1497, pp. 17A, 20A.
93. Ibid. (1930), Downey, Los Angeles Co., Calif., roll 126, e.d. 924, p. 12B; Harrison McDougal death cert. (1930), COVR.
94. U.S. Census (1900), Washington, D.C., roll 161, p. 16A, e.d. 69; "Official Register of the United States, Containing a List of Officers and Employees in the Civil, Military and Naval Service on the First of July, 1883" (48th Cong., 1st sess.), 547; Frederick D. Wilkinson, comp., *Directory of Graduates, Howard University, 1870–1963* (Washington, D.C., 1965), 127, 511; *Washington Bee*, Mar. 10, 1883; "List of Registered Physicians," in *Annual Report of the Commissioners of the District of Columbia for the Year Ended June 30, 1887* (H. Exec. Doc., 50th Cong., 1st sess.), 883.
95. *Washington Bee*, June 27, 1885; ibid., Nov. 30, 1886.
96. *Critic-Record* (Washington, D.C.), Sept. 5, 1888; *St. Louis Republic*, Sept. 6, 1888; *Newark* (Ohio) *Advocate*, Sept. 6, 1888; *Hamilton* (Ohio) *Daily Democrat*, Sept. 6, 1888; *Dunkirk* (N.Y.) *Observer-Journal*, Sept. 6, 1888; *Decatur* (Ill.) *Republican*,

Sept. 7, 1888; *Milwaukee Sentinel*, Sept. 9, 1888; *Syracuse* (N.Y.) *Weekly Express*, Sept. 12, 1888; *Edwardsville* (Ill.) *Intelligencer*, Sept. 19, 1888.

97. *St. Louis Republic*, Sept. 6, 1888; Washington, D.C., directory, 1890–94, 1896; Nashville, Tenn., directory, 1890–91.

98. U.S. Census (1900), Washington, D.C., roll 161, p. 16A, e.d. 69; ibid. (1910), Washington, D.C., roll 149, e.d. 29, p. 8A; ibid. (1920), Washington, D.C., roll 206, e.d. 70, p. 11A; ibid. (1930), Washington, D.C., roll 292, e.d. 11, p. 17A.

99. *Indianapolis Freeman*, Oct. 1, 1892.

100. U.S. Census (1900), Proviso Township, Cook Co., Ill., roll 294, e.d. 1181, p. 9B; ibid. (1910), Ward 4, Indianapolis, Ind., roll 367, e.d. 77, p. 2A.

101. Ibid. (1920), St. Louis, Ward 25, roll 961, e.d. 502, p. 3B; ibid., Chicago, Ward 7, roll 316, e.d. 440, p. 9B; ibid. (1930), Indianapolis, Ind., roll 609, e.d. 57, p. 7B.

102. Mo. Death Cert. no. 14077 (1937). When John died three years later, his daughter registered his death and she said he was still married to her mother. Mo. Death Cert. no. 34065 (1940).

12. On the Fringes

1. *St. Louis Post-Dispatch*, June 10, 1911; *St. Louis Globe-Democrat*, June 10, 1911; *St. Louis Star*, June 10, 1911.

2. Howard J. Jones, "Biographical Sketches of the Members of the 1868 Louisiana State Senate," *LH* 19 (Winter 1978): 67–70, 91–92.

3. *New Orleans Times*, Sept. 2, 1868; *New Orleans Commercial Bulletin*, Sept. 2, 1868.

4. *Daily True Delta*, Feb. 2 and Apr. 10, 1862.

5. Reuben F. Briggs to Abraham Lincoln, Mar. 15, 1864, in Ser. 1, Gen. Corr., 1833–1916, Abraham Lincoln Papers, Library of Congress, www.memory.loc.gov.

6. *Daily Delta*, June 19, 1862.

7. In "The Origins of Black Leadership in New Orleans During Reconstruction," *JSH* 40 (Aug. 1974): 439, David C. Rankin refers to one C. Clay Morgan as having been a pioneering African American attorney in New Orleans. Other authors have cited Rankin. See, for instance, J. Clay Smith, Jr., *Emancipation: The Making of the Black Lawyer, 1844–1944* (Philadelphia: University of Pennsylvania Press, 1993), 282. Paul Finkelman's research has established conclusively that no one of that name was admitted to the Louisiana Bar either before or after the Civil War. ("Not Only the Judges' Robes Were Black: African-American Lawyers as Social Engineers," *Stanford Law Review* 47 [Nov. 1994]: 173.) Cyprian Clamorgan, alias C. Clay Morgan, did practice law, but as a white man, and without being a member of the Bar.

8. *New Orleans Times*, Mar. 11, 1872, in James Haskins, *Pinckney Benton Stewart Pinchback* (New York: Macmillan, 1973), 21–22.

9. *Daily True Delta*, June 19, 1862; Joy J. Jackson, "Keeping Law and Order in New Orleans Under General Butler, 1862," *LH* 34 (Winter 1993): 54–55.

10. "From New Orleans," in *Philadelphia Inquirer*, July 16, 1862.

11. *Times-Picayune*, Mar. 10, 1863; ibid., Mar. 13, 1863.

12. Ibid., Jan. 21, 1864.

13. Ibid., Jan. 24, 1864; C. C. Morgan to the Public, Feb. 1, 1864, enclosed with Reuben F. Briggs to Abraham Lincoln, Mar. 15, 1864.

14. C. C. Morgan to the Public.

15. Briggs to Lincoln, Mar. 15, 1864.

16. *Daily True Delta*, Dec. 4, 1864.

17. Ibid., Nov. 30, 1864; ibid., Dec. 3, 1864; ibid., Dec. 4, 1864; ibid., Dec. 9, 1864; *Times-Picayune*, Dec. 4, 1864; *New Orleans Tribune*, Dec. 4, 1864; ibid., Dec. 6, 1864.

18. Cyprian found another ally in George H. Hanks, the white colonel of a regiment of U.S. Colored Troops, who wrote a glowing letter of recommendation for him in February 1865. Hanks and "C. C. Morgan" had met in the summer of 1864. Hanks knew Cyprian to be a man of mixed racial ancestry, but he obviously considered this fact to be irrelevant. He certainly made no mention of it in his letter. *Claim of Heirs of Jacques Clamorgan, House Bill 17888, 61st Congress* (Washington, D.C.: Government Printing Office, 1910), 20; *L'Union*, June 14, 1864; "U.S. Civil War Soldiers, 1861–1865" (www.ancestry.com); U.S. Census (1860), Hartford, Conn., roll 78, p. 922.

19. Haskins, *Pinchback*, 26–27.

20. On the mounting pressure for civil rights, especially the right to vote, see Donald E. Everett, "Demands of the New Orleans Free Colored Population for Political Equality, 1862–1865," *LHQ* 38 (Apr. 1955): 43–64.

21. *L'Union*, June 14, 1864.

22. *State Convention of the Colored People of Louisiana, Jan. 9th, 10th, 11th, 12th, 13th and 14th, 1865*, in Philip S. Foner and George E. Walker, eds., *Proceedings of the Black State Conventions, 1840–1865* (Philadelphia: Temple University Press, 1980), vol. 2, p. 244.

23. *New Orleans Tribune*, Mar. 18, 1865.

24. Ibid., Sept. 12, 1865; ibid., Sept. 13, 1865; ibid., Oct. 8, 1865; ibid., Oct. 18, 1865; ibid., Oct. 19, 1865.

25. *Times-Picayune*, Nov. 7, 1867.

26. *New Orleans Tribune*, July 11, 1867.

27. Ibid., May 15, 1867.

28. Ibid., May 21, 1867; ibid., May 28, 1867; ibid., May 29, 1867; *Cincinnati Daily Gazette*, May 29, 1867.

29. *New Orleans Tribune*, May 30, 1867.

30. He spoke a couple of times in St. John the Baptist Parish. *New Orleans Tribune*, June 6, 1867; ibid., June 11, 1867.

31. Ibid., July 9, 1867; ibid., July 12, 1867; ibid., July 21, 1867.

32. Ibid., Dec. 5, 1867; ibid., Dec. 7, 1867.

33. *Daily National Intelligencer* (Washington, D.C.), Sept. 7, 1868.

34. *Milwaukee Daily Sentinel*, Sept. 7, 1868; *Daily National Intelligencer*, Sept. 7, 1868; *New Orleans Times*, Sept. 2, 1868; ibid., Sept. 3, 1868; *Times-Picayune*, Sept. 2, 1868.

35. *Daily National Intelligencer*, Sept. 7, 1868.

36. *Milwaukee Daily Sentinel*, Sept. 7, 1868.

37. *New Orleans Times*, Sept. 11, 1868; Haskins, *Pinchback*, 64–65.

38. *New Orleans Commercial Bulletin*, Sept. 11, 1868; *New Orleans Times*, Sept. 5, 1868; ibid., Sept. 11, 1868.

39. *Times-Picayune*, Sept. 11, 1868.

40. The letter from Charles D. Drake, written from Washington, D.C., and dated January 19, 1869, was referred to in *Claims of Heirs of Jacques Clamorgan*, 20 to refute any suggestion that Cyprian had been a Confederate sympathizer at any point in his long career.

41. 41st Cong., 2nd sess., H.R., Misc. Doc. No. 154, *Testimony Taken by the Sub-Committee on Elections in Louisiana* (Washington, D.C., 1870), vol. 5, pp. 309–10.

42. *Times-Picayune*, Mar. 21, 1872; ibid., May 5, 1872.

43. Ibid., Mar. 24, 1872.

44. Ibid., May 9, 1872.

45. *New Orleans Tribune*, Jan. 20, 1875.

46. *Daily Arkansas Gazette*, July 30, 1873; St. Louis Deeds, Book 492, p. 271 (CSLRD); *St. Louis Globe-Democrat*, Apr. 7, 1876.

47. *St. Louis Globe-Democrat*, July 11, 1876; ibid., July 27, 1876; St. Louis directory, 1879.

48. St. Peter's Church, New Iberia, Register, vol. 1, pp. 263, 291.

49. Glenn R. Conrad, *New Iberia—Essays on the Town and Its People* (Lafayette: Center for Louisiana Studies, University of Southwestern Louisiana, 1979), 114, 305, 327–28. I am grateful to Soulier family historian Steve Navaro for the information on Hebe's date of death (e-mail communication with the author, Jan. 8, 2008).

50. U.S. Census (1870), New Iberia, La., roll 513, p. 194; St. Louis Death Registers, vol. K, p. 295 (www.ancestry.com).

51. St. Peter's Church, Register, vol. 2, pp. 174, 179.

52. Registre de St. Thomas de Montmagny (1844), 16, Quebec Vital and Church Records, 1621–1967, Drouin Collection (www.ancestry.com); Canadian Census (1851), St. Thomas, L'Islet County, Canada East, roll C-1124, p. 49 (www.ancestry.com).

53. Opelousas Church, vol. 2, p. 433, *Southwest Louisiana Records, 1750–1900* CD (Hébert Publications); U.S. Census (1880), Ward 6, Iberia, La., roll 454, p. 430, e.d. 31; ibid., St. Louis, roll 735, p. 210, e.d. 408; ibid., Texas City, Whitman, Wash., roll 1398, p. 381, e.d. 58; St. Louis Death Registers, vol. 12, p. 597.

54. Massachusetts Deaths (1908), vol. 69, p. 456 (MSA).

55. *New Orleans Daily Picayune*, May 24, 1889.

56. *New Orleans Times*, Oct. 28, 1876.

57. A copy of Minor's baptismal certificate was kindly supplied by Ronda Barnes, his great-granddaughter. In the 1910 census, Mary Belle reported that she had borne four children (U.S. Census, Ward 4, New Bedford, Mass., roll 579, e.d. 198, p. 11A), but there is no record of her fourth child's name, gender, or dates of birth and death.

58. Passenger Lists of Vessels Arriving at New York, 1820–97, M237, roll 396, list no. 104; roll 419, list no. 932; roll 447, list no. 256 (www.ancestry.com).

59. Ibid., roll 428, list no. 2; Passenger Lists of Vessels Arriving at New Orleans, 1820–1902 (www.ancestry.com).

60. Registre de St. Thomas de Montmagny (1853), 9; ibid. (1880), 12; Registre de Cap-St-Ignace (1884), 6, Drouin Collection.

61. Registre de St. Thomas de Montmagny (1862), 23; ibid. (1864), 4. Registre de Trois Pistoles (1887), 10–11.

62. New Orleans Passenger Lists.

63. Massachusetts Deaths (1889), vol. 400, p. 177; Registre de Cap-St-Ignace (1889), 32.

64. New York Passenger Lists, roll 441, list no. 1215.

65. On Jules's new business ties, see *Daily Picayune*, May 24, 1889.

66. Massachusetts Marriages (1889), vol. 397, p. 167 (MSA).

67. *New Bedford Evening Standard*, Mar. 16, 1909.

68. U.S. Census (1850), Boston, Ward 1, roll 522, p. 11; New Bedford directories, 1889–90.

69. New Bedford directories, 1889–1909.

70. St. Louis directories, 1893, 1894.

71. St. Louis Deeds, Book 1240, p. 487; St. Louis Death Registers, vol. 26, p. 342.

72. St. Louis Death Registers, vol. 34, p. 366; U.S. Census (1900), St. Louis, Ward 10, roll 893, p. 1A, e.d. 436; St. Louis directory, 1900. Donna Carl Dahl, archivist of the Alexian Brothers' Immaculate Conception Province, kindly searched the Patient Registers of the Alexian Brothers' Hospital in St. Louis and supplied the information on Cyprian's hospitalization.

73. St. Louis Deeds, Book 1586, p. 262; ibid., Book 1617, p. 490.

74. St. Louis Death Register, vol. 44, p. 68; St. Louis Burial Permit (1902) no. 9186 (www.ancestry.com).

75. *New Bedford Evening Standard*, Jan. 1, 1908; ibid., Jan. 2, 1908; Massachusetts Deaths (1908), vol. 69, p. 456.

76. Massachusetts Deaths (1909), vol. 70, p. 315; *New Bedford Evening Standard*, Mar. 16, 1909.

77. *Boston Journal*, Dec. 10, 1908; *Pawtucket Times*, Dec. 11, 1908.

78. U.S. Census (1910), New Bedford, Mass., roll 579, e.d. 198, p. 11A.

79. New Bedford directories, 1889–1911.

80. *New Orleans Daily Picayune*, Feb. 24, 1899; *New York Times*, Aug. 8, 1900.

81. *Morning Oregonian*, Feb. 21, 1899; *New Orleans Daily Picayune*, Feb. 24, 1899; ibid., Mar. 9, 1899.
82. New Orleans Passenger Lists.
83. U.S. Army, Register of Enlistments, 1798–1914 (www.ancestry.com).
84. Duplicate of discharge certificate (kindly supplied by Ronda Barnes).
85. Massachusetts Marriages (1904), vol. 546, p. 240; Armand Letourneau and Mary Letourneau, comps., *Franco-American Marriages of New Bedford* (New Bedford, Mass.: American-French Genealogical Society, 1986), 21. On Etta's parentage, see Alphabetical Index of the Births, Marriages and Deaths Recorded in Providence, Rhode Island, Births (1901–10), vol. 14, p. 188 (NEHGS); U.S. Census (1850), Hallowell, Kennebec Co., Maine, roll 256, p. 177; Maine Marriages (www.ancestry.com).
86. Philadelphia Death Certificates (1906), no. 4198 (PCA); Records of Hillside Cemetery, Roslyn, Pennsylvania. (Hillside's family service counselor, Douglas Pierson, kindly supplied a list of the Bélanger family interments.)
87. New York Passenger Lists, 1908 (www.ancestry.com). The captain of the *Altai* misstated the year as 1907.
88. New Bedford directory, 1908.
89. U.S. Census (1910), New Bedford, Ward 6, Bristol Co., Mass., roll 579, p. 21B, e.d. 211.
90. Bristol County Naturalization Index, vol. 17, no. 4001 (MSA); New Bedford directories, 1908–16.
91. U.S. Census (1860), Jackson, Polk Co., Mo., roll 641, p. 210; ibid. (1870), Jackson, Polk Co., Mo., roll 800, p. 49; ibid. (1880), Jackson, Polk Co., Mo., roll 710, p. 233, e.d. 113.
92. Ibid. (1900), Haynesville, Pratt Co., Kans., roll 495, p. 1A, e.d. 179; ibid. (1910), Colton, San Bernardino Co., Calif., roll 93, p. 1A, e.d. 94; Calif. Voter Registrations, San Bernardino Co., 1912–16 (www.ancestry.com); Calif. Deaths (www.vitalsearch-ca.com); Los Angeles Marriages, vol. 227, p. 310 (no. 6927) (www.vitalsearch-ca.com).
93. Promissory note from Thomas B. and Mary Belle Coats to Samuel P. Coats, Nov. 1, 1916; May Coats to Neva Coats Staples, Mar. 23, 1972 (courtesy of Audrey Nation Staples); Los Angeles directory, 1918.
94. U.S. Census (1920), Lake County, Calif., roll 101, p. 6A, e.d. 80. Calif. Voter Registrations, Lake Co., 1918, 1920, 1922.
95. Calif. Voter Registrations, Lake Co., 1918, 1920, 1922; ibid., Santa Barbara Co., 1920–28; Calif. Deaths; Santa Barbara Cemetery, Burials, www.sbgen.org/Santa_Barbara-Cemetery-2010.
96. Neva Maxine Coats Staples, *My Coats Family* (Kismet, Kans.: J. P. Staples, 1989), 256–57.
97. U.S. Census (1930), Compton, Los Angeles Co., Calif., roll 125, p. 9B, e.d. 885; Calif. Voter Registrations, Los Angeles Co., 1930, 1934, 1936; Mary Bell [*sic*] Guilbert Death Cert., COVR.

98. Minor Arthur Bélanger, World War I draft registration (www.ancestry.com); U.S. Census (1920), Philadelphia, Ward 22, roll 1623, p. 2B, e.d. 553; Records of Hillside Cemetery.

99. Philadelphia directories, 1922–27, 1929, 1935; U.S. Census (1930), Philadelphia, Ward 41, roll 2132, p. 28B, e.d. 1014.

100. U.S. Census (1930), Philadelphia, Ward 41, roll 2132, p. 28A, e.d. 1014; Calif. Births (www.vitalsearch-ca.com).

101. U.S. National Homes for Disabled Volunteer Soldiers, 1866–1938 (www.ancestry.com).

102. Calif. Deaths; Records of Hillside Cemetery.

103. Calif. Voter Registrations, Los Angeles Co., 1942, 1944, 1946, 1948, 1954.

104. Minor Arthur Bélanger death certificate (COVR).

Bibliography

Manuscript Sources

Boston Public Library, Boston, Massachusetts
  Draper Manuscript Collection (microfilm)
California Office of Vital Records, Sacramento
  California Death Certificates
Church of Jesus Christ of Latter-Day Saints, Family History Library
  Milwaukee, Wisconsin, Mortgages (microfilm)
  Nashville, Tennessee, Death Records, 1874–1913 (microfilm)
  New Orleans Registers of Free Colored Persons
  St. Martin's Parish, Louisiana, Marriage Licenses
Church of the Epiphany, New Iberia, Louisiana
  Baptismal Registers
Hillside Cemetery, Roslyn, Pennsylvania
  Records of Interments
Illinois State Archives, Southern Illinois University, Carbondale
  Madison County Emancipation Records
  Madison County Marriages
  Madison County Probate Case Files, 1813–1903
Illinois State Archives, Springfield
  Database of Illinois Death Certificates, 1916–50
  Kaskaskia Manuscripts

Kentucky State Archives, Frankfort
    Franklin County Deeds
Louisiana State Archives, Baton Rouge
    New Orleans Birth Records
Massachusetts State Archives, Boston
    Bristol County Naturalization Index, 1907–92
    Massachusetts Deaths
    Massachusetts Marriages
Missouri Historical Society, St. Louis
    Albert Todd Papers
    Census Collection
    Clamorgan Papers
    COLARCH, Colonial Archives of St. Louis (microfilm)
    B. G. Farrar Account Book
    Hamilton R. Gamble Papers
    Livres Terrien
    St. Louis City Census, 1840
    Tiffany Papers
Missouri State Archives, Jefferson City
    Gasconade County Marriages
    Jefferson County Circuit Court Records, 1831–46
    Minutes of the First Board of Land Commissioners, 1805–12
    Minutes of the Second Board of Land Commissioners Covering the Period October 2,
        1832, to September 30, 1835
    Missouri Death Certificates
    Missouri Judicial Records Database
    Missouri Soldiers' Database
    Missouri Superior Court Cases
    St. Charles Circuit Court Records
    St. Charles County Deeds
    St. Louis Birth Registers
    St. Louis City and County Wills, 1804–1900
    St. Louis County Guardianship Records
    St. Louis Criminal Court Record Books
    St. Louis Probate Court Records
Missouri State Archives–St. Louis
    St. Louis Circuit Court Case Files
    St. Louis Circuit Court Records
New England Historic Genealogical Society, Boston, Massachusetts
    Alphabetical Index of the Births, Marriages, and Deaths Recorded in Providence,
        Rhode Island
Philadelphia City Archives, Philadelphia, Pennsylvania
    Death Certificates

St. Louis, Missouri, City of, Office of the Recorder of Deeds
  Deeds, 1804–1940
  Tax Records, 1826, 1828, 1829, 1831
St. Louis County Library, St. Louis, Missouri
  Church of St. Francis Xavier
    Marriages, 1863–88
  Church of St. Thomas of Aquin
    Baptisms, 1882–1908
    Marriages, 1882–96, 1897–1908
  Church of St. Vincent de Paul
    Baptisms, 1852–67, 1867–77, 1881–92
    Marriages, 1867–91, 1892–1935
    Burials, 1845–66, 1867–1905
  St. Louis County Court Records
  St. Louis, Old Cathedral
    Baptisms, 1769–1804, 1804–14, 1814–23, 1823–35, 1835–44, 1844–51
    Marriages, 1781–1828, 1828–39, 1840–49, 1849–55, 1855–81, 1881–1932
    Burials, 1781–1832, 1832–47, 1847–52, 1852–70
St. Peter's Catholic Church, New Iberia, Louisiana
  Baptismal Registers
  Marriage Registers

Electronic Databases

Abraham Lincoln Papers, Library of Congress (www.memory.loc.gov)
Border Crossings from Canada to the United States, 1895–1956 (www.ancestry.com)
California Births Database, 1905–96 (www.vitalsearch-ca.com)
California Death Records, 1940–97 (www.vitalsearch-ca.com)
California Voter Registrations (www.ancestry.com)
Canadian Censuses, 1851–91 (www.ancestry.com)
"Forde Morgan" (www.americasgreatestbrands.com)
Interments at Calvary Cemetery, St. Louis (www.search.stlcathcem.org)
International Genealogical Index (www.familysearch.org)
Los Angeles Marriages, 1914 (www.vitalsearch-ca.com)
Maine Marriages (www.ancestry.com)
Montgomery County, Tennessee, Marriages (www.ancestry.com)
Passenger Lists of Vessels Arriving at New Orleans, 1820–1902 (www.ancestry.com)
Passenger Lists of Vessels Arriving at New York City, 1820–97, 1907–1908 (www
  .ancestry.com)
Passport Applications, January 2, 1906, to March 31, 1925 (www.ancestry.com)
Petitions for Naturalization, Los Angeles, California (www.ancestry.com)
Quebec Vital and Church Records, 1621–1967, Drouin Collection (www.ancestry.com)
St. Louis Burial Permits (www.ancestry.com)

St. Louis Burials (CD, St. Louis Genealogical Society)
St. Louis Death Registers (www.ancestry.com)
St. Louis Marriages (www.ancestry.com)
Santa Barbara Cemetery, Burials (www.sbgen.org/Santa_Barbara_Cemetery-2010)
Social Security Death Index (www.ancestry.com)
Southwest Louisiana Records, 1750–1900 (CD, Hébert Publications)
U.K. Census, 1841–81 (www.ancestry.com)
U.S. Army, Register of Enlistments, 1798–1914 (www.ancestry.com)
U.S. Census, 1830–1930 (www.ancestry.com)
U.S. Civil War Soldiers, 1861–65 (www.ancestry.com)
U.S. IRS Tax Assessment Lists, 1862–1918 (www.ancestry.com)
U.S. National Homes for Disabled Volunteer Soldiers, 1866–1938 (www.ancestry.com)
Washington State Census, 1892 (www.ancestry.com)
World War I Draft Registrations (www.ancestry.com)

City Directories

Chicago, Ill.
Glendale, Calif.
Inglewood, Calif.
Kansas City, Mo.
Los Angeles, Calif.
Nashville, Tenn.
New Bedford, Mass.
New Orleans, La.
New York City, N.Y.
St. Louis, Mo.
South Pasadena, Calif.

Law Cases

United States Supreme Court

Isaac Landes, Plaintiff in Error, v. Joshua Brant (51 U.S. 348)
John Glenn and Charles M. Thruston, Appellants, v. The United States (54 U.S. 250)
United States v. Clamorgan; Clamorgan v. United States (101 U.S. 822)

Missouri Supreme Court

Clamorgan, Appellant, v. The Baden & St. Louis Railway Company (72 Mo 139)
Clamorgan et al., Plaintiffs in Error, v. Hornsby et al. (94 Mo 83)
Clamorgan et al. v. Lane (9 Mo 446)
Clamorgan v. O'Fallon & Lindell (10 Mo 112)
Collins v. Administrator of Pauline Clamorgan (5 Mo 272)
Collins v. Administrator of Pauline Clamorgan (6 Mo 169)

Crevier v. Bertrand et al. (1858)

Dougal v. Fryer (3 Mo 39)

Finney, Respondent, v. Brant, Appellant (19 Mo 42)

George Speers, Adm. of Ester, A Free Mulatto Woman, v. William C. Carr (1842)

H. Clamorgan et al., Plaintiffs in Error, v. D. C. Hornsby et al., Defendants (13 Mo App. 550)

Henry Clamorgan et al., Defendants in Error, v. Isaac T. Greene, Plaintiff in Error (32 Mo 285)

John Magwire, Respondent, v. Mary L. Tyler et al., Appellants (40 Mo 406)

John Magwire v. Mary Tyler et al. (25 Mo 433)

Landes et al. v. Perkins (12 Mo 238)

Lindell, Respondent, v. Brant, Appellant (19 Mo 50)

Theresa Speers v. Thomas Fleck (34 Mo 101)

Government Reports

American State Papers: Public Lands. Washington, D.C.: Gales and Seaton, 1861; repr. Greenville, S.C.: Southern Historical Press, 1994 (8 vols).

Annual Report of the Commissioner of the District of Columbia for the Year Ended June 30, 1887. House Executive Document, 50th Congress, 1st session.

Claim of Heirs of Jacques Clamorgan, House Bill 17888, 61st Congress. Washington, D.C.: Government Printing Office, 1910.

Official Register of the United States, Containing a List of Officers and Employees in the Civil, Military and Naval Service on the First of July, 1883. House Miscellaneous Document, 48th Congress, 1st session.

Report No. 22 to Accompany Bill H.R. No. 214. 35th Congress, 1st session.

Report on Claim of Heirs of Jacques Clamorgan. Senate Reports, No. 328, 30th Cong., 2nd session.

Report to Accompany Senate Bill No. 551. 32nd Congress, 1st session.

Testimony Taken by the Sub-Committee on Elections in Louisiana (Washington, D.C., 1870). 41st Congress, 2nd session, H.R., Misc. Doc. No. 154.

Newspapers and Periodicals

Appleton (Wisconsin) *Post-Crescent,* 1925

Arkansas Gazette, 1834

Atchison (Kansas) *Globe,* 1891

Baltimore Patriot, 1826

Biloxi Herald, 1895

Bismarck (North Dakota) *Daily Tribune,* 1888

Boston Journal, 1908

Chicago Tribune, 1964

Chillicothe (Ohio) *Telegraph,* 1813

Cincinnati Daily Gazette, 1867

Cleveland Gazette, 1885–86, 1890

Cleveland Morning Daily Herald, 1873

Columbus (Georgia) *Daily Enquirer*, 1911

The Crisis (New York City), 1911

Critic-Record (Washington, D.C.), 1888

Daily Arkansas Gazette (Little Rock), 1873

Daily Evening Bulletin (San Francisco), 1880

Daily Inter-Ocean (Chicago), 1880, 1888

Daily Missouri Republican (St. Louis), 1851

Daily National Intelligencer (Washington, D.C.), 1849–68

Daily Picayune (New Orleans), 1892

Daily True Delta (New Orleans), 1862–64

Decatur (Illinois) *Republican*, 1888

Dunkirk (New York) *Observer Journal*, 1888

Edwardsville (Illinois) *Intelligencer*, 1888

Essex (Massachusetts) *Register*, 1813

Frank Leslie's Illustrated Newspaper, 1868

Frederick Douglass' Paper, 1854

Galveston (Texas) *Daily News*, 1910

Georgia Telegraph, 1846

Hamilton (Ohio) *Daily Democrat*, 1888

Indianapolis Freeman, 1890, 1892

Irish World and American Industrial Liberator (New York), 1892

Kansas City Journal, 1911

Kansas City Star, 1911

Little Rock Daily Republican, 1872

Los Angeles Times, 1911–48

Louisville Public Advertiser, 1823

L'Union (New Orleans), 1864

Milwaukee Daily Sentinel, 1845, 1868, 1888

Missouri Gazette, 1809–16

Missouri Republican, 1826–63

Morning Oregonian, 1895–99

National Intelligencer and Washington Advertiser, 1809

Newark (Ohio) *Advocate*, 1888

New Bedford (Massachusetts) *Evening Standard*, 1908–1909

New Haven (Connecticut) *Register*, 1888–92

New Jersey Gazette, 1780

New Orleans Commercial Bulletin, 1868

New Orleans Daily Picayune, 1889–99

New Orleans Times, 1868–76, 1911

New Orleans Tribune, 1864–67, 1875

New York Daily Tribune, 1871

New York Herald, 1857

New York Times, 1852–1949

North American (Philadelphia), 1880

Ohio Repository (Canton), 1842

Pawtucket (Rhode Island) *Times,* 1908–11

Pennsylvania Gazette, 1780

Philadelphia Inquirer, 1862

Providence (Rhode Island) *Gazette,* 1817

St. Louis Argus, 1918

St. Louis Daily New Era, 1849

St. Louis Daily Times, 1868

St. Louis Globe-Democrat, 1868–1929

St. Louis Palladium, 1904

St. Louis Post-Dispatch, 1883–1944

St. Louis Republic, 1889–1911

St. Louis Star, 1911

St. Paul (Minnesota) *Daily News,* 1889

Sunday Republican (St. Louis), 1850

Syracuse (New York) *Daily Journal,* 1911

Syracuse (New York) *Weekly Express,* 1888

Times-Picayune (New Orleans), 1863–72, 1889

Trenton (New Jersey) *Times,* 1911

Tulsa World, 1911

Washington Bee, 1883, 1885–86

Washington Post, 1880, 1911

Weekly Patriot and Union (Harrisburg, Pennsylvania), 1868

Western Appeal (St. Paul, Minnesota), 1888

Wilkes-Barre (Pennsylvania) *Times-Leader,* 1911

Wisconsin Rapids Daily Tribune, 1925

Printed Primary Sources

Alvord, Clarence Walworth, ed. *Cahokia Records, 1778–1790.* Springfield: Illinois State Historical Library, 1907.

"An Address of the Colored People of Missouri to the Friends of Equal Rights, October 12, 1865." In Philip S. Foner and George E. Walker, eds. *Proceedings of the Black State Conventions, 1840–1865.* Philadelphia: Temple University Press, 1980. Vol. 2, pp. 279–82.

André Michaux's Travels into Kentucky, 1793–96. In Reuben Gold Thwaites, ed., *Early Western Travels, 1748–1846.* Cleveland, Ohio: A. H. Clark, 1904–1907.

Argument on Behalf of the Claimants in the Claim of the Representatives of Jacques Clamorgan, to a Tract on the Rivers Cuivre and Dardenne, in the State of Missouri. Np., n.d. [1837].

Billon, Frederic Louis. *Annals of St. Louis in Its Early Days Under the French and Spanish Dominations.* St. Louis: self-published, 1886.

————. *Annals of St. Louis in Its Territorial Days, from 1804 to 1821.* St. Louis: self-published, 1888.

Blattner, Teresa, comp. *People of Color: Black Genealogical Records and Abstracts from Missouri Sources.* Bowie, Md.: Heritage Books, 1998.

Carter, Clarence Edwin, ed. *The Territorial Papers of the United States.* Vols. 13–14. Washington, D.C.: Government Printing Office, 1948.

"Chronological Statement of Papers and Documents Relative to Louisiana in the National Historical Archives of Madrid." *Louisiana Historical Quarterly* 4 (January 1908): 121–44.

Clamorgan Land Association. *Papers Relating to the Clamorgan Grant.* N.p., n.d. [1838]. Available at www.jstor.org/stable/60207085.

Conrad, Glenn R., and Carl A. Brasseaux, comps. *"Gone but Not Forgotten": Records from South Louisiana Cemeteries.* Lafayette: Center for Louisiana Studies, University of Southwestern Louisiana, 1983.

Directory of Graduates of the University of California, 1864–1916. Berkeley: University of California, 1916.

Edwards, Richard, and Menra Hopewell. *Edwards's Great West and Her Commercial Metropolis, Embracing a General View of the West and a Complete History of St. Louis.* St. Louis: Office of *Edwards's Monthly,* 1860.

Fenner, B. *Fenner's Complete Formulary.* 6th ed. Westfield, N.Y.: self-published, 1888.

Foner, Philip S., and George E. Walker, eds. *Proceedings of the Black State Conventions, 1840–1865.* 2 vols. Philadelphia: Temple University Press, 1980.

General Alumni Catalogue of New York University, 1833–1907: Medical Alumni. New York: General Alumni Society, 1908.

Hill, Joseph J. "An Unknown Expedition to Santa Fé in 1807." *Mississippi Valley Historical Review* 6 (March 1920): 560–62.

Hogan, John. *Thoughts About the City of St. Louis, Her Commerce and Manufactures, Railroads, &c.* St. Louis, Mo.: Republican Steam Press, 1854.

"Index to the Spanish Judicial Records of Louisiana, August–September 1781." *Louisiana Historical Quarterly* 17 (January 1934): 203–23.

"Index to the Spanish Judicial Records of Louisiana, October 1783." *Louisiana Historical Quarterly* 22 (January 1939): 259–309.

"Index to the Spanish Judicial Records of Louisiana, March 1784." *Louisiana Historical Quarterly* 23 (January 1940): 299–347.

James, Thomas. *Three Years Among the Indians and Mexicans.* Waterloo, Ill., printed at the Office of the "War Eagle," 1846. Reprint Walter B. Douglas, ed. St. Louis: Missouri Historical Society, 1916.

Jensen, Richard E., and James S. Hutchins, eds. *Wheel Boats on the Missouri: The Journals and Documents of the Atkinson-O'Fallon Expedition, 1824–26*. Helena: Montana Historical Society, 2001.

Johnson, E. P., and G. W. Hall. *Henry Clamorgan et al., Appellants, v. The Baden & St. Louis R. R. Co., Respondent: Statement and Brief of Appellants*. St. Louis: Chancy R. Barns, 1880.

Jones, Landon Y., ed. *The Essential Lewis and Clark*. New York: HarperCollins, 2000.

"Journal of Jean Baptiste Truteau on the Upper Missouri, Première Partie." *American Historical Review* 19 (January 1914): 299–333.

Kinnaird, Lawrence, ed. *Spain in the Mississippi Valley, 1765–1794. Annual Report of the American Historical Association for the Year 1945, Vol. 4*. Washington, D.C.: Government Printing Office, 1946.

Krum, J. M., and C. H. Krum, *Henry Clamorgan, Cyprian Clamorgan, Leon A. Clamorgan, and Julius Clamorgan, Appellants, v. The Baden and St. Louis Railway Company: Statement and Brief for Respondent*. St. Louis: Chancy R. Barns, 1878.

————. *Henry Clamorgan, Cyprian Clamorgan, Leon A. Clamorgan and Julius Clamorgan, Appellants, v. The Baden and St. Louis Railway Company, Respondent: Statement and Brief for Respondent*. St. Louis: Chancy R. Barns, 1880.

Laws of the State of Missouri, Passed at the First Session of the Fourteenth General Assembly. Jefferson City: James Lusk, 1847.

Laws of the State of Missouri, Passed at the Session of the Sixteenth General Assembly Begun and Held at the City of Jefferson, on Monday the Thirtieth Day of December, A.D. 1850. Jefferson City: James Lusk, 1851.

Laws of the State of Missouri, Passed at the Regular Session of the Twenty-Second General Assembly, Begun and Held at the City of Jefferson on Monday, December 29, 1862. Jefferson City: J. P. Ament, 1863.

Letourneau, Armand, and Mary Letourneau, comps. *Franco-American Marriages of New Bedford*. New Bedford, Mass.: American-French Genealogical Society, 1986.

Marsh, Helen C., and Timothy R. Marsh, comps. *Davidson County, Tennessee, Wills and Inventories, vol. 1 (1783–1816)*. Greenville, S.C.: Southern Historical Press, 1990.

Marshall, Thomas Maitland, ed. *The Life and Papers of Frederick Bates*. St. Louis: Missouri Historical Society, 1926.

Missouri State Legislature, 22nd General Assembly, 1st Session.
  Journal of the House. Jefferson City, 1863.
  Journal of the Senate. Jefferson City, 1863.

Nasatir, Abraham P., ed. *Before Lewis and Clark: Documents Illustrating the History of the Missouri, 1785–1804*. St. Louis: St. Louis Historical Documents Foundation, 1952; reprint. Norman: University of Oklahoma Press, 1990.

Opinion in the Case of Charles Lyons, A Free Negro, Determined in the St. Louis Circuit Court, November Term, 1846. St. Louis, 1846.

Petition of Clamorgan's Representatives. N.p., 1818.

Piesse, G. W. Septimus. *The Art of Perfumery, and Method of Obtaining the Odors of Plants*. Philadelphia: Lindsay and Blakiston, 1857.

Prospectus for Raising a Loan of £54,000 Upon Shares in the Clamorgan Land Association, U.S., at Six Per Cent Interest, with a Valuable Bonus to the Lenders. N.p., ca. 1837. Available at www.jstor.org/stable/60206421.

Representation and Petition of the Representatives Elected by the Freemen of the Territory of Louisiana. Washington, D.C.: William Duane and Son, 1805.

Revised Statutes of Missouri. 1909.

Riffel, Judy, comp. "Register of Free Colored Persons (1840–1864)." *Le Raconteur* 22 (August 2002): 161–64.

Ripley, C. Peter, et al., eds. *The Black Abolitionist Papers*. Vol. 2. Chapel Hill: University of North Carolina Press, 1986.

"St. Geneviève Co., Missouri, Slave Bills of Sale, 1766–1827." In Sherida K. Eddleman, comp. *Missouri Genealogical Records and Abstracts*. Vol. 1 (1766–1839). Bowie, Md.: Heritage Books, 1990.

Schweninger, Loren, ed. *From Tennessee Slave to St. Louis Entrepreneur: The Autobiography of James Thomas*. Columbia: University of Missouri Press, 1984.

Sharpe, W. C., comp. *Vital Statistics of Seymour, Connecticut*. Seymour, Conn.: Record Printing, 1883.

Sistler, Byron, and Barbara Sistler, comps. *Early Middle Tennessee Marriages, vol. 1: Grooms*. Nashville: Byron Sistler and Associates, 1988.

Skillman, W. D. *The Western Metropolis of St. Louis in 1846*. St. Louis: W. D. Skillman, 1846.

Stanley, Lois, George F. Wilson, and Maryellen Wilson, comps. *Death Records from Missouri Newspapers: The Civil War Years (January 1861–December 1865)*. Greenville, S.C.: Southern Historical Press, 1990.

———. *More Death Records from Missouri Newspapers, 1810–1857*. Greenville, S.C.: Southern Historical Press, 1990.

Taylor, J. N., and M. O. Crooks. *Sketch Book of St. Louis*. St. Louis, Mo.: George Knapp and Co., 1858.

Title Papers of the Clamorgan Grant of 536,904 Arpents of Alluvial Lands in Missouri and Arkansas. New York: T. Snowden, 1837.

Wells, Carole, comp. *Davidson County, Tennessee—County Court Minutes, 1783–1792*. Bowie, Md.: Heritage Books, 1990.

White, Joseph M., and Victor Monroe. *Clamorgan's Case*. N.p., n.d. [1836]. In Collections of the St. Louis Mercantile Library, University of Missouri–St. Louis.

Wilkinson, Frederick D., ed. *Directory of Graduates, Howard University, 1870–1963*. Washington, D.C., 1965.

Winch, Julie, ed. *Cyprian Clamorgan's "The Colored Aristocracy of St. Louis."* Columbia: University of Missouri Press, 1999.

———. ed. *"The Elite of Our People": Joseph Willson's Sketches of Black Upper-Class Life in Antebellum Philadelphia*. University Park, Pa.: Penn State University Press, 2000.

Secondary Works

Books

Adler, Jeffry S. *Yankee Merchants and the Making of the Urban West: The Rise and Fall of Antebellum St. Louis.* New York: Cambridge University Press, 1991.

Canu, Jean. *Les mille ans d'une famille normande: Les Clamorgan, 1066–1980.* St. Lô: Société d'archéologie de la Manche, 1980.

Christian, Shirley. *Before Lewis and Clark: The Story of the Chouteaus, the French Dynasty That Ruled America's Frontier.* New York: Farrar, Straus and Giroux, 2004.

Conrad, Glenn R. *New Iberia: Essays on the Town and Its People.* Lafayette: Center for Louisiana Studies, University of Southwestern Louisiana, 1979.

Cunningham, Mary B., and Jeanne C. Blythe, comps. *The Founding Family of St. Louis.* St. Louis, Mo.: Piraeus Publishers, 1977.

Dictionnaire des familles françaises anciennes ou notables à la fin du XIXe siècle. Evreux: Charles Hérissey, 1912.

Douglas, Walter B. *Manuel Lisa.* Annotated and edited by Abraham P. Nasatir. New York: Argosy-Antiquarian, 1964.

Ekberg, Carl J. *Colonial Ste. Genevieve: An Adventure on the Mississippi Frontier.* Gerald, Mo.: Patrice Press, 1985.

Foley, William E., and C. David Rice. *The First Chouteaus: River Barons of Early St. Louis.* Urbana and Chicago: University of Illinois Press, 1983.

Gerteis, Louis S. *Civil War St. Louis.* Lawrence: University Press of Kansas, 2001.

Gitlin, Jay. *The Bourgeois Frontier: French Towns, French Traders, and American Expansion.* New Haven, Conn.: Yale University Press, 2010.

Greene, Lorenzo J., Gary R. Kremer, and Antonio F. Holland. *Missouri's Black Heritage.* Columbia: University of Missouri Press, 1993.

Haskins, James. *Pinckney Benton Stewart Pinchback.* New York: Macmillan, 1973.

Hodes, Frederick A. *Beyond the Frontier: A History of St. Louis to 1821.* Tucson, Ariz.: Patrice Press, 2004.

Hoig, Stan. *The Chouteaus: First Family of the Fur Trade.* Albuquerque: University of New Mexico Press, 2008.

Houck, Louis. *A History of Missouri, From Its Earliest Explorations and Settlements Until the Admission of the State into the Union.* Chicago: R. R. Donnelly and Sons, 1908.

Kinzie, Juliette Augusta Magill. *Wau-Bun: The Early Day in the Northwest.* Philadelphia: J. B. Lippincott, 1873.

Kukla, Jon. *A Wilderness So Immense: The Louisiana Purchase and the Destiny of America.* New York: Random House, 2003.

Lavender, David. *The Southwest.* New York: Harper and Row, 1980.

Little Compton Historical Society. *Little Compton Families, from Records Compiled by Benjamin Franklin Wilbour.* Little Compton, R.I.: self-published, 1967.

Loomis, Noel M., and Abraham P. Nasatir. *Pedro Vial and the Roads to Santa Fé.* Norman: University of Oklahoma Press, 1967.

McDermott, John Francis. *Private Libraries in Creole Saint Louis*. Baltimore, Md.: Johns Hopkins University Press, 1938.

Nasatir, Abraham P. *Borderland in Retreat: From Spanish Louisiana to the Far Southwest*. Albuquerque: University of New Mexico Press, 1976.

Norton, W. T., comp. *Centennial History of Madison County, Illinois, and Its People, 1812 to 1912*. Chicago and New York: Lewis Publishing Co., 1912.

Oglesby, Richard Edward. *Manuel Lisa and the Opening of the Missouri Fur Trade*. Norman: University of Oklahoma Press, 1963.

Peterson, Charles E. *Colonial St. Louis: Building a Creole Capital*. St. Louis: Missouri Historical Society, 1949.

Primm, James Neal. *Lion of the Valley: St. Louis, Missouri*. 3rd ed. Columbia: University of Missouri Press, 1998.

Quaife, Milo M. *Checagou: From Indian Wigwam to Modern City, 1673–1835*. Chicago: University of Illinois Press, 1933.

Rittenhouse, John D. *The Santa Fé Trail: A Historical Bibliography*. Albuquerque: University of New Mexico Press, 1971.

Rodabough, John. *Frenchtown*. St. Louis: Sunrise Publishing, 1980.

Smith, J. Clay, Jr. *Emancipation: The Making of the Black Lawyer, 1844–1944*. Philadelphia: University of Pennsylvania Press, 1993.

Staples, Neva Maxine Coats. *My Coats Family*. Kismet, Kans.: J. P. Staples, 1989.

Tillyard, Stella. *Citizen Lord: The Life of Edward Fitzgerald, Irish Revolutionary*. New York: Farrar, Straus and Giroux, 1997.

Van Ravenswaay, Charles, and Candace O'Connor. *St. Louis: An Informal History of the City and Its People, 1764–1865*. St. Louis: University of Illinois Press for the Missouri Historical Society, 1991.

Weber, David J. *The Spanish Frontier in North America*. New Haven, Conn.: Yale University Press, 1992.

Articles and Book Chapters

Abendanon, E. C. "An Important Atlas in the British Museum." *The Geographical Journal* 57 (April 1921): 284–89.

Adler, Jeffrey S. "Streetwalkers, Degraded Outcasts, and Good-for-Nothing Huzzies: Women and the Dangerous Class in Antebellum St. Louis." *Journal of Social History* 25 (Summer 1992): 737–55.

Bailey, Howald. "Baron Renfrew Captivates America." *History Teacher* 4 (November 1970): 37–46.

Banner, Stuart. "Written Law and Unwritten Norms in Colonial St. Louis." *Law and History Review* 14 (Spring 1996): 33–80.

Bellamy, Donnie D. "Free Blacks in Antebellum Missouri, 1820–1860." *Missouri Historical Review* 67 (January 1973): 198–226.

Bloom, Lansing B. "The Death of Jacques D'Eglise." *New Mexico Historical Review* 2 (October 1927): 369–79.

Broadhead, G. C. "The Location of the Capital of Missouri." *Missouri Historical Review* 2 (January 1908): 158–63.

Capers, Gerald M., Jr. "Confederates and Yankees in Occupied New Orleans, 1862–1865." *Journal of Southern History* 30 (November 1964): 405–26.

Christensen, Lawrence O. "Cyprian Clamorgan, *The Colored Aristocracy of St. Louis* (1858)." *Bulletin of the Missouri Historical Society* 31 (October 1974): 3–31.

Day, Judy, and M. James Kedro. "Free Blacks in St. Louis: Antebellum Conditions, Emancipation, and the Postwar Era." *Bulletin of the Missouri Historical Society* 30 (January 1974): 117–35.

Everett, Donald E. "Demands of the New Orleans Free Colored Population for Political Equality, 1862–1865." *Louisiana Historical Quarterly* 38 (April 1955): 43–64.

Finkelman, Paul. "Not Only the Judges' Robes Were Black: African-American Lawyers as Social Engineers." *Stanford Law Review* 47 (November 1994): 161–209.

Floyd, Samuel A. "J. W. Postlewaite of St. Louis: A Search for His Identity." *Black Perspective in Music* 6 (Autumn 1978): 151–67.

———. "A Black Composer in Nineteenth-Century St. Louis." *19th-Century Music* 4 (Autumn 1980): 121–33.

Furstenberg, François. "The Significance of the Trans-Appalachian Frontier in Atlantic History." *American Historical Review* 113 (June 2008): 647–77.

Gahan, Daniel. "'Journey After My Own Heart': Lord Edward Fitzgerald in America, 1788–90." *New Hibernia Review* 8 (Summer 2004): 85–105.

Gates, Paul Wallace. "Private Land Claims in the South." *Journal of Southern History* 22 (May 1956): 183–204.

Gilbert, Judith A. "Esther and Her Sisters: Free Women of Color as Property Owners in Colonial St. Louis, 1765–1803." *Gateway Heritage* 17 (Summer 1996): 14–23.

Gregg, Kate L. "Building the First American Fort West of the Mississippi." *Missouri Historical Review* 30 (July 1936): 345–64.

Holt, Glen E. "St. Louis's Transition Decade, 1819–1830." *Missouri Historical Review* 76 (July 1982): 365–81.

Hunter, Lloyd A. "Slavery in St. Louis, 1804–1860." *Bulletin of the Missouri Historical Society* 30 (July 1974): 233–65.

Jackson, Joy J. "Keeping Law and Order in New Orleans under General Butler, 1862." *Louisiana History* 34 (1993): 51–67.

Jones, Breckinridge. "One Hundred Years of Banking in Missouri." *Missouri Historical Review* 15 (January 1921): 345–92.

Jones, Howard J. "Biographical Sketches of Members of the 1868 Louisiana State Senate." *Louisiana History* 19 (1978): 65–110.

Lindberg, Richard C. "Jean Baptiste Point Du Sable." In John A. Garraty and Mark C. Carnes, eds., *American National Biography*. New York: Oxford University Press, 1999, vol. 7, pp. 166–68.

Lohrenz, Otto. "The Reverend Ichabod Camp: First American Preacher on the Ohio and Mississippi Rivers." *Filson Club History Quarterly* 65 (July 1991): 358–86.

"Missouriana." *Missouri Historical Review* 30 (January 1936): 177–78.

Nasatir, A. P. "Anglo-Spanish Rivalry on the Upper Missouri, Part 1." *Mississippi Valley Historical Review* 16 (December 1929): 359–82.

———. "Anglo-Spanish Rivalry on the Upper Missouri, Part 2." *Mississippi Valley Historical Review* 16 (March 1930): 507–28.

———. "The Formation of the Missouri Company." *Missouri Historical Review* 25 (October 1930): 10–22.

———. "Jacques Clamorgan: Colonial Promoter of the Northern Border of New Spain." *New Mexico Historical Review* 17 (April 1942): 101–12.

———. "Jacques Clamorgan." In Leroy R. Hafen, ed., *French Fur Traders and Voyageurs in the American West*. Lincoln: University of Nebraska Press, 1997, pp. 124–37.

Rader, Perry S. "The Location of the Permanent Seat of Government." *Missouri Historical Review* 21 (October 1927): 9–18.

Rankin, David C. "The Origins of Black Leadership in New Orleans During Reconstruction." *Journal of Southern History* 40 (August 1974): 417–40.

Reichard, Maximilian. "Black and White on the Urban Frontier: The St. Louis Community in Transition, 1800–1830." *Bulletin of the Missouri Historical Society* 33 (October 1976): 3–17.

Richardson, Lemont K. "Private Land Claims in Missouri, Part 1." *Missouri Historical Review* 50 (January 1956): 132–44.

———. "Private Land Claims in Missouri, Part 2." *Missouri Historical Review* (April 1956): 271–86.

———. "Private Land Claims in Missouri, Part 3." *Missouri Historical Review* (July 1956): 387–99.

Tansey, Richard. "Out-of-State Free Blacks in Late Antebellum New Orleans." *Louisiana History* 22 (Fall 1981): 369–86.

"Town of Osage." *Missouri Historical Review* 2 (October 1907): 78–80.

Viles, Jonas. "Missouri Capitals and Capitols (Part 1)." *Missouri Historical Review* 13 (January 1919): 135–56.

Williams, Christine. "Prosperity in the Face of Prejudice: The Life of a Free Black Woman in Frontier St. Louis." *Gateway Heritage* 19 (Fall 1998): 4–11.

Williams, David. "John Evans' Strange Journey: Part I. The Welsh Indians." *American Historical Review* 54 (January 1949): 277–95.

———. "John Evans' Strange Journey: Part II. Following the Trail." *American Historical Review* 54 (April 1949): 508–29.

Williams, Gwyn A. "Welsh Indians: The Madoc Legend and the First Welsh Radicalism." *History Workshop* 1 (Spring 1976): 136–54.

Dissertations

Christensen, Lawrence Oland. "Black St. Louis: A Study in Race Relations, 1865–1916." University of Missouri, 1972.

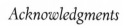

Acknowledgments

When you have been working on a project for eight years and seen that project take as many unexpected changes of direction as this one has, the list of people and organizations you need and want to thank grows by the day.

First, I owe a tremendous debt of gratitude to the National Endowment for the Humanities for awarding me a yearlong fellowship. Hurried research trips squeezed into a few days of vacation are no substitute for more in-depth explorations of the wealth of material that is out there. Of course, you need teams of librarians and archivists to guide you along the way, and I was fortunate to run into some of the best there are.

Had it not been for Michael Everman and his staff at the Missouri State Archives–St. Louis, and Kathy Grillo, the records manager at the St. Louis Circuit Court, I would never have come close to understanding the history of a family that positively thrived on litigation. The Clamorgans fought over the possession of land, and that spawned hundreds of property deeds. Every visit to St. Louis's Office of Recorder of Deeds was made memorable by the warmth of the welcome I received from Dusty Reese and Ann Grisham. Charles E. Brown, the head of reference services at the St. Louis Mercantile Library, could not have been more helpful, and the library itself is a veritable treasure trove. I also spent many hours in the Special Collections at the St. Louis County Library, and the librarians and volunteers there were quite simply wonderful. Another of my favorite venues was the Missouri Historical Society. The opportunity to work with such rich collections in such a beautiful building and with such a great bunch of people was something I truly appreciate. I want to say a special word of thanks to Dennis Northcott.

Anyone with an interest in the past who has not yet delved into the superb online databases maintained by the Missouri State Archives in Jefferson City has a real treat awaiting them. Teams of dedicated archivists and volunteers have digitized vast amounts of data . . . and it's all free. I enjoyed my visits to Jefferson City, and the time I spent in the "real" archives, and I also enjoyed, and continue to enjoy, my excursions into the "virtual" archives. Missouri's website is the gold standard for other state archives.

When it comes to individuals, I must begin by thanking Ronda Barnes, a Clamorgan descendant who is justifiably proud of her remarkable forebears. Thank you, Ronda, for always being ready and willing to share your family's history with me.

Other people whose own genealogies intersected with the Clamorgans aided me in navigating the twists and turns of the Clamorgan saga. Gwen and Gary Jonas, Steve Navaro, Nancy Lees, Nicholas Schaefer, Jacqueline J. Riley-Jennings, and Audrey Staples all contributed in their different ways, as did several informants who prefer not to be publicly recognized. I thank each and every one of them.

I found an enthusiastic band of Clamorgan devotees in and around St. Louis. For Clark Hickman, trekking around a cemetery or sleuthing a land title was never too much trouble. Mary Seematter always found time in her busy schedule to ferry me around St. Louis and share with me the heritage of the city and its people. Jack Ulrich, a true urban pioneer, lovingly restored one of the Clamorgan homes—and knew when he found a box of "old stuff" in a crawl space that it should *not* go out with the trash. The "house that Jack built"—or rescued from ruin—is now in the hands of two people who love it for its past as much as its present. The Clamorgan spirits are reportedly happy to have Josh and Sara Schipkowski in what was once *their* home.

Louis Gerteis, Professor of History at the University of Missouri–St. Louis, not only gave me invaluable insights into Civil War St. Louis but recruited for me two research assistants, Derek Kluba and Mark A. Neels. I was also lucky enough to find three great assistants in my own department at the University of Massachusetts Boston. Alfie Paul, Rita Hutchinson, and Robert Goodwin helped me work through mounds of data and keep everything organized. I would like to say a special word of thanks to Rob and his wife, Julie Kiernan, who prepared the Clamorgan family trees. My computer skills don't come close to theirs. Another UMB graduate student, Wayne Soini, a member of the Massachusetts Bar, was always on hand to aid me in translating the language of the law into everyday English.

Thomas LeBien, my editor at Hill and Wang, is a model of patience and encouragement. He never lost faith that *The Clamorgans* would be wrapped up one day, even as the multigenerational saga threatened at times to spiral out of control.

I cannot end without thanking my husband, Louis S. Cohen. In addition to living with the Clamorgan clan for eight long years, he has twice driven this nondriving Brit from Bunker Hill to the Gateway Arch and back. Yes, I had seen a great deal of the United States from thirty-five thousand feet as I flew back and forth from Boston to St. Louis. It was Lou's insistence that I see it from ground level that truly enriched my research and writing experience. Lou, this book is for you.

Index